Lecture Notes of the Institute for Computer Sciences, Social Informatics and Telecommunications Engineering 56

Xuejia Lai Dawu Gu Bo Jin
Yongquan Wang Hui Li (Eds.)

Forensics in Telecommunications, Information, and Multimedia

Third International ICST Conference,
e-Forensics 2010
Shanghai, China, November 11-12, 2010
Revised Selected Papers

Springer

Volume Editors

Xuejia Lai
Dawu Gu
Shanghai Jiao Tong University, Department of Computer
Science and Engineering, 200240 Shanghai, P.R. China
E-mail: lai-xj@cs.sjtu.edu.cn; dwgu@sjtu.edu.cn

Bo Jin
The 3rd Research Institute of Ministry of Public Security
Zhang Jiang, Pu Dong, 210031 Shanghai, P.R. China
E-mail: jinbo@stars.org.cn

Yongquan Wang
East China University of Political Science and Law
Shanghai 201620, P. R. China
E-mail: wangyquan@sina.com

Hui Li
Xidian University Xi'an, Shaanxi 710071, P.R. China
E-mail: xd.lihui@gmail.com

ISSN 1867-8211
e-ISSN 1867-822X
ISBN 978-3-642-23601-3
e-ISBN 978-3-642-23602-0
DOI 10.1007/978-3-642-23602-0

Springer Heidelberg Dordrecht London New York

Library of Congress Control Number: 2011935336

CR Subject Classification (1998): C.2, K.6.5, D.4.6, I.5, K.4, K.5

Typesetting: Camera-ready by author, data conversion by Scientific Publishing Services, Chennai, India

Printed on acid-free paper

Springer is part of Springer Science+Business Media (www.springer.com)

Preface

E-Forensics 2010, the Third International ICST Conference on Forensic Applications and Techniques in Telecommunications, Information and Multimedia, was held in Shanghai, China, November 11-12, 2010. The conference was sponsored by ICST in cooperation with Shanghai Jiao Tong University (SJTU), the Natural Science Foundation of China (NSFC), Science and Technology Commission of Shanghai Municipality, Special Funds for International Academic Conferences of Shanghai Jiao Tong University, the 3rd Research Institute of the Ministry of Public Security, China, East China University of Political Science and Law, China, NetInfo Security Press and Xiamen Meiya Pico Information Co. Ltd.

The aim of E-Forensics conferences is to provide a platform for the exchange of advances in areas involving forensics such as digital evidence handling, data carving, records tracing, device forensics, data tamper identification, mobile device locating, etc. The first E-Forensics conference, E-Forensics 2008, was held in Adelaide, Australia, January 21–22, 2008; the second, E-Forensics 2009, was held in Adelaide, Australia, January 19–21, 2009.

This year, the conference received 42 submissions and the Program Committee selected 32 papers after a thorough reviewing process, appear in this volume, together with 5 papers from the Workshop of E-Forensics Law held during the conference. Selected papers are recommended for publication in the journal *China Communications*.

In addition to the regular papers included in this volume, the conference also featured three keynote speeches: "Intelligent Pattern Recognition and Applications" by Patrick S. P. Wang of Northeastern University, USA, "Review on Status of Digital Forensic in China" by Rongsheng Xu of the Chinese Academy of Sciences, China, and "Interdisciplinary Dialogues and the Evolution of Law to Address Cybercrime Issues in the Exciting Age of Information and Communication Technology" by Pauline C. Reich of Waseda University School of Law, Japan.

The TPC decided to give the Best Paper Award to Xiaodong Lin, Chenxi Zhang, and Theodora Dule for their paper "On Achieving Encrypted File Recovery" and the Best Student Paper Award to Juanru Li, Dawu Gu, Chaoguo Deng, and Yuhao Luo for their paper "Digital Forensic Analysis on Runtime Instruction Flow."

Here, we want to thank all the people who contributed to this conference. First, all the authors who submitted their work; the TPC members and their external reviewers, the organizing team from the Department of Computer Science and Engineering of Shanghai Jiao Tong University—Zhihua Su, Ning Ding,

Jianjie Zhao, Zhiqiang Liu, Shijin Ge, Haining Lu, Huaihua Gu, Bin Long, Kai Yuan, Ya Liu, Qian Zhang, Bailan Li, Cheng Lu, Yuhao Luo, Yinqi Tang, Ming Sun, Wei Cheng, Xinyuan Deng, Bo Qu, Feifei Liu, and Xiaohui Li—for their great efforts in making the conference run smoothly.

November 2010

Xuejia Lai
Dawu Gu
Bo Jin
Yongquan Wang
Hui Li

Organization

Steering Committee Chair

Imrich Chlamtac	President Create-Net Research Consortium

General Chairs

Dawu Gu	Shanghai Jiao Tong University, China
Hui Li	Xidian University, China

Technical Program Chair

Xuejia Lai	Shanghai Jiao Tong University, China

Technical Program Committee

Xuejia Lai	Shanghai Jiao Tong University, China
Barry Blundell	South Australia Police, Australia
Roberto Caldelli	University of Florence, Italy
Kefei Chen	Shanghai Jiao Tong University, China
Thomas Chen	Swansea University, UK
Liping Ding	Institute of Software, Chinese Academy of Sciences, China
Jordi Forne	Technical University of Catalonia, Spain
Zeno Geradts	The Netherlands Forensic Institute, The Netherlands
Pavel Gladyshev	University College Dublin, Ireland
Raymond Hsieh	California University of Pennsylvania, USA
Jiwu Huang	Sun Yat-Sen University, China
Bo Jin	The 3rd Research Institute of the Ministry of Public Security, China
Tai-hoon	Kim Hannam University, Korea
Richard Leary	Forensic Pathway, UK
Hui Li	Xidian University, China
Xuelong Li	University of London, UK
Jeng-Shyang	Pan National Kaohsiung University of Applied Sciences, Taiwan
Damien Sauveron	University of Limoges, France
Peter Stephenson	Norwich University, USA
Javier Garcia	Villalba Complutense University of Madrid, Spain

Jun Wang	China Information Technology Security Evaluation Center
Yongquan Wang	East China University of Political Science and Law, China
Che-Yen Wen	Central Police University, Taiwan
Svein Y. Willassen	Norwegian University of Science and Technology, Norway
Weiqi Yan	Queen's University Belfast, UK
Jianying Zhou	Institute for Infocomm Research, Singapore
Yanli Ren	Shanghai University, China

Workshop Chair

Bo Jin	The 3rd Research Institute of the Ministry of Public Security, China
Yongquan Wang	East China University of Political Science and Law, China

Publicity Chair

Liping Ding	Institute of Software, Chinese Academy of Sciences, China
Avinash Srinivasan	Bloomsburg University, USA
Jun Han	Fudan University, China

Demo and Exhibit Chairs

Hong Su	NetInfo Security Press, China

Local Chair

Ning Ding	Shanghai Jiao Tong University, China

Publicity Chair

Yuanyuan Zhang	East China Normal University, China
Jianjie Zhao	Shanghai Jiao Tong University, China

Web Chair

Zhiqiang Liu	Shanghai Jiao Tong University, China

Conference Coordinator

Tarja Ryynanen	ICST

Workshop Chairs

Bo Jin	The 3rd Research Institute of the Ministry of Public Security, China
Yongquan Wang	East China University of Political Science and Law, China

Workshop Program Committee

Anthony Reyes	Access Data Corporation, Polytechnic University, USA
Pauline C. Reich	Waseda University, Japan
Pinxin Liu	Renmin University of China, China
Jiang Du	Chongqing University of Posts and Telecommunications, China
Denis Edgar-Nevill	Canterbury Christ Church University, UK
Yonghao Mai	Hubei University of Police, China
Paul Reedy	Manager Forensic Operations Forensic and Data Centres, Australia
Shaopei Shi	Institute of Forensic Science, Ministry of Justice, China
Man Qi	Canterbury Christ Church University, UK
Xufeng Wang	Hangzhou Police Bureau, China
Lin Mei	The 3rd Research Institute of the Ministry of Public Security, China

Table of Contents

On Achieving Encrypted File Recovery

Xiaodong Lin[1], Chenxi Zhang[2], and Theodora Dule[1]

[1] University of Ontario Institute of Technology, Oshawa, Ontario, Canada
{Xiaodong.Lin,Theodora.Dule}@uoit.ca
[2] University of Waterloo, Waterloo, Ontario, Canada
c14zhang@engmail.uwaterloo.ca

Abstract. As digital devices become more prevalent in our society, evidence relating to crimes will be more frequently found on digital devices. Computer forensics is becoming a vital tool required by law enforcement for providing data recovery of key evidence. File carving is a powerful approach for recovering data especially when file system metadata information is unavailable. Many file carving approaches have been proposed, but cannot directly apply to encrypted file recovery. In this paper, we first identify the problem of encrypted file recovery, and then propose an effective method for encrypted file recovery through recognizing the encryption algorithm and mode in use. We classify encryption modes into two categories. For each category, we introduce a corresponding mechanism for file recovery, and also propose an algorithm to recognize the encryption algorithm and mode. Finally, we theoretically analyze the accuracy rate of recognizing an entire encrypted file in terms of file types.

Keywords: Data Recovery, File Carving, Computer Forensics, Security, Block Cipher Encryption/Decryption.

1 Introduction

Digital devices such as cellular phones, PDAs, laptops, desktops and a myriad of data storage devices pervade many aspects of life in today's society. The digitization of data and its resultant ease of storage, retrieval and distribution have revolutionized our lives in many ways and led to a steady decline in the use of traditional print mediums. The publishing industry, for example, has struggled to reinvent itself by moving to online publishing in the face of shrinking demand for print media. Today, financial institutions, hospitals, government agencies, businesses, the news media and even criminal organizations could not function without access to the huge volumes of digital information stored on digital devices.

Unfortunately, the digital age has also given rise to digital crime where criminals use digital devices in the commission of unlawful activities like hacking, identity theft, embezzlement, child pornography, theft of trade secrets, etc. Increasingly, digital devices like computers, cell phones, cameras, etc. are found at crime scenes during a criminal investigation. Consequently, there is a growing need for investigators to search digital devices for data evidence including

X. Lai et al. (Eds.): E-Forensics 2010, LNICST 56, pp. 1–13, 2011.

emails, photos, video, text messages, transaction log files, etc. that can assist in the reconstruction of a crime and identification of the perpetrator. One of the decade's most fascinating criminal trials against corporate giant Enron was successful largely due to the digital evidence in the form of over 200,000 emails and office documents recovered from computers at their offices. Digital forensics or computer forensics is an increasingly vital part of law enforcement investigations and is also useful in the private sector for disaster recovery plans for commercial entities that rely heavily on digital data, where data recovery plays an important role in the computer forensics field.

Traditional data recovery methods make use of file system structure on storage devices to rebuild the device's contents and regain access to the data. These traditional recovery methods become ineffective when the file system structure is corrupted or damaged, a task easily accomplished by a savvy criminal or disgruntled employee. A more sophisticated data recovery solution which does not rely on the file system structure is therefore necessary. These new and sophisticated solutions are collectively known as file carving. File carving is a branch of digital forensics that reconstructs data from a digital device without any prior knowledge of the data structures, sizes, content or type located on the storage medium. In other words, the technique of recovering files from a block of binary data without using information from the file system structure or other file metadata on the storage device.

Carving out deleted files using only the file structure and content could be very promising [3] due to the fact that some files have very unique structures which can help to determine a file's footer as well as help to correct and verify a recovered file, e.g., using a cyclic redundancy check (CRC) or polynomial code checksum. Recovering contiguous files is a trivial task. However, when a file is fragmented, data about the file structure is not as reliable. In these cases, the file content becomes a much more important factor than the file structure for file carving. The file contents can help us to collect the features of a file type, which is useful for file fragment classification. Many approaches [4,5,6,7,8] of classification for file recovery have been reported and are efficient and effective. McDaniel et al. [4] proposed algorithms to produce file fingerprints of file types. The file fingerprints are created based on byte frequency distribution (BFD) and byte frequency cross-correlation (BFC). Subsequently, Wang et al. [5] created a set of modes for each file type in order to improve the technique of creating file fingerprint and thus to enhance the recognition accuracy rate: 100% accuracy for some file types and 77% accuracy for JPEG file. Karresand et al. [7,8] introduced a classification approach based on individual clusters instead of entire files. They used the rate of change (RoC) as a feature, which can recognize JPEG file with the accuracy up to 99%.

Although these classification approaches are efficient, they have no effect on encrypted files. For reasons of confidentiality, in some situations, people encrypt their private files and then store them on the hard disk. The content of encrypted files is a random bit stream, which provides no clue about original file features or useful information for creating file fingerprints. Thus, traditional classification approaches cannot be directly applied to encrypted file recovery. In this paper, we introduce a recovering mechanism for encrypted files. To the best of our knowledge, this is the first study of encrypted file recovery. Firstly, we categorize block cipher encryption mode into two groups: block-decryption-dependant, and block-decryption-independent. For each group, we present an approach for file recovery. Secondly, we present an approach for recognizing block cipher mode and encryption algorithm. Based on the introduced approach, encrypted files can be recovered. Lastly, we analyze our proposed scheme theoretically.

The rest of the paper is organized as follows. Section 2 briefly introduces problem statement, objective and preliminaries that include file system, file fragmentation, and file encryption/decryption. According to different block cipher encryption modes, Section 3 presents a corresponding mechanism for file recovering. Section 4 introduces an approach of recognizing a block cipher mode and an encryption algorithm. Section 5 theoretically analyzes our proposed approach. Finally, we draw the conclusions of this study and give the future work in Section 6.

2 Preliminaries and Objective

2.1 File System and File Fragmentation

We use the FAT file system as an example to introduce general concepts about file systems. In a file system, a file is organized into two main parts: (1) The first part is the file identification and metadata information, which tell an operating system (OS) where a file is physically stored; (2) The second part of a file is its physical contents that are stored in a disk data area. In a file system, a cluster (or block) is the smallest data unit of transfer between the OS and disk. The name and starting cluster of a file is stored in a directory entry, which presents the first cluster of the file. Each entry of a file allocation table (FAT) records its next cluster number where a file is stored and a special value is used to indicate the end of file (EOF), for example, 0xfffffff as end of cluster chain markers for one of three versions of FAT, i.e., FAT32. As shown in Fig. 1, the first cluster number of file a.txt is 32, and the following cluster number is 33, 39, 40. When a file is deleted, its corresponding entries at the file allocation table are wiped out to zero. As shown in Fig. 1, if a.txt is deleted, the entries, 32, 33, 39, and 40, are set to "0". However, the contents of a.txt in the disk data area remain. The objective of a file carver is to recover a file without the file allocation table.

When files are first created, they may be allocated in disk entirely and without fragmentation. As files are modified, deleted, and created over time, it is highly possible that some files become fragmented. As shown in Fig. 1, a.txt and b.txt are fragmented, and each of them are fragmented into two fragments.

2.2 Problem Statement and Objective

We will now give an example to properly demonstrate the issue we will address in this paper. Suppose that there are several files in a folder. Some files are

Directory entries:

File name:	a.txt	b.txt
Starting cluster :	32	34

File allocation table:

32	33	34	35	36	37	38	39	40	41	42
33	39	35	36	41	0	0	40	EOF	42	EOF

Disk data area:

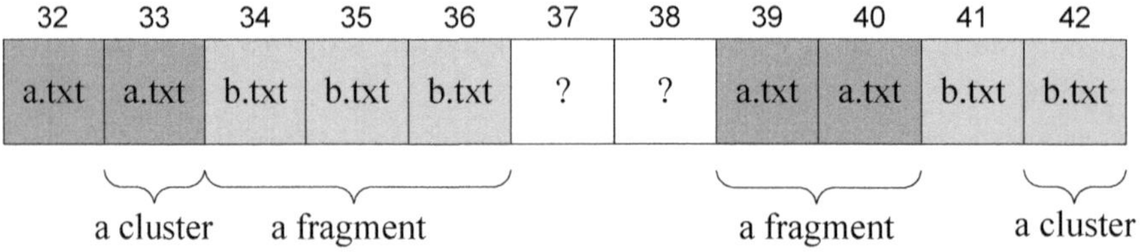

Fig. 1. The illustration of a file system and file fragmentation

unencrypted while some files are encrypted due to some security and privacy reasons. It is worth noting that the encrypted files are encrypted by a user not an operating system. Now assume that all of these files are deleted inadvertently. Our objective is to recover these files, given that the user still remembers the encryption key for each encrypted file.

First of all, let us consider the situation where the files are unencrypted. As shown in Fig. 2(a), file F_1 and F_2, which are two different file types, are fragmented and stored in the disk. In this case, a file classification approach can be used to classify the file F_1 and F_2, and then the two files can be reassembled. The reason why F_1 and F_2 can be classified is that the content features of F_1 and F_2 are different. Based on the features, such as keyword, rate of change (RoC), byte frequency distribution (BFD), and byte frequency cross-correlation (BFC), file fingerprints can be created easily and used for file classification.

However, when we consider the situation where the files are encrypted, the solution of using file classification does not work any more. As illustrated in Fig. 2(b), the encrypted content of files is a random bit stream, and it is difficult to find file features from the random bit stream in order to classify the files accurately. The only information we have is the encryption/decryption keys. Even given these keys, we still cannot simply decrypt the file contents like from Fig. 2(b) to Fig. 2(a). It is not only because the cipher content of a file is fragmented, but also because we cannot know which key corresponds to which random bit stream.

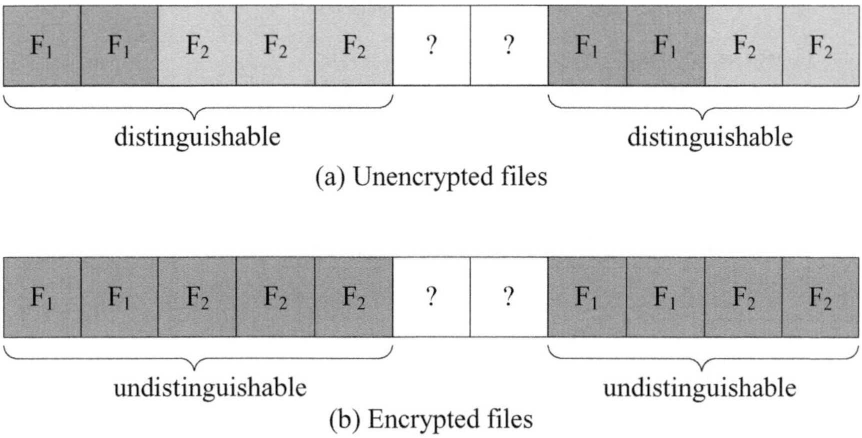

Fig. 2. File F_1 and F_2 have been divided into several fragments. (a) shows the case that F_1 and F_2 are unencrypted, and (b) shows the case that F_1 and F_2 are encrypted.

The objective of this paper is to find an efficient approach to recover encrypted files. Recovering unencrypted files is beyond the scope of this paper because it can be solved with existing approaches.

2.3 File Encryption/Decryption

There is no difference between file encryption/decryption and data stream encryption/decryption. In a cryptosystem, there are two kinds of encryption: symmetric encryption and asymmetric encryption. Symmetric encryption is more suitable for data streams. In symmetric cryptograph, there are two categories of encryption/decryption algorithms: stream cipher and block cipher. Throughout this paper, we focus on investigating the block cipher to address the issue of file carving. There are many block cipher modes of operation in existence. Cipher-block chaining (CBC) is one of the representative cipher modes. To properly present block cipher, we take CBC an example in this subsection.

Fig. 3 illustrates the encryption and decryption processes of CBC mode. To be encrypted, a file is divided into blocks. The size of a block could be 64, 128, or 256 bits, depending on which encryption algorithm is being used. For example, in DES, the block size is 64 bits. If 128- bit AES encryption is used, then the block size is 128 bits. Each block can be encrypted with its previous block cipher and the key. Also, each block can be decrypted with its previous block cipher and the key. The symbol "$\oplus$" in Fig. 3 stands for Exclusive OR (XOR).

3 Encrypted-File Carving Mechanism

For encrypted-file caving, the most important part is to know what block cipher operation mode is used when a file is encrypted. A user intending to recover

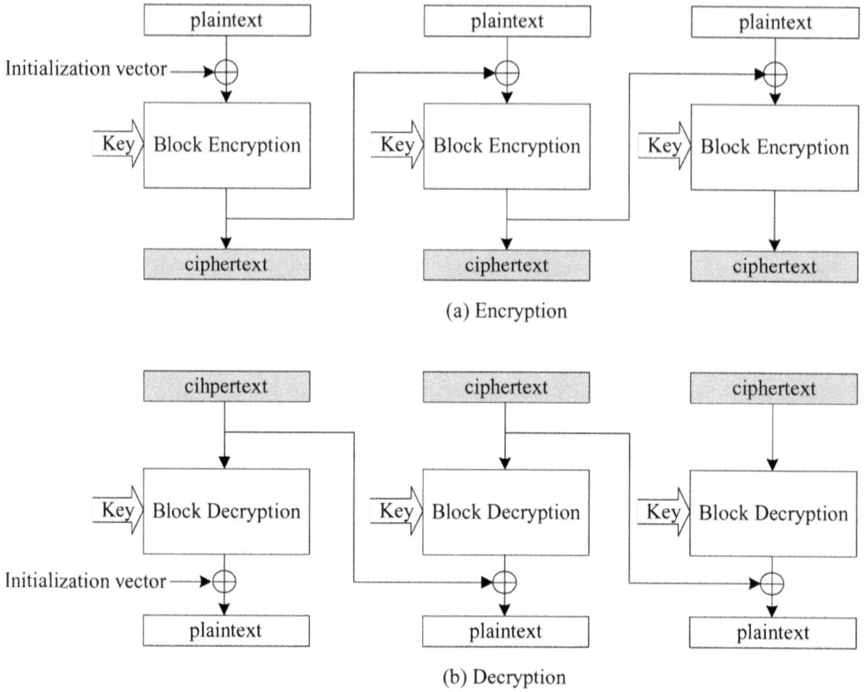

Fig. 3. The encryption and decryption processes of CBC mode

the deleted files may still remember the encryption key, but is unlikely to have any knowledge about the details of the encryption algorithm. In this section, we present a mechanism to recover encrypted files under different block cipher operation modes.

3.1 Recovering Files Encrypted with CBC Mode

In this section, we suppose the file to be recovered is encrypted using CBC mode. From the encryption process of CBC, as shown in Fig. 3(a), we can see that encrypting each block depends on its previous cipher block. As such, the encryption process is like a chain, in which adjacent blocks are connected closely. For example, if we want to get the cipher block i (e.g., $i = 100$), we have to encrypt the plaintext block 1 and get the cipher block 1. Then, we can get the cipher block 2, the cipher block 3, until get the cipher block $i = 100$.

However, the decryption process is different from the encryption process. As shown in Fig. 3(b), to decrypt a cipher block, we only need to know its previous cipher block in addition to the key. For example, if we intent to decrypt the cipher block i (e.g., $i = 100$), we do not have to obtain the cipher block 1 while we only need the cipher block $i - 1 = 99$. We call this feature *block-decryption-independent*.

Based on the block-decryption-independent feature of CBC, we recover an encrypted file according to the following steps.

1. Estimate the physical disk data area where an encrypted file to be recovered could be allocated.
2. Perform brute-force decryption: decrypt each block in the estimated disk data area using the remembered encryption key.
3. Recognize the decrypted fragments, collect the recognized fragments, and reassemble the fragments.

In file systems, the size of a cluster depends on the operating system, e.g., 4KB. However, the size is always larger than and multiple of the size of an encryption block, e.g., 64 or 128 bits. Thus, we can always decrypt a cluster from the beginning of a cluster.

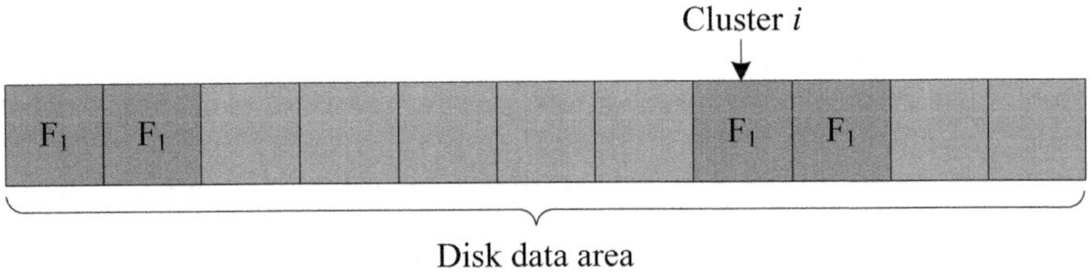

Fig. 4. Decrypted clusters in disk data area

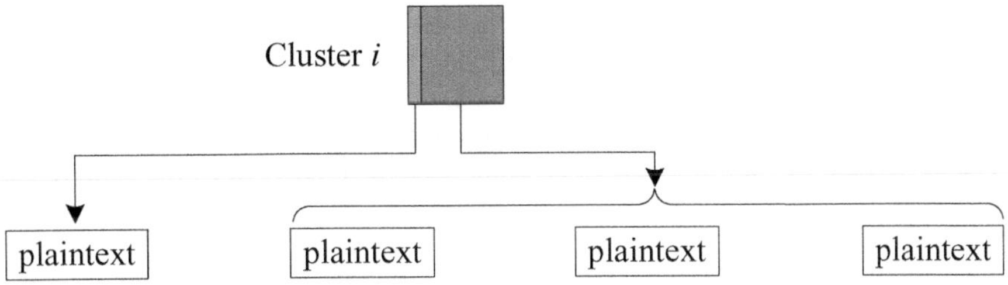

Fig. 5. The first block of Cluster i in Fig. 4 is not decrypted correctly

The encrypted file is a double-edged sword. On the one hand, ciphertext makes us unable to create file fingerprint for file classification. On the other hand, decrypted content makes it easier to classify decrypted file in the disk data area. For example, suppose we intent to recover the file F_1 in Fig. 2(b), and we know the encryption key, K. Using key K, we perform decryption on all clusters. The decrypted clusters of F_1 are shown in Fig. 4. For the clusters that are not part of F_1, the decryption can be treated as encryption using key K. Hence, the clusters that are not parts of F_1 become random bit streams, which are presented using gray squares in Fig. 4. The random bit streams have no feature of a file type and thus decryption is helpful for us to classify the fragments of F_1 from the disk data area.

Since F_1 is fragmented, cluster i in Fig. 4 cannot be decrypted completely. However, only the first CBC block in cluster i is not decrypted correctly, and the blocks following cluster i can be decrypted correctly according to the block-decryption-independent feature of CBC mode, shown in Fig. 5. This fact does not affect file classification because a block size is far smaller than a cluster size. It is worth noticing that we adopt the existing classification approaches [4,5,6,7,8] for file carving in the file classification process (Step 3). Designing a file classification algorithm is beyond the scope of this paper.

3.2 Recovering Files Encrypted with PCBC Mode

For block cipher, in addition to CBC mode, there are many other modes. Propagating cipher block chaining (PCBC) is another representative mode. The encryption and decryption processes of PCBC mode are shown in Fig. 6. Let C denote a block of cipher text in Fig. 6, P denote a block of plain text, i denote a block index, and $D_K()$ denote block decryption with key K. Observing the decryption process in Fig. 6(b), we can see the following relationship.

$$P_i = C_{i-1} \text{ XOR } P_{i-1} \text{ XOR } D_K(C_i)$$

Clearly, obtaining each block of plain text P_i not only depends on its corresponding cipher text C_i, but also depends on its previous cipher text C_{i-1} and plain text P_{i-1}. To obtain P_i, we have to know P_{i-1}, and to obtain P_{i-1}, we have to know P_{i-2} and so on. As such, to decrypt any block of cipher text, we have to do the decryption from the beginning of a file. In contrast to CBC mode, we call this feature *block-decryption-dependent.*

Compared with recovering files encrypted with CBC mode, recovering files encrypted with PCBC mode is more difficult. We recover files encrypted with PCBC mode according to the following steps.

1. Estimate the physical disk data area where an encrypted file to be recovered could be allocated.
2. Find the first cluster of the file. Decrypt each cluster with an initialization vector and the remembered key K, and use individual cluster recognition approach [7,8] to find and decrypt the first cluster. Alternately, the first cluster can also be found from the directory entry table as shown in Fig. 1
3. Having the first cluster, we can find the second cluster. Decrypt each cluster with P and C of the last block of the first cluster and key K, and then use the individual cluster recognition approach to recognize the second cluster.
4. As such, we can find and decrypt the clusters 3, 4, ..., i.

Clearly, recovering files encrypted with PCBC mode is more difficult because failing to recover the ith cluster leads to failing to recover all clusters following the ith cluster.

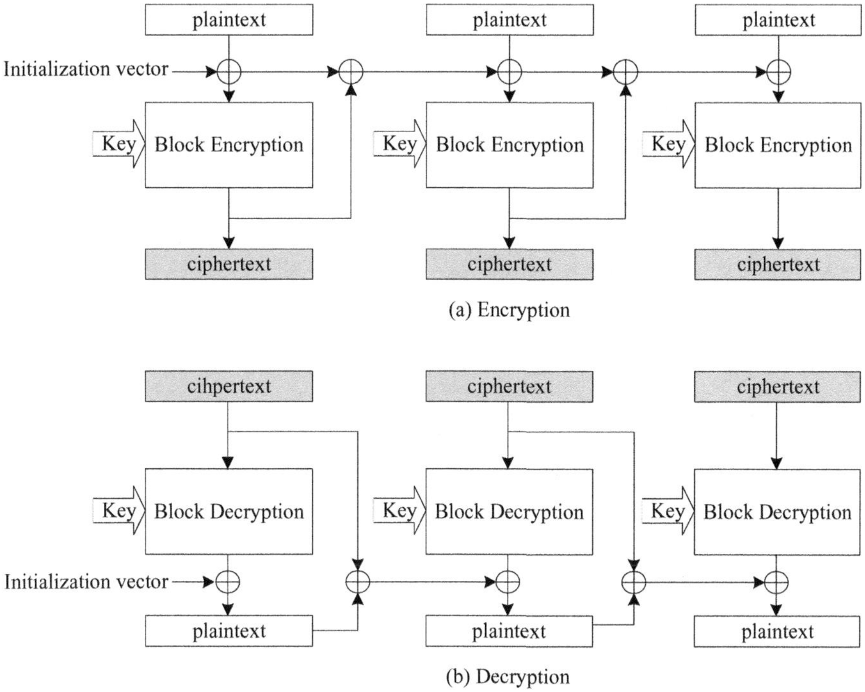

Fig. 6. Encryption and decryption processes of PCBC mode

4 Cipher Mode and Encryption Algorithm Recognition

In the previous section, we have presented the recovering approaches respectively for CBC and PCBC modes. The precondition is that we already know which mode was used to encrypt the file. In reality, however, the encryption mode is not known ahead of time. Furthermore, even if we know the cipher mode, we would still need to know what encryption algorithm is used inside a block encryption module. This section introduces an approach to recognize a cipher mode and an encryption algorithm.

Table 1. Classification of cipher modes

Feature	Cipher mode
block-decryption-dependent	PCBC, OFB
block-decryption-independent	CBC, ECB, CFB , CTS

In a cryptosystem, in addition to CBC and PCBC, there are other block cipher encryption modes. However, the number is limited. For example, Windows CryptoAPI [9] supports the cipher modes including, CBC, cipher feedback

(CFB), cipher text stealing (CTS), electronic codebook (ECB), output feedback (OFB). According to the decryption dependency, we classify these modes, as shown in Table 1. Since mode CBC, ECB, CFB, and CTS are in the same group, the approach of recovering files using mode ECB, CFB, and CTS is the same as that of recovering files using mode CBC, which has been presented in Section III-A. Similarly, the approach of recovering files using mode OFB is the same as that of recovering files using mode PCBC, which has been presented in Section III-B. Similar to cipher mode, the number of encryption algorithm for block cipher is also limited. Windows CryptoAPI [9] supports RC2, DES, and AES.

Algorithm 1: Cipher mode Recognition

```
Input: The first fragment of an encrypted file
Output: Cipher mode and encryption algorithm

    Step 1: Use RC2 as the encryption algorithm. Decrypt the
    first fragment respectively using mode CBC, ECB, CFB ,
    CTS, PCBC, and OFB, and save the corresponding decrypted
    plaintext fragments.

    Step 2: Use DES as the encryption algorithm. Decrypt the
    first fragment respectively using mode CBC, ECB, CFB ,
    CTS, PCBC, and OFB, and save the corresponding decrypted
    plaintext fragments.

    Step 3: Use AES as the encryption algorithm. Decrypt the
    first fragment respectively using mode CBC, ECB, CFB ,
    CTS, PCBC, and OFB, and save the corresponding decrypted
    plaintext fragments.

    Step 4: Recognize the first fragment from all plaintext
    fragments that are obtained from Step 1, 2, 3.

    Step 5: Output the cipher mode and the encryption algorithm
    corresponding to the recognized first fragment in Step 4.
```

We use an exhaustive algorithm to recognize the cipher mode and the encryption algorithm that are used to encrypt a to-be-recovered file. Algorithm **1** presents the steps of the recognition process. In Algorithm **1**, the beginning cluster number of the first fragment can be obtained from the directory entry table as shown in Fig. 1. If the used cipher mode and the encryption algorithm are included in Algorithm **1**, Step 5 must return correct results. It is worth noting that in Step 4 of Algorithm **1** we do not introduce a new file classification algorithm and we adopt the existing solutions [5].

5 Theoretical Analysis

In this section, we theoretically analyze the accuracy of recovering an entire encrypted file. For ease of presentation, we call this accuracy *Recovering Accuracy* (RA).

For recovering files with block-decryption-independent cipher mode, such as CBC and EBC, RA only depends on the recognition accuracy of a file because all contents (except the first block of a fragment as shown in Fig.5) of an encrypted file can be decrypted as plaintext. According to [6], based on the results, the recognition accuracy is variant for different file types. Table 2 [6] shows the results. Clearly, HTML file can be recognized with 100% accuracy and BMP file has the lowest accuracy. Nevertheless, as we present in Section III-A, the decrypted clusters that are not part of the to-be-recovered file become a random bit stream, which is favorable to classifying a decrypted file. Theoretically, RA should be higher than the results in Table 2.

Table 2. Recognition accuracy of different types of files [6]

Type	AVI	BMP	EXE	GIF	HTML	JPG	PDF
Accuracy	0.95	0.81	0.94	0.98	1.00	0.91	0.86

For recovering files with block-decryption-dependent cipher mode, such as PCBC and OFB, RA not only depends on the recognition accuracy of a file, but also on the number of clusters of an encrypted file. It is because recovering the ith cluster depends on whether the (i-1)th cluster can be recovered correctly. For ease of our analysis, we define some variables. Let k be the total number of clusters that a file has, p be the recognition accuracy, which is variant for different file types as shown in Table 2. Since the first cluster of a file can be found in a directory entry table, recognition accuracy on the first cluster is 100%. Therefore, we can derive RA related to k and p.

$$RA = p^{k-1}$$

Fig. 7 clearly shows the relationship between RA and p as increasing the number of clusters of a file (the size of a cluster is 4kb). As the number of clusters increases, RA decreases. On the other hand, the higher p is, the higher RA is. For some file types such as BMP file, since the recognition accuracy is relatively low ($p = 0.81$), RA becomes very low. However, for HTML file, since the recognition accuracy is relatively high ($p = 1$), RA is also high.

For cipher mode and encryption algorithm recognition, the recognition accuracy rate is the same as recognizing files with block-decryption-independent cipher mode, because only the first fragment of a file needs to be recognized. Also, this rate depends on the file type as shown in Table 2.

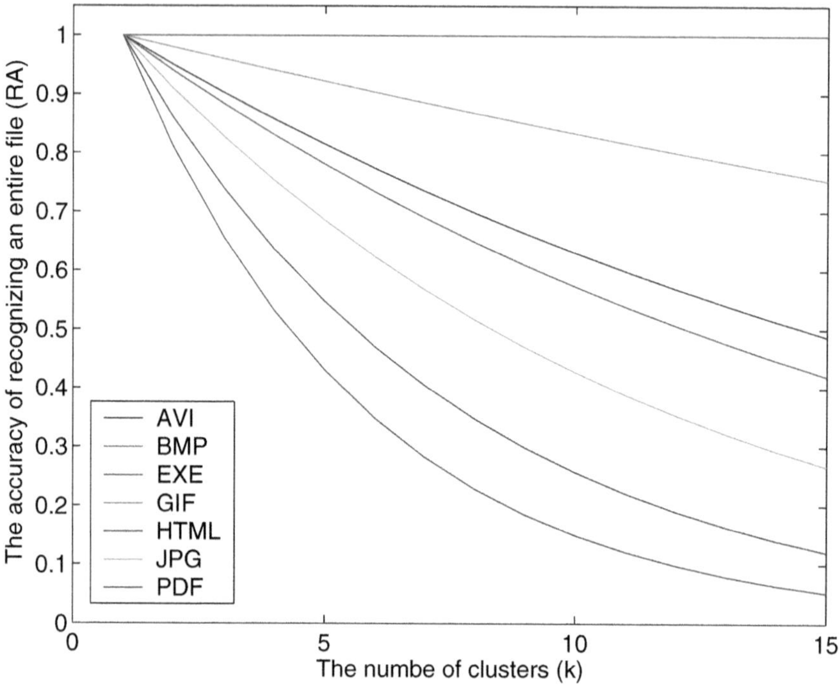

Fig. 7. Encryption and decryption processes of PCBC mode

6 Conclusions and Future Work

In this paper, we have identified the problem of recovering encrypted files, which depends on the encryption cipher mode and encryption algorithm. We have classified encryption cipher modes into two groups, block-decryption-dependant and block-decryption-independent. For each group, we have introduced a corresponding mechanism for file recovery. We have also proposed an algorithm to recognize the encryption cipher mode and the encryption algorithm with which a file is encrypted. Finally, we have theoretically analyzed the accuracy rate of recognizing an entire encrypted file.

We have reported a mechanism and an overall framework of recovering encrypted files. In the future, we will establish and implement an entire system for encrypted file recovery, especially, investigating the applicability of the proposed approaches on the various file/disk encryption solutions available currently, such as TrueCrypt [11], Encrypting File System (EFS) [12], which is a component of the New Technology File System (NTFS) file system on Windows for storing encrypted files. Further, in our system, we will include as many encryption algorithms as possible, including 3DES, AES-128, AES-192 and AES-256, and will also include stream cipher encryption mode. In addition, we will explore more promising recovery algorithms to accelerate the recovery speed.

Acknowledgements. We would like to thank the anonymous reviewers for their helpful comments. This work is partially supported by the grants from the Natural Sciences and Engineering Research Council of Canada (NSERC).

References

1. The MathWorks – MATLAB and Simulink for Technical Computing, `http://www.mathworks.com/`
2. MapleSoft – Mathematics, Mmodeling, and Simulation, `http://www.maplesoft.com/`
3. Pal, A., Memon, N.: The evolution of file carving. IEEE Signal Processing Magazine 26, 59–71 (2009)
4. McDaniel, M., Heydari, M.: Content based file type detection algorithms. In: 36th Annu. Hawaii Int. Conf. System Sciences (HICSS 2003), Washington, D.C (2003)
5. Wang, K., Stolfo, S.J.: Anomalous payload-based network intrusion detection. In: Jonsson, E., Valdes, A., Almgren, M. (eds.) RAID 2004. LNCS, vol. 3224, pp. 203–222. Springer, Heidelberg (2004)
6. Veenman, C.J.: Statistical disk cluster classification for file carving. In: IEEE 3rd Int. Symp. Information Assurance and Security, pp. 393–398 (2007)
7. Karresand, M., Shahmehri, N.: File type identification of data fragments by their binary structure. In: IEEE Information Assurance Workshop, pp. 140–147 (2006)
8. Karresand, M., Shahmehri, N.: Oscar - file type identification of binary data in disk clusters and RAM pages. IFIP Security and Privacy in Dynamic Environments 201, 413–424 (2006)
9. Windows Crypto API, `http://msdn.microsoft.com/enus/library/aa380255(VS.85).aspx`
10. FAT – File Allocation Table, `http://en.wikipedia.org/wiki/File_Allocation_Table`
11. TrueCrypt – Free Open-source On-the-fly Encryption, `http://www.truecrypt.org/`
12. EFS – Encrypting File System, `http://www.ntfs.com/ntfs-encrypted.htm`

Behavior Clustering for Anomaly Detection

Xudong Zhu, Hui Li, and Zhijing Liu

Xidian University, 2 South Taibai Road, Xi'an, Shaanxi, China
zhudongxu@vip.sina.com

Abstract. This paper aims to address the problem of clustering behaviors captured in surveillance videos for the applications of online normal behavior recognition and anomaly detection. A novel framework is developed for automatic behavior modeling and anomaly detection without any manual labeling of the training data set. The framework consists of the following key components: 1) Drawing from natural language processing, we introduce a compact and effective behavior representation method as a stochastic sequence of spatiotemporal events, where we analyze the global structural information of behaviors using their local action statistics. 2) The natural grouping of behaviors is discovered through a novel clustering algorithm with unsupervised model selection. 3) A run-time accumulative anomaly measure is introduced to detect abnormal behaviors, whereas normal behaviors are recognized when sufficient visual evidence has become available based on an online Likelihood Ratio Test (LRT) method. This ensures robust and reliable anomaly detection and normal behavior recognition at the shortest possible time. Experimental results demonstrate the effectiveness and robustness of our approach using noisy and sparse data sets collected from a real surveillance scenario.

Keywords: Computer Vision, Anomaly Detection, Hidden Markov Model, Latent Dirichlet Allocation.

1 Introduction

In visual surveillance, there is an increasing demand for automatic methods for analyzing an extreme number of surveillance video data produced continuously by video surveillance system. One of the key goals of deploying an intelligent video surveillance system (IVSS) is to detect abnormal behaviors and recognize the normal ones. To achieve this objective, one need to analyze and cluster previously observed behaviors, upon which a criterion on what is normal/abnormal is drawn and applied to newly captured patterns for anomaly detection. Due to the large amount of surveillance video data to be analyzed and the real-time nature of many surveillance applications, it is very desirable to have an automated system that requires little human intervention. In the paper, we aim to develop such a system that is based on fully unsupervised behavior modeling and robust anomaly detection.

X. Lai et al. (Eds.): E-Forensics 2010, LNICST 56, pp. 14–27, 2011.

Let us first define the problem of automatic behavior clustering for anomaly detection. Given a collection of unlabeled videos, the goal of automatic behavior clustering is to learn a model that is capable of detecting unseen abnormal behaviors while recognizing novel instances of expected normal ones. In this context, we define an anomaly as an atypical behavior that is not represented by sufficient samples in a training data set but critically satisfies the specificity constraint to an abnormal behavior. This is because one of the main challenges for the model is to differentiate anomaly from outliers caused by noisy visual features used for behavior representation. The effectiveness of an behavior clustering algorithm shall be measured by 1) how well anomalies can be detected (that is, measuring specificity to expected patterns of behavior) and 2) how accurately and robustly different classes of normal behaviors can be recognized (that is, maximizing between class discrimination).

To solve the problem, we develop a novel framework for fully unsupervised behavior modeling and anomaly detection. Our framework has the following key components:

1. A event-based action representation. Due to the space-time nature of actions and their variable durations, we need to develop a compact and effective action representation scheme and to deal with time warping. We propose a discrete event-based image feature extraction approach. This is different from most previous approaches such as [1], [2], [3] where features are extracted based on object tracking. A discrete event-based action representation aims to avoid the difficulties associated with tracking under occlusion in noisy scenes. Each action is modeled using "bag of events" representation [4], which provides a suitable means for time warping and measure the affinity between actions.
2. Behavior clustering based on discovering the natural grouping of behavior using Hidden Markov Model with Latent Dirichlet Allocation (HMM-LDA). A number of clustering techniques based on local word-statistics of a video have been proposed recently [5], [4], [6]. However, these approaches only capture the content of a video sequence and ignore its order. But generally behaviors are not fully defined by their action-content alone; however, there are preferred or typical action-orderings. This problem is addressed by the approach proposed in [4]. However, since discriminative prowess of the approach proposed in [4] is a function of the order over which action-statistics are computed, it comes at an exponential cost of computation complexity. In this work, we address these issues by proposing the usage of HMM-LDA to classify action instances of an behavior into states and topics, constructing a more discriminative feature space based on the context-dependent labels, and resulting in potentially better behavior-class discovery and classification.
3. Online anomaly detection using a runtime accumulative anomaly measure and normal behavior recognition using an online Likelihood Ratio Test (LRT) method. A runtime accumulative measure is introduced to determine an unseen normal or abnormal behavior. The behavior is then recognized as one

of the normal behavior classes using an online LRT method which holds the decision on recognition until sufficient visual features have become available. This is in order to overcome any ambiguity among different behavior classes observed online due to insufficient visual evidence at a given time instance. By doing so, robust behavior recognition and anomaly detection are ensured as soon as possible, as opposed to previous work such as [7], [8], which requires completed behavior being observed. Our online LRT-based behavior recognition approach is also advantageous over previous ones based on the Maximum Likelihood (ML) method [8], [9]. An ML-based approach makes a forced decision on behavior recognition without considering the reliability and sufficiency of the visual evidence. Consequently, it can be error prone.

Note that our framework is fully unsupervised in that manual data labeling is avoided in both the feature extraction and the discovery of the natural grouping of behaviors. There are a number of motivations for performing behavior clustering: First, manual labeling of behaviors is laborious and often rendered impractical given the vast amount of surveillance video data to be processed. More critically though, manual labeling of behaviors could be inconsistent and error prone. This is because a human tends to interpret behaviors based on the a priori cognitive knowledge of what should be present in a scene rather than solely based on what is visually detectable in the scene. This introduces a bias due to differences in experience and mental states.

The rest of the paper is structured as follows: Section 2 addresses the problem of behavior representation. The behavior clustering process is described in Section 3. Section 4 centers about the online detection of abnormal behavior and recognition of normal behavior. In Section 5, the effectiveness and robustness of our approach is demonstrated through experiments using noisy and sparse data sets collected from both indoor and outdoor surveillance scenarios. The paper concludes in Section 6.

2 Behavior Representation

2.1 Video Segmentation

The goal is to automatically segment a continuous video sequence $\mathbf{V}$ into N video segments $\mathbf{V} = \{\mathbf{v}_1, \ldots, \mathbf{v}_i \ldots, \mathbf{v}_N\}$ such that, ideally, each segment contains a single behavior pattern. The nth video segment $\mathbf{v}_n$ consisting of T_n image frames is represented as $\mathbf{v}_n = [\mathbf{I}_{n1}, \ldots, \mathbf{I}_{nt}, \ldots, \mathbf{I}_{nT_n}]$, where $\mathbf{I}_{nt}$ is the tth image frame. Depending on the nature of the video sequence to be processed, various segmentation approaches can be adopted. Since we are focusing on surveillance video, the most commonly used shot change detection-based segmentation approach is not appropriate. In a not-too-busy scenario, there are often nonactivity gaps between two consecutive behavior patterns that can be utilized for behavior segmentation. In the case where obvious nonactivity gaps are not available, the online segmentation algorithm proposed in [3] can be adopted. Specifically, video content is represented as a high-dimensional trajectory based on automatically detected visual events. Breakpoints on the trajectory are then detected online using a Forward-Backward Relevance (FBR) procedure. Alternatively, the video can be simply sliced into overlapping segments with a fixed time duration [5].

2.2 Behavior Representation

First, moving pixels of each image frame in the video are detected directly via spatiotemporal filtering of the image-frames:

$$\begin{aligned} M_t(x,y,t) &= (I(x,y,t) * G(x,y;\sigma) * h_{ev}(t;\tau,\omega))^2 \\ &+ (I(x,y,t) * G(x,y;\sigma) * h_{od}(t;\tau,\omega))^2 > Th_a \end{aligned} \quad (1)$$

where $G(x,y;\sigma) = e^{((\frac{x}{\sigma_x})+(\frac{y}{\sigma_y}))}$ is the 2D Gaussian smoothing kernel, applied only along the spatial dimensions (x,y), and h_{ev} and h_{od} are a quadrature pair of 1D Gabor filters applied temporally, which are defined as $h_{ev}(t;\tau,\omega) = -cos(2\pi t\omega)e^{-t^2/\tau^2}$ and $h_{od}(t;\tau,\omega) = -sin(2\pi t\omega)e^{-t^2/\tau^2}$. The two parameters σ and τ correspond to the spatial and temporal scales of the detector respectively. This convolution is linearly separable in space and time and is fast to compute.

Second, each frame is defined as a event. A detected event is represented as the spatial histogram of the detected objects. Let $H_t(i,j)$ be an $m \times m$ spatial histogram, with m typically equal to 10.

$$H_t(i,j) = \sum_{x,y} M(x,y,t) \cdot \delta(b_i^x \le x < b_{i+1}^x) \cdot \delta(b_i^y \le y < b_{i+1}^y) \quad (2)$$

where b_i^x,b_j^y $(i,j = 1,\ldots,m)$ are the boundaries of the spatial bins. The spatial histograms indicate the rough area of object movement. The process is demonstrated in figure 1(a)-(c).

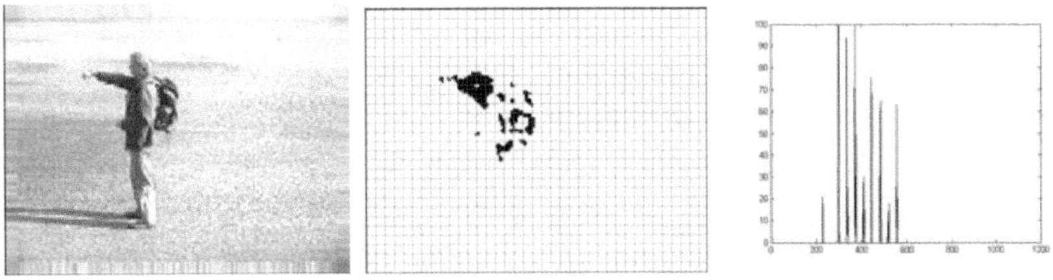

(a) (b) (c)

Fig. 1. Feature extraction from video frames. (a) original video frame. (b) binary map of objects. (c) spatial histogram of (b).

Third, vector quantization is applied to the histogram feature vectors classifying them into a dictionary of K_e event classes $\mathbf{w} = \{w_1,\ldots,w_K\}$ using K-means. So each detected event is classified into one of the K_e event classes.

Finally, the behavior captured in the nth video segment v_n is represented as an event sequence $\mathbf{P}_n$, given as

$$\mathbf{w}_n = [w_{n1}, \ldots, w_{nt}, \ldots, w_{nT_n}] \tag{3}$$

where T_n is the length of the nth video segment. w_{nt} corresponds to the tth image frame of v_n, where $w_{nt} = w_k$ indicates that an event of the kth event class has occurred in the frame.

3 Behavior Clustering

The behavior clustering problem can now be defined formally. Consider a training data set $\mathbf{D}$ consisting of N feature vectors

$$\mathbf{D} = \{\mathbf{w}_1, \ldots, \mathbf{w}_n, \ldots, \mathbf{w}_N\} \tag{4}$$

where $\mathbf{w}_n$ is defined in (6), represents the behavior captured by the nth video $\mathbf{v}_n$. The problem to be addressed is to discover the natural grouping of the training behaviors upon which a model for normal behavior can be built. This is essentially a data clustering problem with the number of clusters unknown. There are a number of aspects that make this problem challenging: 1) Each feature vector $\mathbf{w}_n$ can be of different lengths. Conventional clustering approaches require that each data sample is represented as a fixed length feature vector. 2) Model selection needs to be performed to determine the number of cluster. To overcome the above mentioned difficulties, we propose a clustering algorithm with feature and model selection based on modeling each behavior using HMM-LDA.

3.1 Hidden Markov Model with Latent Dirichlet Allocation (HMM-LDA)

Suppose we are given a collection of M video sequences $D = \{\mathbf{w}_1, \mathbf{w}_2, \ldots, \mathbf{w}_M\}$ containing action words from a vocabulary of size V $(i = 1, \ldots, V)$. Each video $\mathbf{w}_j$ is represented as a sequence of N_j action words $\mathbf{w}_j = (w_1, w_2, \ldots, w_{N_j})$, where w_i is the action word representing the i-th frame. Then the process that generates each video $\mathbf{w}_j$ in the corpus D is:

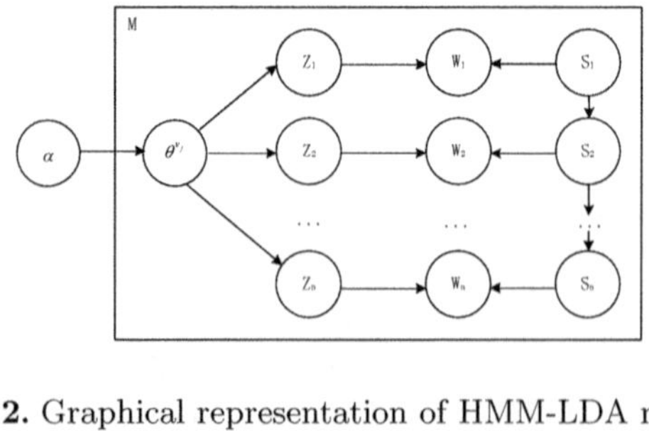

Fig. 2. Graphical representation of HMM-LDA model

1. Draw topic weights $\theta^{(\mathbf{w}_j)}$ from $Dir(\alpha)$
2. For each word w_i in video $\mathbf{w}_j$
   (a) Draw z_i from $\theta^{(\mathbf{w}_j)}$
   (b) Draw c_i from $\pi^{(c_{i-1})}$
   (c) If $c_i = 1$, then draw w_i from $\phi^{(z_i)}$, else draw w_i from $\phi^{(c_i)}$

Here we fixed the number of latent topic K to be equal to the number of behavior categories to be learnt. Also, α is the parameter of a K-dimensional Dirichlet distribution, which generates the multinomial distribution $\theta^{(\mathbf{w}_j)}$ that determines how the behavior categories (latent topics) are mixed in the current video $\mathbf{w}_j$. Each spatial-temporal action word w_i in video $\mathbf{w}_j$ is mapped to a hidden state s_i. Each hidden state s_i generates action words w_i according to a unigram distribution $\phi^{(c_i)}$ except the special latent topic state z_i, where the z_ith topic is associated with a distribution words $\phi^{(z_i)}$. $\phi^{(z_i)}$ corresponds to the probability $p(w_i|z_k)$. Each video $\mathbf{w}_j$ has a distribution over topic $\theta^{(\mathbf{w}_j)}$, and transitions between classes c_{i-1} and c_i follow a distribution $\pi^{s_{i-1}}$. The complete probability model is

$$\theta \sim Dirichlet(\alpha) \tag{5}$$

$$\phi^{(z)} \sim Dirichlet(\beta) \tag{6}$$

$$\pi \sim Dirichlet(\gamma) \tag{7}$$

$$\phi^{(c)} \sim Dirichlet(\delta) \tag{8}$$

Here, α, β, γ and δ are hyperparameters, specifying the nature of the priors on θ, $\phi^{(z)}$, π and $\phi^{(c)}$.

3.2 Learning the Behavior Models

Our strategy for learning topics differs from previous approaches [12] in not explicitly representing θ, $\phi^{(z)}$, π and $\phi^{(c)}$ as parameters to be estimated, but instead considering the posterior distribution over the assignments of words to topics, $p(\mathbf{z}|\mathbf{c}, \mathbf{w})$. We then obtain estimates of θ, $\phi^{(z)}$, π and $\phi^{(c)}$ by examining this posterior distribution. Computing $p(\mathbf{z}|\mathbf{c}, \mathbf{w})$ involves evaluating a probability distribution on a large discrete state space. We evaluate $p(\mathbf{z}|\mathbf{c}, \mathbf{w})$ by using a Monte Carlo procedure, resulting in an algorithm that is easy to implement, requires little memory, and is competitive in speed and performance with existing algorithms.

In Markov chain Monte Carlo, a Markov chain is constructed to converge to the target distribution, and samples are then taken from Markov chain. Each state of the chain is an assignment of values to the variable being sampled and transitions between states follow a simple rule. We use Gibbs sampling where the next state is reached by sequentially sampling all variable from their distribution when conditioned on the current values of all other variables and the data. To apply this algorithm we need two full conditional distributions, $p(z_i|\mathbf{z}_{-i}, \mathbf{c}, \mathbf{w})$ and $p(c_i|\mathbf{c}_{-i}, \mathbf{z}, \mathbf{w})$. These distributions can be obtained by using the conjugacy of the Dirichlet and multinomial distributions to integrate out the parameters θ and ϕ, yielding

$$p(z_i|\mathbf{z}_{-i}, \mathbf{c}, \mathbf{w}) \propto \begin{cases} n_{z_i}^{w_j} + \alpha, & c_i \neq 1 \\ (n_{z_i}^{w_j} + \alpha)\dfrac{n_{w_i}^{(z_i)} + \beta}{n^{(z_i)} + W\beta}, & c_i = 1 \end{cases} \tag{9}$$

where $n_{z_i}^{(\mathbf{w}_j)}$ is the number of words in video $\mathbf{w}_j$ assigned to topic z_i, $n_{w_i}^{(z_i)}$ is the number of words assigned to topic z_i that are the same as w_i, and all counts include only words for which $c_i = 1$ and exclude case i.

$$p(c_i|\mathbf{c}_{-i}) = \frac{(n_{c_i}^{(c_{i-1})} + \gamma)(n_{c_{i+1}}^{(c_i)} + I(c_{i-1} = c_i)I(c_i = c_{i+1}) + \gamma)}{n^{(c_i)} + I(c_{i-1} = c_i) + C_\gamma} \tag{10}$$

$$p(c_i|\mathbf{c}_{-i}, \mathbf{z}, \mathbf{w}) \propto \begin{cases} \dfrac{n_{w_i}^{(c_i)} + \delta}{n^{(c_i)} + W\delta} p(c_i|\mathbf{c}_{-i}), & c_i \neq 1 \\ \dfrac{n_{w_i}^{(z_i)} + \beta}{n^{(z_i)} + W\beta} p(c_i|\mathbf{c}_{-i}), & c_i = 1 \end{cases} \tag{11}$$

where $n_{w_i}^{(z_i)}$ is as before, $n_{w_i}^{(c_i)}$ is the number of words assigned to class c_i that are the same as w_i, excluding case i, and $n_{c_i}^{(c_i)}$ is the number of transitions from class c_{i-1} to class c_i, and all counts of transitions exclude transitions both to and from c_i. $I(.)$ is an indicator function, taking the value 1 when its argument is true, and 0 otherwise. Increasing the order of the HMM introduces additional terms into $p(c_i|\mathbf{c}_i)$, but does not otherwise affect sampling.

The z_i variables are initialized to values in $\{1, 2, \ldots, K\}$, determining the initial state of the Markov chain. We do this with an online version of the Gibbs samples, using Eq.12 to assign words to topics, but with counts that are computed from the subset of the words seen so far rather than the full data. The chain is then run for a number of iterations, each time finding a new state by sampling each z_i from the distribution specified by Eq.12. Because the only information needed to apply Eq.12 is the number of times a word is assigned to a topic and the number of times a topic occurs in a document, the algorithm can be run with minimal memory requirements by caching the sparse set of nonzero counts and updating them whenever a word is reassigned. After enough iteration for the chain to approach the target distribution, the current values of the z_i variables are recorded. Subsequent samples are taken after an appropriate lag to ensure that their autocorrelation is low.

With a set of samples from the posterior distribution $p(\mathbf{z}|\mathbf{c}, \mathbf{w})$, statistics that are independent of the content of individual topics can be computed by integrating across the full set of samples. For any single sample we can estimate θ, $\phi^{(z)}$, π and $\phi^{(c)}$ from the value $\mathbf{z}$ by

$$\widehat{\phi}^{(z)} = \frac{n_{w_i}^{(z_i)} + \beta}{n^{(z_i)} + W\beta} \tag{12}$$

$$\widehat{\phi}^{(c)} = \frac{n_{w_i}^{(c_i)} + \delta}{n^{(c_i)} + W\delta} \tag{13}$$

$$\theta = n_{z_i}^{w_j} + \alpha \tag{14}$$

$$\pi = \frac{(n_{c_i}^{(c_i-1)} + \gamma)(n_{c_{i+1}}^{(c_i)} + I(c_{i-1} = c_i)I(c_i = c_{i+1}) + \gamma)}{n^{(c_i)} + I(c_{i-1} = c_i) + C_\gamma} \tag{15}$$

3.3 Model Selection

Given values of α, β and γ, the problem of choosing the appropriate value for K is a problem of model selection, which we address by using a standard method from Bayesian statistics. For a Bayesian statistician faced with a choice between a set of statistical models, the natural response is to compute the posterior probability of the set of models given the observed data. The key constituent of this posterior probability will be the likelihood of the data given the model, integrating over all parameters in the model. In our case, the data are the words in the corpus, $\mathbf{w}$, and the model is specified by the number of topics, K, so we wish to compute the likelihood $p(\mathbf{w}|K)$. The complication is that this requires summing over all possible assignments of words to topics $\mathbf{z}$. However, we can approximate $p(\mathbf{w}|K)$ by taking the harmonic mean of a set of values of $p(\mathbf{w}|\mathbf{z}, K)$ when $\mathbf{z}$ is sampled from the posterior $p(\mathbf{z}|\mathbf{c}, \mathbf{w}, K)$. Our Gibbs sampling algorithm provides such samples, and the value of $p(\mathbf{w}|\mathbf{z}, K)$ can be computed.

4 Online Anomaly Detection and Normal Behavior Recognition

Given a unseen behavior pattern $\mathbf{w}$, we calculate the likelihood $l(\mathbf{w}; \alpha, \beta) = P(\mathbf{w}|\alpha, \beta)$. The likelihood can be used to detect whether an unseen behavior pattern is normal using a runtime anomaly measure. If it is detected to be normal, the behavior pattern is then recognized as one of the K classes of normal behavior patterns using an online LRT method.

An unseen behavior pattern of length T is represented as $\mathbf{w} = (w_1, \ldots, w_t, \ldots, w_T)$. At the tth frame, the accumulated visual information for the behavior pattern, represented as $\mathbf{w}_t = (w_1, \ldots, w_t)$, is used for online reliable anomaly detection. First, the normalized likelihood of observing $\mathbf{w}$ at the tth frame is computed as

$$l_t = P(\mathbf{w}_t|\alpha, \beta) \tag{16}$$

l_t can be easily computed online using the variational inference method.

We then measure the anomaly of $\mathbf{w}_t$ using an online anomaly measure Q_t

$$Q_t = \begin{cases} l_t, & if\ t = 1 \\ (1-\alpha)Q_{t-1} + \alpha(l_t - l_{t-1}), & otherwise \end{cases} \tag{17}$$

where α is an accumulating factor determining how important the visual information extracted from the current frame is for anomaly detection. We have $0 < \alpha \leq 1$. Compared to l_t as an indicator of normality/anomaly, Q_t could add more weight to more recent observations. Anomaly is detected at frame t if

$$Q_t < Th_A \tag{18}$$

where Th_A is the anomaly detection threshold. The value of Th_A should be set according to the detection and false alarm rates required by each particular surveillance application.

At each frame t, a behavior pattern needs to be recognized as one of the K behavior classes when it is detected as being normal, that is, $Q_t > Th_A$. This is achieved by using an online LRT method. More specifically, we consider a hypotheses test between the following

H_k:$\mathbf{w}_t$ is from the hypothesized model z_k and belongs to kth normal behavior class;

H_0:$\mathbf{w}_t$ is from a model other than z_k and does not belong to the kth normal behavior class;

where H_0 is called the alternative hypothesis. Using LRT, we compute the likelihood ratio of accepting the two hypotheses as

$$r_k = \frac{P(\mathbf{w}_t; H_k)}{P(\mathbf{w}_t; H_0)} \tag{19}$$

The hypothesis H_k can be represented by the model z_k, which has been learned in the behavior clustering step. The key to LRT is thus to construct the alternative model that represents H_0. In a general case, the number of possible alternatives is unlimited; $P(\mathbf{w}_t; H_0$ can thus only be computed through approximation. Fortunately, in our case, we have determined at the tth frame that $\mathbf{w}_t$ is normal and can only be generated by one of the K normal behavior classes. Therefore, it is reasonable to construct the alternative model as a mixture of the remaining of $K-1$ normal behavior classes. In particular, (4) is rewritten as

$$r_k = \frac{P(\mathbf{w}_t|z_k)}{\sum_{i \neq k} P(\mathbf{w}_t|z_i)} \tag{20}$$

Note that r_k is a function of t and computed over time. $\mathbf{w}_t$ is reliably recognized as the kth behavior class only when $1 \ll Th_r < r_k$. When there are more than one r_k greater than Th_r, the behavior pattern is recognized as the class with the largest r_k.

5 Experiments

In this section, we illustrate the effectiveness and robustness of our approach on behavior clustering and online anomaly detection with experiments using data sets collected from the entrance/exit area of an office building.

5.1 Dataset and Feature Extraction

A CCTV camera was mounted on a on-street utility pole, monitoring the people entering and leaving the building (see Fig.3). Daily behaviors from 9a.m. to 5p.m. for 5 days were recorded. Typical behaviors occurring in the scene would be people entering, leaving and passing by the building. Each behavior would normally last a few seconds. For this experiment, a data set was collected from 5 different days consisting of 40 hours of video, totaling to 2880,000 frames. A training set consisting of 568 instances was randomly selected from the overall 947 instances without any behavior class labeling. The remaining 379 instances were used for testing the trained model later.

5.2 Behavior Clustering

To evaluate the number of clusters K, we used the Gibbs sampling algorithm to obtain samples from the posterior distribution over $\mathbf{z}$ for K values of 3, 4, 5, 6, 7, 8, and 12. For all runs of the algorithm, we used $\alpha = 50/T$, $\beta = 0.01$ and $\gamma = 0.1$, keeping constant the sum of the Dirichlet hyper-parameters, which can be interpreted as the number of virtual samples contribution to the smoothing of θ. We computed an estimate of $p(\mathbf{w}|K)$ for each value of K . For all values of K, we ran 7 Markov chains, discarding the first 1,000 iterations, and then took 10 samples from each chain at a lag of 100 iterations. In all cases, the log-likelihood values stabilized within a few hundred iterations. Estimates of $p(\mathbf{w}|K)$ were computed based on the full set of samples for each value of K and are shown in Fig.3.

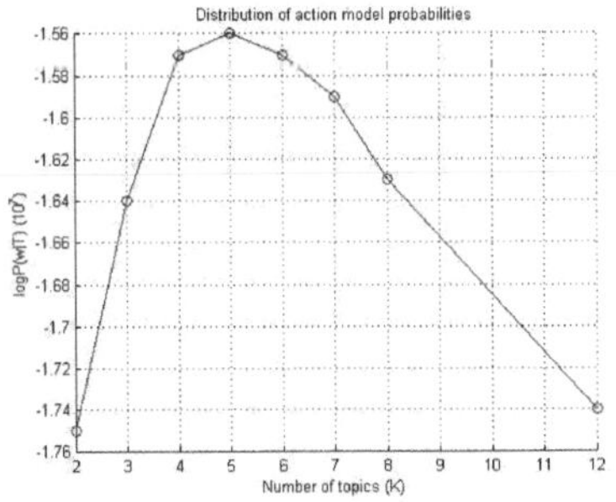

Fig. 3. Model selection results

The results suggest that the data are best accounted for by a model incorporating 5 topics. $p(\mathbf{w}|K)$ initially increases as function of K, reaches a peak at $K = 5$, and then decreases thereafter. By observation, each discovered data cluster mainly contained samples corresponding to one of five behavior classes listed in Table 1.

Table 1. The Five Classes of Behaviors that Most Commonly Occurred in the entrance/exit area of an office building

C1	going into the office building
C2	leaving the office building
C3	passing by the office building
C4	getting off a car and entering the office building
C5	leaving the office building and getting on a car

5.3 Anomaly Detection

The behavior model built using both labeled and unlabeled behaviors were used to perform online anomaly detection. To measure the performance of the learned models on anomaly detection, each behavior in the testing sets was manually labeled as normal if there were similar behaviors in the corresponding training sets and abnormal otherwise. A testing pattern was detected as being abnormal when (18) was satisfied. The accumulating factor α for computing Q_t was set to 0.1. Fig.4. demonstrates one example of anomaly detection in the entrance/exit area of an office building.

We measure the performance of anomaly detection using the anomaly detection rate, which equals to $\frac{\#(abnormal\ detected\ as\ abnormal)}{\#(abnormal\ patterns)}$, and the false alarm rate, which equals to $\frac{\#(normal\ detected\ as\ abnormal)}{\#(normal\ patterns)}$. The detection rate and false alarm rate of anomaly detection are shown in the form of a Receiver Operating Characteristic (ROC) curve by varying the anomaly detection threshold Th_A, as Fig.5(a).

5.4 Normal Behavior Recognition

To measure the recognition rate, the normal behaviors in the testing sets were manually labeled into different behavior classes. A normal behavior was recognized correctly if it was detected as normal and classified into a behavior class containing similar behaviors in the corresponding training set by the learned

Fig. 4. Example of anomaly detection in the entrance/exit area of an office building. (a) An abnormal behavior where one people attempted to destroy the car parking the area. It resembles C3 in the early stage. (b) The behavior was detected as an anomaly from Frame 62 till the end based on Q_t.

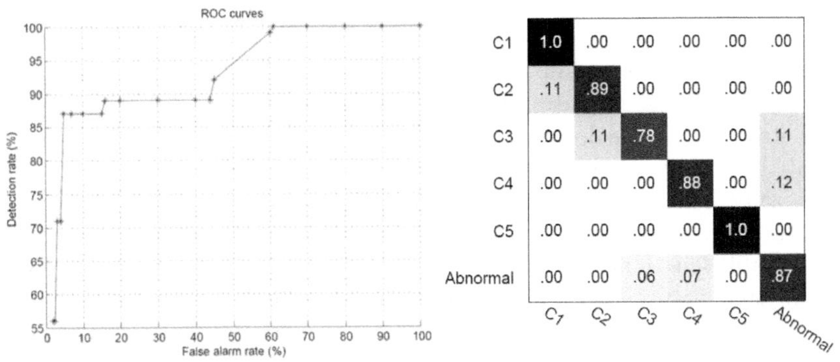

(a) **(b)**

Fig. 5. (a) the mean ROC curves for our dataset. (b)confusion matrix for our dataset; rows are ground truth, and columns are model results.

behavior model. Fig.5(b) shows that when a normal behavior was not recognized correctly by a model trained using unlabeled data, it was most likely to be recognized as belonging to another normal behavior class. On the other hand, for a model trained by labeled data, a normal behavior was most likely to be wrongly detected as an anomaly if it was not recognized correctly. This contributed to the higher false alarm rate for the model trained by labeled data.

5.5 Result Analysis and Discussion

To compare our approach with six other methods, we use exactly the same experiment setup and list the comparison results in Table 2. Each of these is a anomalous behavior detection algorithm that is capable of dealing with low resolution and noisy data. We implement the algorithms of Xiang *et al.* [3], Wang *et al.* [6], Niebles *et al.* [13], Boiman *et al.* [7], Hamid *et al.* [4] and Zhong *et al.* [5]. The key findings of our comparison are summarized and discussed as follows:

1. Table 2 shows that the precision of our HMM-LDA is superior to the HMM method [3], the LDA method [6], the MAP-based method [7] and two

Table 2. Comparison of different methods

methods	Anomaly Detection Rate (%)
Our method	89.26
Xiang *et al.* [3]	85.76
Wang *et al.* [6]	84.46
Niebles *et al.* [13]	83.50
Boiman *et al.* [7]	83.32
Hamid *et al.* [4]	88.48
Zhong *et al.* [5]	85.56

co-clustering algorithms [5],[4]. HMM [3] outperforms the LDA [6] on our scenario, but HMM [3] require explicit modeling of anomalous behaviors structure with minimal supervision. Some recent methods ([5] using Latent Semantic Analysis, [13] using probabilistic Latent Semantic Analysis, [6] using Latent Dirichlet Allocation, [4] using n-grams) extract behavior structure simply by computing local action-statistics, but are limited by their ability to capture behavior structure only up to some fixed temporal resolution. Our HMM-LDA provided the best account, being able to efficiently extract the variable length action-subsequence of behavior, constructing a more discriminative feature space, and resulting in potentially better behavior-class discovery and classification.

2. Work done in [5] clusters behaviors into its constituent sub-class, labeling the clusters with low internal cohesiveness as anomalous cluster. This makes it infeasible for online anomaly detection. The anomaly detection method proposed in [4] was claimed to be online. Nevertheless, in [4], anomaly detection is performed only when the complete behavior pattern is observed. In order to overcome any ambiguity among different behavior classes observed online due to different visual evidence at a given time instance, our online LRT method holds the decision on recognition until sufficient visual features have become available.

6 Conclusions

In conclusion, we have proposed a novel framework for robust online behavior recognition and anomaly detection. The framework is fully unsupervised and consisted of a number of key components, namely, a behavior representation based on spatial-temporal actions, a novel clustering algorithm using HMM-LDA based on action words, a runtime accumulative anomaly measure, and an online LRT-based normal behavior recognition method. The effectiveness and robustness of our approach is demonstrated through experiments using data sets collected from real surveillance scenario.

References

1. Yamato, J., Ohya, J., Ishii, K.: Recognizing human action in time-sequential images using hidden markov model. In: IEEE Computer Society Conference on Computer Vision and Pattern Recognition (1992)
2. Bobick, A.F., Wilson, A.D.: A state-based approach to the representation and recognition of gesture. IEEE Transactions on Pattern Analysis and Machine Intelligence 19(12), 1325–1337 (1997)
3. Xiang, T., Gong, S.: Beyond tracking: Modelling activity and understanding behaviour. International Journal of Computer Vision 67(1), 21–51 (2006)
4. Hamid, R., Johnson, A., Batta, S., Bobick, A., Isbell, C., Coleman, G.: Detection and Explanation of Anomalous Activities: Representing Activities as Bags of Event n-Grams. In: IEEE Computer Society Conference on Computer Vision and Pattern Recognition, pp. 1031–1038 (2005)

5. Zhong, H., Shi, J., Visontai, M.: Detecting Unusual Activity in Video. In: IEEE Computer Society Conference on Computer Vision and Pattern Recognition, pp. 819–826 (2004)
6. Wang, Y., Mori, G.: Human Action Recognition by Semi-Latent Topic Models. IEEE Transactions on Pattern Analysis and Machine Intelligence (2009)
7. Boiman, O., Irani, M.: Detecting irregularities in images and in video. In: IEEE International Conference on Computer Vision, pp. 462–469 (2005)
8. Oliver, N., Rosario, B., Pentland, A.: A Bayesian computer vision system for modelling human interactions. IEEE Transactions on Pattern Analysis and Machine Intelligence 22(8), 831–843 (2000)
9. Zelnik-Manor, L., Irani, M.: Event-based video analysis. In: IEEE Conference on Computer Vision and Pattern Recognition, pp. 123–130 (2001)
10. Comaniciu, D., Meer, P.: Mean Shift Analysis and Applications. In: Proceedings of the International Conference on Computer Vision, Kerkyra, pp. 1197–1203 (1999)
11. Efros, A.A., Berg, A.C., Mori, G., Malik, J.: Recognizing action at a distance. In: IEEE International Conference on Computer Vision, pp. 726–733 (2003)
12. Blei, D.M., Ng, A.Y., Jordan, M.I.: Latent dirichlet allocation. Journal of Machine Learning Research 3, 993–1022 (2003)
13. Niebles, J.C., Wang, H., Fei-Fei, L.: Unsupervised Learning of Human Action Categories Using Spatial-Temporal Words. In: Proc. British Machine Vision Conference, pp. 1249–1258 (2006)

A Novel Inequality-Based Fragmented File Carving Technique

Hwei-Ming Ying and Vrizlynn L.L. Thing

Institute for Infocomm Research, Singapore
{hmying,vriz}@i2r.a-star.edu.sg

Abstract. Fragmented File carving is an important technique in Digital Forensics to recover files from their fragments in the absence of the file system allocation information. In this paper, the fragmented file carving problem is formulated as a graph theoretic problem. Using this model, we describe two algorithms, "Best Path Search" and "High Fragmentation Path Search", to perform file reconstruction and recovery. The best path search algorithm is a deterministic technique to recover the best file construction path. We show that this technique is more efficient and accurate than existing brute force techniques. In addition, a test was carried out to recover 10 files scattered into their fragments. The best path search algorithm was able to successful recover all of them back to their original state. The high fragmentation path search technique involves a trade-off between the final score of the constructed path of the file and the file recovery time to allow a faster recovery process for highly fragmented files. Analysis show that the accurate eliminations of paths have an accuracy of up to greater than 85%.

1 Introduction

The increasing reliance on digital storage devices such as hard disks and solid state disks for storing important private data and highly confidential information has resulted in a greater need for efficient and accurate data recovery of deleted files during digital forensic investigation.

File carving is the technique to recover such deleted files, in the absence of file system allocation information. However, there are often instances where files are fragmented due to low disk space, file deletion and modification. In a recent study [10], FAT was found to be the most popular file system, representing 79.6% of the file systems analyzed. From the files tested on the FAT disks, 96.5% of them had between 2 to 20 fragments. This scenario of fragmented and subsequently deleted files presents a further challenge requiring a more advanced form of file carving techniques to reconstruct the files from the extracted data fragments.

The reconstruction of objects from a collection of randomly mixed fragments is a common problem that arises in several areas, such as archaeology [9], [12], biology [15] and art restoration [3], [2]. In the area of fragmented file craving, research efforts are currently on-going. A proposed approach is known as the Bifragment gap carving(BGC) [13]. This technique searches and recovers files,

X. Lai et al. (Eds.): E-Forensics 2010, LNICST 56, pp. 28–39, 2011.

fragmented into two fragments that contain identifiable headers and footers. An idea of using a graph theoretic approach to perform file craving has also been studied in [8], [14], [4] and [5]. In graph theoretic carving, the fragments are represented by the vertices of a graph and the edges are assigned weights which are values that indicate the likelihood that two fragments are adjacent in the original file. For example in image files, we list two possible techniques to evaluate the candidate weighs between any two fragments [8]. The first is pixel matching whereby the total number of pixels matching along the edges for the two fragments are summed. Each pixel value is then compared with the corresponding pixel value in the other fragment. The closer the values, the better the match. The second is median edge detection. Each pixel is predicted from the value of the pixel above, to the left and left diagonal to it [11]. Using median edge detection, we would sum the absolute value of the difference between the predicted value in the adjoining fragment and the actual value. The carving is then based on obtaining the path of the graph with the best set of weights. In addition, Cohen, 2007 introduced a technique of carving involving mapping functions and discriminators in [6], [7]. These mapping functions represent various ways for which a file can be reconstructed and the discriminators will then check on the validity of them until the best one is obtained. We discuss these methods further in Section 3 on related work.

In this paper, we model the problem in a graph theoretic form which is not restricted by the limitation of the number of fragments. We assume that all the fragments belonging to a file are known. This can be achieved through identification of fragments for a file based on groups of fragments belonging to an image of same scenery (i.e. edge pixel difference detection) or context based modelling for document fragments [4].

We define a file construction path as one passing through all the vertices in the graph. In a graph, there are many different possible file construction paths. An optimal path is one which gives the largest sum of weight (i.e. final score) for all the edges it passes through. The problem of finding the optimum path is intractable [1]. Furthermore, it is well known that applying the greedy algorithm does not give good results and that computing all the possible paths is resource-intensive and not feasible for highly fragmented files. In this paper, we present two main algorithms namely the "Best Path Search" and the "High Fragmentation Path Search". Best Path search is an inequality-based method which will reduce the required computations. This algorithm is more efficient and faster than brute force which computes all the possible path combinations. It is suitable for relative small values of n. For larger values of n, we introduce the High Fragmentation Path Search, which is a tradeoff algorithm to allow a flexible control over the complexity of the algorithm, while at the same time, obtain sufficiently good results for fragmented file carving.

2 Statement of Problem

In fragmented file carving, the objective is to arrange a file back to its original structure and recover the file in as short a time as possible. The technique should not rely on the file system information, which may not exist (e.g. deleted fragmented file, corrupted file system). We are presented with files that are not arranged in its proper original sequence from its fragments. The goal in this paper is to arrange them back to its original state in a short a time as possible.

The core approach would be to test each fragment against one another to check how likely any two fragments is a joint match. They are then assigned weights and these weights represent the likelihood that two fragments are a joint match. Since the header can be easily identified, any edge joining the header is considered a single directional edge while all other edges are bi-directional. Therefore, if there are n fragments, there will be a total of $(n\text{-}1)^2$ weights. The problem can thus be converted into a graph theoretic problem where the fragments are represented by the vertices and the weights are represented by the edges. The goal is to find a file construction path which passes each vertex exactly once and has a maximum sum of edge weights, given the starting vertex. In this case, the starting vertex will correspond to the header.

A simple but tedious approach to solve this problem is to try all path combinations, compute their sums and obtain the largest value which will correspond to the path of maximum weight. Unfortunately, this method will not scale well when n is large since the number of computations of the sums required will be $(n\text{-}1)!$. This complexity increases exponentially as n increases.

3 Related Work

Bifragment gap carving [13] was introduced as a fragmented file carving technique that assumed most fragmented files comprise of the header and footer fragments only. It exhaustively searched for all the combinations of blocks between an identified header and footer, while incrementally excluded blocks that result in unsuccessful decoding/validation of the file. A limitation of this method was that it could only support carving for files with two fragments. For files with more than two fragments, the complexity could grow extremely large.

Graph theoretic carving was implemented as a technique to reassemble fragmented files by constructing a k-vertex disjoint graph. Utilizing a matching metric, the reassembly was performed by finding an optimal ordering of the file blocks/sectors. The different graph theoretic file carving methods are described in [8]. The main drawback of the greedy heuristic algorithms was that it failed to obtain the optimal path most of the time. This was because they do not operate exhaustively on all the data. They made commitments to certain choices too early which prevented them from finding the best path later.

In [6], the file fragments were "mapped" into a file by utilizing different mapping functions. A Mapping function generator generated new mapping functions which were tested by a discriminator. The goal of this technique was to derive a mapping function which minimizes the error rate in the discriminator. It is of great importance to construct a good discriminator for it to localize errors within the file, so that discontinuities can be determined more accurately. If the discriminator failed to indicate the precise locations of the errors, then all the permutations need to be generated which could become intractable.

4 Inequality-Based File Carving Technique

The objective of our work is to devise a method to produce the optimum file construction path and yet achieve a lesser complexity than the brute force approach which requires the computation of all possible paths.

In this section, we do an investigation of the non-optimal paths that can be eliminated. In doing so, the complexity can be reduced when doing the final evaluations of possible candidates for the optimal path. The general idea is described below.

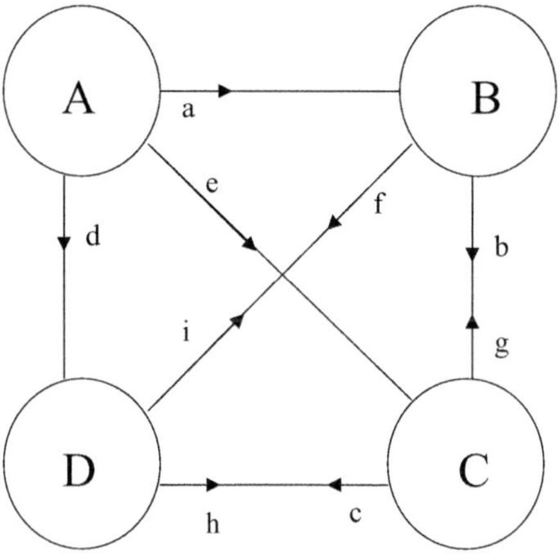

Fig. 1. n=4 (General Case)

In Figure 1, we show an example of a file with 4 fragments (n=4). A, B, C and D represent the file fragments. The letters, a to i, assigned to the edges represent the numbered values of the likelihood of a match between two adjacent fragments in a particular direction. Assume that A is the header fragment which can be easily identified. Let *f(x)* represent the sum of the edges of a path where x is a path. Computing the values of *f(x)* for all the possible paths, we obtain:

f(ABCD) $= a + b + c$
f(ABDC) $= a + f + h$
f(ACBD) $= e + g + f$
f(ACDB) $= e + c + i$
f(ADBC) $= d + i + b$
f(ADCB) $= d + h + g$

Arrange the values of each individual a to i in ascending order. From this chain of inequalities formed from these nine variables, it is extremely unlikely that the optimal path can identified immediately except in very rare scenarios. However, it is possible to eliminate those paths (without doing any additional computations) which we can be certain are non optimal. The idea is to extract more information that can be deduced from the construction of these inequalities. Doing these eliminations will reduce the number of evaluations which we need to compute at the end and hence will result in a reduction in complexity while still being able to obtåin the optimal path.

5 Best Path Search Algorithm

The general algorithm is as follows:

1) For a fixed n, assign $(n\text{-}1)^2$ variables to the directed edges.
2) Work out f(each path) in terms of the sum of n-1 of these variables and arrange the summation in ascending order.
3) Establish the chain of inequalities based on the actual values of the directed edges.
4) Pick the smallest value and identify the paths which contain that value.
5) Do a comparison of that path with other paths at every position of the summation. If the value at each position of this path is less than the corresponding positions with any other path, then the weaker path that has been chosen can be eliminated.
6) Repeat steps 4 to 6 for other paths to determine if they can be eliminated.
7) The remaining paths that remain are then computed to determine the optimal path.

6 Analysis of Best Path Search Algorithm

The algorithm is an improvement over the brute force method in terms of reduced complexity and yet can achieve a 100% success rate of obtaining the optimal path.

Let n = 3. Assign four variables, a, b, c, d to the four directed weights. There are a total of 4! = 24 ways in which the chain of inequality can be formed. Without loss of generality, we can assume that the values of the 2 paths are a+c and b+d. Hence, there are a total of 8 possible chains of inequalities such that no paths can be eliminated. This translates to a probability of $\frac{8}{24} = \frac{1}{3}$. Therefore, there is a probability of $\frac{1}{3}$ that 2 computations are necessary to evaluate the optimal paths and a probability of $\frac{2}{3}$ that no computations are needed to do likewise. Hence, the average complexity required for the case n = 3 is $\frac{1}{3} * 2 + \frac{2}{3} * 0 = \frac{2}{3}$. Since brute force requires 2 computations, this method of carving on average will require only 33% of the complexity of brute force.

To calculate an upper bound for the number of comparisons needed, assume that every single variable of all possible paths have to compared against one another. Since there are (n-1)! possible paths and each path contains (n-1) variables, an upper bound for the number of comparisons required

$= (n\text{-}1)!* \frac{[(n-1)!-1]}{2} * (n\text{-}1)$
$= (n\text{-}1)!* (n\text{-}1)* \frac{[(n-1)!-1]}{2}$

For general n, when all the paths are written down in terms of their variables, it is observed that each path has exactly n -1 other paths such that they have one variable in common.

By using the above key observation, it is possible to evaluate the number of pairs of paths such that they have a variable in common.

No. of pairs of paths such that they have a variable in common = (n-1)! * $\frac{n-1}{2}$
Since there are a total of (n-1)!* $\frac{(n-1)!-1}{2}$ possible pair of paths, the percentage of pairs of paths which will have a variable in common = $\frac{100n-100}{(n-1)!-1}$%

The upper bound which was obtained earlier can now be strengthened to

(n-1)!* (n-1)* $\frac{(n-1)!-1}{2}$ - (n-1)! * $\frac{n-1}{2}$
= (n-1)!* (n-1)* $\frac{(n-1)!-2}{2}$

The implementation to do these eliminations is similar to the general algorithm given earlier but with the added step of ignoring the extra comparison whenever a common variable is present. For any general n, apply the algorithm to determine the number of paths k that cannot be eliminated. This value of k will depend on the configurations of the weights given.

To compute the time complexity of this carving method, introduce functions g(x) and h(x) such that g represents the time taken to do x comparisons and h represents the time taken to do x summations of (n-1) values.

The least number of comparisons needed such that k paths remain after implementing the algorithm

= [(n-1)! - k]* (n-1) + $\frac{k(k-1)}{2}$
= (n-1)!* (n-1) - k* (n-1) + $\frac{k(k-1)}{2}$
= (n-1)!* (n-1) + k* (k-3)* $\frac{n-1}{2}$
− (n-1)[(n-1)! + $\frac{k(k-3)}{2}$]

The greatest number of comparisons needed such that k paths remain after implementing the algorithm

= [(k-1) * (n-1)! - $\frac{k(k-1)}{2}$]* (n-1) + [(n-1)! - k]* (n-1)
= (n-1)[k*(n-1)! - $\frac{k(k-1)}{2}$]

Hence, the average number of comparisons needed in the implementation

= 1/2 * (n-1)[(n-1)! + $\frac{k(k-3)}{2}$] + 1/2 * (n-1)[k*(n-1)! - $\frac{k(k-1)}{2}$]
= (n-1)* [(k+1)* $\frac{(n-1)!}{2}$ - k]

The total average time taken to implement the algorithm is equal to the sum of the time taken to do the comparisons and the time taken to evaluate the remaining paths

= g((n-1)* [(k+1)* $\frac{(n-1)!}{2}$ - k]) + h(k)

Doing comparisons of values take a shorter time compared to evaluating the sum of n-1 values and hence, the function g is much smaller than the function h. Thus, this time complexity can be approximated to be h(k) and since h(k) < h((n-1)!), this carving method is considerably better than brute force.

A drawback of this method is that even after the eliminations, the number of paths that need to be computed might still be exceedingly large. In this case, we can introduce a high fragmentation path search algorithm as described below.

7 High Fragmentation Path Search Algorithm

In the previous sections, we introduced a deterministic way of obtaining the best path. It is suitable for relatively small values of n where the computational complexity is minimal. For larger values of n, we propose a probabilistic algorithm which offers a tradeoff between obtaining the best path and the computational complexity.

The algorithm is described as follows.

1) For a fixed n, assign $(n-1)^2$ variables to the directed edges.
2) Work out f(each path) in terms of the sum of n-1 of these variables and arrange the summation in ascending order.
3) Establish the chain of inequalities based on the actual values of the directed edges.
4) Pick the smallest value and identify the paths which contain that value.
5) Do a comparison of that path with other paths at every position of the summation. If the value at each position of this path is less than the corresponding positions with any other path, then the weaker path that has been chosen can be eliminated.
6) Repeat steps 4 to 6 for other paths to determine if they can be eliminated.
7) The remaining paths are then compared pairwise at their corresponding positions. The ones that have lesser values in more positions are then eliminated.
8) If both the paths have an equal number of lesser and greater values at the corresponding positions, then neither of the paths are eliminated.
9) Repeat step 7 for the available paths until the remaining number of paths is a small enough number to do computations.
10) Compute all remaining paths to determine "optimal path"

This probabilistic algorithm is similar to the general algorithm from step 1 to 6. The additional steps 7 to 9 are added to reduce the complexity of the algorithm.

8 Analysis of High Fragmentation Path Algorithm

We shall use a mathematical statistical method to do the analysis of the general case. Instead of arranging the variables of each path in ascending order, we can also skip this step which will save a bit of time. So now instead of comparing the variables at each position between 2 paths, we can just take any variable from each path at any position to do the comparison.

Since the value of each variable is uniformly distributed in the interval (0,1), the difference of two such independent variables will result in a triangular distribution. This triangular distribution has probability density function of f(x) = 2 - 2x and a cumulative distribution function of 2x - x^2. Its expected value is $\frac{1}{3}$ and its variance is $\frac{1}{18}$. Let the sum of the edges of a valid path A be $x_1 + x_2 + ... + x_{n-1}$ and let the sum of edges of a valid path B be $y_1 + y_2 + ... + y_{n-1}$ where n is the number of fragments to be recovered including the header. If $x_i - y_i > 0$ for more than $\frac{n-1}{2}$ values of i, then we eliminate path B. Similarly, if path $x_i - y_i < 0$ for less than $\frac{n-1}{2}$ values of i, then we eliminate path A. The aim is to evaluate the probability of f(A) > f(B) in the former case and the probability of f(A) < f(B) in the latter case. Assume $x_i - y_i > 0$ for more than $\frac{n-1}{2}$ values of i, then we can write $P(x_1 + x_2 + ... + x_{n-1} > y_1 + y_2 + ... + y_{n-1}) = P(M > N)$ where M is the sum of all $z_i = x_i - y_i > 0$ and N is the sum of all $w_i = y_i - x_i > 0$. From the assumption, the number of variables in M is greater than the number of variables in N. Both z_i and w_i in both M and N are random variables of triangular distribution and thus since the sum of independent random variable with a triangular distribution approximates to a normal distribution (by the Central Limit Theorem), both Z and W approximates to a normal distribution. Let k be the number of z_i and (n-1-k) be the number of w_i.

Then, the expected value of Z = E(Z) = E(kX) = kE(X) = $\frac{k}{3}$.

The variance of Z = Var(Z) = Var(kX) = k^2Var(X) = $k^2/18$.

Expected values of W = E(W) = E((n-1-k)Y) = (n-1-k)E(Y) = $\frac{n-1-k}{3}$.

Variance of W = Var(W) = Var((n-1-k)Y) = $(n\text{-}1\text{-}k)^2$Var(Y) = $(n\text{-}1\text{-}k)^2/18$.

Hence, the problem of finding $P(x_1 + x_2 + ... + x_{n-1} > y_1 + y_2 + ... + y_{n-1})$ is equivalent to finding the P(Z > W) where Z and W are normally distributed with mean = $\frac{k}{3}$, variance = $k^2/18$ and mean = $\frac{n-1-k}{3}$ and variance = $(n\text{-}1\text{-}k)^2/18$ respectively.

Therefore, P(Z > W) = P(Z - W > 0) = P(U > 0) where U = Z - W. Since U is a difference of two normal distributions, U has a normal distribution with mean = E(Z) - E(W) = $\frac{k}{3}$ - $\frac{n-1-k}{3}$ = $\frac{2k-n+1}{3}$ and

variance = Var(Z) + Var(W) = $k^2/18 + (n\text{-}1\text{-}k)^2/18 = [(n\text{-}1\text{-}k)^2 + k^2]/18$. P(U > 0) can now be found easily since the exact distribution of U is obtained and finding P(W > 0) is equivalent to P(f(A) > f(B)) which gives the probability of f(A) > f(B) (the probability of the value of path A greater than B for a general n).

For example, let n = 20 and k = 15. Then P(f(A) > f(B)) = P(W > 0) where U is normally distributed with mean $\frac{11}{3}$ and variance = $\frac{241}{18}$. Hence, P(W > 0) = 0.8419. This implies that path A has a 84% chance of being the higher valued path compared to path B.

A table for n =30 and various values of k is constructed below:

Table 1. Probability for corresponding k when n=30

k	P(f(A) > f(B))
25	87.96%
24	86.35%
23	84.41%
22	82.09%
21	79.33%
20	76.10%
19	72.33%
18	68.05%

9 Results and Evaluations

We conducted some tests on 10 image files of 5 fragments each. Each pair of directional edge is evaluated and assigned a weight value, with a lower weight representing a higher likelihood of a correct match. The 10 files are named A, B,......, J and the fragments are numbered 1 to 5. X(i,j) denote the edge linking i to j in that order of file X. The original files are in the order of X(1,2,3,4,5) where 1 represents the known header. The results of the evaluation of weights are given in Table 2.

Considering file A, we have the following 24 paths values:

$$
\begin{aligned}
f(12345) &= A(1,2) + A(2,3) + A(3,4) + A(4,5)\\
f(12354) &= A(1,2) + A(2,3) + A(3,5) + A(3,4)\\
f(12435) &= A(1,2) + A(2,4) + A(4,3) + A(3,5)\\
f(12453) &= A(1,2) + A(2,4) + A(4,5) + A(5,3)\\
f(12534) &= A(1,2) + A(2,5) + A(5,3) + A(3,4)\\
f(12543) &= A(1,2) + A(2,5) + A(5,4) + A(4,3)\\
f(13245) &= A(1,3) + A(3,2) + A(2,4) + A(4,5)\\
f(13254) &= A(1,3) + A(3,2) + A(2,5) + A(5,4)\\
f(13425) &= A(1,3) + A(3,4) + A(4,2) + A(2,5)\\
f(13452) &= A(1,3) + A(3,4) + A(4,5) + A(5,2)\\
f(13524) &= A(1,3) + A(3,5) + A(5,2) + A(2,4)\\
f(13542) &= A(1,3) + A(3,5) + A(5,4) + A(4,2)\\
f(14235) &= A(1,4) + A(4,2) + A(2,3) + A(3,5)\\
f(14253) &= A(1,4) + A(4,2) + A(2,5) + A(5,3)\\
f(14325) &= A(1,4) + A(4,3) + A(3,2) + A(2,5)\\
f(14352) &= A(1,4) + A(4,3) + A(3,5) + A(5,2)\\
f(14523) &= A(1,4) + A(4,5) + A(5,2) + A(2,3)\\
f(14532) &= A(1,4) + A(4,5) + A(5,3) + A(3,2)\\
f(15234) &= A(1,5) + A(5,2) + A(2,3) + A(3,4)\\
f(15243) &= A(1,5) + A(5,2) + A(2,4) + A(4,3)\\
f(15324) &= A(1,5) + A(5,3) + A(3,2) + A(2,4)\\
f(15342) &= A(1,5) + A(5,3) + A(3,4) + A(4,2)\\
f(15423) &= A(1,5) + A(5,4) + A(4,2) + A(2,3)\\
f(15432) &= A(1,5) + A(5,4) + A(4,3) + A(3,2)
\end{aligned}
$$

The chain of inequalities is given as below:

A(1,2) < A(2,3) < A(4,5) < A(3,4) < A(1,3) < A(5,3) < A(5,2) < A(3,5) < A(4,2) < A(1,5) < A(4,3) < A(2,5) < A(5,4) < A(1,4) < A(3,2) < A(2,4)

Applying the best path search algorithm will indicate that f(12345) will result in the minimum value among all the paths. Hence, the algorithm outputs the optimal path as 12345 which is indeed the original file. The other files from B to J are done in a similar way and the algorithm is able to recover all of them accurately.

Table 2. Weight values of edges

Edges	Weights	Edges	Weights	Edges	Weights	Edges	Weights	Edges	Weights
A(1,2)	25372	B(1,2)	26846	C(1,2)	1792	D(1,2)	1731	E(1,2)	20295
A(1,3)	106888	B(1,3)	255103	C(1,3)	189486	D(1,3)	169056	E(1,3)	170011
A(1,4)	411690	B(1,4)	238336	C(1,4)	234623	D(1,4)	170560	E(1,4)	461661
A(1,5)	324065	B(1,5)	274723	C(1,5)	130208	D(1,5)	34583	E(1,5)	516498
A(2,3)	27405	B(2,3)	26418	C(2,3)	29592	D(2,3)	11546	E(2,3)	15888
A(2,4)	463339	B(2,4)	211579	C(2,4)	282775	D(2,4)	169162	E(2,4)	404686
A(2,5)	361142	B(2,5)	262210	C(2,5)	259358	D(2,5)	179053	E(2,5)	391823
A(3,2)	421035	B(3,2)	242422	C(3,2)	234205	D(3,2)	168032	E(3,2)	470644
A(3,4)	66379	B(3,4)	37416	C(3,4)	35104	D(3,4)	25275	E(3,4)	33488
A(3,5)	294658	B(3,5)	309995	C(3,5)	278213	D(3,5)	169954	E(3,5)	191333
A(4,2)	322198	B(4,2)	278721	C(4,2)	130525	D(4,2)	34434	E(4,2)	521456
A(4,3)	358088	B(4,3)	259830	C(4,3)	261451	D(4,3)	176501	E(4,3)	395452
A(4,5)	57753	B(4,5)	19728	C(4,5)	20939	D(4,5)	1484	E(4,5)	12951
A(5,2)	279017	B(5,2)	274992	C(5,2)	113995	D(5,2)	101827	E(5,2)	584460
A(5,3)	253033	B(5,3)	276129	C(5,3)	240769	D(5,3)	163356	E(5,3)	465384
A(5,4)	374883	B(5,4)	295966	C(5,4)	211830	D(5,4)	113634	E(5,4)	169112

Edges	Weights	Edges	Weights	Edges	Weights	Edges	Weights	Edges	Weights
F(1,2)	67998	G(1,2)	42018	H(1,2)	18153	I(1,2)	8459	J(1,2)	4004
F(1,3)	213617	G(1,3)	301435	H(1,3)	181159	I(1,3)	231029	J(1,3)	166016
F(1,4)	194851	G(1,4)	185411	H(1,4)	215640	I(1,4)	202608	J(1,4)	115094
F(1,5)	165275	G(1,5)	165869	H(1,5)	325518	I(1,5)	89197	J(1,5)	57867
F(2,3)	106293	G(2,3)	67724	H(2,3)	44721	I(2,3)	36601	J(2,3)	13662
F(2,4)	233053	G(2,4)	271544	H(2,4)	284600	I(2,4)	218702	J(2,4)	191048
F(2,5)	211497	G(2,5)	242194	H(2,5)	296134	I(2,5)	190189	J(2,5)	152183
F(3,2)	200732	G(3,2)	183942	H(3,2)	210413	I(3,2)	200946	J(3,2)	118273
F(3,4)	103039	G(3,4)	54623	H(3,4)	88262	I(3,4)	13523	J(3,4)	10557
F(3,5)	209739	G(3,5)	126607	H(3,5)	342848	I(3,5)	168190	J(3,5)	81922
F(4,2)	180667	G(4,2)	170638	H(4,2)	328548	I(4,2)	89695	J(4,2)	58634
F(4,3)	213518	G(4,3)	241621	H(4,3)	289364	I(4,3)	191023	J(4,3)	150592
F(4,5)	35972	G(4,5)	18323	H(4,5)	23165	I(4,5)	1859	J(4,5)	2667
F(5,2)	159007	G(5,2)	167898	H(5,2)	366394	I(5,2)	136627	J(5,2)	84547
F(5,3)	198318	G(5,3)	241149	H(5,3)	301614	I(5,3)	183217	J(5,3)	160503
F(5,4)	162130	G(5,4)	124795	H(5,4)	339541	I(5,4)	130938	J(5,4)	63671

10 Conclusions

In this paper, we modeled the file recovery problem using a graph theoretic approach. We took into account the weight values of two directed edges connected to an edge to perform the file carving. We proposed two new algorithms to perform fragmented file recovery. The first algorithm, best path search, is suitable for files which have been fragmented into a small number of fragments. The second algorithm, high fragmentation path, is applicable in the cases where a file is fragmented into a large number of fragments. It introduces a trade-off between time and success rate of optimal path construction. This flexibility enables a user to adjust the settings according to his available resources. Analysis of the best path search technique reveals that it is much superior to brute force in complexity and at the same time, able to achieve accurate recovery. A sample of 10 files with their fragments were tested and the optimal carve is able to recover all of them back to their original correct state.

References

1. Leiserson, C.E.: Introduction to algorithms. MIT Press, Cambridge (2001)
2. da Gama Leito, H.C., Soltfi, J.: Automatic reassembly of irregular fragments. In: Univ. of Campinas, Tech. Rep. IC-98-06 (1998)
3. da Gama Leito, H.C., Soltfi, J.: A multiscale method for the reassembly of two-dimensional fragmented objects. IEEE Transections on Pattern Analysis and Machine Intelligence 24 (September 2002)
4. Shanmugasundaram, K., Memon, N.: Automatic reassembly of document fragments via context based statistical models. In: Proceedings of the 19th Annual Computer Security Applications Conference, p. 152 (2003)
5. Shanmugasundaram, K., Memon, N.: Automatic reassembly of document fragments via data compression. Presented at the 2nd Digital Forensics Research Workshop, Syracuse (July 2002)
6. Cohen, M.I.: Advanced jpeg carving. In: Proceedings of the 1st International Conference on Forensic Applications and Techniques in Telecommunications, Information, and Multimedia and Workshop, Article No.16 (2008)
7. Cohen, M.I.: Advanced carving techniques. Digital Investigation 4(supplement 1), 2–12 (2007)
8. Memon, N., Pal, A.: Automated reassembly of file fragmented images using greedy algorithms. IEEE Transactions on Image Processing, 385–393 (February 2006)
9. Sablatnig, R., Menard, C.: On finding archaeological fragment assemblies using a bottom-up design. In: Proc. of the 21st Workshop of the Austrain Association for Pattern Recognition Hallstatt, Austria, Oldenburg, Wien, Muenchen, pp. 203–207 (1997)
10. Garfinkel, S.: Carving contiguous and fragmented files with fast object validation. In: Proceedings of the 2007 Digital Forensics Research Workshop, DFRWS, Pittsburgh, PA (August 2007)
11. Martucci, S.A.: Reversible compression of hdtv images using median adaptive prediction and arithmetic coding. In: IEEE International Symposium on Circuits and Systems, pp. 1310–1313 (1990)

12. Kampel, M., Sablatnig, R., Costa, E.: Classification of archaeological fragments using profile primitives. In: Computer Vision, Computer Graphics and Photogrammetry - a Common Viewpoint, Proceedings of the 25th Workshop of the Austrian Association for Pattern Recognition (OAGM), pp. 151–158 (2001)
13. Pal, A., Sencar, H.T., Memon, N.: Detecting file fragmentation point using sequential hypothesis testing. In: Proceedings of the Eighth Annual DFRWS Conference. Digital Investigation, vol. 5(supplement 1), pp. S2–S13 (September 2008)
14. Pal, A., Shanmugasundaram, K., Memon, N.: Automated reassembly of fragmented images. Presented at ICASSP (2003)
15. Stemmer, W.P.: DNA shuffling by random fragmentation and reassembly: in vitro recombination for molecular evolution. Proc. Natl. Acad. Sci. (October 25, 1994)

Using Relationship-Building in Event Profiling for Digital Forensic Investigations

Lynn M. Batten and Lei Pan

School of IT, Deakin University, Burwood, Victoria 3125, Australia
{lmbatten,l.pan}@deakin.edu.au

Abstract. In a forensic investigation, computer profiling is used to capture evidence and to examine events surrounding a crime. A rapid increase in the last few years in the volume of data needing examination has led to an urgent need for automation of profiling. In this paper, we present an efficient, automated event profiling approach to a forensic investigation for a computer system and its activity over a fixed time period. While research in this area has adopted a number of methods, we extend and adapt work of Marrington et al. based on a simple relational model. Our work differs from theirs in a number of ways: our object set (files, applications etc.) can be enlarged or diminished repeatedly during the analysis; the transitive relation between objects is used sparingly in our work as it tends to increase the set of objects requiring investigative attention; our objective is to reduce the volume of data to be analyzed rather than extending it. We present a substantial case study to illuminate the theory presented here. The case study also illustrates how a simple visual representation of the analysis could be used to assist a forensic team.

Keywords: digital forensics, relation, event profiling.

1 Introduction

Computer profiling, describing a computer system and its activity over a given period of time, is useful for a number of purposes. It may be used to determine how the load on the system varies, or whether it is dealing appropriately with attacks. In this paper, we describe a system and its activity for the purposes of a forensic investigation.

While there are many sophisticated, automated ways of determining system load [15] or resilience to attacks [13,16], forensic investigations have, to date, been largely reliant on a manual approach by investigators experienced in the field. Over the past few years, the rapid increase in the volume of data to be analyzed has spurred the need for automation in this area also. Additionally, there have been arguments that, in forensic investigations, inferences made from evidence are too subjective [8] and therefore automated methods of computer profiling have begun to appear [8,10]; such methods rely on logical and consistent analysis from which to draw conclusions.

X. Lai et al. (Eds.): E-Forensics 2010, LNICST 56, pp. 40–52, 2011.

There have been two basic approaches in the literature to computer profiling — one based on the raw data, captured as evidence on a hard drive for instance [3], the other examining the events surrounding the crime as in [11,12]. We refer to the latter as ***event profiling***.

In this paper, we develop an automated event profiling approach to a forensic investigation for a computer system and its activity over a fixed time period. While, in some respects, our approach is similar to that of Marrington et al. [11,12], our work both extends theirs and differs from it in fundamental ways described more fully in the next section.

In Sections 4 and 5, we present and analyze a case study to demonstrate the building of relationships between events which then lead to isolation of the most relevant events in the case. While we have not implemented it at this point, a computer graphics visualization of each stage of the investigation could assist in managing extremely large data sets.

In Section 2, we describe the relevant literature in this area. In Section 3, we develop our relational theory. Section 6 concludes the paper.

2 Background and Motivation

Models representing computer systems as finite state machines have been presented in the literature for the purposes of digital event reconstruction [3,5]. While such models are useful in understanding how a formal analysis leading to an automated approach can be established, the computational needs for carrying out an investigation based on a finite state representation are too large and complex to be practical.

The idea of linking data in large databases by means of some kind of relationship between the data goes back about twenty years to work in data mining. In [2], a set-theoretic approach is taken to formalize the notion that if certain data is involved in an event, then certain other data might also be involved in the same event. Confidence thresholds to represent the certainty of conclusions drawn are also considered. Abraham and de Vel [1] implement this idea in a computer forensic setting dealing with log data.

Since then, a number of inference models have been proposed. In [4], Garfinkel proposes cross-drive analysis which uses statistical techniques to analyze data sets from disk images. The method permits identification of data likely to be of relevance to the investigation and assigns it a high priority. While the author's approach is efficient and simple, at this stage, the work seems to apply specifically to data features found on computer drives.

In 2006, Hwang, Kim and Noh [7] proposed an inference process using Petri Nets. The principal contribution of this work is the addition of confidence levels to the inferences which accumulate throughout the investigation and the result is taken into consideration in the final drawing of conclusions. The work also permits inclusion of partial or damaged data as this can be accommodated by the confidence levels. However, the cost of analysis is high for very large data sets.

Bayesian methods were used by Kwan et al. [8] again to introduce confidence levels related to inferences. The probability that one event led to another is measured and taken into consideration as the investigation progresses. The investigative model follows that of a rooted tree where the root is a hypothesis being tested. The choice of root is critical to the model, and, if it is poorly chosen, can lead to many resource-consuming attempts to derive information.

Liu et al. [9] return to the finite state automata representation of [3,5] and introduce a transit process between states. They acknowledge that a manual check of all evidential statements is only possible when the number of intermediate states is small. Otherwise, independent event reconstruction algorithms are needed.

While methods in this area vary widely, in this paper, we follow the work of Marrington [12]. The relational device used in his work is simple and makes no restrictive assumptions. We believe, therefore, that it is one of the most efficient methods to implement.

Marrington begins by generating some information about a (computer) system based on embedded detection instruments such as log files. He then uses these initial 'relationships' to construct new information by using equivalence relations on objects which form part of a computer system's operation. These objects include hardware devices, applications, data files and also users [12, p. 69]. Marrington goes on to divide the set of all objects associated with a specific computer into four types: content, application, principal and system [12, p. 71]. A content item includes such things as documents, images, audio etc; an application includes such items as browsers, games, word processors; a principal includes users, groups and organizations; a system includes devices, drivers, registries and libraries.

In this paper, we begin with the same basic set-up as Marrington. However, our work differs in several essential ways. First, unlike Marrington, we do not assume global knowledge of the system: our set of 'objects' can be enlarged or reduced over the period of the investigation. Secondly, while Marrington uses relations to enlarge his information database, we use them primarily to reduce it; thus, we attempt to eliminate data from the investigation rather than add it. Finally, we do not assume, as in Marrington's case, that transitivity of a relation is inherently good in itself, rather, we analyze its usefulness from a theoretical perspective, and implement it when it brings useful information to the investigation.

The next section describes the relational setting.

3 Relational Theory

We begin with a set of objects **O** which is designed to be as comprehensive as possible in terms of the event under investigation. For example, for an incident in an office building, **O** would comprise all people and all equipment in the building at the time. It may also include all those off-site personnel who had access to the building's computer system at the time. In case the building has a website which interacts with clients, **O** may also include all clients in contact with the building at the time of the event.

Marrington defines two types of relationships possible between two elements of **O**. One is a 'defined' relationship, such as 'Tom is related to document D because Tom is the author of D'. Another type of relationship is an 'inferred' relationship: suppose that 'document D is related to computer C' because D is stored in C and 'D is related to printer X' because X printed D. We can thus infer a relationship between C and X — for instance, that C is connected to X. Note that the precise relationship between elements of a pair here is not necessarily the same. The inferred relationship is one that must make sense between the two object types to which it refers.

In [12], the objective is to begin an investigation by establishing a set of objects and then determining the 'defined' relationships between them. Given those relationships, inferred relationships can then be constructed. In gaining new information by means of these inferred relationships, the transitivity property is crucial; it is the basis of inference. We define these concepts formally below.

In our context, **O** is the set of items perceived to be in the vicinity of, or connected to, a forensic investigation. The definitions below are standard definitions used in set theory or the theory of binary relations and can be found in [6].

Definition 1. *A* ***relation*** $\mathbb{R}$ *on* **O** *is a subset of ordered pairs of* $\mathbf{O} \times \mathbf{O}$.

Example 1. If $\mathbf{O}=\{a, b, c, d\}$, then the set of pairs $\{(a, c), (b, c)\}$ is a relation on **O**.

Notation. If a pair (a, b) belongs to a relation $\mathbb{R}$, we also write $a\mathbb{R}b$.

Definition 2. *A relation* $\mathbb{R}$ *on* **O** *is* ***reflexive*** *if* $a\mathbb{R}a$ *for all* a *in* **O**.

We can assume without any loss of generality that any relation on **O** in our context is reflexive since this property neither adds nor deletes information in a forensic investigative sense.

Definition 3. *A relation* $\mathbb{R}$ *on* **O** *is* ***symmetric*** *if* $a\mathbb{R}b$ *implies* $b\mathbb{R}a$ *for all objects* a *and* b *in* **O**.

Again, without loss of generality, in our context we assume that any relation on **O** is symmetric. This assumption is based on an understanding of how objects in **O** are related. So for instance, a printer and PC are related bi-directionally in the sense that they are connected to each other.

Example 2. Let **O** be the set {printer, Joanne, laptop, memory stick, Akura}. Consider $\mathbb{R} = \{(a, a) \text{ for all } a \in \mathbf{O}\} \cup \{$(printer, laptop), (laptop, printer), (Akura, laptop), (laptop, Akura)$\}$. This relation is reflexive and also symmetric. The interpretation of the symmetric relation in practice is that the printer and laptop are physically connected to each other, and that the laptop belongs to Akura (and Akura to the laptop).

Definition 4. *Given a reflexive and symmetric relation* $\mathbb{R}$ *on* **O**, *for each element* $a \in \mathbf{O}$, *we define a* ***relational class*** *for* a *by* $(a) = \{b \mid a\mathbb{R}b, b \in \mathbf{O}\}$.

In Example 2 above, (Akura) = {Akura, laptop}. Note that, because of reflexivity, a is always an element of the relational class (a).

Definition 5. *A relation $\mathbb{R}$ on* **O** *is* ***transitive*** *if $a\mathbb{R}b$ and $b\mathbb{R}c$ implies $a\mathbb{R}c$ for all a, b, c in* **O**.

Example 3. The relation of Example 2 is easily seen not to be transitive. However, we can add some pairs to it in order to have the transitivity property satisfied: $\mathbb{R}' = \{(a, a)$ for all $a \in \mathbf{O}\} \cup \{$(printer, laptop), (laptop, printer), (Akura, laptop), (laptop, Akura), (Akura, printer), (printer, Akura)$\}$. This example now satisfies all three properties of reflexive, symmetric and transitive.

Example 3 demonstrates the crux of Marrington's work [12] and how he builds on known relationships between objects to determine new relationships between them. The facts that Akura owns the laptop and that the laptop is connected to the printer may be used to infer that Akura prints to the printer, or at least has the potential to do so. Any relation on a finite set of objects which is both reflexive and symmetric can be developed into a transitive relation by adding the necessary relationships. This is known as *transitive closure* [14] and may involve several steps before it is achieved. We formalize this statement in the following (well-known) result:

Theorem 1. *Let $\mathbb{R}$ be a reflexive and symmetric relation on a finite set* **O**. *Then the transitive closure of $\mathbb{R}$ exists.*

We note that for infinite sets, Theorem 1 can be false [14, p. 388, 389].

Definition 6. *A relation on a set* **O** *is an* ***equivalence relation*** *if it is reflexive, symmetric and transitive.*

Lemma 1. *If $\mathbb{R}$ is an equivalence relation on a set* **O**, *then for all a and b in* **O**, *either $(a) = (b)$ or $(a) \cap (b) = \emptyset$.*

Proof. Suppose that there is an element x in $(a) \cap (b)$. So $a\mathbb{R}x$ and $x\mathbb{R}b$ results in $a\mathbb{R}b$. Then for any y such that $a\mathbb{R}y$, we obtain $b\mathbb{R}y$, and for any z such that $b\mathbb{R}z$, we obtain $a\mathbb{R}z$. Thus $(a) = (b)$. □

Lemma 2. *Let $\mathbb{R}$ be both reflexive and symmetric on a finite set* **O**. *Then the transitive closure of $\mathbb{R}$ is an equivalence relation on* **O**.

Proof. It is only necessary to show that as transitive closure is implemented, symmetry is not lost. We use induction on the number of stages used to achieve the transitive closure. Since **O** is finite, this number of steps must be finite.

In the first step, suppose that a new relational pair $a\mathbb{R}c$ is introduced. Then this pair came from two pairs, $a\mathbb{R}b$ and $b\mathbb{R}c$ for some b. Moreover, these pairs belonged to the original symmetric relation and so $b\mathbb{R}a$ and $c\mathbb{R}b$ hold; now $c\mathbb{R}b$ and $b\mathbb{R}a$ produce $c\mathbb{R}a$ by transitive closure, and so the relation is still symmetric.

Inductively, suppose that to step $k-1$, the relation achieved is still symmetric. Suppose also that at step k, the new relational pair $a\mathbb{R}c$ is introduced. Then this pair came from two pairs, $a\mathbb{R}b$ and $b\mathbb{R}c$ in step $k-1$ for some b. Because of symmetry in step $k-1$, the pairs $b\mathbb{R}a$ and $c\mathbb{R}b$ hold. Thus, $c\mathbb{R}b$ and $b\mathbb{R}a$ produce $c\mathbb{R}a$ by transitive closure, and so the relation remains symmetric at step k. This completes the proof. □

Equivalence relations have an interesting impact on the set **O**. They partition it into equivalence classes — every element of **O** belongs to exactly one of these classes [6]. We illustrate this partition on the set **O** of Example 2 above in Figure 1.

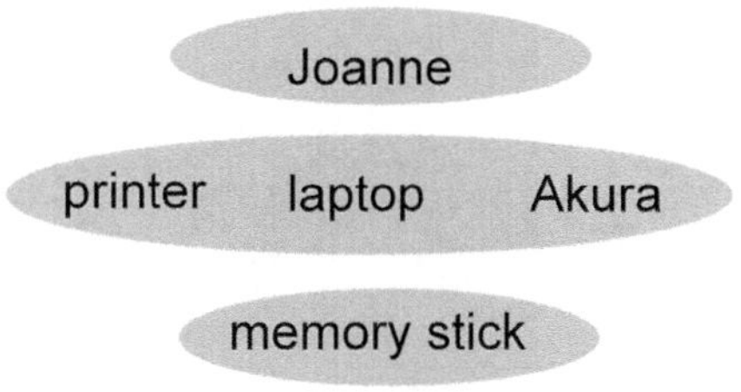

Fig. 1. A Partition Induced by an Equivalence Relation

The transitive property is the crux of the inference of relations between objects in **O**. However, we argue that one of the drawbacks is that, in taking the transitive closure, it may be the case that eventually all objects become related to each other and this provides no information about the investigation. This is illustrated in the following example.

Example 4. Xun has a laptop L and PC1, both of which are connected to a server S. PC1 is also connected to a printer P. Elaine has PC2 which is also connected to S and P. Thus, the relation on the object set **O** = {Xun, Elaine, PC1, PC2, L, S, P} is $\mathbb{R} = \{\{(a, a) \text{ for all } a \in \mathbf{O}\}, \{$(Xun, L), (L, Xun), (Xun, PC1), (PC1, Xun), (Xun, S), (S, Xun), (Xun, P), (P, Xun), (L, S), (S, L), (PC1, P), (P, PC1), (PC1, S), (S, PC1), (Elaine, PC2), (PC2, Elaine), (Elaine, S), (S, Elaine), (Elaine, P), (P, Elaine), (PC2, P), (P, PC2), (PC2, S), (S, PC2)}}. Figure 2 describes the impact of $\mathbb{R}$ on **O**.

Note that (S, P), (Elaine, PC1) and a number of other pairs are not part of $\mathbb{R}$.

We compute the transitive closure of $\mathbb{R}$ on **O** and so the induced equivalence relation. Since (S, PC1) and (PC1, P) hold, we deduce (S, P) and (P, S). Since (Elaine, S) and (S, PC1) hold, we deduce (Elaine, PC1) and (PC1, Elaine). Continuing in this way, we derive all possible pairs and so every object is related to every other object, giving a single equivalence class which is the entire object set **O**. We argue that this can be counter-productive in an investigation.

Our goal is in fact to isolate only those objects in **O** of specific investigative interest. We tackle this by re-interpreting the relationship on **O** in a different way from Marrington et al. [11] and by permitting the flexibility of the addition of elements to **O** as an investigation proceeds.

Below, we describe a staged approach to an investigation based on the relational method. We require that the forensic investigator set a maximal amount of time t_{max} to finish the investigation. The investigator will abort the procedure if it exceeds the pre-determined time limit or a fixed number of steps. Regarding each case, the investigator chooses the set $\mathbf{O}_1$ to be as comprehensive as possible

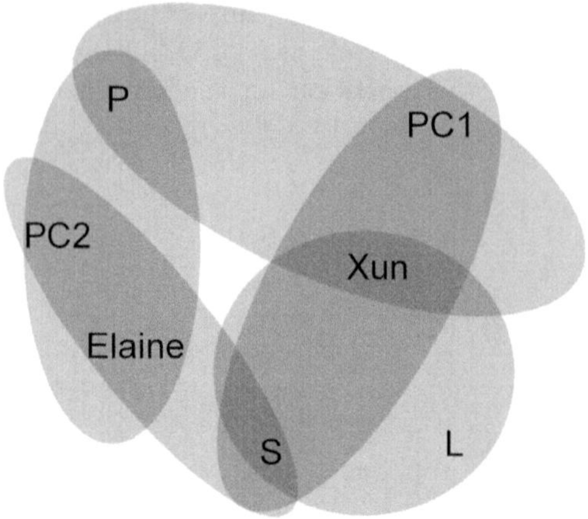

Fig. 2. The Relation $\mathbb{R}$ on the set $\mathbf{O}$ of Example 4

in the context of known information at a time relevant to the investigation and establishes a reflexive and symmetric relation $\mathbb{R}_1$ on $\mathbf{O}_1$. This should be based on relevant criteria. (See Example 4.)

We propose the following three-stage process.
Process input: A set $\mathbf{O}_1$ and a corresponding relation $\mathbb{R}_1$.
Process output: A set $\mathbf{O}_{i+1}$ and a corresponding relation $\mathbb{R}_{i+1}$.

STAGE 1. Based on the known information about the criminal activity and $\mathbb{R}_i$, investigate further relevant sources such as log files, e-mails, applications and individuals. Adjust $\mathbb{R}_i$ and $\mathbf{O}_i$ accordingly to (possibly new) sets $\mathbb{R}'_i$ and $\mathbf{O}'_i$. (If files are located hidden inside files in $\mathbf{O}_i$ these should be added to the object set; if objects not in $\mathbf{O}_i$ are now expected to be important to the investigation, these should be placed in $\mathbf{O}'_i$.)

STAGE 2. From $\mathbf{O}'_i$, determine the most relevant relational classes and discard the non-relevant ones. Call the resulting set of objects $\mathbf{O}_{i+1}$ and the corresponding relational class $\mathbb{R}_{i+1}$. (Note that $\mathbb{R}_{i+1}$ will still be reflexive and symmetric on $\mathbf{O}_{i+1}$.)

STAGE 3. If possible, draw conclusions at this stage. If further investigation is warranted and time $t < t_{max}$, return to STAGE 1 and repeat with $\mathbf{O}_{i+1}$ and $\mathbb{R}_{i+1}$. Otherwise, stop.

Note that transitivity is not used in our stages. This is to ensure that the investigator is able to focus on a small portion of the object set as the investigation develops. However, at some point, one of the $\mathbb{R}_i$ may well be an equivalence relation. This has no impact on our procedure.

Stage 1 can be viewed as a screening test which assists the investigator by establishing a baseline ($\mathbb{R}_i$ and $\mathbf{O}_i$) against which to compare other information. The baseline is then adjusted accordingly for the next stage (to $\mathbb{R}'_i$ and $\mathbf{O}'_i$). In Stage 2, this new baseline is examined to see if all objects in it are still relevant and all relations still valid. The investigator deletes any objects deemed to be unimportant and adjusts the relations accordingly. This process continues in several rounds until the investigator is satisfied that the resulting sets of objects and relations are the most relevant to the investigation. If necessary, a cut-off time can be used to establish the stopping point either for the entire process or for each of the rounds.

Our methodology can be used either alone, or as part of a multi-facets approach to an investigation with several team members. It provides good organization of the data leading to a focus on the area likely to be of most interest. It can be structured to meet an overall time target by adopting time limits to each stage. The diagrammatic approach used lends itself to a visualization of the data (as in Figures 1 and 2) which provides a simple overview of the relationships between objects, and which assists in the decision making process. We give a detailed case study in the next section.

4 Case Study

Joe operates a secret business to traffic illegal substances to several customers. One of his regular customers, Wong, sent Joe an email to request a phone conversation. The following events happened chronologically —

2009-05-01 07:30 Joe entered his office and switched on his laptop.

2009-05-01 07:31 Joe successfully connected to the Internet and started retrieving his emails.

2009-05-01 07:35 Joe read Wong's email and called Wong's land-line number.

2009-05-01 07:40 Joe started the conversation with Wong. Wong gave Joe a new private phone number and requested continuation of their business conversations through the new number.

2009-05-01 07:50 Joe saved Wong's new number in a text file named "Where.txt" on his laptop where his customers' contact numbers are stored.

2009-05-01 07:51 Joe saved Wong's name in a different text file called "Who.txt" which is a name list of his customers.

2009-05-01 08:00 Joe hid these two newly created text files in two graphic files ("1.gif" and "2.gif") respectively by using S-Tools with password protection.

2009-05-01 08:03 Joe compressed the two new GIF files into a ZIP archive file named "1.zip" which he also encrypted.

2009-05-01 08:04 Joe concatenated the ZIP file to a JPG file named "Cover.jpg".

2009-05-01 08:05 Joe used Window Washer[1] to erase 2 text files ("Who.txt" and "Where.txt"), 2 GIF files ("1.gif" and "2.gif") and 1 ZIP file ("1.zip"). (Joe did not remove the last generated file "Cover.jpg".)

2009-05-01 08:08 Joe rebooted the laptop so that all cached data in the RAM and free disk space were removed.

Four weeks later, Joe's laptop was seized by the police due to suspicion of drug possession. As part of a formal investigation procedure, police officers made a

[1] Window Washer, by Webroot, available at `http://www.webroot.com.au`

forensic image of the hard disk of Joe's laptop. Moti, a senior officer in the forensic team, is assigned the analysis task.

The next section describes Moti's analysis of the hard disk image.

5 Analysis

Moti firstly examines the forensic image file by using Forensic Toolkit[2] to filter out the files with known hash values. This leaves Moti with 250 emails, 50 text files, 100 GIF files, 90 JPG files and 10 application programs. Moti briefly browses through these files and finds no evidence against Joe. However, he notices that the program S-Tools[3] installed on the laptop is not a commonly used application and decides to investigate further.

To work more efficiently, Moti decides to use our method described in Section 3 and limits his investigation to 3 rounds. Moti includes all of the 500 items, all emails, all text files, all GIF and JPG files and all applications in a set $\mathbf{O}_1$. Because S-Tools operates on GIF files and text files, Moti establishes the relation $\mathbb{R}_1$ with the following two relational classes $\mathbb{R}_1 = \{\{$S-Tools program, 100 GIF files, 50 text files$\}, \{$250 emails, 90 JPG files, 9 programs$\}\}$. Now, Moti starts the investigation.

Round 1

Stage 1. Moti runs a data carving tool Scalpel[4] over the 500 items. He carves out 10 encrypted ZIP files, each of which is concatenated to a JPG file; Moti realizes that he has overlooked these 10 JPG files during the initial investigation. Adding the newly discovered files, Moti has $\mathbf{O}_1' = \mathbf{O}_1 \cup \{$10 encrypted ZIP files$\}$ and defines $\mathbb{R}_1'$ based on three relational classes $\mathbb{R}_1' = \{\{$10 ZIP files, WinZIP program$\}, \{$S-Tools program, 100 GIF files, 50 text files$\}, \{$250 emails, 90 JPG files, 8 programs$\}\}$.

Stage 2. Moti tries to extract the 10 ZIP files by using WinZIP[5]. But he is given the error messages indicating that each of the 10 ZIP files contains two GIF files all of which are password-protected. Moti suspects that these 20 GIF files contain important information and hence should be the focus of the next round. So he puts two installed programs, the 10 ZIP files and the 20 newly discovered GIF files in the set $\mathbf{O}_2 = \{$10 ZIP files, 20 compressed GIF files, 100 GIF files, 50 text files, WinZIP program, S-Tools program$\}$ and refines the relational classes $\mathbb{R}_2 = \{\{$10 ZIP files, 20 compressed GIF

[2] Forensic Toolkit (FTK), by AccessData, version 1.7, available at `http://www.accessdata.com`

[3] Steganography Tool (S-Tools), version 4.0, available at `http://www.jjtc.com/Security/stegtools.htm`

[4] Scalpel, by Golden G. Richard III, version 1.60, available at `http://www.digitalforensicssolutions.com/Scalpel/`

[5] WinZIP, by WinZip Computing, version 12, available at `http://www.winzip.com/index.htm`

files, WinZIP program}, {20 compressed GIF files, 100 GIF files, 50 text files, S-Tools program}}. (As shown in Figure 3.)

Stage 3. Moti cannot draw any conclusions to proceed with the investigation based on the current discoveries. He continues to the second round.

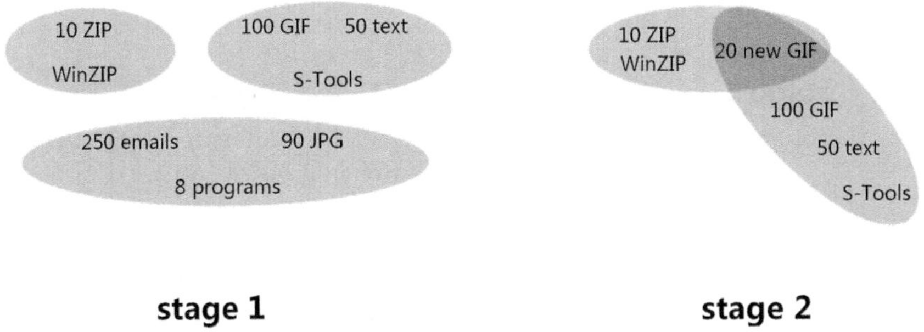

Fig. 3. Relational Classes in the Round 1 Investigation

Stage 1 of Round 1 indicates an equivalence relation on $\mathbf{O}_1$ as there is a partition of $\mathbf{O}_1$. However, in stage 2, the focus of the investigation becomes S-Tools, and so one of the relational (equivalence) classes is dropped and the new GIF files discovered are now placed in the intersection of two relational classes. Figure 3 emphasizes that there is no reason at this point to link the WinZIP program or the ZIP files with S-Tools or the other GIF and text files.

Round 2

Moti decides to explore the ten encrypted ZIP files.

Stage 1. Moti obtains the 20 compressed GIF files from the 10 ZIP files by using PRTK[6]. So, Moti redefines the set $\mathbf{O}'_2 = \{$10 ZIP files, 20 new GIF files, 100 GIF files, 50 text files, WinZIP program, S-Tools program$\}$ and modifies the relational classes $\mathbb{R}'_2 = \{\{$10 ZIP files, 20 new GIF files, WinZIP program$\}, \{$20 new GIF files, 100 GIF files, 50 text files, S-Tools program$\}\}$.

Stage 2. Moti decides to focus on the newly discovered GIF files. Moti is confident he can remove the ZIP files from the set because he proves that every byte in the ZIP files has been successfully recovered. Moti modifies the set $\mathbf{O}'_2$ to $\mathbf{O}_3 = \{$20 new GIF files, 100 GIF files, 50 text files, S-Tools program$\}$ and the relational classes $\mathbb{R}_3 = \{\{$20 new GIF files, 50 text files, S-Tools program$\}, \{$100 GIF files, 50 text files, S-Tools program$\}\}$. (As shown in Figure 4.)

Stage 3. Moti still cannot draw any conclusions based on the current discoveries. He wishes to extract some information in the last investigation round.

[6] Password Recovery Toolkit (PRTK), by AccessData, available at `http://www.accessdata.com`

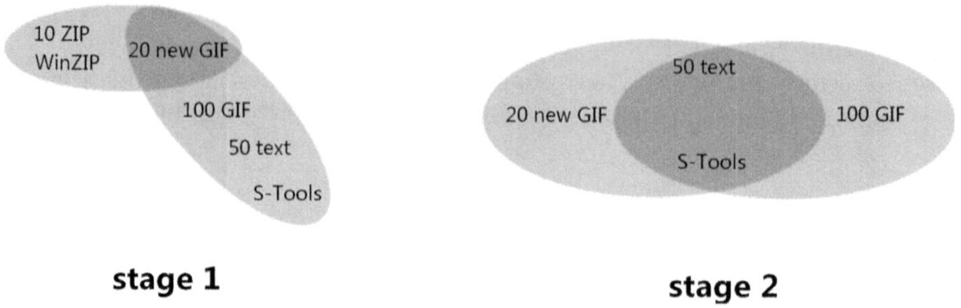

Fig. 4. Relational Classes in the Round 2 Investigation

In the first stage of Round 2, Moti recovers the GIF files identified in Round 1. In stage 2 of this round, he can now eliminate the WinZIP program and the ZIP files from the investigation, and focus on S-Tools and the GIF and text files.

Round 3

Moti tries to reveal hidden contents in the new GIF files by using the software program S-Tools found installed on Joe's laptop.

Stage 1. Since none of the password recovery tools in Moti's toolkit works with S-Tools, Moti decides to take a manual approach. As an experienced officer, Moti hypothesizes that Joe is very likely to use some of his personal details as passwords because people cannot easily remember random passwords for 20 items. So Moti connects to the police database and obtains a list of numbers and addresses related to Joe. After several trial and error attempts, Moti reveals two text files from the two GIF files extracted from one ZIP file by using Joe's medical card number. These two text files contain the name "Wong" and the mobile number 0409267531. So, Moti has the set $\mathbf{O}_3' = \{$"Wong", "0409267531", 18 remaining new GIF files, 100 GIF files, 50 text files, S-Tools program$\}$ and the relational classes $\mathbb{R}_3' = \{\{$"Wong", "0409267531"$\}, \{$18 remaining new GIF files, 50 text files, S-Tools program$\}, \{$100 GIF files, 50 text files, S-Tools program$\}\}$.

Stage 2. Moti thinks that the 20 new GIF files should have higher priority than the 100 GIF files and the 50 text files found in the file system because Joe might have tried to hide secrets in them. Therefore, Moti simplifies the set $\mathbf{O}_3'$ to $\mathbf{O}_4 = \{$"Wong", "0409267531", 18 remaining new GIF files, S-Tools program$\}$ and the relational classes $\mathbb{R}_4 = \{\{$"Wong", "0409267531"$\}, \{$18 remaining new GIF files, S-Tools$\}\}$. (As shown in Figure 5.)

Stage 3. Moti recommends that communications and financial transactions between Joe and Wong should be examined and further analysis is required to examine the remaining 18 new GIF files.

In the first stage of Round 3, Moti is able to eliminate two of the GIF files from the object set $\mathbf{O}_3$ as he has recovered new, apparently relevant data from them. The diagram in Figure 5 represents a non-transitive relation as there is still no

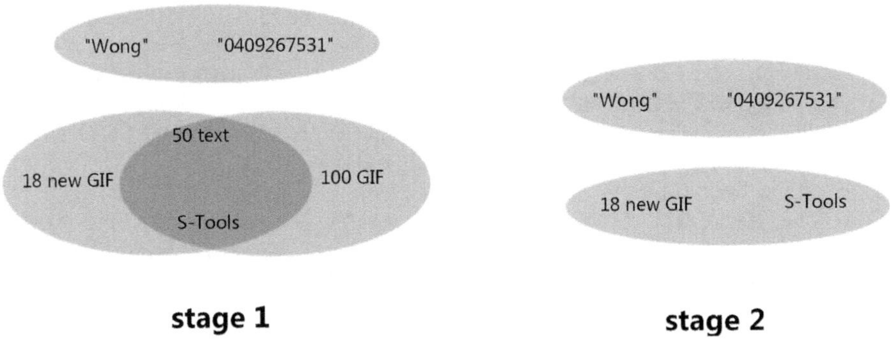

Fig. 5. Relational Classes in the Round 3 Investigation

clear connection between the 100 original GIF files and the newly discovered ones. In stage 2 of this round Moti then focuses only on the newly discovered GIF files along with S-Tools and the new information regarding "Wong". This is represented in Figure 3 by retaining one of the relational classes, completely eliminating a second and eliminating part of the third. These eliminations are possible in the relational context because we do not have transitivity.

In summary, Moti starts with a cohort of 500 digital items and ends up with two pieces of information regarding a person alongside 18 newly discovered GIF files. Moti finds useful information to advance the investigation within his limit of three rounds. Thus Moti uses three stages to sharpen the focus on the relevant evidence. This is opposite to the approach of Marrington et al. who expand the object set and relations at each stage.

6 Conclusions

We have presented relational theory designed to facilitate and automate forensic investigations into events surrounding a digital crime. This is a simple methodology which is easy to implement and which is capable of managing large volumes of data since it isolates data most likely to be of interest.

We demonstrated our theoretical model in a comprehensive case study and have indicated through this study how a visualization of the stages of the investigation can be established by means of Venn diagrams depicting relations between objects (*e.g.*, see Figures 3, 4 and 5). Future work by the authors will include development of a visualization tool to better manage data volume and speed up investigation analysis.

References

1. Abraham, T., de Vel, O.: Investigative Profiling with Computer Forensic Log Data and Association Rules. In: Proceedings of the 2002 IEEE International Conference on Data Mining, pp. 11–18 (2002)
2. Agrawal, R., Imielinski, T., Swami, A.: Mining Association Rules between Sets of Items in Large Databases. In: Proceedings of the 1993 ACM SIGMOD International Conference on Management of Data, pp. 207–216 (1993)

3. Carrier, B.: File System Forensic Analysis. Upper Saddle River, Addison-Wesley (2005)
4. Garfinkel, S.L.: Forensic Feature Extraction and Cross-Drive Analysis. Digital Investigation 3, 71–81 (2006)
5. Gladyshev, P., Patel, A.: Finite State Machine Approach to Digital Event Reconstruction. Digital Investigation 1, 130–149 (2004)
6. Herstein, I.N.: Topics in Algebra, 2nd edn. Wiley, New York (1975)
7. Hwang, H.-U., Kim, M.-S., Noh, B.-N.: Expert System Using Fuzzy Petri Nets in Computer Forensics. In: Szczuka, M.S., Howard, D., Ślęzak, D., Kim, H.-k., Kim, T.-h., Ko, I.-s., Lee, G., Sloot, P.M.A. (eds.) ICHIT 2006. LNCS (LNAI), vol. 4413, pp. 312–322. Springer, Heidelberg (2007)
8. Kwan, M., Chow, K.-P., Law, F., Lai, P.: Reasoning about Evidence Using Bayesian Networks. In: Proceedings of IFIP International Federation for Information Processing. Advances in Digital Forensics IV, vol. 285, pp. 275–289. Springer, Heidelberg (2008)
9. Liu, Z., Wang, N., Zhang, H.: Inference Model of Digital Evidence based on cFSA. In: Proceedings IEEE International Conference on Multimedia Information Networking and Security, pp. 494–497 (2009)
10. Marrington, A., Mohay, G., Morarji, H., Clark, A.: Computer Profiling to Assist Computer Forensic Investigations. In: Proceedings of RNSA Recent Advances in Security Technology, pp. 287–301 (2006)
11. Marrington, A., Mohay, G., Morarji, H., Clark, A.: Event-based Computer Profiling for the Forensic Reconstruction of Computer Activity. In: Proceedings of AusCERT 2007, pp. 71–87 (2007)
12. Marrington, A.: Computer Profiling for Forensic Purposes. PhD thesis, QUT, Australia (2009)
13. Tian, R., Batten, L., Versteeg, S.: Function Length as a Tool for Malware Classification. In: Proceedings of 3rd International Conference on Malware 2008, pp. 79–86. IEEE Computer Society, Los Alamitos (2008)
14. Welsh, D.J.A.: Matroid Theory. Academic Press, London (1976)
15. Wolf, J., Bansal, N., Hildrum, K., Parekh, S., Rajan, D., Wagle, R., Wu, K.-L., Fleischer, L.K.: SODA: An Optimizing Scheduler for Large-Scale Stream-Based Distributed Computer Systems. In: Issarny, V., Schantz, R. (eds.) Middleware 2008. LNCS, vol. 5346, pp. 306–325. Springer, Heidelberg (2008)
16. Yu, S., Zhou, W., Doss, R.: Information Theory Based Detection against Network Behavior Mimicking DDoS Attacks. IEEE Communication Letters 12(4), 319–321 (2008)

A Novel Forensics Analysis Method for Evidence Extraction from Unallocated Space

Zhenxing Lei, Theodora Dule, and Xiaodong Lin

University of Ontario Institute of Technology, Oshawa, Ontario, Canada
{Zhenxing.Lei,Theodora.Dule,Xiaodong.Lin}@uoit.ca

Abstract. Computer forensics has become a vital tool in providing evidence in investigations of computer misuse, attacks against computer systems and more traditional crimes like money laundering and fraud where digital devices are involved. Investigators frequently perform preliminary analysis at the crime scene on these suspect devices to determine the existence of target files like child pornography. Hence, it is crucial to design a tool which is portable and which can perform efficient preliminary analysis. In this paper, we adopt the space efficient data structure of fingerprint hash table for storing the massive forensic data from law enforcement databases in a flash drive and utilize hash trees for fast searches. Then, we apply group testing to identify the fragmentation points of fragmented files and the starting cluster of the next fragment based on statistics on the gap between the fragments.

Keywords: Computer Forensics, Fingerprint Hash Table, Bloom Filter, Fragmentation, Fragmentation Point.

1 Introduction

Nowadays a variety of digital devices including computers and cell phones have become pervasive, bringing comfort and convenience to our daily lives. Consequently, unlawful activities such as fraud, child pornography, etc., are facilitated by these devices. Computer forensics has become a vital tool in providing evidence in cases where digital devices are involved [1].

In a recent scandal involving Richard Lahey, a former Bishop of the Catholic Church from Nova Scotia, Canada, the evidence of child pornography was discovered on his personal laptop by members of the Canada Border Agency during a routine border crossing check. Preliminary analysis of the laptop was first performed on-site and revealed images of concern which necessitated seizure of the laptop for more comprehensive analysis later. The results of the comprehensive analysis confirmed the presence of child pornography images and formal criminal charges were brought against Lahey as a result.

Law enforcement agencies around the world collect and store large databases of inappropriate images like child pornography to assist in the arrests of perpetrators that possess the images, as well as to gather clues about the whereabouts of the victimized children and the identity of their abusers. In determining whether a suspect's computer contains inappropriate images, a forensic investigator compares the files

X. Lai et al. (Eds.): E-Forensics 2010, LNICST 56, pp. 53–65, 2011.

from the suspect's device with these databases of known inappropriate materials. These comparisons are time consuming due to the large volume of the source material and so a methodology for preliminary screening is essential to eliminate devices that are of no forensic interest. Also, it is crucial that tools used for preliminary screening are portable and can be carried by forensic investigators from one crime scene to another easily to facilitate efficient forensic inspections. Some tools are available today which have these capabilities. One such tool created by Microsoft in 2008 is called Computer Online Forensic Evidence Extractor (COFEE) [2]. COFEE is loaded on a USB flash drive, and performs automatic forensic analysis of storage devices at crime scenes by comparing hash values of target files on the suspect device calculated on site with hash values of source files compiled from the law enforcement which we call alert database and stored on the USB flash drive. COFEE was created through a partnership with law enforcement and is available free of charge to law enforcement agencies around the world. As a result it is increasing prevalent in crime scenes requiring preliminary forensic analysis.

Unfortunately, COFEE becomes ineffective in cases where forensic data has been permanently deleted on the suspect's device, e.g., by emptying the recycle bin. This is a common occurrence in crime scenes where the suspect has had some prior warning of the arrival of law enforcement and attempts to hide evidence by deleting incriminating files. Fortunately, although deleted files are no longer accessible by the file system, their data clusters may be wholly or partially untouched and are recoverable. File carving is an area of research in digital forensics that focuses on recovering such files. Intuitively, one way to enhance COFEE to also analyze these deleted files is to first utilize a file carver to recover all deleted files and then runs COFEE against them. This solution is constrained by the lengthy recovery speed of existing file caring tools especially when recovering files that are fragmented into two or more pieces, which is a challenge that existing forensic tools face. Hence, the recovery timeframe may not be suitable for the fast preliminary screening for which COFEE was designed. Another option is to enhance COFEE to perform direct analysis on all the data clusters on disk for both deleted and existing files. However this option is again hampered by the difficulty in parsing files fragmented into two or more pieces.

Nevertheless, we can simply extract those unallocated space and leave those allocated space checked by COFEE. Then, similar to COFEE, we calculate the hash value for the data clusters of unallocated space. In order to cope with this design, each file in the alert database must be stored as multiple hash values instead of one in COFEE. As a result, the required storage space will be a very challenging issue. Suppose the alert database contains 10 million images which we would like to compare with files on the devices at the crime scene and suppose also that the source image files are 1MB in size on average. Assuming that the cluster size is 4KB on the suspect device, we can estimate the size of the USB device for storing all 10 million images from the alert databases. We assume that the result of a secure hash algorithm used is128-bit length, we would require 38.15GB storage capacity for all 10 million images. A 256-bit hash algorithm would require 76.29GB storage and a 512-bit hash algorithm such as SHA-512 would require 152.59GB (see Table 1). The larger the alert database, the larger storage space is needed for a USB drive such that 20 million images would require twice the storage previous calculated.

Table 1. The required storage space for different methods of storing alert database

Storage Method		10 million photos
Without using cryptographic hash		10^3GB
Hash Algorithms	SHA-256	76.29GB
	SHA-512	152.59GB

Motivated by aforementioned observations in terms of the size of the storage medium and the requirement for analysis of deleted files, we propose an efficient evidence extracting method which supplements COFEE. The contributions of this paper are twofold. First, we propose efficient data structures based on hash trees and Fingerprint Hash Table (FHT) to achieve both better storage efficiency and faster lookups. The FHT is a space-efficient data structure that is used to test the existence of a given element from a known set. Also, the hash tree indexing structure ensures that the lookups are fast and efficient. Second, we apply group testing technique based on statistics about the size of gaps between two fragments of a file [3] for effectively searching the unallocated space of the suspect device to extract fragmented files that were permanently deleted.

The rest of this paper is organized as follows: in Section 2 we briefly introduce some preliminaries and background knowledge. In Section 3 we present our proposal in detail and in Section 4 we discuss false positive rates and how we handle some special cases like unbalanced hash trees and slack space. In Section 5, we analyze the time complexity and storage efficiency of the proposed scheme. Finally, we draw our conclusions and directions for future work.

2 Preliminaries

In this section we will briefly introduce bloom filters and fingerprint hash table, which serve as important background of the proposed forensics analysis method for unallocated space. Then, we discuss file fragmentation issue and file deletion in file systems.

2.1 Bloom filter and Fingerprint Hash Table

A bloom filter is a hash based space efficient data structure used for querying a large set of items to determine whether a given item is a member of the set. When we query an item in the bloom filter, false negative matches are not possible but false positives occur with a pre-determined acceptable false positive rate. A bloom filter is developed by inserting a given set of items $E = \{e_1, \ldots, e_n\}$ into a bit array of m bits $B=(b_1, b_2 \ldots b_m)$ which is initially set to 0. K independent hash functions $(H_1, H_2 \ldots H_k)$ are applied to each item in the set to produce k hash values $(V_1, V_2 \ldots V_k)$ and all corresponding bits in the bit array are set to 1 as illustrated in Figure 1.

The main properties of a bloom filter are as follows [4]: (1) the space for storing the Bloom filter is very small as well as the size of a bit array B; (2) the time to query whether an element is in the Bloom filter is constant and is not affected by the number of items in the set; (3) false negatives are impossible, and (4) false positives are possible, but the rate can be controlled. As one space-efficient data structure for representing a set of elements, bloom filter has been widely used in web cache sharing [5, 6], package routing [7], and so on.

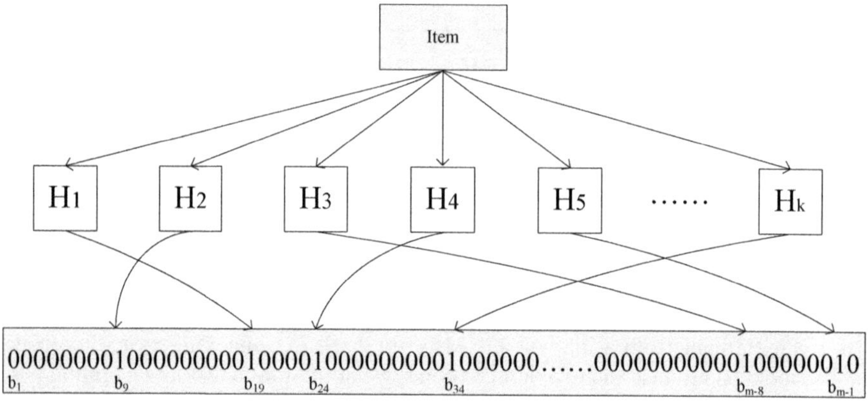

Fig. 1. m-bit standard Bloom filter

An alternative construction of Bloom filter is fingerprint hash table show as follows [8]:

$$\begin{cases} P(x): E \rightarrow \{1, 2, \ldots, n\} & (1) \\ F(x): E \rightarrow 1^{\iota} & (2) \end{cases}$$

Where P(x) is a perfect hash function [8] which maps each element $e \in E$ to an element at the unique location in an array of size n, F(x) is a hash function which calculates a fingerprint with $l=[\log 1/\varepsilon]$ bits of a given element $e \in E$, ε is the probability of a false positive, 1^{ι} denotes a bit stream with a length l. For example, given the desired false positive probability of $\varepsilon=2^{-10}$, only 10 bits are needed to represent each element. In this case, the required storage space for the scenario in Table 1 is 2.98GB, which takes much less space compared to traditional cryptographic hash methods.

2.2 File System

2.2.1 File Fragmentation

When a file is newly created in an operating system, the file system attempts to store the file contiguously in a series of sequential clusters large enough to hold the entire file in order to improve the performance of file retrieval and other operations later on. Most files are stored in this manner but some conditions like low disk space cause files to become fragmented over time and split over two or more sequential blocks of clusters. Garfinkel's corpus investigation in 2008 of over 449 hard disks collected over an 8 year period from different regions around the world provided the first published findings about fragmentation statistics in real-world datasets. According to his findings, fragmentation rates were not evenly distributed amongst file systems and hard drives and roughly half of all the drives in the corpus contained only contiguous files. Only 6% of all the recoverable files were fragmented at all with bifragmented files accounting for about 50% of fragmented files and files fragmented into three and as many as one thousand fragments accounted for the remaining 50% [3].

2.2.2 File Deletion

When a file is permanently deleted (e.g. by emptying the recycle bin), the file system no longer provides any means for recovering the file and marks the clusters previously assigned to the deleted file as unallocated and available for reuse. Although the file appears to have been erased, its data is still largely intact until it is overwritten by another file. For example, in the FAT file system each file and directory is allocated a data structure called a directory (DIR) entry that contains the file name, size, starting cluster address and other metadata. If a file is large enough to require multiple clusters, only the file system has the information to link one cluster to another in the right order to form a cluster chain. When the file is deleted, the operating system only updates the DIR entry and does not erase the actual contents of the data clusters [10]. It is therefore possible to recover important files during an investigation by analyzing the unallocated space of the device. Recovering fragmented files that have been permanently deleted is a challenge which existing forensic tools face.

3 Proposed Scheme

In this section we will first introduce our proposed data structure based on FHTs and hash trees for efficiently storing the alert database and fast lookup in the database. Then we will present an effective forensics analysis method for unallocated space even in the presence of file fragmentation.

3.1 Proposed Data Structure

3.1.1 Constructing Alert Database

In order to insert a file into alert database, we first divide the file size by 4096 bytes (cluster size) to create separate data items $\{e_1, e_2, e_3 \ldots e_n\}$ that are fed into P(x) so that we can map each element $e_i \in E$, $1 \leq i \leq n$, to a unique location in an array of size n. Later on, we store the fingerprint $l=[\log 1/\varepsilon]$ bits which is the F(x) value of a given element in each unique location. The process is repeated for the rest of the data items of each file; finally each file takes n*l bits in the alert database. In this manner, we store all the files into alert database.

3.1.2 Hash Tree Indexing

In order to get rapid random lookups and efficient access of records from the alert database, we construct a Merkle tree based on all cluster fingerprints of the files processed by the FHT and index each fingerprint as a single unit. In the Merkle tree, data records are stored only in leaf nodes but internal nodes are empty. Indexing the cluster fingerprints is easily achieved in the alert database using existing indexing algorithms, for example binary searching. The hash tree can be computed online while the indexing should be completed offline when we store the file into the alert database.

Figure 2 shows an example of an alert database with m files divided into 8 clusters each. Each file in the database has a hash tree and all the cluster fingerprints are indexed. It is worth noting that in a file hash tree, the value of the internal nodes and file roots can be computed online quickly due to the fact that the hash value can be calculated very fast.

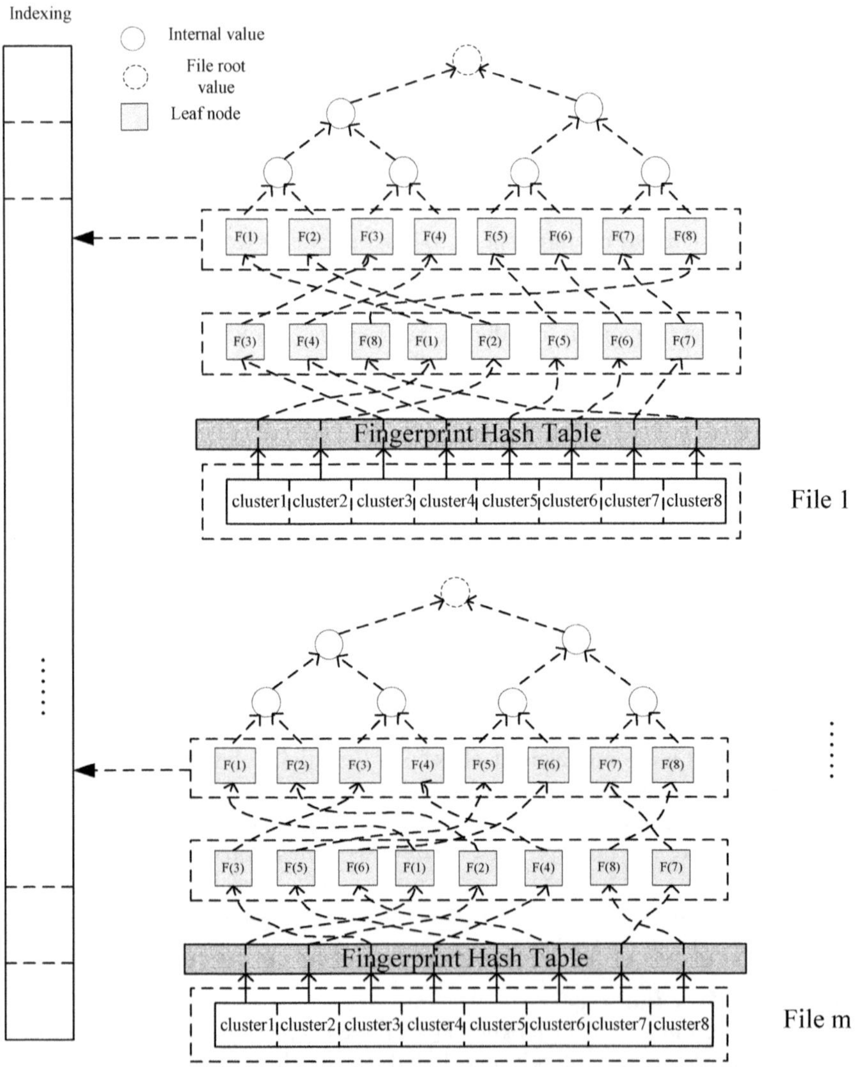

Fig. 2. Hash Tree Indexing

3.2 Group Testing Query Based on the Storage Characteristics

Group testing was first introduced by Dorfman [10] in World War II to provide efficient testing of millions of blood samples from US Army recruits being screened for venereal diseases. Dorfman realized that it was inefficient to test each individual blood sample and proposed to pool a set of blood samples together prior to running the screening test. If the test comes back negative, then all the samples that make up the pool are cleared of the presence of the venereal disease. If the test comes back positive however, additional tests can be performed on the individual blood samples until the infected source samples are identified. Group testing is an efficient method for separating out desired elements from a massive set using a limited number of tests. We adopt the use of group testing for efficiently identifying the fragmentation point of a known target file.

From Garfinkel's corpus investigation, there appears to be a trend in the relationship between the file size and the gap between the fragments that make up the file. Let us examine JPEG files from the corpus as an example. 16% of recoverable JPEG files were fragmented. With bifragmented JPEG files, the gap between the fragments were 8, 16, 24, 32, 56, 64, 240, 256 and 1272 sectors with corresponding file sizes of 4096, 8192, 12288,16384, 28672, 32768, 122880, 131072, and 651264 bytes as illustrated in Figure 3. Using this information, we can build search parameters for the first sector of the next fragment based on the size of the file which we know from the source database.

In limited case, the file is fragmented into two and more than two fragmentations. We suppose a realistic fragmentation scenario in which fragments are not randomly distributed but have multiple clusters sequentially stored. Under these characteristics, we can quickly find out the fragmentation point and the starting cluster of the next fragmentation.

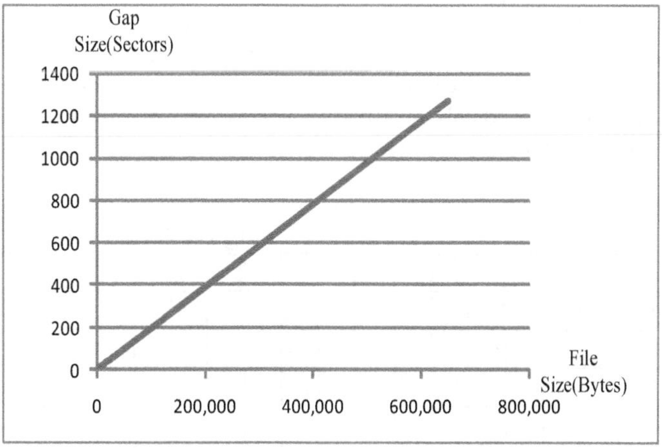

Fig. 3. The relation between the gap and the file size

3.3 Description of Algorithm

In the rest of this section, we discuss our proposed forensic analysis method with the assumption that the deleted file is still wholly intact and that no slack space exists on the last cluster, which is considered the basic algorithm of our proposed scheme. Discussions on cases involving partially overwritten files and slack space trimming are presented in Section 4.

During forensic analysis when any cluster of a file is found in the unallocated space of the suspect's machine, we compute its fingerprint and search the alert database containing indexed cluster fingerprints for a match. If no match is found it means that the cluster is not part of the investigation and can be safely ignored. Recall that the use of FHTs to calculate the fingerprint guarantees that false negatives are not possible. If a match is found in the alert database then we can proceed to further testing to determine if the result is a false positive or a true match. We begin by checking if the target cluster is part of a contiguous file by pooling together a group of clusters corresponding to the known file size and then computing the root value of the hash tree in both the alert database and the target machine. If the root values match, then it means that a complete file of forensic interest has been found on the suspect's machine. If the root values do not match, then either the file is fragmented or the result is a false positive. For non-contiguous files, our next set of tests search for the fragmentation point of the file and as well the first cluster of the next fragment.

Finding the fragmentation point of a fragment is achieved in a similar manner as finding contiguous files with the use of root hash values. Rather than computing a root value using all the clusters that make up the file however, we begin with a pool of *d* clusters and calculate its partial root value and then compare it with the partial root value from the alert database. If a match is found, we continue adding clusters *d* at a time to the previous pool until there a negative result is returned which indicates that the fragmentation point is somewhere in the last *d* clusters processed. The last *d* clusters processed can then be either divided into two groups (with a size of d/2) and tested, or processed one cluster at a time and tested at each stage until the last cluster for that fragment, i.e., fragmentation point, is found.

In order to find the starting cluster of the next fragment, we apply statistics about gap distribution introduced in the previous section to select a narrow range of clusters to begin searching and perform simple binary comparisons using the target cluster fingerprint from the alert database. Binary comparisons are very fast and as such we can ignore the time taken for searching for the next fragment when calculating the

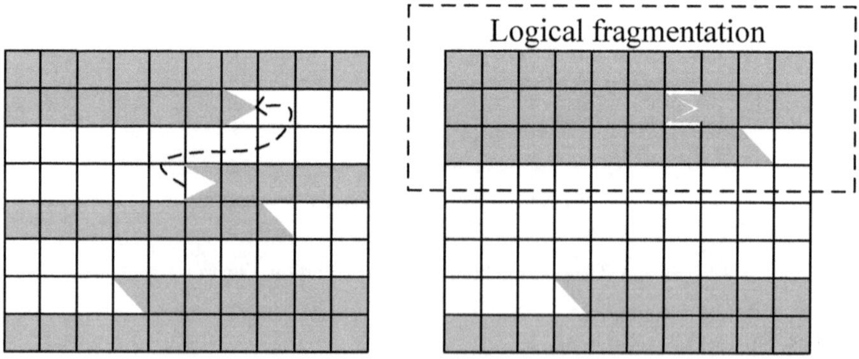

Fig. 4. Logical fragmentation for files of several fragments

time complexity. If the starting cluster of the next fragment cannot be successfully identified based on the gap distribution, brute-force cluster search is conducted on the suspect's device until a successful match occurs. Afterwards, the first two fragments are logically combined together by removing the clusters which separate them as shown in Figure 4 to form a single logical/virtual fragment. Verification of a match can be performed at this point using the aforementioned method for contiguous files. If the test returns a negative result, then we can deduce that the file is further fragmented. Otherwise, we successfully identify a file of interest.

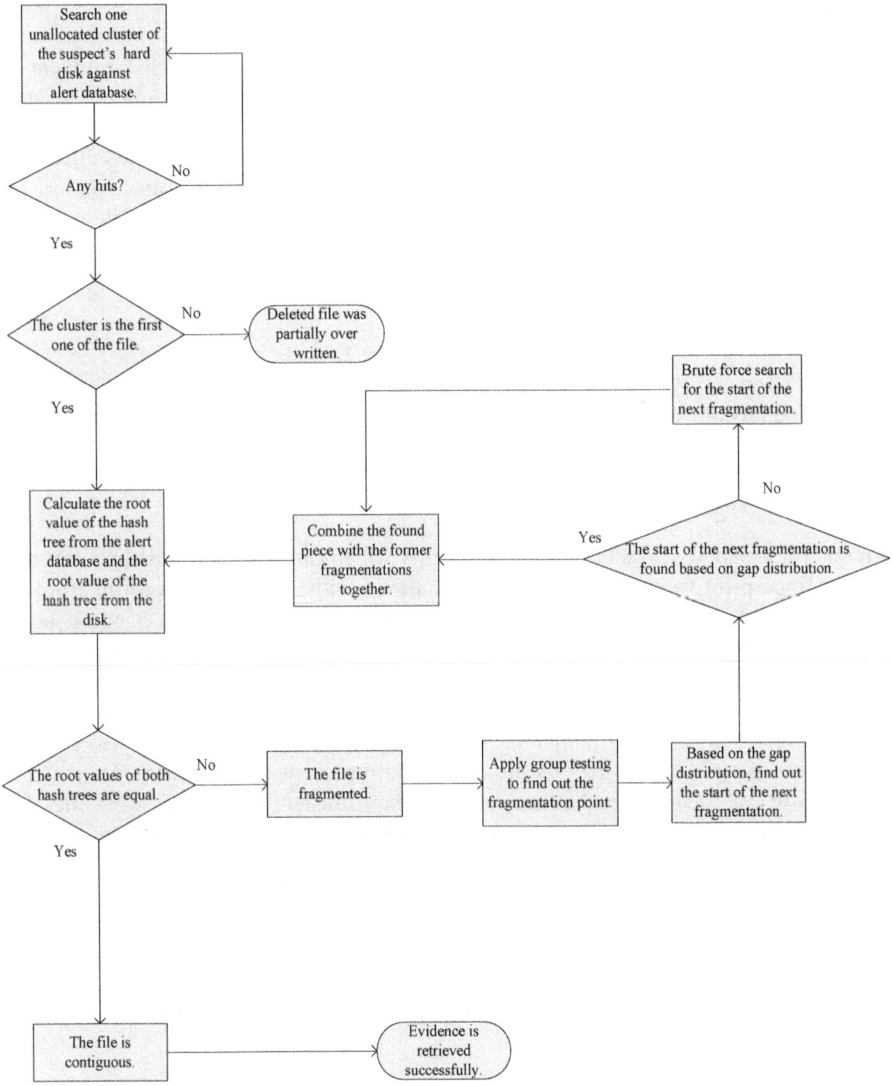

Fig. 5. The basic efficient unallocated space evidence extracting algorithm

Forensic analysis of contiguous files using this method has a time complexity of O (log (N)) while bifragmented files has a time complexity of O (log(N) + log(d)), where N=m*n, m is the total number of files in alert database, n is the number of clusters which each file in alert database contains. For simplicity, we consider the situation where the files in alert database have the same size. In the worst case where the second fragment of a bifragmented file is no longer available on the suspect's device (see Section 4 for additional discussion), every cluster on the device would be exhaustively searched before such conclusion could be reached. The time complexity in this case would be O(log(N) + log(d)+M), where M is the number of unallocated clusters on the suspect's harddisk.

For the small percentage (or 3%) of files that are fragmented into three or more pieces, once we logically combine detected fragments as a single fragment as illustrated in Figure 4, the fragmentation point of the logical fragment and the location of the starting cluster for the third fragment can be determined using statistics about the gap between fragments and binary comparisons as with bifragmented files. The rest of the fragmentation detection algorithm can follow the same pattern as bifragmenetd files until the complete file is detected. Figure 5 illustrates the efficient unallocated space evidence extracting algorithm discussed in this section.

4 Discussions

In this section we will discuss the effect of false positives from the FHT, handling unbalanced hash trees caused by an odd number of clusters in a file, and some special cases to be considered in the proposed algorithm.

4.1 False Positive in Alert Database

Bloom filter and it variants have a possibility of producing false positives where a cluster fingerprint from the alert database matches with a cluster fingerprint from the suspect's device that is actually part of an unrelated file. However, it could be an excellent space saving solution if the probability of an error is controlled. In fingerprint hash table, the probability of false positive is related to the size of the fingerprint representing an item. If the false positive probability is ε, the required size of the fingerprint is $l=[\log 1/\varepsilon]$ bits. For example, given the desired false positive probability of $\varepsilon=2^{-10}$, only 10 bits are needed to represent each element. Hence, The false positive ε' is shown in the function (3) when *d* cluster fingerprints from the alert database match with *d* fingerprints from the suspect's device but actually not

$$\varepsilon' = \varepsilon^d, \text{ where } l=[\log 1/\varepsilon] \tag{3}$$

The false positive will decrease when d or l increases. Therefore, we can simply choose the right d and l to control the false positive in order to achieve a good balance between the size of the cluster fingerprint and the probability of a false positive.

4.2 Unbalanced Hash Tree

An unbalanced hash tree will occur in cases where the clusters that form a file do not add up to a power of 2. In these cases, we can promote the node up in the tree until a sibling is found [11]. For example the file illustrated in Figure 6 is divided into 7 clusters and the corresponding fingerprints are F(1), F(2), … F(7), but the value F(7) of the seventh cluster does not have a sibling. Without being rehashed, we can promote F(7) up until it can be paired with value *K*. The values *K* and *G* are then concatenated and hashed to produce value *M*.

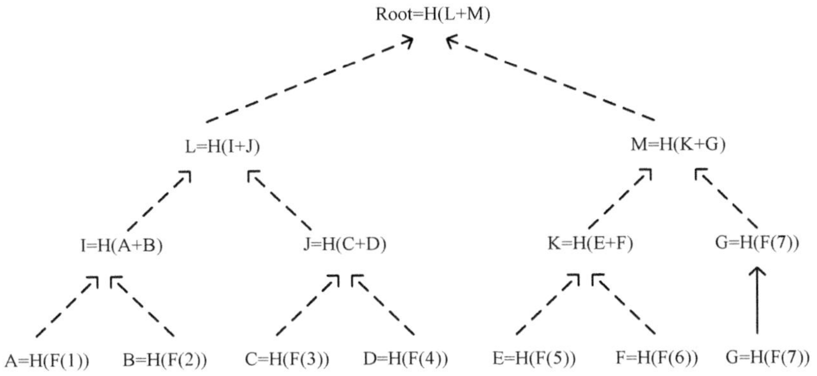

Fig. 6. An example of unbalanced hash tree

4.3 Slack Space Trimming

In a digital device clusters are equal-sized data units typically pre-set by the operating system. A file is spread over one or more clusters equal in size or larger than the size of the file being stored. This means that often there are unused bytes at the end of the last cluster which are not actually part of the file; this is called slack space. For example, on an operating system with 4 KB cluster size (4096bytes) and 512 byte sector, a 1236 byte file would require one cluster with first 1236 bytes containing file data and the remaining 2560 bytes are slack space as illustrated in Figure 7. The first two sectors of the cluster would be filled with file data and only 212 bytes of the third sector would be filled with data with the remaining 300 bytes and the entirety of clusters 4, 5, 6, 7 and 8 as slack space.

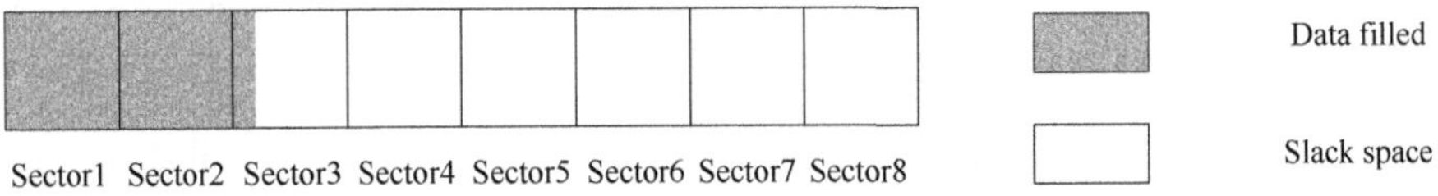

Fig. 7. Slack space in the cluster

Depending on the file system and operating system, slack space may be padding with zeros, may contain data from a previously deleted file or system memory. For files that are not a multiple of the cluster size, the slack space is the space after the file footer. Slack space would cause discrepancies in the calculated hash value of a file cluster when creating the cluster fingerprint. In this paper we are working on the assumption that the file size can be determined ahead of time from the information in the law enforcement source database and as a result, slack space can be easily detected and trimmed prior to the calculation of the hash values.

4.4 Missing File Fragments

As discussed earlier when a file is deleted, the operating system marks the clusters belonging to the file as unallocated without actually erasing the data contained in the clusters. In some cases some clusters may have since been assigned to other files and overwritten with data. In these cases, part of the file may still be recoverable and decisions on how many recovered clusters of a file constitute evidence of the prior existence of the entire file is up to the law enforcement agencies. For example, a search warrant may indicate that thresholds above 40% are sufficient for seizure of the device for more comprehensive analysis at an offsite location.

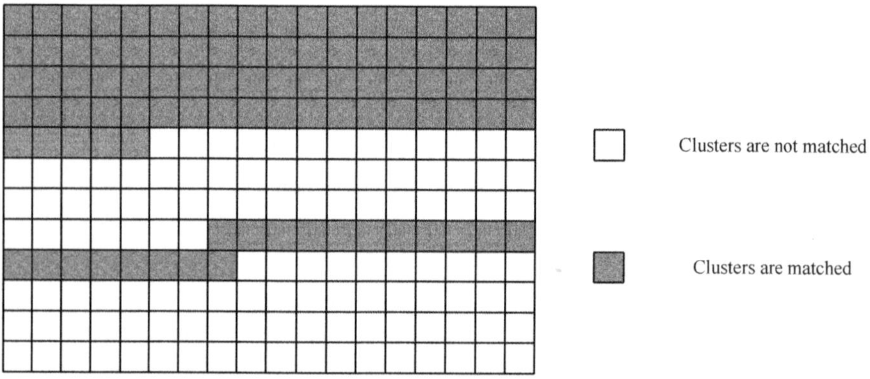

Fig. 8. 44.44% of one file are found, it can be seen as a warrant application evidence

Suppose the file in Figure 8 has four fragments and that the dark clusters (fragments 1 and 3) are still available on the suspect disk and the white clusters (fragments 2 and 4) have been overwritten with other information. Once the first fragment is detected using the techniques discussed in Section 3, detecting the second fragment will require the time consuming option of searching every single cluster when the targeted region sweep based on gap size statistics fails. After this search also fails to find the second fragment and we can conclusively say that the fragment is missing, we can either continue searching for the third fragment or prioritize these types of cases with missing fragments to the end after all other possible lucrative searches have been exhausted.

5 Complexity Analysis

Compared to the time complexity of the other query methods, such as classical hash tree traversal of O(2log(N)), where N=m*n, our proposed scheme is very promising as a result. Classical hash tree traversal for bifragmented files have a time complexity of O(2log(N)+2log(d/2)), and our scheme has only O(log(N)+log(d/2)). For file with multiple fragments the time complexity will be much more complicated as a result of utilizing sequential tests to query for the fragmented file cluster by cluster.

Nevertheless, very large fragments are typically seen only with very large files and the file information recovered from the first few during preliminary analysis may exceed the set threshold alleviating the need to continue exhaustive searching of the remaining fragments.

As we discussed in the section 4.1, when the false positive is 2^{-10}, the storage space for 10 million images each averaging 1MB is 2.98GB. It provides us a big advantage on choosing the storage device.

6 Conclusion and Future Work

In this paper we proposed a new approach to storing large amounts of data for easy portability in a space efficient data structure of FHT and used group testing and hash trees to efficiently query for the existence of files of interest and for detecting the fragmentation point of a file. The gap distribution statistics between the file fragments was applied to narrow down the region where searching for the next fragment begins. This approach helps us quickly query for relevant files from the suspect's device during preliminary analysis at the crime scene. After successful detection of target file using preliminary forensic tools that are fast and efficient, a warrant for further time consuming comprehensive analysis can be granted.

References

1. An introduction to Computer Forensics, `http://www.dns.co.uk`
2. Computer Online Forensic Evidence Extractor (COFEE), `http://www.microsoft.com/industry/government/solutions/cofee/default.aspx`
3. Garfinkel, S.L.: Carving contiguous and fragmented files with fast object validation. Digital Investigation 4, 2–12 (2007)
4. Antognini, C.: Bloom Filters, `http://antognini.ch/papers/BloomFilters20080620.pdf`
5. Fan, L., Cao, P., Almeida, J., Broder, A.: Summary Cache: A Scalable Wide-Area Web Cache Sharing Protocol. In: ACM SIGCOMM 1998, Vancouver, Canada (1998)
6. Squid Web Cache, `http://www.squid-cache.org/`
7. Broder, A., Mitzenmacher, M.: Network Applications of Bloom Filters: A Survey, `http://www.eecs.harvard.edu/~michaelm/NEWWORK/postscripts/BloomFilterSurvey.pdf`
8. Cormen, T.H., Leiserson, C.E., Rivest, R.L., Stein, C.: Introduction to Algorithms. The MIT Press, Cambridge (2001)
9. Hua, N., Zhao, H., Lin, B., Xu, J.: Rank-Indexed Hashing: A Compact Construction of Bloom Filters and Variants. In: IEEE Conference on Network Protocols (ICNP), pp. 73–82 (2008)
10. Carrier, B.: File System Forensic Analysis. Addison Wesley Professional, Reading (2005)
11. Hong, Y.-W., Scaglione, A.: Generalized group testing for retrieving distributed information. In: IEEE International Conference on Acoustics, Speech, and Signal Processing (ICASSP), Philadelphia, PA (2005)
12. Chapweske, J., Mohr, G.: Tree Hash EXchange format (THEX), `http://zgp.org/pipermail/p2p-hackers/2002-June/000621.html`

An Efficient Searchable Encryption Scheme and Its Application in Network Forensics

Xiaodong Lin[1], Rongxing Lu[2], Kevin Foxton[1], and Xuemin (Sherman) Shen[2]

[1] Faculty of Business and Information Technology, University of Ontario Institute of Technology, Oshawa, Ontario, Canada L1H 7K4
{xiaodong.lin,kevin.foxton}@uoit.ca

[2] Department of Electrical and Computer Engineering, University of Waterloo, Waterloo, Ontario, Canada N2L 3G1
{rxlu,xshen}@bbcr.uwaterloo.ca

Abstract. Searchable encryption allows an encrypter to send a message, in an encrypted form, to a decryptor who can delegate to a third party to search the encrypted message for keywords without losing encrypted message content's privacy. In this paper, based on the bilinear pairings, we propose a new efficient searchable encryption scheme, and use the provable security technique to formally prove its security in the random oracle model. Since some time-consuming operations can be pre-computed, the proposed scheme is very efficient. Therefore, it is particularly suitable for time-critical applications, such as network forensics scenarios, especial when the content is encrypted due to privacy concerns.

Keywords: Searchable encryption, Network forensics, Provable security, Efficiency.

1 Introduction

Network forensics is a newly emerging forensics technology aiming at the capture, recording, and analysis of network events. This is done in order to discover the source of security attacks or other incidents occurring in networked systems [1]. There has been a growing interest in this field of forensics in recent years. Network forensics can help provide evidence to investigators to track back and prosecute the attack perpetrators by monitoring network traffic, determining a traffic anomaly, and ascertaining the attacks [2]. However, as an important element of a network investigation, network forensics is only applicable to environment where network security policies such as authentication, firewall, and intrusion detection systems have already been deployed. Large-volume traffic storage units are necessary as well, in order to hold the large amount of network information that is gathered during network operations. Once a perpetrator attacks a networked system, network forensics should immediately be launched by investigating the traffic data kept in the data storage units.

In order for effective network forensics, the storage units are required to maintain a complete record of all network traffic; unfortunately this slows down the investigation due to the amount of data that needs to be reviewed. In addition, to meet the security and privacy goals of a network, the network traffic needs to be encrypted and not removable

X. Lai et al. (Eds.): E-Forensics 2010, LNICST 56, pp. 66–78, 2011.

from the storage units. The network architecture needs to be setup in such way so that if an attacker compromises the storage unit, they still cannot view or edit the data's plaintext. Since the policy on storing traffic data in an encrypted manner produces negative effects on the efficiency of an investigation; we therefore need to determine how to efficiently make a post-mortem investigation on a large volume of encrypted traffic data. This is an ongoing challenge in the network forensics field.

Boneh et al. first introduced the concept of searchable encryption in 2004 [3]. They state that it is possible for an encryptor to send an encrypted message, in its encrypted form, to a decryptor who has the rights to decrypt the message, and that receiving decryptor can delegate to a third party to search for keywords in the encrypted message without losing the confidentiality of the message's content. Due to this promising feature, searchable encryption has been very active and many searchable encryption schemes have been proposed in recent years [4,5,6,7,8,9,10,11]. Obviously, searchable encryption can be applied in data forensics so that an authorized party can help collect the required encrypted evidence without the loss of confidentiality of the information. Before putting searchable encryption into use in data forensics, the efficiency issue must be resolved. For example, a large volume of network traffic could simultaneously come into a network/system; an encryptor should be able to quickly encrypt the network traffic and store it on storage units. However, many previously reported searchable encryption schemes require time-consuming pairing and MapToPoint hash operations [12] during the encryption process, which make them inefficient for data forensics scenarios. In this paper, motivated by the above mentioned points, we propose a new efficient searchable encryption scheme based on bilinear pairing. Due to its ability to handle some of the time-consuming operations in advance, and only requiring one point multiplication during real-time encryption, the proposed scheme is particularly suitable for data forensics applications. Specifically, the contributions of this paper are twofold:

- We propose an efficient searchable encryption scheme based on bilinear pairing, and use the provable security technique to formally prove its security through the use of the random oracle model [13].
- Due to the proposed scheme's efficiency in terms of the speed of encryption, we also discuss how to apply it to data forensics scenarios to resolve the challenging issue of data privacy while effectively locating valuable forensic data of interest.

The remainder of this paper is organized as follows. In Section 2, we review several related works on public key based searchable encryption. In Section 3, we formalize the definition of public key based searchable encryption and its corresponding security model. In Section 4, we review bilinear pairing and the complexity assumption, which is the basis of our proposed scheme. We present our efficient public key based searchable encryption scheme based on bilinear pairing, together with its formal security proof and efficiency analysis in Section 5. We discuss how to apply the proposed scheme in several network forensics scenarios that require the preservation of information confidentiality in Section 6. Finally, we draw our conclusions in Section 7.

2 Related Work

Recently, many research works on public key based searchable encryption have been appeared in literature [3,4,5,6,7,8,9,10,11]. The pioneering work of public-key based searchable encryption scheme is due to Boneh et al [3], where an entity, which is granted with some search capability, can search for encrypted keywords without revealing the content of the original data. Shortly after Boneh et al's work [3], Golle et al. [4] propose some provably secure schemes to allow for conjunctive keywords queries on encrypted data, and Park et al. [5] also propose public key encryption with conjunctive field keyword search in 2004. In 2005, Abdalla et al [6] further discuss the consistency property of searchable encryption, and give a generic construction by transforming an anonymous identity-based encryption scheme. In 2007, Boneh and Waters [7] extend the searchable encryption scheme to support conjunctive, subset, and range queries on encrypted data. Both Fuhr and Paillier [8] and Zhang et al. [9] investigate how to combine searchable encryption and public key encryption in a generic way. In [10], Hwang and Lee study the public key encryption with conjunctive keyword search and its extension to a multi-user system. In 2008, Bao et al. [11] further systematically study searchable encryption in a practical multi-user setting.

Differencing from the above works, we investigate a provably secure and efficient searchable encryption scheme and apply it to network forensics. Specifically, our proposed scheme does not require any costly MapToPoint hash operations [12], and supports pre-computation to improve the efficiency.

3 Definition and Security Model

3.1 Notations

Let $\mathbb{N} = \{1, 2, 3, \ldots\}$ denote the set of natural numbers. If $l \in \mathbb{N}$, then 1^l is the string of l 1s. If x, y are two strings, then $|x|$ is the length of x and $x\|y$ is the concatenation of x and y. If S is a finite set, $s \overset{R}{\leftarrow} S$ denotes sampling an element x uniformly at random from S. And if $\mathcal{A}$ is a randomized algorithm, $y \leftarrow \mathcal{A}(x_1, x_2, \ldots)$ means that $\mathcal{A}$ has inputs $x_1, x_2, \ldots$ and outputs y.

3.2 Definition and Security Model of Searchable Encryption

Informally, a searchable encryption ($\mathcal{SE}$) allows a receiver to delegate some search capability to a third-party so that the latter can help the receiver to search some keywords in an encrypted message without losing the message content's privacy. According to [3], a $\mathcal{SE}$ can be formally defined as follows.

Definition 1. *(Searchable Encryption) A searchable encryption ($\mathcal{SE}$) scheme consists of the following polynomial time algorithms:* SETUP, KGEN, PEKS, TRAPDOOR, *and* TEST, *where*

- SETUP*(l): Given the security parameter l, this algorithm generates the system parameter $params$.*

- KGEN(*params*): *Given the system parameters* $\underline{params}$, *this algorithm generates a pair of public and private keys* (pk, sk).
- PEKS($params, pk, w$): *On input of the system parameters* $\underline{params}$, *a public key* pk, *and a word* $w \in \{0,1\}^l$, *this algorithm produces a searchable encryption* C *of* w.
- TRAPDOOR($params, sk, w$): *On input of the system parameters* $\underline{params}$, *a private key* sk, *and a word* w, *this algorithm produces a trapdoor* S_w *with respect to* w.
- TEST($params, s_w, C$): *On input of the system parameters* $\underline{params}$, *a searchable encryption ciphertext* $C = \text{PEKS}(pk, w)$, *and a trapdoor* $S_{w'} = \text{TRAPDOOR}(sk, w')$, *this algorithm outputs "*`Yes`*" if* $w = w'$ *and "*`No`*" otherwise.*

Next, we define the security of $\mathcal{SE}$ in the sense of semantic-security under the adaptively chosen keyword attacks (IND-CKA), which ensures that $C = \text{PEKS}(pk, w)$ does not reveal any information about the keyword w unless S_w is available [3]. Especially, we consider the following interaction game run between an adversary $\mathcal{A}$ and a challenger. First, the adversary $\mathcal{A}$ is fed with the system parameters and public key, and can adaptively ask the challenger for the key trapdoor S_w for any keyword $w \in \{0,1\}^l$ of his choice. At a certain time, the adversary $\mathcal{A}$ chooses two un-queried keywords $w_0^\star, w_1^\star \in \{0,1\}^l$, on which it wishes to be challenged. The challenger flips a coin $b \in \{0,1\}$ and returns $C^\star = \text{PEKS}(pk, w_b^\star)$ to $\mathcal{A}$. The adversary $\mathcal{A}$ can continue to make key trapdoor query for any keyword $w \notin \{w_0^\star, w_1^\star\}$. Eventually, $\mathcal{A}$ outputs its guess $b' \in \{0,1\}$ on b and wins the game if $b = b'$.

Definition 2. *(IND-CKA Security) Let* l *and* t *be integers and* ϵ *be a real in* $[0,1]$, *and* $\mathcal{SE}$ *a secure searchable encryption scheme with security parameter* l. *Let* $\mathcal{A}$ *be an IND-CKA adversary, which is allowed to access the key trapdoor oracle* $\mathcal{O}_K$ *(and random oracle* $\mathcal{O}_H$ *in the random oracle model), against the semantic security of* $\mathcal{SE}$. *We consider the following random experiment:*

$$
\begin{array}{l}
\texttt{Experiment } \mathbf{Exp}_{\mathcal{SE},\mathcal{A}}^{\textsf{IND-CKA}}(l) \\
\quad params \xleftarrow{R} \text{SETUP}(l) \\
\quad (pk, sk) \xleftarrow{R} \text{KGEN}(params) \\
\quad (w_0^\star, w_1^\star) \leftarrow \mathcal{A}^{\mathcal{O}_K(,\mathcal{O}_H)}(params, pk) \\
\quad b \xleftarrow{R} \{0,1\}, C^\star \leftarrow \text{PEKS}(pk, w_b^\star) \\
\quad b' \leftarrow \mathcal{A}^{\mathcal{O}_K(,\mathcal{O}_H)}(params, pk, C^\star) \\
\quad \texttt{if } b = b' \texttt{ then return } \ b^* \leftarrow 1 \texttt{ else } b^* \leftarrow 0 \\
\quad \texttt{return } b^*
\end{array}
$$

We define the success probability of $\mathcal{A}$ *via*

$$\mathbf{Succ}_{\mathcal{SE},\mathcal{A}}^{\textsf{IND-CKA}}(l) = 2\Pr\left[\mathbf{Exp}_{\mathcal{SE},\mathcal{A}}^{\textsf{IND-CKA}}(l)\right] - 1 = 2\Pr[b = b'] - 1$$

$\mathcal{SE}$ *is said to be* (l, t, ϵ)*-IND-CKA secure, if no adversary* $\mathcal{A}$ *running in time* t *has a success* $\mathbf{Succ}_{\mathcal{SE},\mathcal{A}}^{\textsf{IND-CKA}}(l) \geq \epsilon$.

4 Bilinear Pairing and Complexity Assumptions

In this section, we briefly review the necessary facts about bilinear pairing and the complexity assumptions used in our scheme.

Bilinear Pairing. Let $\mathbb{G}$ be a cyclic additive group generated by P, whose order is a large prime q, and $\mathbb{G}_T$ be a cyclic multiplicative group with the same order q. An *admissible* bilinear pairing $e : \mathbb{G} \times \mathbb{G} \rightarrow \mathbb{G}_T$ is a map with the following properties:

1. *Bilinearity:* For all $P, Q \in \mathbb{G}$ and any $a, b \in \mathbb{Z}_q^*$, we have $e(aP, bQ) = e(P, Q)^{ab}$;
2. *Non-degeneracy:* There exists $P, Q \in \mathbb{G}$ such that $e(P, Q) \neq 1_{\mathbb{G}_T}$;
3. *Computability:* There is an efficient algorithm to compute $e(P, Q)$ for all $P, Q \in \mathbb{G}$.

Such an *admissible* bilinear pairing $e : \mathbb{G} \times \mathbb{G} \rightarrow \mathbb{G}_T$ can be implemented by the modified Weil or Tate pairings [12].

Complexity Assumptions. In the following, we define the quantitative notion of the complexity of the problems underlying the proposed scheme, namely the collusion attack algorithm with k traitors (k-CAA) Problem [14] and the decisional collusion attack algorithm with k traitors (k-DCAA) Problem.

Definition 3. *(k-CAA Problem) Let $(e, \mathbb{G}, \mathbb{G}_T, q, P)$ be a bilinear pairing tuple. The k-CAA Problem in $\mathbb{G}$ is as follows: for an integer k, and $x \in \mathbb{Z}_q$, given*

$$\left\{P, Q = xP, h_1, h_2, \cdots, h_k \in \mathbb{Z}_q, \frac{1}{h_1 + x}P, \frac{1}{h_2 + x}P, \cdots, \frac{1}{h_k + x}P\right\}$$

to compute $\frac{1}{h^* + x}P$ for some $h^* \notin \{h_1, h_2, \cdots, h_k\}$.

Definition 4. *(k-CAA Assumption) Let $(e, \mathbb{G}, \mathbb{G}_T, q, P)$ be a bilinear pairing tuple, and $\mathcal{A}$ be an adversary that takes an input of $P, Q = xP, h_1, h_2, \cdots, h_k \in \mathbb{Z}_q$, $\frac{1}{h_1+x}P$, $\frac{1}{h_2+x}P, \cdots, \frac{1}{h_k+x}P$ for some unknown $x \in \mathbb{Z}_q^*$, and returns a new tuple $(h^*, \frac{1}{h^*+x}P)$ where $h^* \notin \{h_1, h_2, \cdots, h_k\}$. We consider the following random experiment.*

Experiment $\mathbf{Exp}_{\mathcal{A}}^{\text{k-CAA}}$
 $x \xleftarrow{R} \mathbb{Z}_q^*$,
 $(h^*, \alpha) \leftarrow \mathcal{A}\left(P, Q = xP, h_1, h_2, \cdots, h_k \in \mathbb{Z}_q, \frac{1}{h_1+x}P, \frac{1}{h_2+x}P, \cdots, \frac{1}{h_k+x}P\right)$
 if $\alpha = \frac{1}{h^*+x}P$ then $b \leftarrow 1$ else $b \leftarrow 0$
 return b

We define the corresponding success probability of $\mathcal{A}$ in solving the k-CAA problem via

$$\mathbf{Succ}_{\mathcal{A}}^{\text{k-CAA}} = \Pr\left[\mathbf{Exp}_{\mathcal{A}}^{\text{k-CAA}} = 1\right]$$

Let $\tau \in \mathbb{N}$ and $\epsilon \in [0, 1]$. We say that the k-CAA is (τ, ϵ)-secure if no polynomial algorithm $\mathcal{A}$ running in time τ has success $\mathbf{Succ}_{\mathcal{A}}^{\text{k-CAA}} \geq \epsilon$.

Definition 5. *(k-DCAA Problem) Let $(e, \mathbb{G}, \mathbb{G}_T, q, P)$ be a bilinear pairing tuple. The k-DCAA Problem in $\mathbb{G}$ is as follows: for an integer k, and $x \in \mathbb{Z}_q$, given*

$$\left\{P, Q = xP, h_1, h_2, \cdots, h_k, h^* \in \mathbb{Z}_q, \frac{1}{h_1 + x}P, \frac{1}{h_2 + x}P, \cdots, \frac{1}{h_k + x}P, T \in \mathbb{G}_T\right\}$$

to decide whether $T = e(P, P)^{\frac{1}{h^*+x}}$ or a random element R drawn from $\mathbb{G}_T$.

Definition 6. *(k-DCAA Assumption) Let $(e, \mathbb{G}, \mathbb{G}_T, q, P)$ be a bilinear pairing tuple, and $\mathcal{A}$ be an adversary that takes an input of $P, Q = xP, h_1, h_2, \cdots, h_k, h^* \in \mathbb{Z}_q, \frac{1}{h_1+x}P, \frac{1}{h_2+x}P, \cdots, \frac{1}{h_k+x}P, T \in \mathbb{G}_T$ for unknown $x \in \mathbb{Z}_q^*$, and returns a bit $b' \in \{0, 1\}$. We consider the following random experiments.*

Experiment $\mathbf{Exp}_{\mathcal{A}}^{\text{k-DCAA}}$
$x, h_1, h_2, \cdots, h_k, h \xleftarrow{R} \mathbb{Z}_q; R \xleftarrow{R} \mathbb{G}_T$
$\widetilde{b} \leftarrow \{0, 1\}$
if $\widetilde{b} = 0$, *then* $T = e(P, P)^{\frac{1}{h^*+x}}$; *else if* $\widetilde{b} = 1$ *then* $T = R$
$\widetilde{b'} \leftarrow \mathcal{A}\left(P, Q = xP, h_1, h_2, \cdots, h_k, h \in \mathbb{Z}_q, \frac{1}{h_1+x}P, \frac{1}{h_2+x}P, \cdots, \frac{1}{h_k+x}P, T\right)$
return 1 *if* $\widetilde{b'} = \widetilde{b}$, 0 *otherwise*

We then define the advantage of $\mathcal{A}$ via

$$\mathbf{Adv}_{\mathcal{A}}^{\text{k-DCAA}} = \Big|\Pr\left[\mathbf{Exp}_{\mathcal{A}}^{\text{k-DCAA}} = 1 | \widetilde{b} = 0\right] - \Pr\left[\mathbf{Exp}_{\mathcal{A}}^{\text{k-DCAA}} = 1 | \widetilde{b} = 1\right]\Big| \geq \epsilon$$

Let $\tau \in \mathbb{N}$ and $\epsilon \in [0, 1]$. We say that the k-DCAA is (τ, ϵ)-secure if no adversary $\mathcal{A}$ running in time τ has an advantage $\mathbf{Adv}_{\mathcal{A}}^{\text{k-DCAA}} \geq \epsilon$.

5 New Searchable Encryption Scheme

In this section, we will present our efficient searchable encryption scheme based on bilinear pairing, followed by its security proof and performance analysis.

5.1 Description of The Proposed Scheme

Our searchable encryption ($\mathcal{SE}$) scheme mainly consists of five algorithms, namely SETUP, KGEN, PEKS, TRAPDOOR and TEST, as shown in Fig. 1.

SETUP. Given the security parameter l, 5-tuple bilinear pairing parameters ($e, \mathbb{G}$, $\mathbb{G}_T$, q, P) are first chosen such that $|q| = l$. Then, a secure cryptographic hash function $\mathcal{H}$ is also chosen, where $\mathcal{H} : \{0, 1\}^l \rightarrow \mathbb{Z}_q^*$. In the end, the system parameters $params = (e, \mathbb{G}, \mathbb{G}_T, q, P, \mathcal{H})$ are published.

KGEN. Given the system parameters $params = (e, \mathbb{G}, \mathbb{G}_T, q, P, \mathcal{H})$, choose a random number $x \in \mathbb{Z}_q^*$ as the private key, and compute the corresponding public key $Y = xP$.

PEKS. Given a key $w \in \{0, 1\}^l$ and the public key Y, choose a random number $r \in \mathbb{Z}_q^*$, and execute the following steps:

SETUP SETUP(l) $\rightarrow$system parameters $params = (e, \mathbb{G}, \mathbb{G}_T, q, P, \mathcal{H})$	KGEN system parameters $params \rightarrow$ private key $x \in \mathbb{Z}_q^*$ public key $Y = xP$
PEKS for a keyword $w \in \{0,1\}^l$ choose a random number $r \in \mathbb{Z}_q^*$ $\alpha = r \cdot (Y + \mathcal{H}(w)P), \beta = e(P,P)^r$ $C = (\alpha, \beta)$	TRAPDOOR trapdoor for keyword w: $S_w = \frac{1}{x+\mathcal{H}(w)}P$ TEST test if $\beta = e(\alpha, S_w)$ if so, output "Yes"; if not, output "No".

Fig. 1. Proposed searchable encryption ($\mathcal{SE}$) scheme

- compute (α, β) such that $\alpha = r \cdot (Y + \mathcal{H}(w)P), \beta = e(P,P)^r$,
- set the ciphertext $C = (\alpha, \beta)$.

TRAPDOOR. Given the keyword $w \in \{0,1\}^l$ and the public and private key pairs (Y, x), compute the keyword w's trapdoor $S_w = \frac{1}{x+\mathcal{H}(w)}P$.

TEST. Given the ciphertext $C = (\alpha, \beta)$ and the keyword w's trapdoor $S_w = \frac{1}{x+\mathcal{H}(w)}P$, check if $\beta = e(\alpha, S_w)$. If the equation holds, "Yes" is output; otherwise, "No" is output. The correctness is as follows,

$$e(\alpha, S_w) = e\left(r \cdot (Y + \mathcal{H}(w)P), \frac{1}{x + \mathcal{H}(w)}P\right) = e\left(xP + \mathcal{H}(w)P, \frac{1}{x + \mathcal{H}(w)}P\right)^r$$
$$= e(P,P)^r = \beta$$

Consistency. Since $\mathcal{H}()$ is a secure hash function, the probability that $\mathcal{H}(w_0) = \mathcal{H}(w_1)$ can be negligible for any two keywords $w_0, w_1 \in \{0,1\}^l$ and $w_0 \neq w_1$. Therefore, $S_{w_0} = \frac{1}{x+\mathcal{H}(w_0)}P \neq \frac{1}{x+\mathcal{H}(w_1)}P = S_{w_1}$, and the TEST algorithm outputs "Yes" on input of a trapdoor for w_0 and a $\mathcal{SE}$ ciphertext C of w_1 is negligible. As a result, the consistency follows.

5.2 Security Proof

In the following theorem, we will prove that the ciphertext $C = (\alpha, \beta)$ is IND-CKA-secure in the random oracle model, where the hash function $\mathcal{H}$ is modelled as random oracle [13].

Theorem 1. *(IND-CKA Security) Let $k \in \mathbb{N}$ be an integer, and $\mathcal{A}$ be an adversary against the proposed $\mathcal{SE}$ scheme in the random oracle model, where the hash function $\mathcal{H}$ behaves as random oracle. Assume that $\mathcal{A}$ has the success probability $\mathbf{Succ}_{\mathrm{SE},\mathcal{A}}^{\textsf{ind-cka}} \geq \epsilon$ to break the indistinguishability of the ciphertext $C = (\alpha, \beta)$ within the running time τ, after $q_H = k + 2$ and $q_K \leq k$ queries to the random oracle $\mathcal{O}_H$ and the key trapdoor oracle $\mathcal{O}_K$, respectively. Then, there exist $\epsilon' \in [0,1]$ and $\tau' \in \mathbb{N}$ as follows*

$$\epsilon' = \mathbf{Adv}_{\mathcal{A}}^{\mathrm{k-DCAA}}(\tau') \geq \frac{\epsilon}{q_H(q_H - 1)}, \qquad \tau' \leq \tau + \Theta(.) \tag{1}$$

such that the k-DCAA problem can be solved with probability ϵ' within time τ', where $\Theta(.)$ is the time complexity for the simulation.

Proof. We define a sequence of games $\mathbf{Game}_0$, $\mathbf{Game}_1$, $\cdots$ of modified attacks starting from the actual adversary $\mathcal{A}$ [15]. All the games operate on the same underlying probability space: the system parameters $params = (e, \mathbb{G}, \mathbb{G}_T, q, P, \mathcal{H})$ and public key $Y = xP$, the coin tosses of $\mathcal{A}$. Let $(P, xP, h_1, h_2, \cdots, h_k, h^* \in \mathbb{Z}_q^*, \frac{1}{h_1+x}P, \frac{1}{h_2+x}P, \cdots, \frac{1}{h_k+x}P, T \in \mathbb{G}_T)$ be a random instance of k-DCAA problem, we will use these incremental games to reduce the k-DCAA instance to the adversary $\mathcal{A}$ against the IND-CKA security of the ciphertext $C = (\alpha, \beta)$ in the proposed $\mathcal{SE}$ scheme.

$\mathbf{Game}_0$: This is a real attack game. In the game, the adversary $\mathcal{A}$ is fed with the system parameters $params = (e, \mathbb{G}, \mathbb{G}_T, q, P, \mathcal{H})$ and public key $Y = xP$. In the first phase, the adversary $\mathcal{A}$ can access to the random oracle $\mathcal{O}_H$ and the key trapdoor oracle $\mathcal{O}_K$ for any input. At some point, the adversary $\mathcal{A}$ chooses a pair of keywords $(w_0^\star, w_1^\star) \in \{0,1\}^l$. Then, we flip a coin $b \in \{0,1\}$ and produce the message $w^\star = w_b^\star$'s ciphertext $C^\star = (\alpha^\star, \beta^\star)$ as the challenge to the adversary $\mathcal{A}$. The challenge comes from the public key Y and one random number $r^\star \in \mathbb{Z}_q^*$, and $\alpha^\star = r^\star \cdot (Y + \mathcal{H}(w^\star)P)$, $\beta^\star = e(P,P)^{r^\star}$. In the second stage, the adversary $\mathcal{A}$ is still allowed to access to the random oracle $\mathcal{O}_H$, and the key trapdoor oracle $\mathcal{O}_K$ for any input, except the challenge $(w_0^\star, w_1^\star)$. Finally, the adversary $\mathcal{A}$ outputs a bit $b' \in \{0,1\}$. In any $\mathbf{Game}_j$, we denote by $\mathbf{Guess}_j$ the event $b = b'$. Then, by definition, we have

$$\epsilon \leq \mathbf{Succ}_{\mathrm{SE},\mathcal{A}}^{\text{ind-cka}} = 2\Pr[b = b']_{\mathbf{Game}_0} - 1 = 2\Pr[\mathbf{Guess}_0] - 1 \quad (2)$$

$\mathbf{Game}_1$: In the simulation, we know the adversary $\mathcal{A}$ makes a total of $q_H = k+2$ queries on $\mathcal{O}_H$, two of which are the queries of the challenge $(w_0^\star, w_1^\star)$. In this game, we consider that we successfully guess the challenge $(w_0^\star, w_1^\star)$ from q_H queries $(w_1, w_2, \cdots, w_{q_H})$ in advance, then the probability of successful guessing $(w_0^\star, w_1^\star)$ is $1/\binom{q_H}{2} = \frac{2}{q_H(q_H-1)}$. Then, in this game, we have

$$\begin{aligned} \frac{2}{q_H(q_H-1)}\mathbf{Succ}_{\mathrm{SE},\mathcal{A}}^{\text{ind-cka}} &= 2\Pr[b = b']_{\mathbf{Game}_1} - 1 = 2\Pr[\mathbf{Guess}_1] - 1, \\ \Pr[\mathbf{Guess}_1] &= \frac{1}{q_H(q_H-1)} \cdot \mathbf{Succ}_{\mathrm{SE},\mathcal{A}}^{\text{ind-cka}} + \frac{1}{2} \geq \frac{\epsilon}{q_H(q_H-1)} + \frac{1}{2} \end{aligned} \quad (3)$$

$\mathbf{Game}_2$: In this game, we simulate the random oracle $\mathcal{O}_H$ and the key trapdoor oracle $\mathcal{O}_K$, by maintaining the lists $\mathcal{H}$-List and $\mathcal{K}$-List to deal with the identical queries. In addition, we also simulate the way that the challenges $C^\star$ is generated as the challenger would do. The detailed simulation in this game is described in Fig. 2. Because the distribution of $(params, Y)$ is unchanged in the eye of the adversary $\mathcal{A}$, the simulation is perfect, and we have

$$\Pr[\mathbf{Guess}_2] = \Pr[\mathbf{Guess}_1] \quad (4)$$

$\mathbf{Game}_3$: In this game, we modify the rule Key-Gen in the key trapdoor oracle $\mathcal{O}_K$ simulation without resorting to the private key x.

▷ **Rule** Key-Gen$^{(3)}$

look up the item $\frac{1}{h+x}P$ in $\{\frac{1}{h_1+x}P, \frac{1}{h_2+x}P, \cdots, \frac{1}{h_k+x}P\}$
set $S_w = \frac{1}{h+x}P$
answer S_w and add (w, S_w) to $\mathcal{K}$-List

Because q_K, the total key trapdoor query number, is less than or equal to k, the item $S_w = \frac{1}{h+x}P$ always can be found in the simulation due to the k-DCAA problem. Therefore, these two games $\mathbf{Game}_3$ and $\mathbf{Game}_2$ are perfectly indistinguishable, and we have

$$\Pr[\mathbf{Guess}_3] = \Pr[\mathbf{Guess}_2] \quad (5)$$

Game$_4$: In this game, we manufacture the challenge $C^\star = (\alpha^\star, \beta^\star)$ by embedding the k-DCAA challenge $(h^*, T \in \mathbb{G}_T)$ in the simulation. Specifically, after flipping $b \in \{0,1\}$ and choosing $r^\star \in \mathbb{Z}_q^*$, we modify the rule Chal in the Challenger simulation and the rule No-H in the $\mathcal{O}_H$ simulation.

▷ **Rule** Chal$^{(4)}$
| $\alpha^\star = r^\star P, \beta^\star = T^{r^\star}$
| set the ciphertext $C^\star = (\alpha^\star, \beta^\star)$

▷ **Rule** No-H$^{(4)}$
| if $w \notin (w_0^\star, w_1^\star)$
| | randomly choose a fresh h from the set $\mathbb{H} = \{h_1, h_2, \cdots, h_k\}$
| | the record (w, h) will be added in $\mathcal{H}$-List
| else if $w \in (w_0^\star, w_1^\star)$
| | if $w = w_b^\star$
| | | set $h = h^*$, the record (w, h) will be added in $\mathcal{H}$-List
| | else if $w = w_{b-1}^\star$
| | | randomly choose a fresh random number h from $\mathbb{Z}_q^*/(\mathbb{H} \cup \{h^*\})$
| | | the record (w, h) will be added in $\mathcal{H}$-List

Based on the above revised rules, if T in the k-DCAA challenge is actually $e(P,P)^{\frac{1}{h^*+x}}$, i.e., $\widetilde{b} = 0$ in the Experiment $\mathbf{Exp}_{\mathcal{A}}^{\text{k-DCAA}}$, we know that

$$C^\star = \left(\alpha^\star = r^\star P, \beta^\star = T^{r^\star} = e(P,P)^{\frac{r^\star}{h^*+x}}\right)$$

is a valid ciphertext, which will pass the Test equation $\beta^\star = e(\alpha^\star, S_{w_b^\star})$, where $S_{w_b^\star} = T = e(P,P)^{\frac{1}{h^*+x}}$. Therefore, we have

$$\Pr[\mathbf{Guess}_4 | \widetilde{b} = 0] = \Pr[\mathbf{Guess}_3]. \quad (6)$$

and

$$\Pr\left[\mathbf{Exp}_{\mathcal{A}}^{\text{k-DCAA}} = 1 | \widetilde{b} = 0\right] = \Pr[\mathbf{Guess}_4 | \widetilde{b} = 0] \quad (7)$$

If T in the k-DCAA challenge is a random element in $\mathbb{G}_T$ other than $e(P,P)^{\frac{1}{h^*+x}}$, i.e., $\widetilde{b} = 1$ in the Experiment $\mathbf{Exp}_{\mathcal{A}}^{\text{DBDH}}$, $C^\star = \left(\alpha^\star = r^\star P, \beta^\star = T^{r^\star}\right)$ is not a valid ciphertext, and thus is independent on b. Therefore, we will have

$$\Pr\left[\mathbf{Exp}_{\mathcal{A}}^{\text{k-DCAA}} = 1 | \widetilde{b} = 1\right] = \Pr[\mathbf{Guess}_4 | \widetilde{b} = 1] = \frac{1}{2}. \quad (8)$$

As a result, from Eqs. (3)-(8), we have

$$\begin{aligned} \epsilon' &= \mathbf{Adv}_{\mathcal{A}}^{\text{k-DCAA}} \\ &= \left| \Pr\left[\mathbf{Exp}_{\mathcal{A}}^{\text{k-DCAA}} = 1 | \widetilde{b} = 0 \right] - \Pr\left[\mathbf{Exp}_{\mathcal{A}}^{\text{k-DCAA}} = 1 | \widetilde{b} = 1 \right] \right| \\ &\geq \left| \frac{\epsilon}{q_H(q_H - 1)} + \frac{1}{2} - \frac{1}{2} \right| = \frac{\epsilon}{q_H(q_H - 1)} \end{aligned} \tag{9}$$

In addition, we can obtain the claimed bound for $\tau' \leq \tau + \Theta(.)$ in the sequence games. Thus, the proof is completed. □

Query to Oracle $\mathcal{O}_H$

Query $\mathcal{H}(w)$: if a record (w, h) has already appeared in $\mathcal{H}$-List, the answer is returned with the value of h.

Otherwise the answer h is defined according to the following rule:

▷ **Rule** No-H$^{(2)}$
- if $w \notin (w_0^\star, w_1^\star)$
  - randomly choose a fresh h from the set $\mathbb{H} = \{h_1, h_2, \cdots, h_k\}$
  - the record (w, h) will be added in $\mathcal{H}$-List
- else if $w \in (w_0^\star, w_1^\star)$
  - randomly choose a fresh random number h from $\mathbb{Z}_q^*/(\mathbb{H} \cup \{h^*\})$
  - the record (w, h) will be added in $\mathcal{H}$-List

Query to Oracle $\mathcal{O}_K$

Query $\mathcal{O}_K(w)$: if a record (w, S_w) has already appeared in $\mathcal{K}$-List, the answer is returned with S_w.

Otherwise the answer S_w is defined according to the following rules:

▷ **Rule** Key-Init$^{(2)}$
- Look up for $(w, h) \in \mathcal{H}$-List
- if the record (w, h) is unfound
  - same as the rule of query to Oracle $\mathcal{O}_H$

▷ **Rule** Key-Gen$^{(2)}$
- Use the private key $sk = x$ to compute $S_w = \frac{1}{x+h} P$

Answer S_w and add (w, S_w) to $\mathcal{K}$-List

Challenger

For two keywords $(w_0^\star, w_1^\star) \in \mathbb{Z}_q^*$, flip a coin $b \in \{0, 1\}$ and set $w^\star = w_b^\star$, randomly choose $r^\star \in \mathbb{Z}_q^*$, then answer $C^\star$, where

▷ **Rule** Chal$^{(2)}$
- $\alpha^\star = r^\star \cdot (Y + \mathcal{H}(w_b^\star)P)$, $\beta^\star = e(P, P)^{r^\star}$
- set the ciphertext $C^\star = (\alpha^\star, \beta^\star)$

Fig. 2. Formal simulation of the IND-CKA game against the proposed $\mathcal{SE}$ scheme

5.3 Efficiency

Our proposed $\mathcal{SE}$ scheme is particularly efficient in terms of the computational costs. As shown in Fig. 1, the PEKS algorithm requires two point multiplications in $\mathbb{G}$ and one pairing operation. Because $\alpha = r \cdot (Y + \mathcal{H}(w)P) = rY + \mathcal{H}(w)(rP)$, the items rY, rP together with $\beta = e(P, P)^r$, which are irrelative to the keyword w, can be pre-computed. Then, only one point multiplication is required at PEKS. In addition, the TRAPDOOR and TEST algorithms also only require one point multiplication, one pairing operation, respectively. Table 1 shows the computational complexity between the scheme in [3] and our proposed scheme, where we consider point multiplication in $\mathbb{G}$, exponentiation in $\mathbb{G}_T$, pairing, and MapToPoint hash operation [12], but omit miscellaneously small computation operations such as point addition and ordinary hash function $\mathcal{H}$ operation. Then, from the figure, we can see our proposed scheme is more efficient, especially when the pre-computation is considered since T_{pmul} is much smaller than $T_{\text{pair}} + T_{\text{m2p}}$ in many software implementations.

Table 1. Computational cost comparisons

	Scheme in [3]	Proposed scheme
PEKS (w.o. precomputation)	$2 \cdot T_{\text{pmul}} + T_{\text{pair}} + T_{\text{m2p}}$	$2 \cdot T_{\text{pmul}} + T_{\text{exp}}$
PEKS (with precomputation)	$T_{\text{pair}} + T_{\text{m2p}}$	T_{pmul}
TRAPDOOR	$T_{\text{pmul}} + T_{\text{m2p}}$	T_{pmul}
TEST	T_{pair}	T_{pair}

T_{pmul}: time cost of point multiplication in $\mathbb{G}$; T_{pair}: time cost of one pairing;
T_{m2p}: time cost of MapToPoint hash; T_{exp}: time cost of exponentiation in $\mathbb{G}_T$

6 Application in Network Forensics

In this section, we discuss how to apply our proposed searchable encryption $\mathcal{SE}$ scheme to network forensics. As shown in Fig. 3, the network forensics system that we consider mainly consists of a top-level administrator, an investigator and two security modules resided in each network service. The network service consists of the user authentication module and the traffic monitoring module, where the user authentication module takes the responsibility for the user authentication, and the traffic monitoring module is monitoring and logging all user activities in the system. In general, network forensics used in a system can be divided into three phases: network user authentication phase, traffic logging phase, and network investigation phase. Each of the phases is detailed as follows:

- Network user authentication phase: when an Internet user with identity U_i visits a network service, the residing user authentication module will authenticate the user. If the user passes the authentication, he can access the service. Otherwise, the user is prohibited from accessing the service.

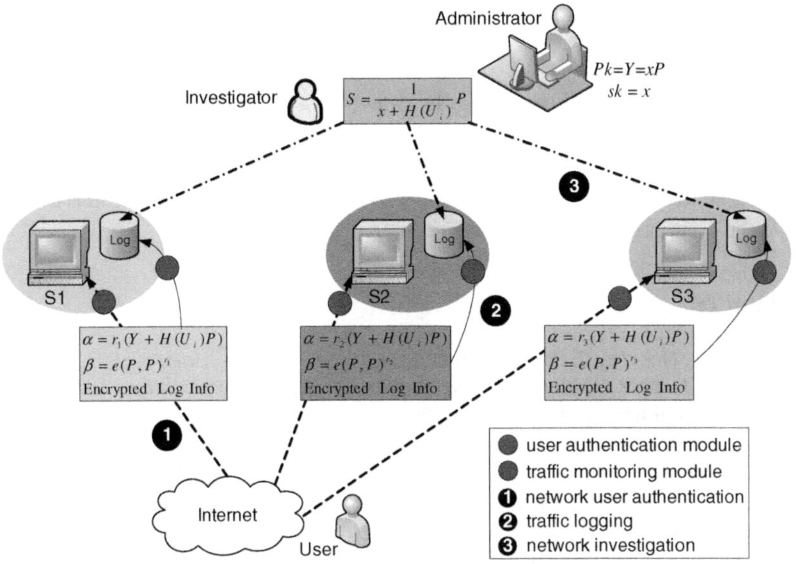

Fig. 3. Network forensics enhanced with searchable encryption

Fig. 4. The format of encrypted record

- Traffic logging phase: when the network service is idle, the traffic monitoring module precomputes a huge number of tuples, each tuple is of the form $(rY, rP, \beta = e(P, P)^r)$, where $r \in \mathbb{Z}_q^*$ and Y is the public key of the administrator. When an authenticated user U_i runs some actions with the service, the traffic monitoring module will pick up a tuple $(rY, rP, \beta = e(P, P)^r)$, compute $\alpha = rY + \mathcal{H}(U_i)rP$, create the logging record in the format as shown in Fig. 4, where Header $:= (\alpha, \beta)$ and EncryptedRecord $:=$ U_i's actions encrypted with the administrator's public key Y. After the user's actions are encrypted, the logged record is stored in the storage units.
- Network investigation phase: once the administrator suspects that an authenticated user U_i could have been compromised by an attacker, he should collect evidence on all actions that U_i did in the past. Therefore, the administrator needs to authorize an investigator to collect the evidences at each service's storage units. However, because U_i is still just under suspicion, the administrator cannot let the investigator know U_i's identity. To address this privacy issue, the administrator grants $S = \frac{1}{x+H(U_i)}P$ to the investigator, and the latter can collect all the required records satisfying $\beta = e(\alpha, S)$. After recovering the collected records from the investigator, the administrator can then do forensics analysis on the data. Obviously, such network forensics enhanced with our proposed searchable encryption can work well in terms of forensics analysis, audit, and privacy preservation.

7 Conclusions

In this paper, we have proposed an efficient searchable encryption ($\mathcal{SE}$) scheme based on bilinear pairings, and have formally shown its security with the provable security technique under k-DCAA assumption. Due to the fact that it supports pre-computation, i.e., only one point multiplication and one pairing are required in PEKS and TEST algorithms, respectively, the proposed scheme is much efficient and particularly suitable to resolve the challenging privacy issues in network forensics.

References

1. Ranum, M.: Network flight recorder, http://www.ranum.com/
2. Pilli, E. S., Joshi, R.C., Niyogi, R.: Network forensic frameworks: Survey and research challenges. Digitial Investigation (in press, 2010)
3. Boneh, D., Di Crescenzo, G., Ostrovsky, R., Persiano, G.: Public key encryption with keyword search. In: Cachin, C., Camenisch, J.L. (eds.) EUROCRYPT 2004. LNCS, vol. 3027, pp. 506–522. Springer, Heidelberg (2004)
4. Golle, P., Staddon, J., Waters, B.: Secure conjunctive keyword search over encrypted data. In: Jakobsson, M., Yung, M., Zhou, J. (eds.) ACNS 2004. LNCS, vol. 3089, pp. 31–45. Springer, Heidelberg (2004)
5. Park, D.J., Kim, K., Lee, P.J.: Public key encryption with conjunctive field keyword search. In: Lim, C.H., Yung, M. (eds.) WISA 2004. LNCS, vol. 3325, pp. 73–86. Springer, Heidelberg (2005)
6. Abdalla, M., Bellare, M., Catalano, D., Kiltz, E., Kohno, T., Lange, T., Malone-Lee, J., Neven, G., Paillier, P., Shi, H.: Searchable encryption revisited: Consistency properties, relation to anonymous IBE, and extensions. In: Shoup, V. (ed.) CRYPTO 2005. LNCS, vol. 3621, pp. 205–222. Springer, Heidelberg (2005)
7. Boneh, D., Waters, B.: Conjunctive, subset, and range queries on encrypted data. In: Vadhan, S.P. (ed.) TCC 2007. LNCS, vol. 4392, pp. 535–554. Springer, Heidelberg (2007)
8. Fuhr, T., Paillier, P.: Decryptable searchable encryption. In: Susilo, W., Liu, J.K., Mu, Y. (eds.) ProvSec 2007. LNCS, vol. 4784, pp. 228–236. Springer, Heidelberg (2007)
9. Zhang, R., Imai, H.: Generic combination of public key encryption with keyword search and public key encryption. In: Bao, F., Ling, S., Okamoto, T., Wang, H., Xing, C. (eds.) CANS 2007. LNCS, vol. 4856, pp. 159–174. Springer, Heidelberg (2007)
10. Hwang, Y.-H., Lee, P.J.: Public key encryption with conjunctive keyword search and its extension to a multi-user system. In: Takagi, T., Okamoto, T., Okamoto, E., Okamoto, T. (eds.) Pairing 2007. LNCS, vol. 4575, pp. 2–22. Springer, Heidelberg (2007)
11. Feng Bao, F., Deng, R.H., Ding, X., Yang, Y.: Private query on encrypted data in multi-user settings. In: Chen, L., Mu, Y., Susilo, W. (eds.) ISPEC 2008. LNCS, vol. 4991, pp. 71–85. Springer, Heidelberg (2008)
12. Boneh, D., Franklin, M.: Identity-based encryption from the weil pairing. In: Kilian, J. (ed.) CRYPTO 2001. LNCS, vol. 2139, pp. 213–229. Springer, Heidelberg (2001)
13. Bellare, M., Rogaway, P.: Random Oracles are Practical: A Paradigm for Designing Efficient Protocols. In: ACM Computer and Communications Security Conference, CCS 1993, Fairfax, Virginia, USA, pp. 62–73 (1993)
14. Zhang, F., Safavi-Naini, R., Susilo, W.: An efficient signature scheme from bilinear pairings and its applications. In: Bao, F., Deng, R., Zhou, J. (eds.) PKC 2004. LNCS, vol. 2947, pp. 277–290. Springer, Heidelberg (2004)
15. Shoup, V.: OAEP Reconsidered. Journal of Cryptology 15, 223–249 (2002)

Attacks on BitTorrent – An Experimental Study

Marti Ksionsk[1], Ping Ji[1], and Weifeng Chen[2]

[1] Department of Math & Computer Science
John Jay College of Criminal Justice
City University of New York
New York, New York 10019
glassnickels@gmail.com,pji@jjay.cuny.edu
[2] Department of Math & Computer Science
California University of Pennsylvania
California, PA 15419
chen@calu.edu

Abstract. Peer-to-peer (P2P) networks and applications represent an efficient method of distributing various network contents across the Internet. Foremost among these networks is the BitTorrent protocol. While BitTorrent has become one of the most popular P2P applications, attacking BitTorrent applications recently began to arise. Although sources of the attacks may be different, their main goal is to slow down the distribution of files via BitTorrent networks. This paper provides an experimental study on peer attacks in the BitTorrent applications. Real BitTorrent network traffic was collected and analyzed, based on which, attacks were identified and classified. This study aims to better understand the current situation of attacks on BitTorrent applications and provide supports for developing possible approaches in the future to prevent such attacks.

1 Introduction

The demand for media content on the Internet has exploded in recent years. As a result, file sharing through peer-to-peer (P2P) networks has noticeably increased in kind. In a 2006 study conducted by CacheLogic [9], it was found that P2P accounted for approximately 60 percent of all Internet traffic in 2006, a dramatic growth from its approximately 15 percent contribution in 2000. Foremost among the P2P networks is the BitTorrent protocol. Unlike traditional file sharing P2P applications, a BitTorrent program downloads pieces of a file from many different hosts, combining them locally to construct the entire original file. This technique has proven to be extensively popular and effective in sharing large files over the web. In that same study [9], it was estimated that BitTorrent comprised around 35 percent of traffic by the end of 2006. Another study conducted in 2008 [4] similarly concluded that P2P traffic represented about 43.5 percent of all traffic, with BitTorrent and Gnutella contributing the bulk of the load.

During this vigorous shift from predominately web browsing to P2P traffic, concern over the sharing of copyrighted or pirated content has likewise escalated. The Recording Industry Association of America (RIAA), certain movie studios,

X. Lai et al. (Eds.): E-Forensics 2010, LNICST 56, pp. 79–89, 2011.

and the Comcast ISP have attempted to block BitTorrent distribution of certain content or tracking BitTorrent users in hopes of prosecuting copyright violators. In order to curtail the exchange of pirated content through BitTorrent, opposing parties can employ two different attacks that can potentially slow the transfer of files substantially. The first is referred to as a fake-block attack, wherein a peer sends forged content to requesters. The second is an uncooperative peer attack, which consists of peers wasting the time of downloaders by continually sending keep alive messages, but never sending any content. These two attacks can also be used by disapproving individuals who just try to malfunction the BitTorrent system.

Not so many studies ([6,10]) have been conducted to understand the situation and consequences of such attacks. This paper aims to get a first hand look at the potential of fake-block and uncooperative-peer attacks, and to provide supports for developing possible approaches in the future to prevent such attacks. An experiment was set up to download files via BitTorrent applications, during which, BitTorrent traffic was captured and analyzed. We classified the hosts connected during the download process into different categories, and identified attack activities based on the traffic. We observed that the two different attacks mentioned above indeed exist within the BitTorrent. We also found that the majority of peers connected in downloading turn out to be completely useless for file acquisition. This process of culling through the network traces is useful in understanding the issues that cause delays in file acquisition in BitTorrent systems.

The rest of the paper is organized as follows. In Section 2, the BitTorrent protocol is explained and the two different attacks, fake-block attack and uncooperative peer attack, are thoroughly examined. Section 3 describes the experiment design and implementation. We present the experimental results and some discussion in Section 4. Finally, Section 5 concludes the paper.

2 BitTorrent Background and Attack Schemes

The BitTorrent protocol consists of four main phases. First, a torrent seed for a particular file is created and uploaded to search sites and message boards. Next, a person who is interested in the file downloads the seed and opens the seed using a BitTorrent client. Then, the BitTorrent client, based on the seed, contacts one or more trackers. Trackers serve as the first contact points of the client. They will point the client to other peers that already have all or some of the file requested. Finally, the client connects to these peers, receives blocks of the file from them, and constructs the entire original file. This section will describe these four stages in details, based on the BitTorrent protocol specification [5,8].

2.1 The Torrent Seed

The torrent seed provides a basic blueprint of the original file and specifies how the file can be downloaded. This seed is created by a user, referred to as the initial seeder, who has the complete data file. Typically, the original file is divided into 256kb pieces, though piece lengths between 64kb and 4mb are acceptable. The seed consists of an "announce" section, which specifies the IP address(es) of the tracker(s), and an "info" section, which contains file names, their lengths, the piece length used, and a SHA-1 hash code for each piece. The SHA-1 hash values for each piece included in the info section of the seed are used by clients to verify the integrity of the pieces they download. In practice, pieces are further broken down into blocks, which are the smallest units exchanged between peers. Figure 1 shows the information found in a torrent seed as displayed in a freely available viewer, TorrentLoader 1.5 [2].

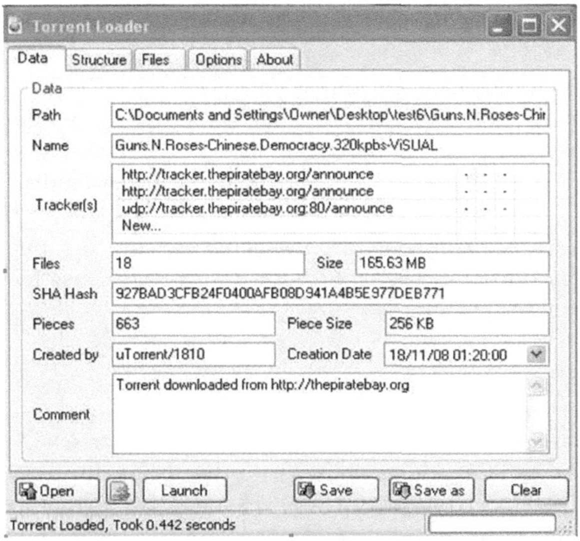

Fig. 1. Torrent File Information

After the seed is created, the initial seeder publishes it on torrent search engines or on message boards.

2.2 Acquiring Torrent Files

Before a user can search and download a file of interest, the user must first install one of several different BitTorrent (BT) clients that can process torrent seeds to connect to trackers, and ultimately other peers that have the file. A BitTorrent client is any program that can create, request, and transmit any type of data using the BitTorrent protocol. Clients vary slightly in appearance and implementation, but can be used to acquire files created by any other clients. Finding the torrent seeds is simply a matter of scanning known torrent hosting sites (such as thepiratebay, isohunt, or torrentz) or search engines. The user then downloads the seed and loads it into the client to begin downloading the file.

2.3 The Centralized Trackers

In BitTorrent systems centralized trackers serve as the first contact points for clients interested in downloading a particular file. IP addresses of the trackers' are listed in the torrent seed. Once a seed is opened in a BT client, the client will attempt to make connections with the trackers. The trackers will then verify the integrity of the seed and generate a list of peers that have a complete or partial copy of the file ready to share. This set of peers constitute the swarm of the seed. Every seed has its swarm. Peers in a swarm can either be seeders or leechers. Seeders are peers that are able to provide the complete file. Leechers are peers that do no yet have a complete copy of the file; however, they are still capable of sharing the pieces that they do have with the swarm. The tracker continually provides updated statistics about the number of seeders and leechers in the swarm.

The BitTorrent protocol also supports trackerless methods for file sharing, such as Distributed Hash Tables (DHT) or Peer Exchange methods. These decentralized methods are also supported by most BT clients. Under a decentralized method, the work of a traditional centralized tracker is distributed across all of the peers in the swarm. Decentralized methods increase the number of discovered peers. A user can configure his/her BT client to support centralized methods, or decentralized methods, or both. In this paper, we focuses solely on the centralized tracker model.

2.4 Joining the Swarm

In order for a new peer to join the swarm of a particular seed, the peer must attempt to establish TCP connections with other peers already in the swarm. After the TCP handshake, two peers then exchange a BitTorrent handshake. The initiating peer sends a handshake message containing a peer id, the type of the BT client being used, and an info_hash of the torrent seed. If the receiving peer responds with corresponding information, the BitTorrent session is considered open. Immediately after the BitTrorrent handshake messages are exchanged, each peer sends the other information about which pieces of the file it possesses. This exchange takes the form of bit-field messages with a stream of bits whose bit index corresponds to a piece index. The exchange is performed only once during the session. After the bit-field messages have been swapped, data blocks can begin to be exchanged over TCP. Figure 2 illustrates the BitTorrent handshake, while Figure 3 summarizes the exchange of data pieces between peers.

2.5 Peer Attacks on the Swarm

From the above description of the BitTorrent protocol, it is evident that someone can manipulate to delay the transmission of a file to an interested peer. The first attack, referred to as the Fake-Block Attack [6], takes advantage of the fact that a piece of a file is not verified via hash until it has been downloaded. Thus, attacking peers can send bad blocks of the file to interested parties, and

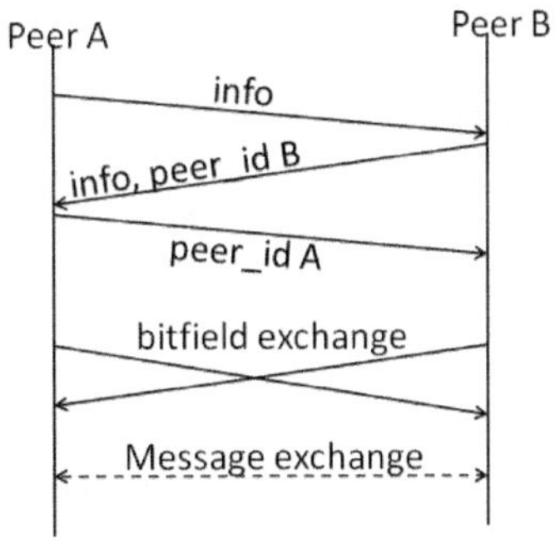

Fig. 2. The BitTorrent Handshake [7]

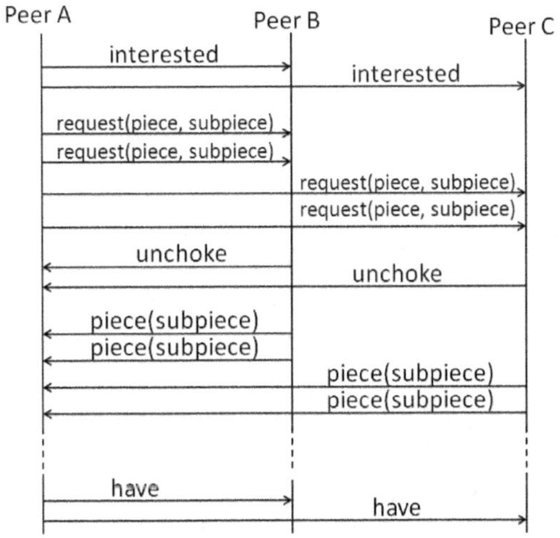

Fig. 3. BitTorrent Protocol Exchange [7]

when these blocks are combined with those from other sources, the completed piece will not be a valid copy since the piece hash will not match that of the original file. This piece will then be discarded by the client and will need to be downloaded again. While this generally only serves to increase the total time of the file transfer, swarms that contain large numbers of fake-blocking peers could potentially cause enough interference that some downloaders would give up.

The second attack is referred to as the Uncooperative, or Chatty, Peer Attack [6]. In this scheme, attacking peers exploit the BitTorrent message exchange protocol to hinder a downloading client. Depending on the client used, these peers can simply keep sending BitTorrent handshake messages without ever sending any content (as is the case in the Azereus client), or they can continually send keep-alive messages without delivering any blocks. Since the number of peer connections is limited, which is often set to 50, connecting to numerous chatty peers can drastically increase the download time of the content.

3 Experiment Design and Implementation

In this section, we describe the design and implementation of our experimental study. The design of this experiment is based heavily on the work in [6]. Three of the most popular album seeds (Beyonce_IAmSasha, GunsNRoses_Chinese, and Pink_Funhouse) were downloaded from thepiratebay.org for the purposes of this experiment. In order to observe the behavior of peers within the swarm and to identify any peers that might be considered attackers as defined in the two attack schemes previously, network traffic during the download process was captured. The traces were then analyzed, with data reviewed on a per host basis.

It is clear from the design of BitTorrent protocol that the efficiency of file distribution relies heavily upon the behavior of peers within the swarm. Peers that behave badly, either intentionally or unintentionally, can cause sluggish download times, as well as poisoned content in the swarm. For the purposes of this experiment, peers were categorized similarly to [6]. Hosts were sorted into different groups as follows:

Table 1. Torrent Properties

Torrent#	File Name	File Size	# of Pieces	Swarm Statistics	Protocol Used
1	Beyonce_IAmSasha	239mb	960	1602	Centralized Tracker
2	GunsNRoses_Chinese	165.63mb	663	493	Centralized Tracker
3	Pink_Funhouse	186.33mb	746	769	Centralized Tracker

- No-TCP-connection Peers: peers with which a TCP connection cannot be established.
- No-BT-handshake Peers: peers with which a TCP connection can be established, but with which a BitTorrent handshake cannot be established.
- Chatty Peers: peers that merely chat with our client. In this experiment, these peers establish a BitTorrent handshake and then only send out BitTorrent continuation data, not any data blocks.
- Fake-Block-Attack Peers: peers that upload forged blocks. These peers are identified by searching hash fails by pieces after the session is completed and then checking which peers uploaded fake blocks for particular pieces.
- Benevolent Peers: peers that communicate normally and upload at least one good block.
- Other Peers: peers that do not fit any of the above categories. This included clients that disconnected during the BT session before sending any data blocks and clients that never sent any data but did receive blocks from the test client

The experiment was implemented using an AMD 2.2 GHz machine with 1GB of RAM, connected to the Internet via a 100 Mbps DSL connection. The three seeds were loaded into the BitTorrent v.6.1.1 client. Based on the seeds, the client connected to trackers and the swarm. Within the client, only the centralized tracker protocol was enabled; DHT and Peer Exchange were both disabled. During each of the three download sessions for the three albums, Wireshark [3] was used to capture network traces, and the BT client's logger was also enabled to capture data for hash fails during a session. A network forensic tool, NetworkMiner [1], was then used to parse the Wireshark data to determine the number of hosts, as well as their IP addresses. Finally, traffic to and from each peer listed in NetworkMiner was examined using filters within Wireshark to determine which category listed above the traffic belonged to.

The properties of the three torrent seeds used in this experiment are shown in Table 1. All three of the torrent seeds listed the same three trackers; however, during the session, only one of the tracker URLs was valid and working. The swarm statistics published in the seed are based on that single tracker.

4 Experiment Results

In this section, we present the experimental results and discuss our observations.

4.1 Results

The three albums were all downloaded successfully, though all three did contain hash fails during the downloading process. Chatty peers were also present in all three swarms. The results of each download are illustrated in Table 2.

Table 2. Download Results

Torrent #	Total Download Time	# Peers Contacted	Hash Fails
1	1 hour 53 minutes	313	21
2	33 minutes	203	2
3	39 minutes	207	7

The classifications of the peers found in the swarm varied only minimally from one seed to another. No-TCP-Connection peers accounted for by far the largest portion of the total number of peers in the swarm. There were three different observable varieties of No-TCP-Connection peers: the peer that never responded to the SYN sent from the initiating client, the peer that sent a TCP RST in response to the SYN, and the peer that sent an ICMP destination unreachable response. Of these three categories, peers that never responded to the initiator's SYN accounted for the bulk of the total. While sending out countless SYN packets without ever receiving a response or receiving only a RST in return certainly utilizes bandwidth that could be otherwise used to establish sessions with active peers, it is important to note that these No-TCP-Connection peers are not necessarily attackers. These peers included NATed peers, firewalled peers, stale IPS returned by trackers, and peers that have reached their TCP connection limit (generally set around 50) [6].

No-BT-Handshake peers similarly fell into two distinct groups: peers that completed the TCP handshake but did not respond to the initiating client's BitTorrent handshake, and peers with whom the TCP connection was ended by the initiating client (via TCP RST) prior to the BitTorrent handshake. The latter case is likely due to a limit on the number of simultaneous BitTorrent sessions allowed per peer. Furthermore, the number of times that the initiating client would re-establish the TCP connection without ever completing a BT handshake ranged from 1 to 25. Clearly, the traffic generated while continually re-establishing TCP connections uses up valuable bandwidth that could be utilized by productive peers.

In this experiment, Chatty peers were classified as such when they repeatedly sent BitTorrent continuation data (keep-alive packets) without ever sending any data blocks to the initiating client. Generally in these connections, the initiator would continually send HAVE piece messages to the peer and would receive only TCP ACK messages in reply. Also, when the initiator would request a piece that the peer revealed that it owned in its initial bitfield message, no response would be sent. In this case, a Chatty peer kept open unproductive BitTorrent sessions that could otherwise have been used for other cooperative peers.

Table 3. Peer Classifications

	No-TCP-Connection			No-BT-Handshake					
Torrent #	No SYN ACK	RST	ICMP	No Handshake Response	RST	Fake Block	Chatty	Benevolent	Other
1	136	43	9	15	19	11	16	57	4
2	90	23	5	13	28	1	4	39	1
3	106	18	6	15	23	2	5	32	0
Total	332	84	20	43	70	14	25	128	5

The number of fake blocks discovered in each swarm varied quite widely, as did the number of unique peers who sent the false blocks. The first seed had 21 different block hash fails that were sent from only 11 unique peers. Among these 21 failed blocks, 9 of them came from a single peer. The other two seeds had far fewer hash fails, but the third seed showed a similar pattern – of the 7 hash fails, 6 were sent by the same individual peer.

The complete overview of peer classification for each torrent is exhibited in Table 3. From this table, it is evident that in all cases the majority of contacted peers in the swarm were not useful to the initiating client. Whether the peer actively fed fake content into the swarm, or merely inundated the client with hundreds of useless packets, all were responsible for slowing the exchange of data throughout the swarm. Figures 4 and 5 show the distribution of each type of peers in the swarms of each seed, as well as the combined distribution across all of the three seeds.

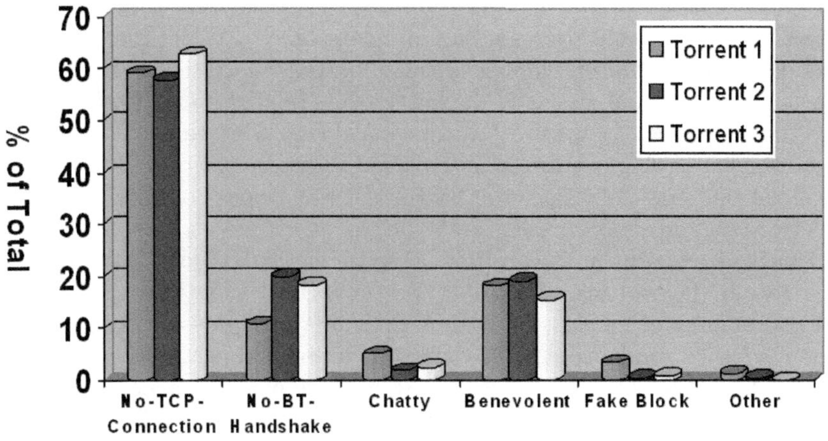

Fig. 4. Peer Classifications by Percent of Total

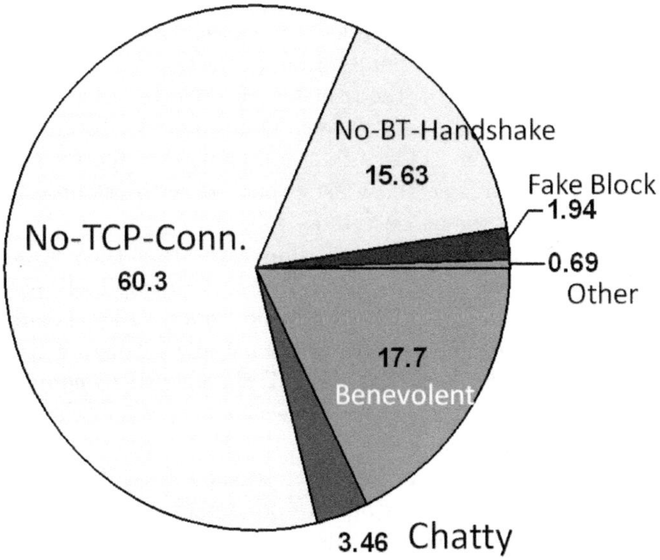

Fig. 5. Peer Distribution Combined Over all Torrents

4.2 Discussion

The experiment yielded interesting results. First, the analysis of network traces during a BitTorrent session demonstrated that while uncooperative/chatty peers do exist within the swarm, they are present in fewer numbers than anticipated. This may be due to the BitTorrent client used, as flaws in the Azereus client allow multiple BT Handshake and bitfield messages to be sent, whereas the client we used does not. The chatty peers observed in this experiment merely sustained the BT session without ever sending any data blocks. While these useless sessions definitely used up a number of the allocated BT sessions, the impact was mitigated by the small quantity of chatty peers relative to the total number of peers in the swarm. However, it can be concluded from these results that if a larger number of chatty peers reside in a single swarm, they can drastically slow download times of a file, since the BitTorrent client does not have a mechanism to detect and end sessions with chatty peers.

From this experiment it can also be seen that Fake-Block attackers indeed exist within the swarms of popular files. The first and third seeds provided perfect examples of the amount of time consumption a single attacking peer can have in a swarm. In both of these cases, one individual peer provided numerous fake blocks to the client. In the first seed, a single peer uploaded 9 failed blocks whereas in the third seed, another single peer uploaded 6 failed blocks. This caused the client to obtain those blocks from other sources after the hash check of the entire piece failed. After the attacking peer in the first seed had sent more than one fake blocks, the connection should have been disconnected to prevent any more time and bandwidth drain. However, the client has no mechanism to recognize which peers have uploaded fake blocks, and should therefore be disconnected. In a swarm with a small number of peers (e.g., a less popular file), a Fake-Block attacker could slow the transfer considerably as more blocks would need to be downloaded from the attacker. There do exist lists of IP addresses associated with uploading bad blocks that can be used to filter traffic in the BT client, but it is difficult to keep those lists updated as the attackers continually change addresses to avoid being detected.

Finally, the results of this experiment illustrated that the majority of peers that were contacted in the swarm turned out to be completely useless for the download. The number of No-TCP-Connection and No-BT-Handshake peers identified during each download was dramatic. While this is not in and of itself surprising, the number of times that the BT client tried to connect to a non-responding peer, or re-establish a TCP connection with a peer that never returns a BT handshake is striking. In some cases, 25 TCP sessions were opened even though the BT handshake was never once returned. TCP SYN messages were sent continually to peers that never once responded or only sent RST responses. In very large swarms such as those in this experiment, it is not necessary to keep attempting to connect with non-responsive peers since there are so many others that are responsive and cooperative.

5 Conclusions

In this paper, we have conducted an experimental study to investigate attacks on BitTorrent applications, which has not yet attracted much research attention. We have designed and implemented the experiment. BitTorrent traffic data has been captured and analyzed. We identified both fake-block attack and uncooperative/chatty attack based on the traffic. We also found that the majority of peers connected in downloading turned out to be completely useless for file acquisition. This experiment would help us to better understand the issues that cause delays in file download in BitTorrent systems. By identifying peer behavior that is detrimental to the swarm, this study is an important exercise to contemplate modification to BitTorrent clients and to develop possible approaches in the future to prevent such attacks.

Acknowledgments. This work is supported in part by National Science Foundation grant CNS-0904901 and National Science Foundation grant DUE-0830840.

References

1. NetworkMiner, http://sourceforge.net/projects/networkminer/
2. TorrentLoader 1.5 (October 2007), http://sourceforge.net/projects/torrentloader/
3. WireShark, http://www.wireshark.org/
4. Sandvine, Incorporated. 2008 Analysis of Traffic Demographics in North American Broadband Networks (June 2008), http://sandvine.com/general/documents/Traffic_Demographics_NA_Broadband_Networks.pdf
5. Cohen, B.: The BitTorrent Protocol Specification (February 2008), http://www.bittorrent.org/beps/bep_0003.html
6. Dhungel, P., Wu, D., Schonhorst, B., Ross, K.: A Measurement Study of Attacks on BitTorrent Leechers. In: The 7th International Workshop on Peer-to-Peer Systems (IPTPS) (February 2008)
7. Erman, D., Ilie, D., Popescu, A.: BitTorrent Session Characteristics and Models. In: Proceedings of HET-NETs 3rd International Working Conference on Performance Modeling and Evaluation of Heterogeneous Networks, West Yorkshire, U.K (July 2005)
8. Konrath, M.A., Barcellos, M.P., Mansilha, R.B.: Attacking a Swarm with a Band of Liars: Evaluating the Impact of Attacks on BitTorrent. In: Proceedings of IEEE P2P, Galway, Ireland (September 2007)
9. ParkerK, A.: P2P Media Summit. CacheLogic Research presentation at the First Annual P2P Media Summit LA, dcia.info/P2PMSLA/CacheLogic.ppt (October 2006)
10. Pouwelse, J., Garbacki, P., Epema, D.H.J., Sips, H.J.: The bittorrent P2P file-sharing system: Measurements and analysis. In: van Renesse, R. (ed.) IPTPS 2005. LNCS, vol. 3640, pp. 205–216. Springer, Heidelberg (2005)

Network Connections Information Extraction of 64-Bit Windows 7 Memory Images

Lianhai Wang*, Lijuan Xu, and Shuhui Zhang

Shandong Provincial Key Laboratory of Computer Network,
Shandong Computer Science Center,
19 Keyuan Road, Jinan 250014, P.R. China
{wanglh,xulj,zhangshh}@Keylab.net

Abstract. Memory analysis technique is a key element of computer live forensics, and how to get status information of network connections is one of the difficulties of memory analysis and plays an important roles in identifying attack sources. It is more difficult to find the drivers and get network connections information from a 64-bit win7 memory image file than its from a 32-bit operating system memory image file. In a this paper, We will describe the approachs to find drivers and get network connection information from windows 7 memory images. This method is reliable and efficient. It is verified on Windows version 6.1.7600.

Keywords: computer forensics, computer live forensics, memory analysis, digital forensics.

1 Introduction

Computer technology has greatly promoted the progress of human society. Meanwhile, it also brought the issue of computer related crimes such as hacking, phishing, online pornography, etc. Now, computer forensics has emerged as a distinct discipline of knowledge in response to the increasing occurrence of computer involvement in criminal activities, both as a tool of crime and as an object of crime and live forensics gains a weight in the area of computer forensics. Live forensics gathers data from running systems, that is to say, collects possible evidence in real time from memory and other storage media, while desktop omputers and servers are running. Physical memory of a computer can be a very useful yet challenging resource for the collection of digital evidence. It contains details of volatile data such as running processes, logged-in users, current network connections, users' sessions, drivers, open files, etc. In some cases, such as encrypted file systems arrive on the scene, the only chance to collect valuable forensic evidence is through physical memory of the computer. We propose a model of computer live forensics based on recent achievements of analysis techniques of physical memory image[1]. The idea is to gather "live" computer evidence through analyzing the raw image of target computer. See Fig. 1. Memory analysis technique is a key element of the model.

* Supported by Shandong Natural Science Foundation (Grant No. Y2008G35).

X. Lai et al. (Eds.): E-Forensics 2010, LNICST 56, pp. 90–98, 2011.

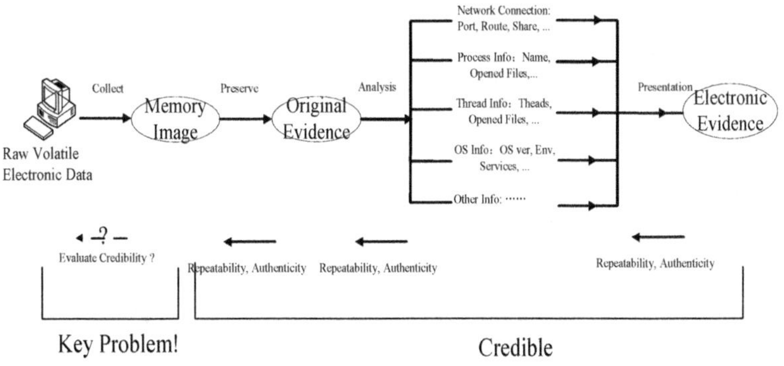

Fig. 1. Model of Computer Live Forensics Based on Physical Memory Analysis

How to get status information of network connections is one of the difficulties of memory analysis and plays an important roles in identifying attack sources. But it is more difficult to get network connections information from a 64-bit win7 memory image file than its from a 32-bit operating system memory image file. There are many difference bewetten the methods for 64-bit system and the method for 32-bit system. We will describe the approachs to get network connection information from 64-bit windows 7 memory images.

2 Related Work

In 2005, the Digital Forensic Research Workshop (DFRWS) organized a challenge of memory analysis (http://dfrws.org/2005/). And then Capture and analysis of the content of physical memory, known as memory forensics, became an area of intense research and experimentation. In 2006, A. Schuster analyzed the in-memory structures and developed search patterns which will then be used to scan the whole memory dump for traces of both linked and unlinked objects [2]. M. Burdach also developed WMFT (Windows Memory Forensics Toolkit) and gave a procedure to enumerate processes [3, 4]· Similar techniques in these works were also being used by A. Walters in developing Volatility tool to analyze memory dumps for an incident response perspective [5]. There are many others articles talked about memory analysis.

Nowadays, there are two methods to acquire network connection status information from physical memory of Windows XP operating system. One is searching for data structure "AddrObjTable" and "ObjTable" from driver "tcpip.sys" to acquire network connection status information. This method is implemented in Volatility[6], a tool to analyze memory which dumps from Windows XP SP2 or Windows XP SP3 for an incident response perpective developed by Walters and Petroni. The other one is proposed by Schuster[7]. Schuster descirbes the steps necessary to detect traces of network activity in a memory dump.His method is searching for pool allocations labeled "TcpA" and a size of 368 bytes (360 bytes for the payload and 8 for the _POOL_HEADER) on Windows XP SP2. These allocations will reside in the non-paged pool.

The first method is feasible on Windows XP. But it doesn't work on Windows Vista and Win 7 ,because there is no data structure "AddrObjTable" or "ObjTable" in driver "tcpip.sys". It is proven that there is no pool allocations labeled "TcpA" on Windows 7 as well.

It is analyzed that there are pool allocations labeled "TcpE" instead of "TcpA" indicating network activity in a memory dump of Windows 7. Therefore, we can acquire network connections from pool allocations labeled "TcpE" on Windows 7.
This paper proposes a method of acquiring current network connection informations from physical memory image of Windows 7 according to memory pool. Network connection informations including IDs of processes which established connections, local address, local port, remote address, remote port, etc., can be get accurately from physical memory image file of Windows 7 with this method.

3 A Method of Network Connections Information Extraction from Windows 7 Physical Memory Images

3.1 The Structure of TcpEndpointPool

A data structure called TcpEndpointPool is found in driver "tcpip.sys" on Windows 7 operating system, and it is similar to its on Windows vista. This pool is a doubly-linked list of which each node is the head of a singly-linked list.

The internal organizational structure of TcpEndpointPool is shown by figure1. The circles represent heads of the singly-linked list. The letters in the circles represent the flag of the head. The rectangles represent the nodes of singly-linked list. The letters in the rectangles represent the type of the node.

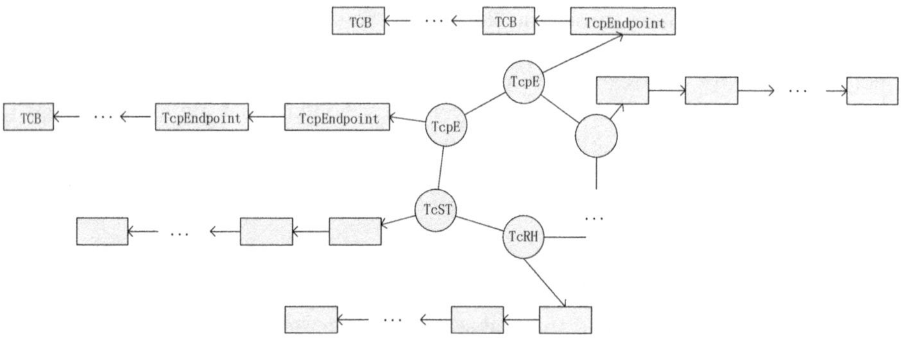

Fig. 2. TcpEndpointPool internal organization

The structure of singly-linked list head is shown by figure 2, in which there is a _LIST_ENTRY structure at the offset 0x40 by which the next head of a singly-linked list can be found .

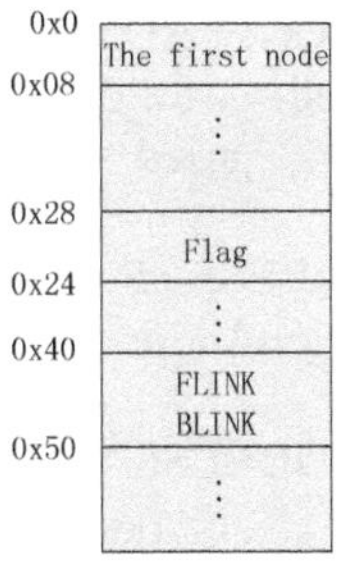

Fig. 3. The structure of singly-linked list head

The relationship of two adjacent heads is shown by figure 4.

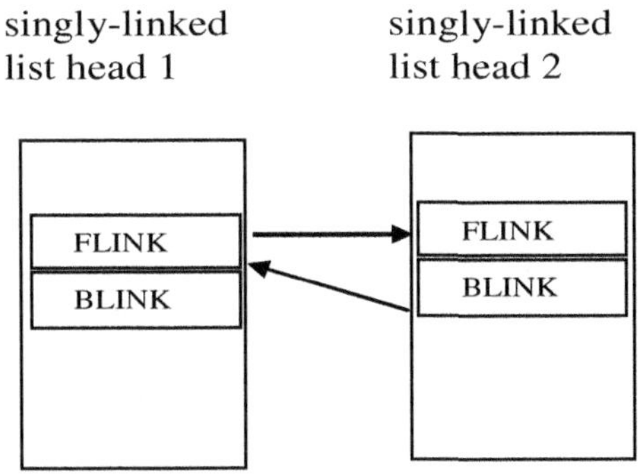

Fig. 4. The linked relationship of two heads

There is a flag at the offset 0x28 of the singly-linked list head by which the node structure of the singly-linked list can be judged. If the flag is "TcpE", the singly-linked list with this head is composed of TcpEndPoint structure and TCB structure which describe the network connection information.

3.2 The Structure of TCB

TCB Structure under Windows 7 is quite different form its under Windows Vista or XP. The definition and the offsets of fields related with network connections in the TCB is shown as follows.

```
typedef struct _TCB {
    CONST NL_PATH *Path;                    +0x30
    USHORT TcbState;                        +0x78
    USHORT EndpointPort                     +0x7a
    USHORT LocalPort;                       +0x7c
    USHORT RemotePort;                      +0x7e
    PEPROCESS OwningProcess ;               +0x238
    } TCB,*PTCB;
```

NL_PATH structure, NL_LOCAL_ADDRESS structure and NL_ADDRESS_IDENTIFIER structure are defined as follows by which network connection local address and remote address can be acquried.

```
typedef struct _NL_PATH {
    CONST NL_LOCAL_ADDRESS *SourceAddress;              +0x00
    CONST UCHAR *DestinationAddress;                    +0x10
} NL_PATH, *PNL_PATH;
typedef struct _NL_LOCAL_ADDRESS {
    ULONG Signature  // Ipla (0x49706c61)
    CONST NL_ADDRESS_IDENTIFIER *Identifier;            +0x10
} NL_LOCAL_ADDRESS, *PNL_LOCAL_ADDRESS;
typedef struct _NL_ADDRESS_IDENTIFIER {
    CONST UCHAR *Address;                               +0x00
} NL_ADDRESS_IDENTIFIER, *PNL_ADDRESS_IDENTIFIER;
```

3.3 Algorithms

The algorithm to find all of TcpE pools is given as follows:

Step1. Get the physical address of KPCR structure and achieve the function of translation from virtual Address to physical address.

Because address stored in image file generally is virtual address, we can not directly get the exact location of its physical address in memory image file via its virutal address . First of all, we should achieve the function of translation from virtual Address to physical address ,which is a difficult problem in memory ananlsis. We can adopt a method, which is similar to the KPCR method[8], to achieve the function ,but It require change as show below:

I) Find KPCR structure according to characteristics as blow: find the two neighboring values is greater than 0xffff000000000000, and the difference between these two values is 0x180, Take away 0x1c from the phyical address of the first value , and we get the KPCR structure address.

II) The offset of CR3 Registe is not 0x410, but 0x1d0.

Step 2. Find dirvers of system ,and get the address of TCPIP.SYS driver

As a 64-bit operating system , it is more difficult to find the drivers of system from a 64-bit win7 memory image file than its from a 32-bit operating system memory image file. In Windows 7 system, KdVersionBlock,a elements of the structure KPCR, is always is zero, so we can't get kernel variables thought it. We find a way to get the dirvers of system as blow:

Step2.1 Locate the address of KPRCB structure

the KPCR structure address add 0x180 ,we will get the address of _KPRCB structure.

```
_KPCR{
    +0x108 KdVersionBlock    : Ptr64 Void
    +0x180 Prcb              : _KPRCB
}
```

Step2.2 Locate the address of pointer pointed to the current thread

CurrentThread ,which is pointed the current thread of system, is a address pointer pointed a KTHREAD structure, and it is stored at the offset 0x08 relative to KPRCB structure address. We can get the phyical address which is pointed by the pointer according to the translation described as Step1

```
_KPRCB{
   +0x008 CurrentThread     : Ptr64 _KTHREAD
}
```

Step2.3 Locate the address of pointer of current process according to the current thread.

The virtual address of current process is stored at the offset 0x210 relative to KTHREAD structure. We will get the phyical address of current process from the virtual address according to the translation.

```
_KTHREAD{
+0x210 Process           : Ptr64 _KPROCESS
}
```

Step 2.4 Locate the address of ActiveProcessLinks

```
_EPROCESS{
  +0x000 Pcb                   : _KPROCESS
  +0x188 ActiveProcessLinks : _LIST_ENTRY
}
```

Step 2.5 Locate the address of the nt!PsActiveProcessHead variable

ActiveProcessLinks is the active process links, Throught it, we can get all of process. When we can the address of system process, we can the the address of the nt!PsActiveProcessHead variable from Blink of its ActiveProcessLinks .

```
_LIST_ENTRY{
   +0x000 Flink          : Ptr64 _LIST_ENTRY
   +0x008 Blink          : Ptr64 _LIST_ENTRY
}
```

Step 2.6 Locate the address of kernel variable psLoadedModuleList

The offset bewteen the virtual address of nt!psLoadedModuleList and the virtual address of nt!PsActiveProcessHead is 0x1e320, so the address of nt!PsActiveProcessHead add 0x1e320, we get the virtual address of nt!psLoadedModuleList. We get the physical address of nt!psLoadedModuleList according to the translation.

Step 2.7 Get the address of TCPIP.SYS driver through the kernel variable psLoadedModuleList.

Step3 Find the virtual address of tcipip!TcpEndpointPool.

We can get the virtual address of tcpip!TcpEndpointPool from the virutal address added 0x18a538.

Step4 Find the virtual address of the first singly-linked list head.

Firstly, transfer the virtual address of TcpEndpointPool to physical address and locate the address in the memory image file, read 8 bytes at this position and transfer the 8 bytes to physical address, locate the address in the memory image file. Secondly , get the the virtual address of the pointer which is the 8 bytes at the offset 0x20 . this pointer points three virtual address pointer pointed the structures in which singly-linked list head is the 8 bytes at the offset 0x40.

The search process on Windbg can be shown in Fig.5

```
fffff880`0198d538 tcpip!TcpEndpointPool = <no type information>
lkd> db  tcpip!TcpEndpointPool
fffff880`0198d538  40 9a 47 04 80 fa ff ff-00 00 00 00 00 00 00 00  @.G.............
fffff880`0198d548  a0 9a 86 01 80 f8 ff ff-00 00 00 00 00 00 00 00  ................
fffff880`0198d558  00 00 00 00 00 00 00 00-a0 ba 47 04 80 fa ff ff  ..........G.....
fffff880`0198d568  00 00 00 00 00 00 00 00-00 00 00 00 00 00 00 00  ................
fffff880`0198d578  00 00 00 00 00 00 00 00-00 00 00 00 00 00 00 00  ................
fffff880`0198d588  50 a3 86 01 80 f8 ff ff-00 00 00 00 00 00 00 00  P...............
fffff880`0198d598  00 00 00 00 00 00 00 00-00 ba 47 04 80 fa ff ff  ..........G.....
fffff880`0198d5a8  00 00 00 00 00 00 00 00-00 00 00 00 00 00 00 00  ................
lkd> db fffffa8004479a40
fffffa80`04479a40  03 00 00 00 00 00 00 00-54 63 70 45 54 63 70 45  ........TcpETcpE
fffffa80`04479a50  10 03 00 00 00 00 00 00-00 00 00 00 00 00 00 00  ................
fffffa80`04479a60  40 88 47 04 80 fa ff ff-00 00 00 00 00 00 00 00  @.G.............
fffffa80`04479a70  00 00 00 00 00 00 00 00-00 00 00 00 00 00 00 00  ................
fffffa80`04479a80  00 00 00 00 00 00 00 00-00 00 00 00 00 00 00 00  ................
fffffa80`04479a90  00 00 00 00 00 00 00 00-00 00 00 00 00 00 00 00  ................
fffffa80`04479aa0  00 00 00 00 00 00 00 00-00 00 00 00 00 00 00 00  ................
fffffa80`04479ab0  00 00 00 00 00 00 00 00-00 00 00 00 00 00 00 00  ................
lkd> db fffffa8004478840
fffffa80`04478840  40 99 47 04 80 fa ff ff-40 98 47 04 80 fa ff ff  @.G.....@.G.....
fffffa80`04478850  00 bb 47 04 80 fa ff ff-00 00 00 00 00 00 00 00  ..G.............
fffffa80`04478860  00 00 00 00 00 00 00 00-00 00 00 00 00 00 00 00  ................
fffffa80`04478870  00 00 00 00 00 00 00 00-00 00 00 00 00 00 00 00  ................
fffffa80`04478880  00 00 00 00 00 00 00 00-00 00 00 00 00 00 00 00  ................
fffffa80`04478890  00 00 00 00 00 00 00 00-00 00 00 00 00 00 00 00  ................
fffffa80`044788a0  08 00 10 02 54 63 44 4d-00 00 00 00 00 00 00 00  ....TcDM........
fffffa80`044788b0  01 00 0f 06 54 63 44 4d-00 00 00 00 00 00 00 00  ....TcDM........
lkd> db fffffa8004479940
fffffa80`04479940  02 00 fb 00 00 00 00 00-71 67 81 06 80 fa ff ff  ........qg......
fffffa80`04479950  04 00 00 01 b1 02 00 00-b8 01 00 00 85 02 00 00  ................
fffffa80`04479960  8a 01 00 00 00 00 00 00-54 63 70 45 10 03 00 00  ........TcpE....
fffffa80`04479970  50 66 e9 03 00 f8 ff ff-ec b1 e9 03 00 f8 ff ff  Pf..............
fffffa80`04479980  80 98 47 04 80 fa ff ff-40 9b 47 04 80 fa ff ff  ..G.....@.G.....
fffffa80`04479990  b1 02 00 00 b8 01 00 00-00 00 00 00 00 00 00 00  ................
fffffa80`044799a0  00 00 00 00 00 00 00 00-00 00 00 00 00 00 00 00  ................
fffffa80`044799b0  00 00 00 00 00 00 00 00-00 00 00 00 00 00 00 00  ................
```

Fig. 5. The process to find the virtual address of the first singly-linked list head on Windbg

Step5 Judge whether the head's type is TcpEndpoint or not by reading the flag which is set at the offset 0x20 relative to the head's address. If the flag is "TcpE", the head's type is TcpEndpoint , go to the step 6, otherwise go to the step 7.

Step6 Analyze the TcpEndpoint structure or TCB structure in the singly-linked list. Analyzing algorithm is shown by figure 6.

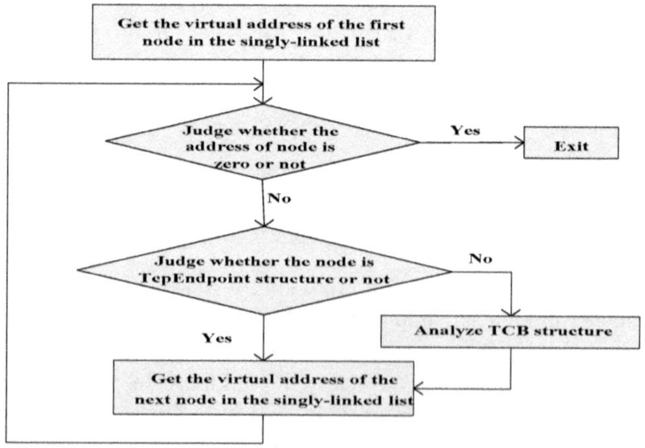

Fig. 6. The flow of analyzing TCB structure or TcpEndpoint structure summary description

Step7 Find the virtual address of the next head.

The virtual address of the next head can be found according to the _LIST_ENTRY structure which is set at the offset 0x30 relative to the address of singly-linked list head. Judging whether the next head's virtual address equals to the first head's address or not. If the next head's virtual address is equal to the first head's address, exit the procedure, otherwise go to the next step.

Step8 Judge whether the head is exactly the first head. If the head is exactly the first head, exit, otherwise go to step 5.

The flow of analyzing TCB structure or TcpEndpoint structure is shown as follows.

Step1 Get the virtual address of the first node in the singly-linked list.

Transfer the virtual address of singly-list head to physical address and locate the address in memory image file. Read 8 bytes from this position which is the virtual address of the first node.

Step2 Judge whether the address of node is zero or not. If the address is zero, exit the procedure, otherwise go to the next step.

Step3 Judge whether the node is Tcb structure or not.

if LocalPort#0 and RemotePort#0 then it is a TCB Structure , furthermore, if TcbState#0 it is valid TCB Structure ,or it is a tcb structure which it indicate the network connection is close.

if LocalPort=0 and RemotePort=0 and EndpointPort#0 then it is a TCP_ENDPOINT structure

Step4 Analyze TCB structure.

Step4.1 Get PID (process id) which is the ID of the process which established this connection. The pointer which points to the process's EPROCESS structure which established this connection is set at the offset +0x238 relative to TCB structure. Firstly, read 8 bytes which represents the virtual address of EPROCESS structure at buffer's offset 0x164 and transfer it to physical address. Secondly, locate the address in the memory image file and read 8 bytes which represents PID at the offset 0x180 relative to EPROCESS structure's physical address.

Step4.3 Get the local port of this connection. The number is set at offset 0x7c of TCB structure. Read 2 bytes at offset 0x7C of the buffer and transfer it to a decimal which is the local port of this connection.

Step4.4 Get the remote port of this connection. The number is set at the offset 0x7e of TCB structure. Read 2 bytes at offset 0x7e of the buffer and transfer it to a decimal which is the remote port of this connection.

Step4.5 Get local address and remote address of this connection. The pointer which points to NL_PATH structure is set at the offset 0x30 of TCB structure. The pointer which points to the remote address is set at the offset 0x10 of NL_PATH structure. The special algorithm is as followes: read 8 bytes which represents the virtual address of NL_PATH structure at the offset 0x30 of TCB structure, transfer the virtual address of NL_PATH structure to physical address, locate the address+0x10 in the memory image file and read 8 bytes which represents remote address at this position. The pointer which points to NL_LOCAL_ADDRESS structure is set at the offset 0x0 of the NL_PATH structure, The pointer which points to NL_ADDRESS_IDENTIFIER structure is set at the offset 0x10 of

NL_LOCAL_ADDRESS structure, local address is set at the offset 0x0 of the NL_ADDRESS_IDENTIFIER structure. Therefore, local address can be acquired from the above three structures.

Step5 Get 8 bytes which represents the next node's virtual at the offset 0 of the buffer and go to step2.

4 Conclusion

In this paper, a method which can acquire network connection information from 64-bit Windows 7 memory image file based on memory pool allocation strategy is proposed. This method is proved to be right for memory image file of Windows version 6.1.7600. This method is reliable and efficient, because the data structure TcpEndpointPool exists in driver tcpip.sys for different Win7 operation system versions and TcpEndpointPool structure will not change when Win 7 operation system version changed.

References

1. Wang, L., Zhang, R., Zhang, S.: A Model of Computer Live Forensics Based on Physical Memory Analysis. In: ICISE 2009, Nanjing China (December 2009)
2. Schuster, A.: Searching for Processes and Threads in Microsoft Windows Memory Dumps. In: Proceedings of the 2006 Digital Forensic Research Workshop, DFRWS (2006)
3. Burdach, M.: An Introduction to Windows Memory Forensic[OL] (July 2005), `http://forensic.seccure.net/pdf/introduction_to_windows_memory_forensic.pdf`
4. Burdachz, M.: Digital Forensics of the Physical Memory [OL] (March 2005), `http://forensic.seccure.net/pdf/mburdach_digital_forensics_of_physical_memory.pdf`
5. Walters, A., Petronni Jr., N.L.: Volatools: Integrating volatile Memory Forensics into the Digital Investigation Process. In: Black Hat DC (2007)
6. Volatile Systems: The Volatility Framework: Volatile memory artifact extraction utility framework (accessed, June 2009), `https://www.volatilesystems.com/default/volatility/`
7. Andreas, S.: Pool allocations as an information source in windows memory forensics. In: Oliver, G., Dirk, S., Sandra, F., Hardo, H., Detlef, G., Jens, N. (eds.) IT-incident management & IT-forensics-IMF 2006, October 18. Lecture notes in informatics, vol. P-97, pp. 104–115 (2006b)
8. Zhang, R., Wang, L., Zhang, S.: Windows Memory Analysis Based on KPCR. In: Fifth International Conference on Information Assurance and Security, IAS 2009, vol. 2, pp. 677–680 (2009)

RICB: Integer Overflow Vulnerability Dynamic Analysis via Buffer Overflow

Yong Wang[1,2], Dawu Gu[2], Jianping Xu[1], Mi Wen[1], and Liwen Deng[3]

[1] Department of Compute Science and Technology,
Shanghai University of Electric Power, 20090 Shanghai, China
[2] Department of Computer Science and Engineering,
Shanghai Jiao Tong University, 200240 Shanghai, China
[3] Shanghai Changjiang Computer Group Corporation, 200001, China
wy616@126.com

Abstract. Integer overflow vulnerability will cause buffer overflow. The research on the relationship between them will help us to detect integer overflow vulnerability. We present a dynamic analysis methods RICB (Run-time Integer Checking via Buffer overflow). Our approach includes decompile execute file to assembly language; debug the execute file step into and step out; locate the overflow points and checking buffer overflow caused by integer overflow. We have implemented our approach in three buffer overflow types: format string overflow, stack overflow and heap overflow. Experiments results show that our approach is effective and efficient. We have detected more than 5 known integer overflow vulnerabilities via buffer overflow.

Keywords: Integer Overflow, Format String Overflow, Buffer Overflow.

1 Introduction

The integer overflow occurs when positive integer changing to negative integer after addition or an arithmetic operation attempts to create a numeric value that is larger than that can be represented within the available storage space. It is old problem, but now faces the security challenge once the integer overflow vulnerabilities are used by hackers. The number of integer overflow vulnerabilities has been increasing rapidly in recent years. With the development of the vulnerabilities exploit technology, the detection methods of integer overflow are made rapid growth.

The IntScope is a systematic static binary analysis tools. It is based approach to particularly focus on detecting integer overflow vulnerabilities. The tool can automatically detect integer overflow vulnerabilities in x86 binaries before an attacker does, with the goal of finally eliminating the vulnerabilities [1]. Integer overflow detection method based on path relaxation is described for avoiding buffer overflow through lightly static program analysis. The solution traces the key variables referring to the size of a buffer allocated dynamically [2].

The methods or tools are classified into two categories: static source code detection and dynamic running detection. Static source code detection methods are composed of IntScope[1], KLEE[3], RICH[4], EXE[5], and the dynamic SAGE[12].

X. Lai et al. (Eds.): E-Forensics 2010, LNICST 56, pp. 99–109, 2011.

KLEE is a symbolic execution tool, which is capable of automatically generating tests that achieve high coverage on a diverse set of complex and environmentally-intensive programs [3]. RICH (Run-time Integer Checking) is a tool for efficiently detecting integer-based attacks against C programs at run time [4]. EXE works well on real code, finding bugs along with inputs that trigger them, which runs it on symbolic input initially [5]. The SAGE (Scalable, Automated, Guided Execution) is a tool employing x86 instruction-level tracing and emulation for white box fuzzing of arbitrary file-reading windows applications [12].

Integer overflow can cause string format overflow, buffer overflow such as stack overflow and heap overflow. CSSV (C String Static Verify) is a tool that statically uncovers all string manipulation errors [6]. FormatGuard is an automatic tools for protection from printf format string vulnerabilities [13]. Buffer overflows in C program language occur easily because C provides little syntactic checking of bounds [7]. Besides static analysis tools, the dynamic buffer overflow analysis tools are used in the detection. Through comparison among tools publicly available for dynamic buffer overflow prevention, we can value the dynamic intrusion prevention efficiently [8].

Research on relationship between the buffer overflow and string format overflow can help us to reveal the buffer overflow internal features [9]. There are some applications such as integer squares with overflow detection [10] and integer multipliers with overflow detection [11].

Our previous related research is focusing on denial of service detection [14] and malicious software behavior detection [15]. The integer overflow vulnerability research can help us to reveal the malware intrusion procedure by exploiting overflow vulnerability to execute shell code. The key idea of our approach is dynamic analysis on the integer overflow via (1) format string overflow; (2) stack overflow; (3) heap overflow.

Our contributions include:

(1) We propose a dynamic method of analyzing the integer overflow via buffer overflow.
(2) We present analysis methods of the buffer overflow interruption change procedure which is caused by integer overflow.
(3) We implement the methods and experiments show that they are effective.

2 Integer Overflow Problem Statement

2.1 Signed Integer and Unsigned Integer Overflow

The register width of a processor determines the range of values that can be represented. Typical binary register widths include: 8 bits, 16 bits, 32 bits. The CF (Carry Flag) and OF (Overflow Flag) in PSW (Program Status Word) represent signed and unsigned integer overflow, respectively. The details are shown in Table 1:

When CF and OF equal to 1, the signed or unsigned integer overflow. If CF=0 and OF=1, the signed integer overflows. If CF=1 and OF=0, the unsigned integer overflow. The integer memory structure is described in Fig. 1, when it overflows.

Table 1. Types and examples of integer overflow

Type	Width	Boundary	Overflow Flag	
char	8 bits	0~255	CF=1	OF=1
Signed Short	16 bits	-32768~32767	CF=0	OF=1
Unsigned Short	16 bits	0 ~ 65535	CF=1	OF=0
Signed Long	32 bits	-2,147,483,648 ~ 2,147,483,64	CF=0	OF=1
Unsigned Long	32 bits	0 ~ 4,294,967,295	CF=1	OF=0

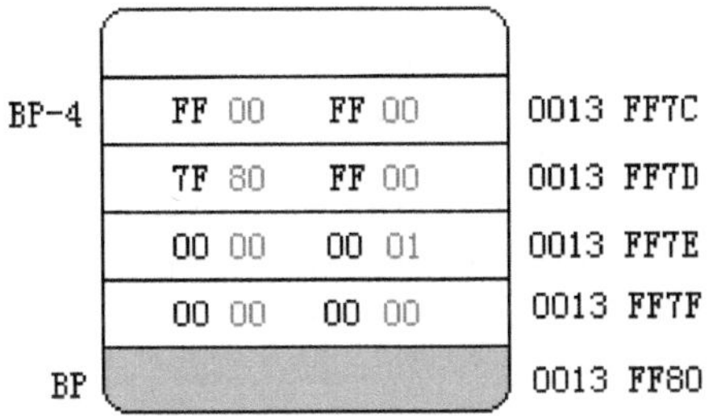

Fig. 1. Integer overflow is composed of signed integer overflow and unsigned integer overflow. The first black column is the signed integer 32767 and the first gray column is -32768. The second black column is the unsigned integer 65535 and the second gray column is 0.

2.2 Relationship between Integer Overflow and Other Overflow

The relation between the integer overflow and other overflows such as string format overflow, stack overflow and heap overflow is shown in formula 1:

$$\begin{cases} \{OV \mid OV_{Integer} \wedge OV_{StringFormat} \wedge OV_{Stack} \wedge OV_{Heap}\} \subset OverFlow \\ \{OV_{stringFormat} \wedge OV_{Stack} \wedge OV_{Heap}\} \cap OV_{Integer} \neq \varnothing \end{cases} \quad (1)$$

The first line in formula (1) means that overflows include integer overflow, string format overflow, stack overflow and heap overflow. The last line in formula (1) means that the integer overflow can cause the other overflow.

The other common overflow types and examples caused by integer overflow are located some special format string or functions, which are listed in Table 2:

Table 2. Overflow types and examples caused by integer overflow

Integer Overflow Type	Boundary	Examples
Format String Overflow	Overwrite memory	printf("format string %s %d %n", s,i);
Stack Overflow	targetBuf < sourceBuf	memcpy(smallBuf, largeBuf, largeSize)
Heap Overflow	heapSize < largeSize	HeapAlloc(hHeap, 0,largeSize)

In Table 2, if the integer in format strings, stack and heap overflow, the integer overflow can cause the corresponding types overflow.

2.3 Problem Scope

In this paper, we focus on the relationship between the integer overflow and the other overflow such as format string overflow, stack overflow, and the heap overflow.

3 Dynamic Analysis via Buffer Overflow

3.1 Format String Overflow Exploitation Caused by Integer Overflow

Format string overflow is one kind of Buffer overflow in some sense. In order to print program results on the screen, program needs to use the printf () function in C language. The function has two types of parameters: format control parameters and output variables parameters. The format control parameters are composed of string format %s, %c, %x, %u and %d. The out variables parameters types may be integer, real, string or address pointer. The common used format string program is presented as below:

```
char *s="abcd";
int i=10;
printf("%s %d",s,i);
```

Char pointer s stores the string address and integer variables I has its initial value 10. Printf () function uses the string format parameters to define the output format. The printf () function will use stack to store its parameters. The printf () has three parameters: the format control string pointer pointing to the string "%s %d", the string pointer variable pointing to the string "abcd" and integer variable I with initial value 10.

String contents can store assembly language instruction by \x format. For instance if the hexadecimal code of assembly language instruction "mov ax,12abH" is B8AB12H, then the shellcode is "\xB8\xAB\x12". When the IP points to the shellcode memory contents, the assembly language instructions will be executed.

The dynamic execute procedure of the program is shown in Fig. 2

Format string will overflow, when data is beyond the string boundary. The vulnerabilities can be used to crash a program or execute the harmful shell code by hacker. The problem exits the C language function, such as printf ().

The malicious may use the parameters to overwrite data in the stack or other memory locations. The dangerous parameter %n in ANSI standard, by which you can write arbitrary data to arbitrary location, is disabled by default in Visual Studio 2005.The following program will make format string overflow.

```
int main(int argc, char *argv[])
{
    char *s="abcd";
    int i=10;
    printf("\x10\x42\x2f\x3A%n",s,i,argv[1]);
    return 0;
}
```

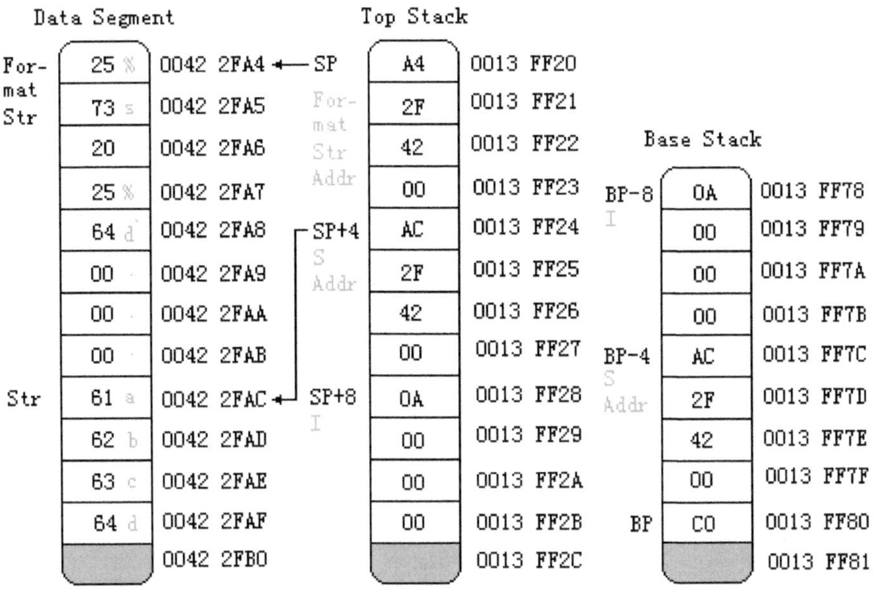

Fig. 2. String Format printf("%s %d", s, i) has three parameters: the format string pointer SP, the s string pointer SP+4, and the integer i saved in 0013FF28H memory address. The black hexadecimal numbers in the box are the memory values. The black side hexadecimal numbers are the memory address.

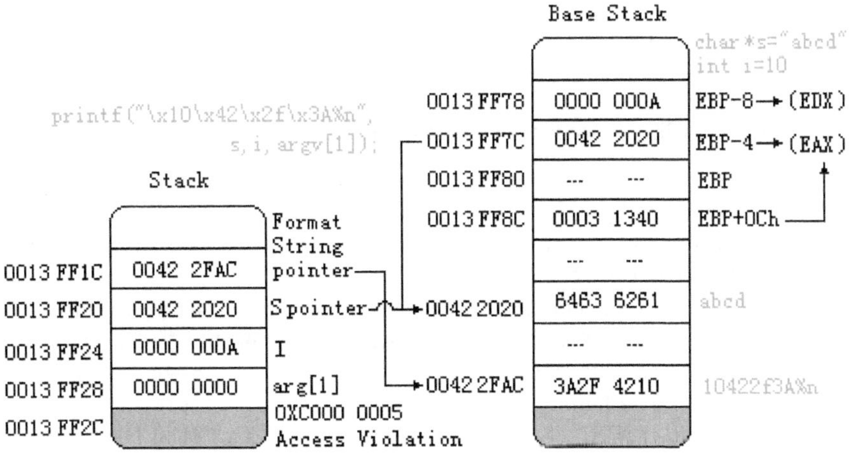

Fig. 3. Format string overflowed at 0XC0000005 physical address. When the char and integer variable are initialed, the base stack memory is shown on the left side. When the printf () function is executed, the stack changing procedure is described on the left side. The first string format control parameter in memory 00422FAC address, the second parameter S pointer to the 00422020 address. Integer variable I and argv[1] pointer are pushed into the stack firstly.

The main function has two parameters: integer variable argc and char integer variable argv[]. If the program executes in console command without input arguments, the argc equals to 1 and the argv[1] is null. The argv[1] is integer down overflow. The execute procedure of the program in stack and base stack memory is shown in Fig.3:

3.2 Stack Overflow Exploitation Caused by Integer Overflow

Stack overflow is the main kind of buffer overflow. As the strcpy () function has not bounds checking, once the source string data beyond the target string buffer bounds and overwrite the function return address in stack buffer, the stack overflow will occur. The integer upper or down overflow will also cause stack overflow. The example program is as shown as bellow.

```
int stackOverflow (char *str)
{
      char buffer[8]="abcdefg";
      strcpy(buffer,str);
      return 0;
}

int main(int argc, char *argv[])
{
      int i;
      char largeStr[16]="12345678abcdefg";
      char str[8]="1234567";
       stackOverflow(str);
      stackOverflow(largeStr);
      stackOverflow(argv[1]);
}
```

The function calling procedure mainly includes six main steps:

(1) The real parameters of called function are pushed into stack from right to left. The example real parameter string address is pushed into stack.
(2) Push instruction: call @ILT+5(stackOverflow) (0040100a) next IP address (00401145) into stack.
(3) Push EBP address into stack; EBP new value equals to ESP by instruction: Mov EBP,ESP; Create new stack space for sub function local variables by instruction: Sub ESP,48H.
(4) Push EBX, ESI, EDI into stack.
(5) Move offset of [EBP-48H] to EDI; Copy 0CCCCCCCCH to DWORD[EDI]; Store local variables in sub function to [EBP-8] and [EBP-4].
(6) POP local variables and return.

The memory change procedure is presented in Fig. 4 during the main function calling the stack overflow sub function.

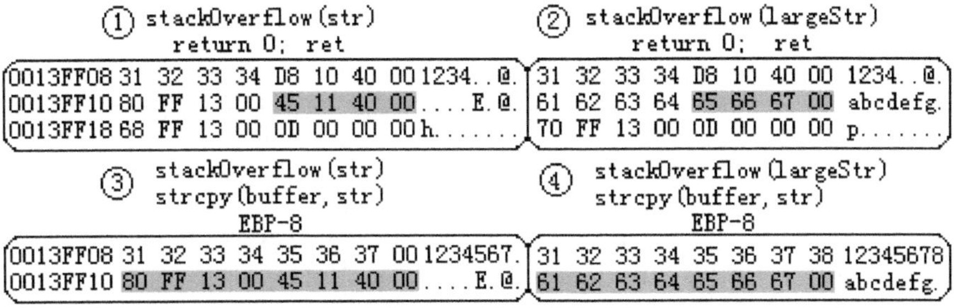

Fig. 4. Stackoverflow(str) return address is 00401145H as shown in figure (1); StackOverflow (largest) return address is 00676665H as shown in figure (2); Base stack memory status of [EBP-8] after strcpy(buffer,str) with str parameter is shown in figure (3); with largest parameter is shown in figure (4).

The access violation is derived from the large string upper integer overflow and argv[1] down integer overflow. The stack overflow caused by integer overflow break the program at the physical address 0xC0000005.

Once the return address content in stack is overwritten by stack buffer overflow or integer overflow, the IP will jump to the overwrite address. If the address points to the shell code, which is the malicious code for intruding or destroying computer system, the original program will execute the malicious shell code. Many kinds of shell codes can be got from shellcode automatic tools.

It is difficult to dynamically locate the overflow instruction physical location. Once finding the location point, you can overwrite the jump instruction into the overflow point. Getting the overflow point has two methods: manually testing methods and insert assembly language. The inserted key assembly language in the front of the return function is: lea ax, shellcode; mov si,sp; mov ss:[si],ax.

The other locating overflow point method is manually testing shown in Table 3:

Table 3. Locate the overflow address point caused by integer upper overflow

Disassembly code	Register value befor running	Register value after running
xor eax,eax	(eax)=0013 FF08H	(eax)=0000 0000H
pop edi	(edi)= 0013 FF10H	(edi)= 0013 FF80H
pop esi	(esi) = 00CF F7F0H	(esi)= 00C FF7F0H
pop ebx	(ebx)=7FFD 6000H	(ebx) =7FFD 6000H
add esp,48h	(esp)= 0013 FEC8H	(esp)= 0013 FF10H
cmp ebp,esp	(ebp)=(esp)= 0013 FF10H	(ebp)=(esp)= 0013 FF10H
call _chkesp	(esp)= 0013 FF10H	(esp) = 0013 FF0CH
ret	(esp) = 0013 FF0CH	(esp)=0013 FF10H
mov ebp,esp	(ebp)=(esp)= 0013 FF10H	(ebp)=(esp)= 0013 FF10H
pop ebp	(ebp)=(esp)= 0013 FF10H	(ebp) = 6463 6261H
ret	(eip) = 0040 10DBH	(eip)= 0067 6655H

3.3 Heap Overflow Exploitation Caused by Integer Overflow

Heap overflow is another important type of buffer overflow. Heap has different data structure from stacks. Stack is FILO (First In Last Out) data structure, which is always used in function calling. Heap is a memory segment that is used for storing dynamically allocated data and global variables. The functions of creating, allocating and free heap are HeapCreate (), HeapAlloc() and HeapFree().

Integer overflow can lead to heap overflow, when the memory addresses are overwritten. The argv[0] is a string pointer. atoi(argv[0]) equals to 0. If the atoi(argv [0]) is the HeapAlloc() function last parameter, It will lead to integer overflow. The program is presented as bellow:

```
int main(int argc, char *argv[])
{
        char *pBuf1,*pBuf2;
        HANDLE hHeap;
        char myBuf[]="intHeapOverflow";
        hHeap=HeapCreate(HEAP_GENERATE_EXCEPTIONS,
                                        0X1000,0XFFFF);
        pBuf1=(char *)HeapAlloc(hHeap,0,8);
        strcpy(pBuf1,myBuf);
        pBuf2=(char *)HeapAlloc(hHeap,0, atoi(argv[0]));
        strcpy(pBuf2,myBuf);
        HeapFree(hHeap,0,pBuf1);
        HeapFree(hHeap,0,pBuf2);
        return 0;
}
```

The program defines two buffer pointers: pBuf1 and pBuf2 and creates a heap with the return hHeap pointer. The variables and heap structure in memory is shown in Fig. 5:

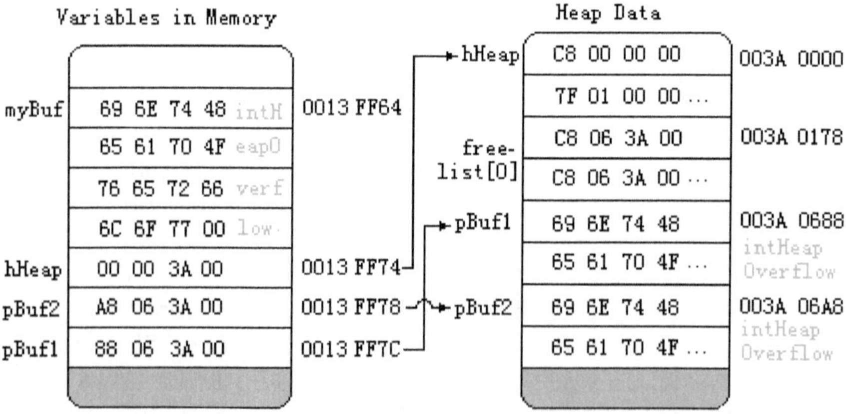

Fig. 5. Variables in memory are shown in left and heap data are in the right. Handle pointer hHeap save heap address. The heap variables pointers pBuf1 and pBuf2 point to their corresponding data in the heap. String variables myBuf save in 0013FF64 address.

The heap next and previous addresses in free list are shown as Fig. 6:

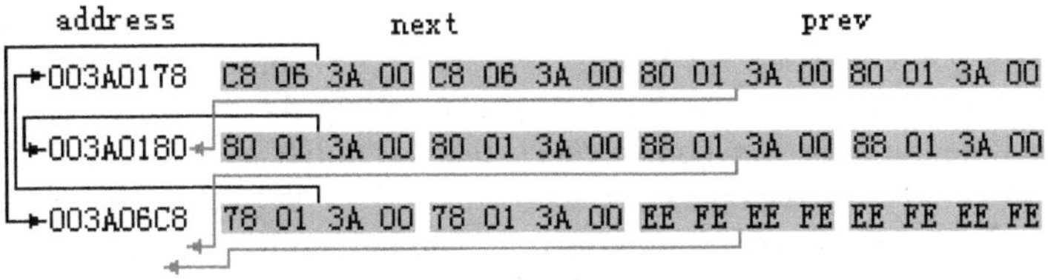

Fig. 6. In the free double link list array, there are next pointer and previous pointer. When allocating a dynamic memory using HeapAlloc () function, a heap free space will be used. Heap overflow will occur if the double link list are destroyed by overwritten string caused by integer overflow.

The program occurs heap overflow which is caused by integer overflow at the IP address 7C92120EH. The integer overflow includes the situation that size of mybuf and is larger than myBuf1 and myBuf2. The max size of myBuf2 allocation is zero as a result of atoi(argv[1]).

4 Evaluation

4.1 Effectiveness

We have applied RICB to analyze integer overflow with format string overflow, stack overflow, heap overflow. RICB methods successfully dynamically detected the integer over flow in examples, and also find the relationship between the integer overflow and buffer overflow.

As RICB is a dynamic analysis method, it may face the difficulties from static C language. To confirm the suspicious buffer overflow vulnerability is really caused by integer overflow, we rely on our CF (Carry Flag) and OF (Overflow Flag) in PSW (Program Status Word).

4.2 Efficiency

The RICB method includes the following steps: decompiling execute file to assembly language; debug the execute file step into and step out; locate the over flow points; check analysis integer overflow via buffer overflow. We measure the three example program on a Intel (R) Core (TM)2 Duo CPU E4600 (2.4GHZ) with 2GB memory running Windows. Table 4 shows the result of efficiency evaluation.

Table 4. Evaluation result on efficiency

File Name	Overflow EIP	Access Violation	Integer Overflow
FormatString.exe	0040 1036	0XC000 0005	argv[1] %n
Stack.exe	0040 1148	0XC000 0005	argv[1] largeStr
Heap.exe	7C92 120E	0X7C92 120E	atoi(argv[0])

5 Conclusions

In this paper, we have presented the use of RICB methods to dynamical analysis of run-time integer checking via buffer overflow. Our approach includes the steps: decompiling execute file to assembly language; debug the execute file step into and step out; locate the over flow points; check analysis buffer overflow caused by integer overflow. We have implemented our approach in three buffer overflow types: format string overflow, stack overflow and heap overflow. Experiment results show that our approach is effective and efficient. We have detected more than 5 known integer overflow vulnerabilities via buffer overflow.

Acknowledgments. The work described in this paper was supported by the National Natural Science Foundation of China (60903188), Shanghai Postdoctoral Scientific Program (08R214131) and World Expo Science and Technology Special Fund of Shanghai Science and Technology Commission (08dz0580202).

References

1. Wang, T.L., Wei, T., Lin, Z.Q., Zou, W.: Automatically Detecting Integer Overflow Vulnerability in X86 Binary Using Symbolic Execution. In: Proceedings of the 16th Network and Distributed System Security Symposium, San Diego, CA, pp. 1–14 (2009)
2. Zhang, S.R., Xu, L., Xu, B.W.: Method of Integer Overflow Detection to Avoid Buffer Overflow. Journal of Southeast University (English Edition) 25, 219–223 (2009)
3. Cadar, C., Dunbar, D., Engler, D.: KLEE: Unassisted and Automatic Generation of High-Coverage Tests for Complex Systems Programs. In: Proceedings of the USENIX Symposium on Operating Systems Design and Implementation (OSDI 2008), San Diego, CA (2008)
4. Brumley, D., Chiueh, T.C., Johnson, R., Lin, H., Song, D.: Rich: Automatically Protecting Against Integer-based Vulnerabilities. In: Proceedings of the 14th Annual Network and Distributed System Security Symposium, NDSS (2007)
5. Cadar, C., Ganesh, V., Pawlowski, P.M., Dill, D.L., Engler, D.R.: Exe: Automatically Generating Inputs of Death. In: Proceedings of the 13th ACM Conference on Computer and Communications Security, CCS 2006, pp. 322–335 (2006)
6. Dor, N., Rodeh, M., Sagiv, M.: CSSV: Towards a Realistic Tool for Statically Detecting all Buffer Overflows. In: Proceedings of the ACM SIGPLAN 2003 Conference on Programming Language Design and Implementation, San Diego, pp. 155–167 (2003)
7. Haugh, E., Bishop, M.: Testing C Programs for Buffer overflow Vulnerabilities. In: Proceedings of the10th Network and Distributed System Security Symposium, NDSS SanDiego, pp. 123–130 (2003)
8. Wilander, J., Kamkar, M.: A Comparison of Publicly Available Tools for Dynamic Buffer Overflow Prevention. In: Proceedings of the 10th Network and Distributed System Security Symposium, NDSS 2003, SanDiego, pp. 149–162 (2003)
9. Lhee, K.S., Chapin, S.J.: Buffer Overflow and Format String Overflow Vulnerabilities, Sofware-Practice and Experience, pp. 1–38. John Wiley & Sons, Chichester (2002)
10. Gok, M.: Integer squarers with overflow detection, Computers and Electrical Engineering, pp. 378–391. Elsevier, Amsterdam (2008)

11. Gok, M.: Integer Multipliers with Overflow Detection. IEEE Transactions on Computers 55, 1062–1066 (2006)
12. Godefroid, P., Levin, M., Molnar, D.: Automated whitebox fuzz testing. In: Proceedings of the 15th Annual Network and Distributed System Security Symposium (NDSS), San Diego, CA (2008)
13. Cowan, C., Barringer, M., Beattie, S., Kroah-Hartman, G.: FormatGuard: Automatic Protection From printf Format String Vulnerabilities. In: Proceedings of the 10th USENIX Security Symposium. USENIX Association, Sydney (2001)
14. Wang, Y., Gu, D.W., Wen, M., Xu, J.P., Li, H.M.: Denial of Service Detection with Hybrid Fuzzy Set Based Feed Forward Neural Network. In: Zhang, L., Lu, B.-L., Kwok, J. (eds.) ISNN 2010. LNCS, vol. 6064, pp. 576–585. Springer, Heidelberg (2010)
15. Wang, Y., Gu, D.W., Wen, M., Li, H.M., Xu, J.P.: Classification of Malicious Software Behaviour Detection with Hybrid Set Based Feed Forward Neural Network. In: Zhang, L., Lu, B.-L., Kwok, J. (eds.) ISNN 2010. LNCS, vol. 6064, pp. 556–565. Springer, Heidelberg (2010)

Investigating the Implications of Virtualization for Digital Forensics*

Zheng Song[1], Bo Jin[2], Yinghong Zhu[1], and Yongqing Sun[2]

[1] School of Software, Shanghai Jiao Tong University, Shanghai 200240, China
[2] Key Laboratory of Information Network Security, Ministry of Public Security, People's Republic of China (The Third Research Institute of Ministry of Public Security), Shanghai 201204, China
{songzheng,zhuyinghong}@sjtu.edu.cn, jinbo@stars.org.cn, yongqing.sun@gmail.com

Abstract. Research in virtualization technology has gained significant momentum in recent years, which brings not only opportunities to the forensic community, but challenges as well. In this paper, we discuss the potential roles of virtualization in the area of digital forensics and conduct an investigation on the recent progresses which utilize the virtualization techniques to support modern computer forensics. A brief overview of virtualization is presented and discussed. Further, a summary of positive and negative influences on digital forensics that are caused by virtualization technology is provided. Tools and techniques that are potential to be common practices in digital forensics are analyzed and some experience and lessons in our practice are shared. We conclude with our reflections and an outlook.

Keywords: Digital Forensics, Virtualization, Forensic Image Booting, Virtual Machine Introspection.

1 Introduction

As virtualization is becoming increasing mainstream, its usage becomes more commonplace. Virtual machines, so far, have a variety of applications. Governments and organizations can have their production systems virtualized to reduce costs on energy, cooling hardware procurements and human resources, enhance availability, robustness and utilization of their systems. Software development and testing is another field that virtual machines are widely used, because virtual machines can be installed, replicated and configured in a short time and support almost all existing operating systems, thus improving the productivity and efficiency. As for security researchers, a virtual machine is a controlled clean environment in which unknown codes from the wild are run and analyzed. Once an undo button is pressed, the virtual machine will roll back to the previous clean states.

* This paper is supported by the Special Basic Research, Ministry of Science and Technology of the People's Republic of China (No. 2008FY240200), and the Key Project Funding, Ministry of Public Security of the People's Republic of China (No. 2008ZDXMSS003).

X. Lai et al. (Eds.): E-Forensics 2010, LNICST 56, pp. 110–121, 2011.

While its benefits are attractive, virtualization also brings challenges to the digital forensics practitioners. With the advent of various virtualization solutions, a lot of work should be done to have a full understanding of all the techniques related with digital forensics. A virtual machine not only can be a suspect's tool for illegal activities, but also become a useful tool for forensic investigator/examiner. Recent years have witnessed a trend of virtualization as a focus in the IT industry and we believe it will have an irreversible influence on the forensic community and their practices as well.

In this paper, we analyze the potential roles that virtual machines will take and investigate several promising forensic techniques that utilize virtualization. A detailed discussion about benefits and limitations of these techniques is provided and lessons learned during our investigation are given.

The next section reviews the idea of virtualization. Section 3 discusses the scenarios where virtual machine is taken as suspect targets. Section 4 introduces several methods that regard virtual machines as forensic tools. We conclude with our reflections on this topic.

2 Overview of Virtualization

The concept of virtualization is not new but its resurgence came only in recent years. Virtualization provides an extra level of abstraction in contrast to the traditional architecture of computer systems, as illustrated in Figure1.

On a broader view, virtualization can be categorized into several types including ISA level, Hardware Abstraction Layer (HAL) level, OS level, Programming language level and Library level, according to the different layer in the architecture where virtualization layer is inserted. HAL-level virtualization, also known as system level virtualization or hardware virtualization, allows the sharing of underlying physical resources between different virtual machines which are based on the same ISA (e.g., x86). Each of the virtual machines is isolated between others and runs its own operating system.

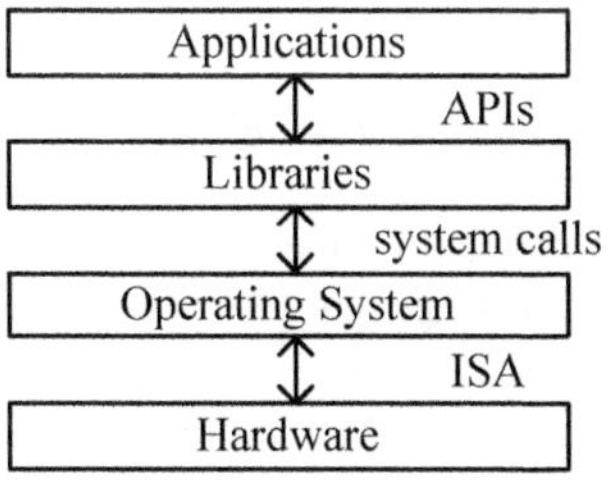

Fig. 1. The hierarchical architecture of modern computer systems

The software layer that provides the virtualization abstraction is called virtual machine monitor (VMM) or hypervisor. Based on the diverse positions where it is implemented, VMM, or hypervisor, can be divided into Type I, which runs on bare metal and Type II, which runs on top of an operating system.

In a Type I system, the VMM runs directly on physical hardware and eliminates an abstraction layer (i.e., host OS layer), so the performance of Type I virtual machines overwhelms that of Type II in general. But Type II systems have closer ties with the underlying host OS and their device drivers; they often have a wider range of functionalities in physical hardware components. This paper involves mainstream virtualization solutions, such as VMware Workstation [39], VMware ESXi [38], and Xen [29]. Figure 2 shows those two architectures. Xen and VMware ESXi belong to the former and VMware Workstation the latter.

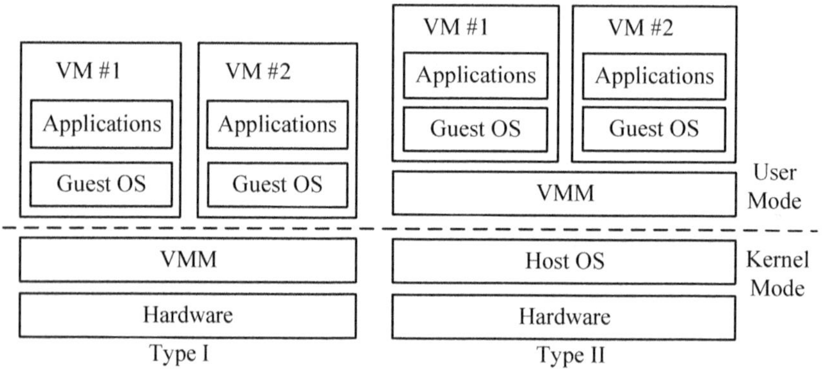

Fig. 2. Different architectures of VMMs, *Type I* on the left and *Type II* on the right

3 Virtual Machines as Suspect Targets

A coin has two sides. With the wide use of virtual machines, it becomes inevitable that virtual machines may become suspect targets for forensic practitioners. The following will present the challenges and problems faced with the forensic society that are found during our research.

3.1 Looking for the Traces of Virtual Machines

The conventional computer forensics process comprises a number of steps, and it can be broadly encapsulated in four key phases [25]: access, acquire, analyze and report. The first step is to find traces of evidences.

There are a variety of virtualization solution products available, not only commercial, but open source and freeware as well. Many of these products are required to be installed on a host machine (i.e., Type II). For these types of solutions, in most cases, it is the simplest situation that both the virtual machine application and virtual machines existing on the target can be found directly. But occasionally, looking for the traces of virtual machines may become a difficult task.

Considering some deleted virtual machines or uninstalled virtual machine applications, they are attractive to examiners, although they are not typically considered as suspicious. Discovering the traces involves careful examination of remnants on a host system: .lnk files, prefetch files, MRU references, registry and sometimes special files left on the hard drive. Shavers [17] showed some experience in looking for the traces: the registry will most always contain remnants of program install/uninstall as well as other associated data referring to virtual machine applications; file associations maintained in the registry will indicate which program will be started based upon a specific file being selected; the existence of "VMware Network Adaptor" without the presence of its application can be a strong indication that the application did exist on the computer in the past. In the book [23], Chapter 5 analyzed the impact of a virtual machine on a host machine. Virtual machines may be deleted directly by the operating system due to its size in Windows, and with today's data recovery means, it might be possible to recover some of these files, but impossible to examine the whole as a physical system. In a nutshell, this kind of recovery work is filled with uncertainty and the larger the size of the virtual machine is, the harder it is to recover in our experiments.

However, with other types of virtualization solutions (Type I), it is totally different to search for traces. For instance, as the Virtual Desktop Infrastructure (VDI) develops, desktop virtualization will gain more popularity. Virtual machine instances can be created, snapshot and deleted quickly and easily, and also can dynamically traverse through the network to different geographical locations. It is similar to the cloud computing environment where you hardly know on which hard disk your virtual machine resides in. Of the above circumstances, maybe only the virtualization application itself knows the answer. Even if you may find a suspect target through tough and arduous work, it could be of a previous version and contains no evidences you want at all. So searching for the existence of the very target is a prerequisite before further investigation is conducted, and it is a valuable field for forensic researchers and practitioners.

It is also important to notice that some virtualization applications do not need to be installed in a host computer and can be accessed and run in external media, including USB flash drivers or even CDs. It is typically considered as an anti-forensic method if he or she wants to disrupt the examinations.

3.2 Acquiring the Evidence

The acquisition of evidence must be conducted under a proper and faultless process; otherwise it will be questionable in court. The traditional forensic procedure, known as static analysis, is to take custody of the target system, shut it down, copy the storage media, and then analyze the image copy using a variety of forensics tools. The shutdown process amounts to either invoking the normal system shutdown sequence, or pulling the power cord from the system to effect an instant shutdown [19].

Type II virtual machines are easier to image, as they typically reside in one hard disk. In theory and practice, there may be more virtual machines in a single disk and a virtual machine may have close ties with the underlying host operating system, such as shared folders and virtual networks. Imaging the "virtual disk" only may miss evidences of vital importance in the host system. It is recommended to image the whole host disk for safety if possible, rather than image the virtual disk only.

An alternate way is to mount the VMDK files of VMware as mounted drives through VMware DiskMount Tool [16], instead of imaging the whole host system. In this way, we can have access to these virtual disks without any VMware applications installed. Being treated as a drive, the virtual disk files can be analyzed with suitable forensic tools. However, it is better to mount a VMDK virtual disk on a write protected external media, which is recommended by Brett Shavers [17]. And further, we believe it is better to use this method if and only if all the evidences exists just in the guest OS, and this situation may be infrequently met.

However, for the Type I virtual machines which are commonly stored in large storage media such as SAN and NAS in production systems in enterprises, the traditional forensic procedure is improper and inappropriate now, as under these circumstances, it is neither practical nor flawless to acquire the evidence in an old fashion: powering off the server could lead to unavailability to other legal users thus become involved in several issues.

The most significant one is the legislative issues as who on earth will account for total losses for the innocents. But we will not continue with it as it is not the focus of this paper. Besides, there are technical issues as well. For example, Virtual Machine File System (VMFS) [20] is a proprietary file system format owned by VMware, and there is a lack of forensic tools to parse this format thoroughly, which brings difficulties for forensic practitioners. What is worse, VMFS is a clustered advanced file system that a single VMFS file system can spread over multiple servers. Although there are some efforts in this field like open source VMFS driver [21], which enables read-only access to files and folders on partitions with VMFS, it is far from satisfying forensic needs. Even if the virtual machine can be exported to an external storage media, it may still arouse suspicions in court as it is reliant on cooperation from the VM administrator and also the help of virtualization management tools. In addition, as we have mentioned earlier, an obstacle to acquire the image of a virtual machine may be in the cloud-computing-alike situation where its virtual disk locates on different disks and has a huge size that imaging it with current technology faces more difficulty.

We also want to point out here that acquiring the virtual machine related evidence with traditional forensic procedure might not be enough or even might be questionable. In the case of a normal shut down of a VM, data is read and written to the virtual hard disk, which may delete or overwrite forensically relevant contents (similar things happens when shut down a physical machine). Another more important aspect lies in that much of the information, such as process list, network ports, encryption keys, or some other sensitive data, may only exist in RAM and it will not appear in the image.

It is recommended to perform a live forensic analysis on the target system in order to get particular information, the same with virtual environments. But note that live forensic analysis virtually faces its own problems and it is discussed in the next section.

3.3 Examining the Virtual Machine

The examination of a virtual machine image is almost the same with that of physical machine, with little differences. The forensic tools and processes are alike. The examination of a virtual machine incurs additional analysis of its related virtual machine files in the perspective of the host OS. The metadata associated with these file may give some useful information.

If further investigation on the associated virtual machine files continues, more detail about the moment when the virtual machine is suspended or closed may be revealed. Figure 3 shows the details of a .vmem file, which is a backup of the virtual machine's paging file. In fact, we believe it is a file storing the contents of "physical" memory. As we know, the virtual addresses used by programs and operating system components are not identical with the true locations of data in physical memory image (dump). It is the examiner's ability to translate the addresses [24]. In our view, the same technique applies to the memory analysis of virtual machines.

It is currently a trend to perform a live forensics [22] when a computer system to examine is in a live state. Useful information of the live system at the moment, such as memory contents, network activities and active process lists will probably not survive after the system is shut down. It is possible to encounter that a live system to be examined involves one or more running virtual machines as well. Running processes or memory contents of a virtual system may as important as, or even more important than that of the host system. But it is highly likely that performing live forensic in the virtual machine will almost certainly affect not only the states of the guest system but also the host system. There is less experience in this situation from literature and we believe it must be tackled carefully.

In addition, encryption is a traditional barrier in front of forensic experts during examination. In order to protect privacy, more and more virtualization providers tend to introduce encryption, which consequently arise the difficulties. This is a new trend which more attentions should be paid to.

```
004D0FF0  00 00 00 00 00 00 00 00  00 00 00 00 00 00 00 00  ................
004D1000  5B 4C 6F 63 61 6C 69 7A  65 64 46 69 6C 65 4E 61  [LocalizedFileNa
004D1010  6D 65 73 5D 0D 0A 57 69  6E 64 6F 77 73 20 D7 CA  mes]..Windows ×Ê
004D1020  D4 B4 B9 DC C0 ED C6 F7  2E 6C 6E 6B 3D 40 25 53  Ô´¹ÜÀíÆ÷.lnk=@%S
004D1030  79 73 74 65 6D 52 6F 6F  74 25 5C 73 79 73 74 65  ystemRoot%\syste
004D1040  6D 33 32 5C 73 68 65 6C  6C 33 32 2E 64 6C 6C 2C  m32\shell32.dll,
004D1050  2D 32 32 30 36 37 0D 0A  C3 FC C1 EE CC E1 CA BE  -22067..ÃüÁîÌáÊ¾
004D1060  B7 FB 2E 6C 6E 6B 3D 40  25 53 79 73 74 65 6D 52  ·û.lnk=@%SystemR
004D1070  6F 6F 74 25 5C 73 79 73  74 65 6D 33 32 5C 73 68  oot%\system32\sh
004D1080  65 6C 6C 33 32 2E 64 6C  6C 2C 2D 32 32 30 32 32  ell32.dll,-22022
004D1090  0D 0A BC C7 CA C2 B1 BE  2E 6C 6E 6B 3D 40 25 53  ..¼ÇÊÂ±¾.lnk=@%S
004D10A0  79 73 74 65 6D 52 6F 6F  74 25 5C 73 79 73 74 65  ystemRoot%\syste
004D10B0  6D 33 32 5C 73 68 65 6C  6C 33 32 2E 64 6C 6C 2C  m32\shell32.dll,
004D10C0  2D 32 32 30 35 31 0D 0A  CD AC B2 BD 2E 6C 6E 6B  -22051..Í¬²½.lnk
```

Fig. 3. The contents of a .vmem file which may include some useful information. A search for the keyword "system32" returned over 1000 hits in a .vmem file of Windows XP virtual machine, and the above figure just show some of them as an example.

4 Virtual Machines as Forensic Tools

Virtualization provides new technologies that promote our forensic tool boxes and we now have more methods in proceeding with the examination. We have focused our attention on the following two fields, forensic image booting and virtual machine introspection.

4.1 Forensic Image Booting

Before forensic image booting with virtual machine comes up, restoration of a forensic image back to disk requires numerous attempts, if the original hardware is not available. And blue screens of death are frequently met. However, with virtual machines solutions, our burden relieves. A forensic image can be booted in a virtual environment, with less manual work as clicking the mouse and the left work is done automatically.

The benefits of booting up a forensic image are various. The obvious one is that it benefits forensic examiners by quick and intuitive insight into the target, which can save a lot of time if nothing valuable exists. Also it provides examiners a convenient way to demonstrate the evidence to the non-experts in the court in a view that is as if seen by the suspect by the time to seizure.

Booting a forensic image requires certain steps. Depending on the format of the image, different tools are prepared. Live View [1] is a forensics tool produced by CERT that creates a VMware virtual machine out of a raw disk image (dd-style) or physical disk. In our practice, dd format and Encase EWF format are mostly used. Encase EWF format (E01) is a proprietary format that is commonly used worldwide and includes additional metadata such as case number, investigator's name, time, notes, checksum and footprint (hash values). Besides, it can reside in multiple segment files or within a single file. So it is not identical with the original hard disk and can not be boot up directly. To facilitate the booting, we developed a small tool to convert Encase EWF files to dd image. Figure 4 illustrates the main steps we use in practice.

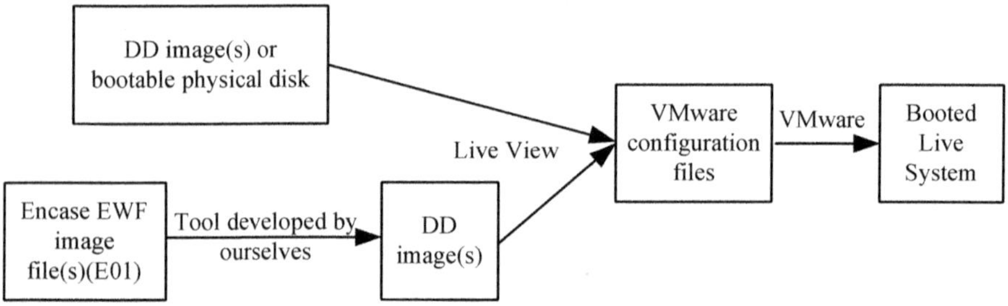

Fig. 4. The main steps to boot forensic image(s) up in our practice

It is recommended to use write-protected devices for safety, in case there would be unexpected accidents. With the support from Live View, investigators can interact with the OS inside the forensic image or physical disk without modifying the evidence, because all the changes to the OS is written to separate virtual machine files, not the original place. Repeated and separate investigations are now available.

Other software tools that can create the files with parameters for virtual machine include ProDiscover Basic [11] and Virtual Forensics Computing [12]. An alternate method to deal with the forensic images with proprietary format is to mount these forensic images as disks beforehand using tools such as Mount Image Pro [13], Encase Forensics Physical Disk Emulator [14] and SmartMount [15].

Based on this forensic image booting technique, a lot of work is done. Bem et al. [10] proposed a new approach where two environments, conventional and virtual, are used independently. After the images are collected in a forensically sound way, two copies are produced. One is protected using the chain of custody rules, and the other is given to a technical worker who works with it in virtual environments. Any findings are documented and passed to a more qualified person who confirms them in accordance with forensic rules. They demonstrated that their approach can considerably shorten the time of the computer forensic investigation analysis phase and allow for better utilization of less qualified personnel.

Mrdovic et al. [26] proposed combinations of static and live analysis. Virtualization is used to bring static data to life. Using data from memory dump, virtual machine created from static data can be adjusted to provide better picture of the live system at the time when the dump was made. Investigator can have interactive session with virtual machine without violating evidence integrity. And their tests with sample system confirm viability of their approach.

As a lot of related work [10, 26, 27] shows, forensic image booting seems to be a promising technology. However, we have found that there exist some anti-forensic methods in the wild during our investigation. One of them is to utilize a small program which uses the virtual machine detection code [2] to shut the system down as soon as a virtualized environment is detected during system startup. Although investigators may finally figure out what has happened and remove this small program to successfully boot the image, extra efforts are made and more time wasted. But this raises our concerns about the covert channels in virtualization solutions, which is still a difficult problem to deal with.

4.2 Virtual Machine Introspection

As we have mentioned before, live analysis has particular strengths over traditional static analysis. But still, live analysis has its own limitations. One limitation, as we have discussed in Section 3.2, which is also known as the observer effect, is that any operation performed during the live analysis process modifies the state of the system, which in turn might result in potential contamination to evidences. The other limitation, as Brian D. Carrier analyzed, is that the current risks in live acquisition [3] lie in the systems to be examined are themselves compromised or incomplete (e.g., by rootkits). Further more, any forensic utilities executed during the live analysis can be detected by a sufficiently careful and skilled attacker, who can at that point change behavior, delete important data, or actively obstruct the investigator's efforts [28]. In that case, live forensic may output inaccurate or even false information. Resolving these issues depends on forensic experts themselves. However, using virtual machines and the Virtual Machine Introspection (VMI) technique, the above limitations may be overcome.

Suppose a computer system runs in a virtual machine, which is supervised by a virtual machine monitor. As VMM has complete read and write access to all memory in VM (in most cases), it is possible for a special tool to reconstruct the contents of a process's memory space, and even the contents of the VM's kernel memory, by using the page table for the VMM and its privileges to obtain an image of the VM's memory. This special tool will gain all memory contents of interest, thus help to fully understand what the target process was doing for the purpose of forensic analysis. The above is just an illustration of the usage of virtual machine introspection and more functionality are possible such as monitoring disk accesses and network activities.

One of the nine research areas identified in the virtualization and digital forensics research agenda [4] is virtual introspection. Specifically, Virtual Machine Introspection is the process by which the state of a virtual machine is observed from either the Virtual Machine Monitor, or from a virtual machine other than the one being examined. This technique was first introduced by Garfinkel and Rosenblum [5].

Research in the application of VMI has typically focused on intrusion detection rather than digital forensics [6]. But there are some associated work in the forensic filed recently. XenAccess [7] project, led by Bryan Payne from Georgia Tech, produced an open source virtual machine introspection library in Xen hypervisor. This library allows a privileged domain to view the runtime state of another domain. It currently focuses on memory access, but also provides proof-of-concept code for disk monitoring. Brian Hay and Kara Nance [8] provide a suite of virtual introspection tools for Xen (VIX tools), which allow an investigator to perform live analysis of an unprivileged Xen [29] virtual machine (DomU) from the privileged Dom0 virtual machine. VMwatcher [30], VMwall [31], and others [32, 33] were developed to monitor VM execution and infer guest states or events, and all of them provide the potential ability to be used in forensics.

However, it seems there is a lack of similar tools in the bare-metal architecture (Type I) solutions of commercial products. Most recently, VMware has introduced VMsafe [9] technology that can allow third-party security vendors to leverage the unique benefits of VMI to better monitor, protect and control guest VMs. But VMsafe mainly addresses security issues, not forensic ones. We believe that VMsafe technology, if gained cooperation with VMware, could be changed and ported to a valuable forensic tool suite on VMware platform.

Nance et al. [28] identified four initial priority research areas in VMI and discussed its potential role in forensics. Virtual Machine Introspection may help the digital forensics community, but it still needs time to be proved and applied, as digital forensics investigation must be serious. We are cautious as we believe that time tries all things. Luckily, our cautions are proved right!

Bahram et al. [18] implemented a proof-of-concept Direct Kernel Structure Manipulation (DKSM) prototype to subvert the VMI tools (e.g., XenAccess). The exploit relies on the assumption that the original kernel data structures are respected by the distrusted guest and thus can directly used to bridge the well-known semantic gap [34]. The semantic gap can be explained as follows: from outside the VM, we can get a view of the VM at the VMM level, which includes its register values, memory pages, disk blocks; whereas from inside the VM, we can observe semantic-level entities (e.g., process and files) and events (e.g., system calls). This semantic gap is formed by the vast difference between external and internal observations. To bridge this gap, a set of data structures (e.g., those for process and file system management) can be used as "templates" to interpret VMM-level VM observations.

We believe current Virtual Machine Introspection has at least several limitations:

The first one is its trustiness. A VMI tool aims to analyze a VM which is not trusted, but still expects a VM to respect the kernel data structure templates, and relies on the VM maintained memory contents. Fundamentally, this is a trust inversion in logic. For the same reason, Bahram et al. [18] believe existing memory snapshop-based memory analysis tools and forensics systems [35, 36, 37] share the same limitation.

The second one is its detectability. There are several possibilities: (1) Timing analysis, as analysis of a running VM typically requires a period of time and might cause an inconsistent view. So a pause to a running VM might be unavoidable, thus might be detectable; (2) Page faults analysis [8], as the VM may be able to detect unusual patterns in the distribution of page faults, caused by the VMI application accessing pages that have been swapped out, or causing pages that were previously swapped out to be swapped back into RAM.

So moving toward the development of next-generation, reliable Virtual Machine Introspection technology is the future direction for researchers interested in this field.

5 Conclusion

On the wave of virtualization, forensic community should adapt themselves to new situations. On one hand, as we have discussed earlier, criminals may use virtual machines as handy tools and desktop computers might be replaced with thin clients in enterprise in the near future; all these will undoubtedly add the difficulties in the forensic process and we should prepare for them. On the other hand, virtualization provides us with new technique that can facilitate the forensic investigation, such as the forensic image booting. However, these techniques should be introduced into this domain carefully with overall tests, as digital forensics can have serious and significant legal and societal consequences.

This paper describes several forensic issues that come along with virtualization and virtual machines, provides experience and lessons in our research and practice.

References

1. Live View, `http://liveview.sourceforge.net/`
2. Detect if your program is running inside a Virtual Machine, `http://www.codeproject.com`
3. Carrier, B.D.: Risks of Live Digital Forensic Analysis. Communications of the ACM 49, 56–61 (2006)
4. Pollitt, M., Nance, K., Hay, B., Dodge, R., Craiger, P., Burke, P., Marberry, C., Brubaker, B.: Virtualization and Digital Forensics: A Research and Education Agenda. Journal of Digital Forensic Practice 2, 62–73 (2008)

5. Garfinkel, T., Rosenblum, M.: A virtual machine introspection based architecture for intrusion detection. In: 10th Annual Symposium on Network and Distributed System Security, pp. 191–206 (2003)
6. Nance, K., Bishop, M., Hay, B.: Virtual Machine Introspection: Observation or Interference? IEEE Security & Privacy 6, 32–37 (2008)
7. XenAccess, `http://code.google.com/p/xenaccess/`
8. Hay, B., Nance, K.: Forensic Examination of Volatile System Data using Virtual Introspection. ACM SIGOPS Operating Systems Review 42, 74–82 (2008)
9. VMsafe, `http://www.vmware.com`
10. Bem, D., Huebner, E.: Computer Forensic Analysis in a Virtual Environment. International Journel of Digital Evidence 6 (2007)
11. ProDiscover Basic, `http://www.techpathways.com/`
12. Virtual Forensics Computing, `http://www.mountimage.com/`
13. Mount Image Pro, `http://www.mountimage.com/`
14. Encase Forensics Physical Disk Emulator, `http://www.encaseenterprise.com/`
15. SmartMount, `http://www.asrdata.com/SmartMount/`
16. VMware DiskMount, `http://www.vmware.com`
17. Shavers, B.: Virtual Forensics (A Discussion of Virtual Machine Related to Forensic Analysis), `http://www.forensicfocus.com/virtual-machines-forensics-analysis`
18. Bahram, S., Jiang, X., Wang, Z., Grace, M., Li, J., Xu, D.: DKSM:Subverting Virtual Machine Introspection for Fun and Profit. Technical report, North Carolina State University (2010)
19. Carrier, B.: File system forensic analysis. Addison-Wesley, Boston (2005)
20. VMFS, `http://www.vmware.com/products/vmfs/`
21. Open Source VMFS Driver, `http://code.google.com/p/vmfs/`
22. Farmer, D., Venema, W.: Forensic Discovery. Addison-Wesley, Reading (2005)
23. Dorn, G., Marberry, C., Conrad, S., Craiger, P.: Advances in Digital Forensics V. IFIP Advances in Information and Communication Technology, vol. 306, p. 69. Springer, Heidelberg (2009)
24. Kornblum, J.D.: Using every part of the buffalo in Windows memory analysis. Digital Investigation 4, 24–29 (2007)
25. Kruse II, W.G., Heiser, J.G.: Computer Forensics: Incident Response Essentials, 1st edn. Addison Wesley Professional, Reading (2002)
26. Mrdovic, S., Huseinovic, A., Zajko, E.: Combining Static and Live Digital Forensic Analysis in Virtual Environment. In: 22nd International Symposium on Information, Communication and Automation Technologies (2009)
27. Penhallurick, M.A.: Methodologies for the use of VMware to boot cloned/mounted subject hard disk image. Digital Investigation 2, 209–222 (2005)
28. Nance, K., Hay, B., Bishop, M.: Investigating the Implications of Virtual Machine Introspection for Digital Forensics. In: International Conference on Availability, Reliability and Security, pp. 1024–1029 (2009)
29. Barham, P., Dragovic, B., Fraser, K., Hand, S., Harris, T.L., Ho, A., Neugebaur, R., Pratt, I., Warfield, A.: Xen and the art of virtualization. In: Nineteenth ACM Symposium on Operating Systems Principles, pp. 164–177. ACM Press, New York (2003)
30. Jiang, X., Wang, X., Xu, D.: Stealthy malware detection through vmm-based "out-of-the-box" semantic view reconstruction. In: 14th ACM conference on Computer and communications security, Alexandria, Virginia, USA, pp. 128–138 (2007)

31. Srivastava, A., Giffin, J.: Tamper-resistant, application-aware blocking of malicious network connections. In: 11th International Symposium on Recent Advances in Intrusion Detection, pp. 39–58. Springer, Heidelburg (2008)
32. Jones, S.T., Arpaci-Dusseau, A.C., Arpaci-Dusseau, R.H.: Antfarm: tracking processes in a virtual machine environment. In: Annual Conference on USENIX 2006 Annual Technical Conference, p. 1. USENIX Association, Berkeley (2006)
33. Litty, L., Lagar-Cavilla, H.A., Lie, D.: Hypervisor support for identifying covertly executing binaries. In: 17th Conference on Security Symposium. USENIX Association (2008)
34. Chen, P.M., Noble, B.D.: When virtual is better than real. In: Eighth Workshop on Hot Topics in Operating Systems, p. 133. IEEE Computer Society, Washington, DC (2001)
35. Volatile systems, https://www.volatilesystems.com/default/volatility
36. Carbone, M., Cui, W., Lu, L., Lee, W., Peinado, M., Jiang, X.: Mapping kernel objects to enable systematic integrity checking. In: 16th ACM Conference on Computer and Communications Security, pp. 555–565. ACM, New York (2009)
37. Dolan-Gavitt, B., Srivastava, A., Trayor, P., Giffin, J.: Robust signatures for kernel data structures. In: 16th ACM Conference on Computer and Communications Security, pp. 566–577 (2009)
38. VMware ESXi, http://www.vmware.com/products/esxi/
39. VMware Workstation, http://www.vmware.com/products/workstation/

Acquisition of Network Connection Status Information from Physical Memory on Windows Vista Operating System

Lijuan Xu, Lianhai Wang, Lei Zhang, and Zhigang Kong

Shandong Provincial Key Laboratory of Computer Network,
Shandong Computer Science Center
19 Keyuan Road, Jinan 250014, P.R. China
{xulj,wanglh,zhanglei,kongzhig}@keylab.net

Abstract. A method to extract information of network connection status information from physical memory on Windows Vista operating system is proposed. Using this method, a forensic examiner can extract accurately the information of current TCP/IP network connection information, including IDs of processes which established connections, establishing time, local address, local port, remote address, remote port, etc., from a physical memory on Windows Vista operating system. This method is reliable and efficient. It is verified on Windows Vista, Windows Vista SP1, Windows Vista SP2.

Keywords: computer forensic, memory analysis, network connection status information.

1 Introduction

In living forensics, network connection status information describes computer's activity communicating with outside world when the computer is investigated. It is important digital evidence judging whether respondents are doing illegal network activity or not. As a volatile data, current network connection status information exist in physical memory of a computer[1]. Therefore, acquiring this digital evidence depends on analyzing physical memory of the computer.

There are a number of memory analysis tools, for examples, WMFT(Windows Memory Forensic Toolkit), volatools, memparser, PTFinder, FTK, etc. WMFT[2] can be used to perform forensic analysis of physical memory images acquired from Windows 2000/2003/XP machines. PTFinder(Process and Thread Finder) is a Perl script created by Andreas Schuster[3] to detect and list all the processes and threads in a memory dump. MemParser tool was programmed by Chris Betz which can enumerate active processes and could also dump their process memory[4]. volatools[5] is a commandline toolkit intended to assist with the Survey Phase of a digital investigation, it is focused on support for Windows XP SP2 and can collect open connections and open ports which could typically be obtained by running netstat on the system under investigation[6,7,8].

X. Lai et al. (Eds.): E-Forensics 2010, LNICST 56, pp. 122–130, 2011.

Windows Vista is the new Microsoft operating system that was released to the public at the beginning of 2007. There are many changes to the new Windows Vista operating system compared to previous versions of Microsoft Windows that has brought new challenges for digital investigations. The tools metioned aboved can not acquire network connection status information from Windows Vista operating system. A memthod to extract network connection status information from physical memory on Windows Vista operating system is not published so far.

2 Related Work

Nowadays, there are two methods to acquire network connection status information from physical memory of Windows XP operating system. One is searching for data structure "AddrObjTable" and "ObjTable" from driver "tcpip.sys" to acquire network connection status information. This method is implemented in Volatility[9], a tool to analyze memory which dumps from Windows XP SP2 or Windows XP SP3 for an incident response perpective developed by Walters and Petroni. The other one is proposed by Schuster[10]. Schuster descirbes the steps necessary to detect traces of network activity in a memory dump. His method is searching for pool allocations labeled "TCPA" and a size of 368 bytes (360 bytes for the payload and 8 for the _POOL_HEADER) on Windows XP SP2. These allocations will reside in the non-paged pool.

The first method is feasible on Windows XP. It doesn't work on Windows Vista, because there is no data structure "AddrObjTable" or "ObjTable" in driver "tcpip.sys". It is proven that there is no pool allocations labeled "TCPA" on Windows Vista as well.

It is analyzed that there are pool allocations labeled "TCPE" instead of "TCPA" indicating network activity in a memory dump of Windows Vista. Therefore, we can acquire network connections from pool allocations labeled "TCPE" on Windows Vista.

This paper proposes a method of acquiring current network connection informations from physical memory image of Windows Vista according to memory pool. Network connection information including IDs of processes which established connections, establishing time, local address, local port, remote address, remote port, etc., can be get accurately from physical memory image file of Windows Vista with this method.

3 Acquisition of Network Connection Status Information from Physical Memory on Windows Vista Operating System

A method of acquiring current network connection information from physical memory image of Windows Vista based on memory pool is proposed.

3.1 The Structure of TcpEndpointPool

A data structure called TcpEndpointPool is found in driver "tcpip.sys" on Windows Vista operating system. This pool is a doubly-linked list of which each node is the head of a singly-linked list.

The internal organizational structure of TcpEndpointPool is shown by figure1. The circles represent heads of the singly-linked list. The letters in the circles represent the flag of the head. The rectangles represent the nodes of singly-linked list. The letters in the rectangles represent the type of the node.

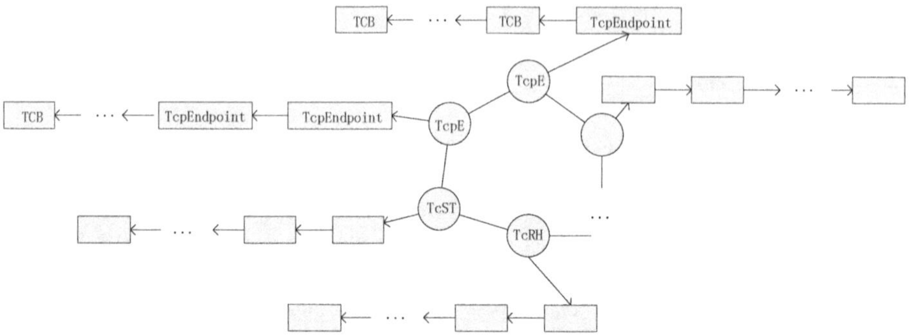

Fig. 1. TcpEndpointPool internal organization

The structure of singly-linked list head is shown by figure 2, in which there is a _LIST_ENTRY structure at the offset 0x30 by which the next head of a singly-linked list can be found.

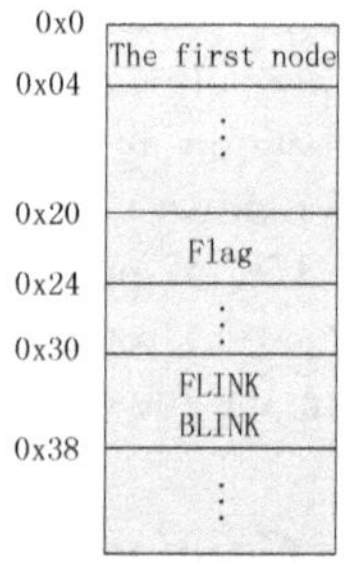

Fig. 2. The structure of singly-linked list head

The relationship of two adjacent heads is shown by figure 3.

There is a flag at the offset 0x20 of the singly-linked list head by which the node structure of the singly-linked list can be judged. If the flag is "TcpE", the singly-linked list with this head is composed of TcpEndPoint structure and TCB structure which describe the network connection information.

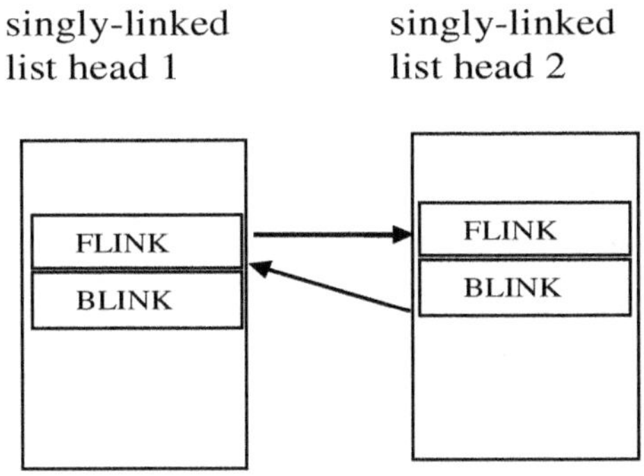

Fig. 3. The linked relationship of two heads

3.2 Searching for TcpEndpointPool

The offset of TcpEndpointPool's address relative to the base address of tcpip.sys is 0xd0d5c for Windows Vista SP1 and 0xd3e9c for Windows Vista SP2. Therefore, the virtual address of TcpEndpointPool can be computed by 0xd0d5c adding the virtual address of tcpip.sys's base address for Windows Vista SP1 and 0xd3e9c adding the virtual address of tcpip.sys's base address for Windows Vista SP2.

The base address of driver tcpip.sys can be acquried by using PsLoadedModuleList which is a global variable. That is because PsLoadedModuleList is a pointer to the list of currently loaded kernel modules, the base address of all loaded drivers can be acquried according to this variable.

3.3 TcpEndpoint and TCB

The definition and the offsets of fields related with network connections in the TcpEndPoint structure is shown as follows.

```
typedef struct _TCP_ENDPOINT {
    PEPROCESS OwningProcess;                    +0x14
    PETHREAD OwningThread;                      +0x18
    LARGE_INTEGER CreationTime;                 +0x20
    CONST NL_LOCAL_ADDRESS* LocalAddress;       +0x34
    USHORT LocalPort;                           +0x3e
} TCP_ENDPOINT, *PTCP_ENDPOINT;
```

From above structure, a pointer points to the process which established network connections at the offset 0x14, and a pointer points to the thread which established network connections at the offset 0x18.

The definition and the offsets of fields related with network connection information in the Tcb structure is shown as follows.

```
typedef struct _TCB {
    CONST NL_PATH *Path;                    +0x10
    USHORT LocalPort;                       +0x2c
    USHORT RemotePort;                      +0x2e
    PEPROCESS OwningProcess;                +0x164
    LARGE_INTEGER CreationTime;             +0x16c
} TCB, *PTCB;
```

NL_PATH structure, NL_LOCAL_ADDRESS structure and NL_ADDRESS_IDENTIFIER structure are defined as follows by which network connection local address and remote address can be acquried.

```
typedef struct _NL_PATH {
    CONST NL_LOCAL_ADDRESS *SourceAddress;          +0x00
    CONST UCHAR *DestinationAddress;                +0x08
} NL_PATH, *PNL_PATH;
typedef struct _NL_LOCAL_ADDRESS {
    CONST NL_ADDRESS_IDENTIFIER *Identifier;        +0x0c
} NL_LOCAL_ADDRESS, *PNL_LOCAL_ADDRESS;
typedef struct _NL_ADDRESS_IDENTIFIER {
    CONST UCHAR *Address;                           +0x00
} NL_ADDRESS_IDENTIFIER, *PNL_ADDRESS_IDENTIFIER;
```

Comparing the definition of TCP_ENDPOINT structure with the definition of TCB structure, we can say that if a pointer points to a EPROCESS structure at the offset 0x14 of the structure (the first 4 bytes of EPROCESS structure is 0x3002000 for windows Vista operating system), this structure is TCP_ENDPOINT, otherwise this structure is TCB.

4 Algorithm

4.1 The Overall Algorithm of Extracting Network Connection Information

The overall flow of extracting network connection information for Windows Vista operating system is shown by figure 4.

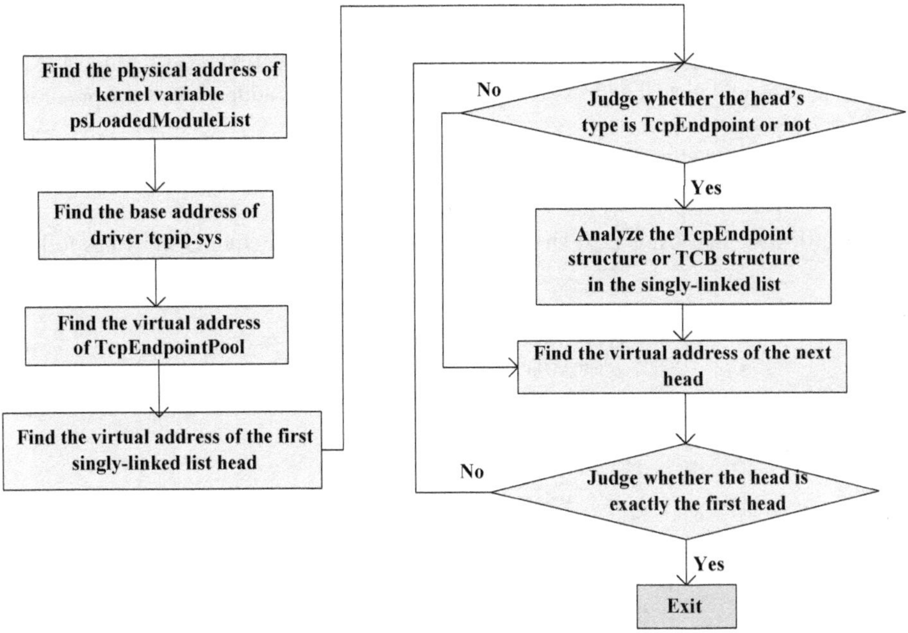

Fig. 4. The flow of extracting network connection information for Windows Vista operating system summary description

The algorithm is given as follows.

Step1 Get the physical address of kernel variable psLoadedModuleList using windows memory analyzing method based on KPCR[11].

Step2 Find the base address of driver tcpip.sys according to physical address of PsLoadedModuleList which point to a doubly-linked list composed of all drivers in the system.

Step3 Find the virtual address of TcpEndpointPool.

Step4 Find the virtual address of the first singly-linked list head.

Firstly, transfer the virtual address of TcpEndpointPool to physical address and locate the address in the memory image file. Secondly, read 4 bytes at this position and transfer the 4 bytes to physical address, locate the address in the memory image file. Lastly, the virtual address of the first singly-linked list head is the 4 bytes at the offset 0x1c.

Step5 Judge whether the head's type is TcpEndpoint or not by reading the flag which is set at the offset 0x20 relative to the head's address. If the flag is "TcpE", the head's type is TcpEndpoint, go to the step 6, otherwise go to the step 7.

Step6 Analyze the TcpEndpoint structure or TCB structure in the singly-linked list. Analyzing algorithm is shown by figure 5.

Step7 Find the virtual address of the next head.

The virtual address of the next head can be found according to the _LIST_ENTRY structure which is set at the offset 0x30 relative to the address of singly-linked list head. Judging whether the next head's virtual address equals to the first head's address or not. If the next head's virtual address is equal to the first head's address, exit the procedure, otherwise go to the next step.

Step8 Judge whether the head is exactly the first head. If the head is exactly the first head, exit, otherwise go to step 5.

The flow of analyzing TCB structure or TcpEndpoint structure is shown as follows.

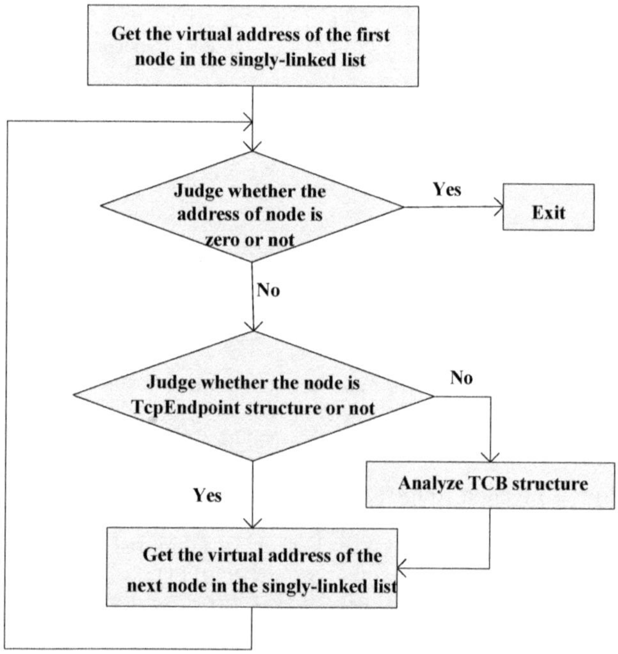

Fig. 5. The flow of analyzing TCB structure or TcpEndpoint structure summary description

Step1 Get the virtual address of the first node in the singly-linked list.

Transfer the virtual address of singly-list head to physical address and locate the address in memory image file. Read 4 bytes from this position which is the virtual address of the first node.

Step2 Judge whether the address of node is zero or not. If the address is zero, exit the procedure, otherwise go to the next step.

Step3 Judge whether the node is TcpEndpoint structure or not.

Transfer the virtual address of the ndoe to physical address and locate the address in the memory image file. Put 0x180 bytes from this position into a buffer. Read 4 bytes at buffer's offset 0x14 and judge whether the value is a pointer which point to a

EPROCESS structure or not. If the value is a pointer which point to a EPROCESS structure, go to step 5, otherwise it indicates that the node's structure is TCB structure, go to the next step.

Step4 Analyze TCB structure.

Step4.1 Get PID (process id) which is the ID of the process which established this connection. The pointer which points to the process's EPROCESS structure which established this connection is set at the offset 0x164 relative to TCB structure. Firstly, read 4 bytes which represents the virtual address of EPROCESS structure at buffer's offset 0x164 and transfer it to physical address. Secondly, locate the address in the memory image file and read 4 bytes which represents PID at the offset 0x9c relative to EPROCESS structure's physical address.

Step4.2 Get establishing time of this connection. The number is set at the offset 0x16c of TCB structure . Read 8 bytes at offset 0x16c of the buffer and it represents establishing time.

Step4.3 Get the local port of this connection. The number is set at offset 0x2c of TCB structure. Read 2 bytes at offset 0x2c of the buffer and transfer it to a decimal which is the local port of this connection.

Step4.4 Get the remote port of this connection. The number is set at the offset 0x2e of TCB structure. Read 2 bytes at offset 0x2e of the buffer and transfer it to a decimal which is the remote port of this connection.

Step4.5 Get local address and remote address of this connection. The pointer which points to NL_PATH structure is set at the offset 0x10 of TCB structure. The pointer which points to the remote address is set at the offset 0x08 of NL_PATH structure. The special algorithm is as followes: read 4 bytes which represents the virtual address of NL_PATH structure at the offset 0x10 of TCB structure, transfer the virtual address of NL_PATH structure to physical address, locate the address+0x08 in the memory image file and read 4 bytes which represents remote address at this position. The pointer which points to NL_LOCAL_ADDRESS structure is set at the offset 0x0 of the TCB structure, The pointer which points to NL_ADDRESS_IDENTIFIER structure is set at the offset 0x0c of TCB structure, local address is set at the offset 0x0 of the NL_ADDRESS_IDENTIFIER structure. Therefore, local address can be acquired from the above three structures.

Step5 Get 4 bytes which represents the next node's virtual at the offset 0 of the buffer and go to step2.

5 Conclusion

In this paper, a method which can acquire network connection information on Windows Vista operating system memory image file based on memory pool allocation strategy is proposed. This method is reliable and efficient, because the data structure TcpEndpointPool exists in driver tcpip.sys for every Windows Vista operation system version and TcpEndpointPool structure will not change when Windows Vista operation system version changed. A software which implements this method is present as follows.

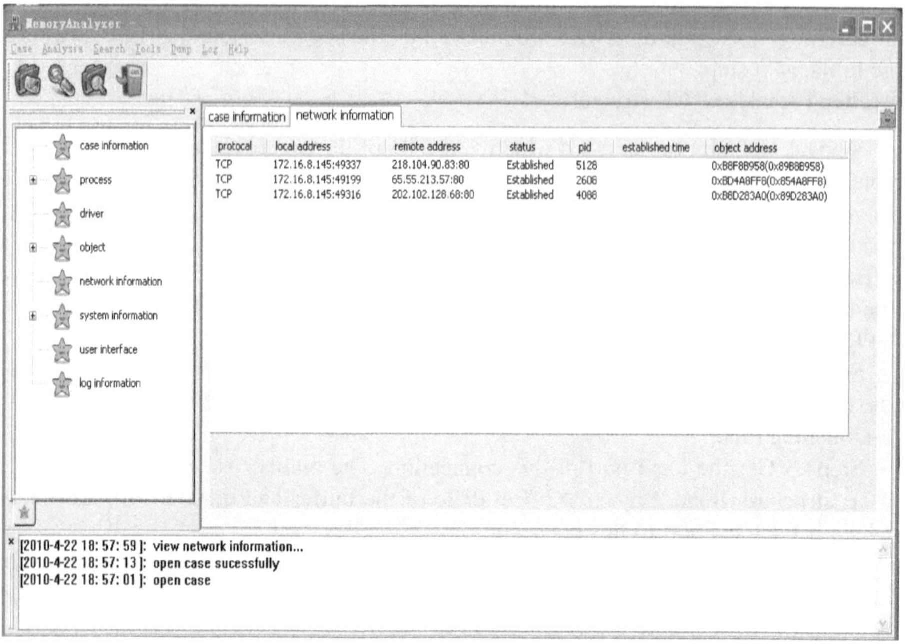

References

1. Brezinski, D., Killalea, T.: Guidelines for evidence collection and archiving. RFC 3227 (Best Current Practice) (February 2002), `http://www.ietf.org/rfc/rfc3227.txt`
2. Burdach, M.: Digital forensics of the physical memory, `http://forensic.seccure.net/pdf/mburdachdigitalforensicsofphysicalmemory.pdf`
3. Schuster, A.: Searching for processes and threads in Microsoft Windows memory dumps. Digital Investigation 3(supplement 1), 10–16 (2006)
4. Betz, C.: memparser, `http://www.dfrws.org/2005/challenge/memparser.shtml`
5. Walters, A., Petronic, N.: Volatools: integrating volatile memory forensics into the digital investigation process. Black Hat DC 2007 (2007)
6. Jones, K.J., Bejtlich, R., Rose, C.W.: Real Digital Forensics. Addison Wesley, Reading (2005)
7. Carvey, H.: Windows Froensics and Incident Recovery. Addison Wesley, Reading (2005)
8. Mandia, K., Prosise, C., Pepe, M.: Incident Response and Computer Forensics. McGrawHill Osborne Media (2003)
9. The Volatility Framework: Volatile memory artifact extraction utility framework, `https://www.volatilesystems.com/default/volatility/`
10. Schuster, S.: Pool allocations as an information source in windows memory forensics. In: Oliver, G., Dirk, S., Sandra, F., Hardo, H., Detlef, G., Jens, N. (eds.) IT-Incident Management & IT-Forensics-IMF 2006. Lecture notes in informatics, vol. P-97, pp. 104–115 (2006)
11. Zhang, R.C., Wang, L.H., Zhang, S.H.: Windows Memory Analysis Based on KPCR. In: 2009 Fifth International Conference on Information Assurance and Security, IAS, vol. 2, pp. 677–680 (2009)

A Stream Pattern Matching Method for Traffic Analysis*

Can Mo, Hui Li, and Hui Zhu

Lab of Computer Networks and Information Security,
Xidian University, Shaanxi 710071, P.R. China

Abstract. In this paper, we propose a stream pattern matching method that realizes a standard mechanism which combines different methods with complementary advantages. We define a specification of the stream pattern description, and parse it to the tree representation. Finally, the tree representation is transformed into the S-CG-NFA for recognition. This method provides a high level of recognition efficiency and accuracy.

Keywords: Traffic Recognition, Stream Pattern, Glushkov NFA.

1 Introduction

The most common traffic recognition method is the port-based method which maps port numbers to applications [1]. With the emergence of new applications, networks exceedingly carry more and more traffic that uses unpredicted port numbers which are dynamically allocated. As a consequence, the port-based method becomes insufficient and inaccurate in many cases.

The most accurate solution is payload-based method which searches the specific byte pattern-called signatures in all or part of the packets using deep packet inspection (DPI) technology[2,3], e.g. Web traffic contains the string 'GET'. However, there are many limits tied to this method. One of them is that some protocols are encrypted.

The statistics-based method utilizes the feature that different protocols correspond to different statistical characteristics [4]. For example, Web traffic is composed of short and small packets, while P2P traffic is usually composed of long and big packets. 289 kinds of statistical features of traffic or packets are presented in [5], including flow duration, payload size, packet inter-arrival time (IAT), and so on. However, this method can just coarsely classify the traffic into several classes, which limits the accuracy of traffic recognition, so this method can not be used alone.

In general, the currently available approaches mentioned above have respective strength and weakness, none of them performs well for all the different network data on the internet nowadays.

* Supported by "the Fundamental Research Funds for the Central Universities"(No.JY10000901018).

X. Lai et al. (Eds.): E-Forensics 2010, LNICST 56, pp. 131–140, 2011.

In this paper we propose a stream pattern matching method which implements a network traffic classification framework that is easy to update and configure. By the definition and specification design of the stream pattern, any kind of data stream with common features can be unambiguously described as a special stream pattern, according to a certain grammar and lexeme. Moreover the designed pattern combines different approaches at present, and can be flexibly written and expanded. In order to be easily understood by computer, a tree representation structure is obtained through a parser for the stream pattern. Then, for the recognition of network traffic, the parse tree is transformed into a Nondeterministic Finite Automata(NFA) with counters, called S-CG-NFA, and a stream pattern engine is built on it. The network traffic is sent to the stream pattern engine to get the matching result using the bit-parallel search algorithm.

The primary contribution of the stream pattern matching method is that three kinds of approaches (i.e, port-based method, payload-based method and statistics-based method) are combined in this method, and the efficiency of recognition is equivalent to a combined effect of these above approaches with complementary advantages, thus a more accurate recognition effect is achieved. Moreover, because of the standard syntax and unified way of parsing and identifying, the updating of the stream pattern is more simple than that of existing methods, so does the way of traffic recognition.

The remainder of this paper is organized as follows. Section 2 puts forward the definition and specification design of the stream pattern. The construction of a special stream parser based on the stream pattern is described in Section 3 and the generation of S-CG-NFA in Section 4. Experimental results can be found in Section 5. Section 6 presents the conclusion and some problems to be further solved.

2 The Design and Definition of the Stream Pattern

The stream pattern matching method proposed in our paper describes a network traffic classification framework that combines several classification approaches at present with complementary advantages and is easy to update and configure. The system framework is shown in Figure 1. First, the network traffic with certain features is described as the stream pattern. Second, a tree representation of the stream pattern is obtained by a stream parser. After that, the tree representation is transformed into S-CG-NFA to get the corresponding stream pattern matching engine. Any traffic to be recognized is first converted into characteristic flow through the collector, and then sent to the stream pattern engine. Finally, the matching result can be got from this engine. In this section, we will discuss the design and definition of the stream pattern.

The stream pattern is designed to be normative, and can unambiguously describe any protocol or behavior with certain characteristics based on the grammar and lexeme defined. Furthermore, for its good expansibility, the stream pattern can conveniently be added with any new characteristic.

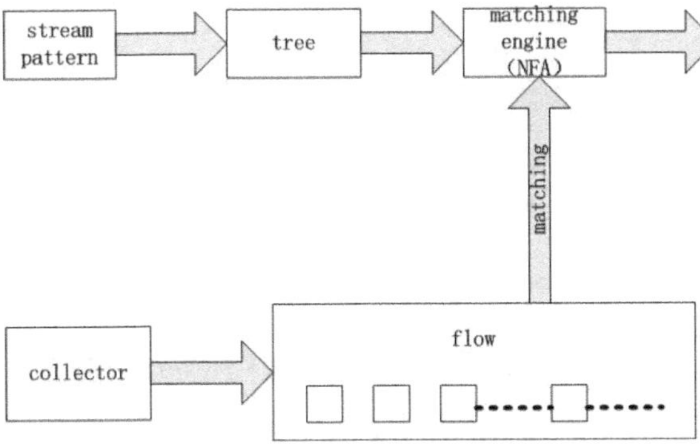

Fig. 1. system framework of the stream pattern matching

A stream pattern describes a whole data flow, and vice versa; that is, the stream pattern and the data flow are a one-to-one mapping. Here, the stream pattern is abstractly denoted as SM. Some formal definitions of the stream pattern are given in the following.

Definition 1. *A stream-character corresponds to a data packet in the data flow. It is the basic component of the stream pattern, which includes recognition features such as head information, payload information, statistical information, etc. The stream character is flexible to extend. The set of stream-character is denoted as $S\Sigma$, $s\omega \in S\Sigma$ denotes a formal stream-character, the empty stream-character is denoted as $s\epsilon$, the wildcards are denoted as "$\textcircled{sw}$".*

Definition 2. *A stream-operator describes the relationship between stream-characters. It is a basic component of the stream pattern including "$\textcircled{(}$", "$\textcircled{)}$", "$\circledast$", "$\oplus$", "$\textcircled{?}$", "$\textcircled{\{\}}$", "$\textcircled{|}$", "$\odot$". The meaning of stream operators is described in Definition 4.*

Definition 3. *A stream pattern is a symbol sequence on the set of symbols $s\omega \in S\Sigma \bigcup \{s\epsilon, \textcircled{sw}, \textcircled{(}, \textcircled{)}, \circledast, \oplus, \textcircled{?}, \textcircled{\{\}}, \textcircled{|}, \odot\}$ which is recursively defined according to a certain generating grammar. The generating grammar is as follows:*

$$
\begin{array}{ll}
SM \longrightarrow s\epsilon; & SM \longrightarrow s\omega \\
SM \longrightarrow \textcircled{(}SM\textcircled{)}; & SM \longrightarrow SM \odot SM \\
SM \longrightarrow SM\textcircled{|}SM; & SM \longrightarrow \circledast \\
SM \longrightarrow SM\oplus; & SM \longrightarrow SM\textcircled{?} \\
SM \longrightarrow SM\textcircled{\{\}}. &
\end{array}
$$

Definition 4. *The network data flow represented by a stream pattern SM is described as $L(SM)$ and the meaning of each stream-operator is described as follows:*

For any $s\omega \in S\Sigma \bigcup s\epsilon$,

$$L(s\omega) = s\omega \tag{1}$$

$$L(SM_1 \oplus SM_2) = L(SM_1) \bigcup L(SM_2) \tag{2}$$

Equation 2 represents a union of the stream pattern SM_1 *and* SM_2.

$$L(SM_1 \odot SM_2) = L(SM_1) \bullet L(SM_2) \tag{3}$$

Equation 3 represents a concatenation of the stream pattern SM_1 *and* SM_2.

$$L(SM^{\circledast}) = \bigcup_{i \geq 0} L(SM)^i \tag{4}$$

Equation 4 represents a concatenation of zero or more sub-stream patterns represented by SM.

$$L(SM^{\oplus}) = \bigcup_{i \geq 1} L(SM)^i \tag{5}$$

Equation 5 represents a concatenation of one or more sub-stream patterns represented by SM.

$$L(SM^{?}) = L(SM) \bigcup L(s\epsilon) \tag{6}$$

Equation 6 represents a concatenation of zero or one sub-stream pattern represented by SM.

$$L(SM^{\{\}}) = \bigcup_{m \leq i \leq n} L(SM)^i \tag{7}$$

Equation 7 represents that the sub-stream pattern is repeated a number of times specified by a lower and upper limit.

The stream-character contains three kinds of characteristics such as head information, payload information and statistics information. The characteristics used are shown in Table 1.

Any additional characteristic to the benefit of recognizing network traffic can be added to the stream pattern based on the specification defined above.

Table 1. Characteristic of stream-character

characteristic classes	feature items
head	source IP, destination IP, source port, destination port
payload	origin, offset, content
statistics	packet size, inter-arrival-time of packet, direction of packet

3 The Construction of the Parse Tree

After the design and definition of the stream pattern, we parse the stream pattern to obtain a tree representation, called parse tree that can be easily understood by computer to perform calculations. The parse tree corresponds to the stream pattern one-to-one: the leaves of the tree are labeled with stream-character, the intermediate nodes are labeled with the stream-operator, and recursively the sub tree corresponds to the sub stream pattern.

The grammar for the stream pattern is too complex for a lexical analyzer and too simple for a full bottom-up parser. Therefore, a special parser for the stream pattern is built, which is shown in Figure 2. Here "θ" represents an empty tree, ST represents an empty stack. The end of the stream is marked with ψ.

Parse($SM = s\omega_1, s\omega_2, \ldots, s\omega_i, \ldots, s\omega_n, last, ST$)
    $\nu \longleftarrow \theta$
    While $SM_{last} \neq \psi$ Do
        If $SM_{last} \in S\Sigma$ OR $SM_{last} = s\epsilon$ Then
            $\nu_r \longleftarrow$Create a node with SM_{last}
            If $\nu \neq \theta$ Then
                $\nu \longleftarrow [\odot](\nu, \nu_r)$
            Else $\nu \longleftarrow \nu_r$
            $last \longleftarrow last + 1$
    Else If $SM_{last} = \textcircled{|}$ Then
        if $\nu = \theta$
            Return Error
        $(\nu_r, last) \longleftarrow$ Parse($SM, last + 1, ST$)
        $\nu \longleftarrow [\textcircled{|}](\nu, \nu_r)$
    Else If $SM_{last} = \circledast$ Then
        $\nu \longleftarrow [\circledast](\nu)$
        $last \longleftarrow last + 1$
    Else If $SM_{last} = \oplus$ Then
        $\nu \longleftarrow [\oplus](\nu)$
        $last \longleftarrow last + 1$
    Else If $SM_{last} = \textcircled{?}$ Then
        $\nu \longleftarrow [\textcircled{?}](\nu)$
        $last \longleftarrow last + 1$
    Else If $SM_{last} = \textcircled{\{\}}$ Then
        $\nu \longleftarrow [\textcircled{\{\}}](\nu)$
        $last \longleftarrow last + 1$
    Else If $SM_{last} = \textcircled{(}$ Then
        PUSH(ST)
        $(\nu_r, last) \longleftarrow$ Parse($SM, last + 1, ST$)
        If $\nu \neq \theta$ Then
            $\nu \longleftarrow [\odot](\nu, \nu_r)$
        Else

```
            ν ⟵ ν_r
            last ⟵ last + 1
      Else If SM_last = ◯) Then
            POP(ST)
            Return(ν,last)
      End of If
End of While
If !EMPTY(ST)
      Return Error
Else Return(ν,last)
```

Fig. 2. The parse algorithm of the stream pattern

4 The Generation of S-CG-NFA

For recognition, the tree representation should be transformed into automata. Considering the features of the stream pattern and network traffic, a special automata for the stream pattern, called S-CG-NFA is presented which is based on Glushkov NFA [6,7] and extended with counters to better resolve numerical constraints. Automata with counter has been proposed in many papers, and has well resolved the problem of constrained repetitions [8,9,10,11,12,13]. Therefore, referred to the method presented in the reference [13], the construction of S-CG-NFA is given in the following.

For simplicity, we first give some statements to better resolve constrained repetitions. A sub-stream pattern of the form ◯{} is called an iterator. Each iterator c contains a lower limit as $lower(c)$, an upper limit as $upper(c)$ and a counter as cv(c). We denote by $iterator(x)$ the list of all the iterated sub stream patterns which contain stream-character x; we denote by $iterator(x, y)$ the list of all the iterated sub stream patterns which contain stream-character x, expect stream-character y. Several functions about iterators are defined as follows.

1. value_test(C): true if $lower(C) \leq cv(C) \leq upper(C)$, else false; check whether the value of cv(C) is between the lower limit and upper limit.
2. reset(C): $cv(C) = 1$; the counter of iterator C is reset to 1.
3. update(C): $cv(C)$++; the counter of iterator C is increased by 1.

Now, we give the construction of S-CG-NFA. S-CG-NFA is generated on the basis of the sets $First$, $Last$, $Empty$, $Follow$ and C. Here, the definitions of sets $First$, $Last$ and $Empty$ are the same as in the standard Glushkov construction, which will not be explained further. However, it is necessary to state that the set of C indicates all the iterators in the stream pattern, and the set $Follow$ being different from the standard set $Follow$ containing a $two-tuples(x, y)$, contains a $triple(x, y, c)$, where x and y are the positions of the stream-character in the stream pattern and c can be null or the iterator in the set C.

So the S-CG-NFA that represents the stream pattern is built in the following way.

$$\text{S-CG-NFA} = (Q_{SM} \bigcup \{q_0\}, S\Sigma^*, C, \delta_{SM}, q_0, F_{SM}) \tag{8}$$

In Equation (8), where

1. Q_{SM} is the set of states and the initial state is $q_0 = 0$;
2. $S\Sigma^*$ is the set of transition conditions, and is constituted with triple(*conid*, *sw*, *actid*). Among them, the element $sw \in S\Sigma$ is a stream-character, the element *conid* represents the set of conditional iterators and the element *actid* represents the set of responding iterators;
3. F_{SM} is the set of final states. For every element $x \in last$, if value_test(iterator(x)) = true, then $q_x \in F_{SM}$;
4. C is the set of all the iterators in the stream pattern;
5. δ_{SM} is the transition function of the automaton. $\delta_{SM} = (q_s, tc, \varphi, \pi, q_f)$; that is, for all $y \in first$, (0, (*null*, sw_y, *null*), true, Φ, y) $\in \delta_{SM}$; for all $x \in$Pos(SM) and (y, SM')$\in follow$, (x, (*conid*, sw_y, *actid*), φ, π, y) $\in \delta_{SM}$ if and only if φ=true. Among them, if $SM' = null$, then *conid* = iterator(x, y); *actid* = *null*, φ= value_test(*conid*), π = reset(*conid*); otherwise, *conid* = iterator(x, SM'); *actid* = SM', φ = value_test(*conid*), π = reset(*conid*)$\bigcup$ update(*actid*).

So far, the whole construction process of S-CG-NFA has been described. Considering the complexity of S-CG-NFA, here we use the one-pass scan algorithm and the bit-parallel search algorithm to recognize the network traffic data.

5 Experimental Evaluation

In the above section, we give the design and realization of the stream pattern matching engine which is implemented in C/C++ development environment and on the basis of function library LibXML2 [14]. In this section, we briefly present an experimental evaluation on the effect of the stream pattern matching technology. We take the HTTP protocol for example and give two kinds of stream patterns describing HTTP. Stream pattern 1 describes HTTP just contains port information which is shown in Figure 3. Stream pattern 2 describes HTTP combined with port information and payload information which is shown in Figure 4.

The two stream patterns are applied in four traces to separately get the total number of HTTP flows recognized. The four traces are from DARPA data sets [15](1998, Tuesday in the third week, 82.9M; 1998, Wednesday in the fourth week, 76.6M; 1998, Friday in the fourth week, 76.1M; 1998, Wednesday in the fifth week, 93.5M). A list file records the number of http flows got by port-based method in each trace which is selected as the base of comparison. The recognition result is shown in Table 2, where the first column corresponds to the number of http flows recorded in the list file, the second column corresponds to the number of http flows recognized by stream pattern 1 and the third column corresponds to the number of http flows recognized by stream pattern 2.

```
 <mode>
      <element type_id=‘‘word">
          <head>
             <dport>80</dport>
         </head>
         <content>NULL</content>
        <statistic>
            <dir>0</dir>
        </statistic>
</mode>
```

Fig. 3. Stream pattern 1 for HTTP

```
 <mode>
     <element type_id=‘‘word">
         <head>
             <dport>80</dport>
         </head>
         <content>
             <within>100</within>
             <offset>0</offset>
             <con>GET</con>
         </content>
         <statistic>
             <dir>0</dir>
         </statistic>
     </element>
     <element type_id=‘‘word">
         <head>
             <sport>80</sport>
         </head>
         <content>
             <within>100</within>
             <offset>0</offset>
             <con>HTTP</con>
         </content>
         <statistic>
             <dir>1</dir>
         </statistic>
     </element>
</mode>
```

Fig. 4. Stream pattern 2 for HTTP

Table 2. recognition result for HTTP

Trace file	list file	stream pattern 1	stream pattern 2
Trace 1	5016	5016	5016
Trace 2	4694	4694	766
Trace 3	2233	2233	158
Trace 4	4833	4833	67

Table 2 shows that the stream pattern matching engine can be reduced to port-based method using stream pattern 1 to achieve 100% recognition rate, that is the stream pattern matching technology can have the same effect as the port-based method. However, due to the existence of incomplete data flows which just contain handshake information and have no transmission content, the number of flows recognized by stream pattern 2 is less than stream pattern 1, since some fake http flows are removed. So at some point, the recognition accuracy of stream pattern 2 which combines both port-based method and payload-based method is higher.

From the above, it is clear that the stream pattern matching technology not only can combine different methods with complementary advantages, but also is easy to expand.

6 Conclusion and Future Work

In this paper, we have introduced a stream pattern matching technology, which provides a recognition framework that combines three kinds of recognition methods with complementary advantages. It is easy to configure and update. We provide a formal definition of the stream pattern, and then convert the text form of the stream pattern into the tree representation. Finally, we transform the parser tree to the S-CG-NFA, a special automata for the stream pattern to generate the stream pattern matching engine. We performed a system test and the test result shows the effectiveness of the stream pattern matching engine.

However, there are some aspects that need further effort.

1. The generation of the stream pattern: the stream pattern is manually written after the manual analysis of network data or the reference to the existing literature, so the validity and reliability of the generation way of the stream pattern are challenging and need to be improved. And also the automatic generation of the stream pattern is a future direction.
2. The speed of matching: Since different protocols correspond to different matching engines and any network data that needs to be recognized should be sent to every engine, so the processing speed of matching engine is highly demanded. Therefore, the study of parallel processing is a vital task.

References

1. IANA, http://www.iana.org/assignments/port-numbers
2. Kang, H.-J., Kim, M.-S., Hong, J.W.-K.: A method on multimedia service traffic monitoring and analysis. In: Brunner, M., Keller, A. (eds.) DSOM 2003. LNCS, vol. 2867, pp. 93–105. Springer, Heidelberg (2003)
3. Levandoski, J., Sommer, E., Strait, M.: Application Layer Packet Classifier for Linux[CP/OL] (2006), http://17-filter.sourceforge.net/
4. Zuev, D., Moore, A.W.: Traffic classification using a statistical approach. In: Dovrolis, C. (ed.) PAM 2005. LNCS, vol. 3431, pp. 321–324. Springer, Heidelberg (2005)
5. Moore A.W., Zuev D., Crogan M.: Discriminators for use in flow based classification. Department of Computer Science, Queen Mary, University of London (2005)
6. Berry, G., Sethi, R.: From regular expression to deterministic automata. Theoretical Computer Science 48(1), 117–126 (1986)
7. Chang, C.H., Paige, R.: From regular expression to DFA's using NFA's. In: Proceedings of the 3rd Annual Symposium on Combinatorial Pattern Matching. LNCS, vol. 664, pp. 90–110. Springer, Heidelberg (1992)
8. Kilpeläinen, P., Tuhkanen, R.: Regular Expressions with Numerical Occurrence Indicators-preliminary results. In: Proceedings of the Eighth Symposium on Programming Languages and Software Tools, SPLST 2003, Kuopio, Finland, pp. 163–173 (2003)
9. Kilpeläinen, P., Tuhkanen, R.: One-unambiguity of regular expressions with numeric occurrence indicators. Inf. Comput 205(6), 890–916 (2007)
10. Becchi, M., Crowley, P.: Extending Finite Automata to Efficiently Match Perl-Compatible Regular Expressions. In: Proceedings of the 2008 ACM Conference on Emerging Network Experiment and Technology, CoNEXT 2008, Madrid, Spain, vol. 25 (2008)
11. Becchi, M., Crowley, P.: A Hybrid Finite Automaton for Practical Deep Packet Inspection. In: ACM CoNEXT 2007, New York, NY, USA, pp. 1–12 (2007)
12. Yun, S., Lee, K.: Regular Expression Pattern Matching Supporting Constrained Repetitions. In: Proceedings of Reconfigurable Computing: Architectures, Tools and Applications, 5th International Workshop, Karlsruhe, Germany, pp. 300–305 (2009)
13. Gelade, W., Gyssens, M., Martens, W.: Regular Expressions with Counting: Weak versus Strong Determinism. In: Proceedings of Mathematical Foundations of Computer Science 2009, 34th International Symposium, Novy Smokovec, High Tatras, Slovakia, pp. 369–381 (2009)
14. LIBXML, http://www.xmlsoft.org/
15. DARPA, http://www.ll.mit.edu/mission/communications/ist/corpora/ideval/data/index.html

Fast in-Place File Carving for Digital Forensics*

Xinyan Zha and Sartaj Sahni

Computer and Information Science and Engineering
University of Florida
Gainesville, FL 32611
{xzha,sahni}@cise.ufl.edu

Abstract. Scalpel, a popular open source file recovery tool, performs file carving using the Boyer-Moore string search algorithm to locate headers and footers in a disk image. We show that the time required for file carving may be reduced significantly by employing multi-pattern search algorithms such as the multipattern Boyer-Moore and Aho-Corasick algorithms as well as asynchronous disk reads and multithreading as typically supported on multicore commodity PCs. Using these methods, we are able to do in-place file carving in essentially the time it takes to read the disk whose files are being carved. Since, using our methods, the limiting factor for performance is the disk read time, there is no advantage to using accelerators such as GPUs as has been proposed by others. To further speed in-place file carving, we would need a mechanism to read disk faster.

Keywords: Digital forensics, Scalpel, Aho-Corasick, multipattern Boyer-Moore, multicore computing, asynchronous disk read.

1 Introduction

The normal way to retrieve a file from a disk is to search the disk directory, obtain the file's metadata (e.g., location on disk) from the directory, and then use this information to fetch the file from the disk. Often, even when a file has been deleted, it is possible to retrieve a file using this method as typically when a file is deleted, a delete flag is set in the disk directory and the remainder of the directory metadata associated with the deleted file unaltered. Of course, the creation of new files or changes to remaining files following a delete may make it impossible to retrieve the deleted file using the disk directory as the new files' metadata may overwrite the deleted file's metadata in the directory and changes to the remaining files may use the disk blocks previously used by the deleted file.

In file carving, we attempt to recover files from a target disk whose directory entries have been corrupted. In the extreme case the entire directory is corrupted and all files on the disk are to be recovered using no metadata. The recovery of disk files in the absence of directory metadata is done using header and footer

* This research was supported, in part, by the National Science Foundation under grants 0829916 and CNS-0963812.

X. Lai et al. (Eds.): E-Forensics 2010, LNICST 56, pp. 141–158, 2011.

information for the file types we wish to recover. Figure 1 gives the header and footer for a few popular file types. This information was obtained from the Scalpel configuration file [9]. \x[0-f][0-f] denotes a hexadecimal value while \[0-3][0-7][0-7] is an octal value. So, for example, "\x4F\123\I\sCCI" decodes to "OSI CCI". In file carving, we view a disk as being serial storage (the serialization being done by sequentializing disk blocks) and extract all disk segments that lie between a header and its corresponding footer as being candidates for the files to be recovered. For example, a disk segment that begins with the string "<html" and ends with the string "</html>" is carved into an *htm* file.

Since a file may not actually reside in a consecutive sequence of disk blocks, the recovery process employed in file carving is clearly prone to error. Nonetheless, file carving recovers disk segments delimited by a header and its corresponding footer that potentially represent a file. These recovered segments may be analyzed later using some other process to eliminate false positives. Notice that some file types may have no associated footer (e.g., *txt* files have a header specified in Figure 1 but no footer). Additionally, even when a file type has a specified header and a footer one of these may be absent in the disk because of disk corruption (for example). So, additional information (such as maximum length of file to be carved for each file type) is used in the file carving process. See [7] for a review of file carving methods.

Scalpel [9] is an improved version of the file carver Foremost [13]. At present, Scalpel is the most popular open source file carver available. Scalpel carves files in two phases. In the first phase, Scalpel searches the disk image to determine the location of headers and footers. This phase results in a database with entries such as those shown in Figure 2. This database contains the metadata (i.e., start location of file, file length, file type, etc.) for the files to be carved. Since the names of the files cannot be recovered (as these are typically stored only in the disk directory, which is presumed to be unavailable), synthetic names are assigned to the carved files in the generated metadata database.

The second phase of Scalpel uses the metadata database created in the first phase to carve files from the corrupted disk and write these carved files to a new disk. Even with maximum file length limits placed on the size of files to be recovered, a very large amount of disk space may be needed to store the carved files. For example, Richard et al. [11] reports a recovery case in which "*carving a wide range of file types for a modest 8GB target yielded over 1.1 million files, with a total size exceeding the capacity of one of our 250GB drives.*"

file type	header	footer
gif	\x47\x49\x46\x38\x37\x61	\x00\x3b
gif	\x47\x49\x46\x38\x39\x61	\x00\x3b
jpg	\xff\xd8\xff\xe0\x00\x10	\xff\xd9
htm	<html	</html>
txt	——BEGIN\040PGP	
zip	PK\x03\x04	\x3c\xac

Fig. 1. Example headers and footers in Scalpel's configuration file

As observed by Richard et al. [11], because of the very large number of false positives generated by the file carving process, file carving can be very expensive both in terms of the time taken and the amount of disk space required to store the carved files. To overcome these deficiencies of file carving, Richard et al. [11] propose in-place file carving, which essentially generates only the metadata database of Figure 2. The metadata database can be examined by an expert and many of the false positives eliminated. The remaining entries in the metadata database may be examined further to recover only desired files. Since the runtime of a file carver is typically dominated by the time for phase 2, on-line file carvers take much less time than do file carvers. Additionally, the size of even a 1 million entry metadata database is less than 60MB [11]. So, in-place carving requires less disk space as well.

Although in-place file carving is considerably faster than file carving, it still takes a large amount of time. For example, in-place file carving of an 16GB flash drive with a set of 48 rules (header and footer combinations) using the first phase of Scalpel 1.6 takes more than 30 minutes on an AMD Athlon PC equipped with a 2.6GHZ Core2Duo processor and 2GB RAM. Marziale et al. [10] have proposed the use of massive threads as supported by a GPU to improve the performance of an in-place file carver. In this paper, we demonstrate that hardware accelerators such as GPUs are of little benefit when doing an in-place file carving. Specifically, by replacing the search algorithm used in Scalpel 1.6 with a multipattern search algorithm such as the multipattern Boyer Moore [15,8,14] and Aho-Corasick [1] algorithms and doing disk reads asynchronously, the overall time for in-place file carving using Scalpel 1.6 becomes very comparable to the time taken to just read the target disk that is being carved. So, the limiting factor is disk I/O and not CPU processing. Further reduction in the time spent searching the target disk for footers and headers, as possibly attainable using a GPU, cannot possibly reduce overall time to below the time needed to just read the target disk. To get further improvement in performance, we need improvement in disk I/O.

The remainder of the paper is organized as follows. Section 2 describes the search process employed by Scalpel 1.6 to identify headers and footers in the target disk. In Sections 3 and 4, respectively, we describe the Boyer-Moore and Aho-Corasick multipattern matching algorithms. Our dual-core search strategy is described in Section 5 and our asynchronous read strategy is described in Section 6. In Section 7 we describe strategies for a multicore in-place file carver. Experimental results demonstrating the effectiveness of our methods are presented in Section 8.

filename	start	truncated	length	image
gif/0000001.gif	27465830	NO	2746	/tmp/linux-image
gif/0000006.gif	45496392	NO	4234	/tmp/linux-image
jpg/0000047.jpg	55645747	NO	675	/tmp/linux-image
htm/0000013.htm	23123244	NO	823	/tmp/linux-image
txt/0000021.txt	34235233	NO	56	/tmp/linux-image
zip/0000008.zip	76452352	NO	1423646	/tmp/linux-image

Fig. 2. Examples of in-place file carving output

2 In-Place Carving Using Scalpel 1.6

There are essentially two tasks associated with in-place carving–(a) identify the location of specified headers and footers in the target disk and (b) pair headers and corresponding footers while respecting the additional constraints (e.g., maximum file length) specified by the user. The time required for (b) is insignificant compared to that required for (a). So, we focus on (a).

Scalpel 1.6 locates headers and footers by searching the target disk using a buffer of size 10MB. Figure 3(a) gives the high-level control flow of Scalpel 1.6. A 10MB buffer is filled from disk and then searched for headers and footers. This process is repeated until the entire disk has been searched. When the search moves from one buffer to the next, care is exercised to ensure that headers/footers that span a buffer boundary are detected. Searching within a buffer is done using the algorithm of Figure 3(b). In each buffer, we first search for headers. The search for headers is followed by a search for footers. Only non-null footers that are within the maximum carving length of an already found header are searched for.

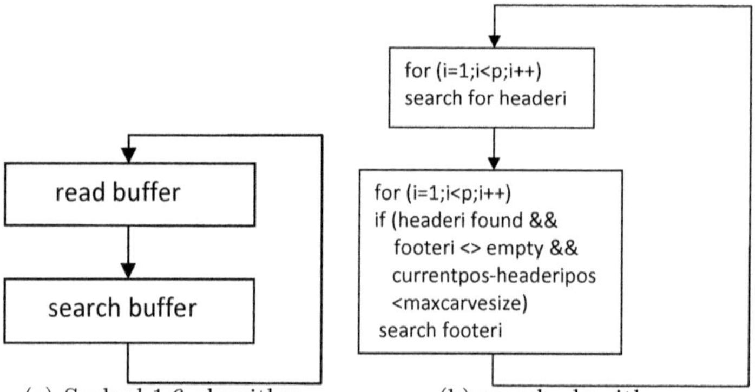

(a) Scalpel 1.6 algorithm (b) search algorithm

Fig. 3. Control flow Scalpel 1.6

To search a buffer for an individual header of footer, Scalpel 1.6 uses the Boyer-Moore pattern matching algorithm [4], which was developed to find all occurrences of a pattern P in a string S.. This algorithm begins by positioning the first character of P at the first character of S. This results in a pairing of the first $|P|$ characters of S with characters of P. The characters in each pair are compared beginning with those in the rightmost pair. If all pairs of characters match, we have found an occurrence of P in S and P is shifted right by 1 character (or by $|P|$ if only non-overlapping matches are to be found). Otherwise, we stop at the rightmost pair (or first pair since we compare right to left) where there is a mismatch and use the *bad character function* for P to determine how many characters to shift P right before re-examining pairs of characters from P and S for a match. More specifically, the bad character function for P gives the distance from the end of P of the last occurrence of each possible character that may appear in S. So, for example, if the characters of S are drawn from the alphabet $\{a, b, c, d\}$, the bad character function, B, for $P =$ "abcabcd" has $B(a) = 4$, $B(b) = 3$, $B(c)= 2$, and $B(d) = 1$. In practice, many of the shifts in the bad character function of a pattern are close to the length, $|P|$, of the pattern P making the Boyer-Moore algorithm a very fast search algorithm. In fact, when the alphabet size is large, the average run time of the Boyer-Moore algorithm is $O(|S|/|P|)$. Galil [5] has proposed a variation for which the worst-case run time is $O(|S|)$. Horspool [6] proposes a simplification to the Boyer-Moore algorithm whose performance is about the same as that of the Boyer-Moore algorithm.

Even though the Boyer-Moore algorithm is a very fast way to find all occurrences of a pattern in a string, using it in our in-place carving application isn't optimal because we must use the algorithm once for each pattern (header/footer) to be searched. So, the time to search for all patterns grows linearly in the number of patterns. Locating headers and footers using the Boyer-Moore algorithm, as is done in Scalpel 1.6, takes $O(mn)$ time where m is the number of file types being searched and n is the size of the target disk. Consequently, the run time for in-place carving grows linearly with both the number of file types and the size of the target disk. Doubling either the number of file types or the disk size will double the expected run time; doubling both will quadruple the run time. However, when a multipattern search algorithm is used, the run time is $O(n)$ (both expected and worst case). That is, the time is independent of the number of file types. Whether we are searching for 20 file types or 40, the time to find the locations of all headers and footers is the same!

3 Multipattern Boyer-Moore Algorithm

Several multipattern extensions to the Boyer-Moore search algorithm have been proposed [2,15,14,8]. All of these multipattern search algorithms extend the basic bad character function employed by the Boyer-Moore algorithm to a bad character function for a set of patterns. This is done by combining the bad character functions for the individual patterns to be searched into a single bad character function for the entire set of patterns. The combined bad character function B for a set of p patterns has

$$B(c) = min\{B_i(c), 1 \leq i \leq p\}$$

for each character c in the alphabet. Here B_i is the bad character function for the ith pattern. The Set-wise Boyer-Moore algorithm of [14] performs multipattern matching using this combined bad function. The multipattern search algorithms of [2,15,8] employ additional techniques to speed the search further. The average run time of the algorithms of [2,15,8] is $O(|S|/minL)$, where $minL$ is the length of the shortest pattern. Baeza and Gonnet [3] extend multipattern matching to allow for don't cares and complements in patterns. This extension isn't required for our in-place file carving application.

abcaabb
abcaabbcc
acb
acbccabb
ccabb
bccabc
bbccabca

Fig. 4. An example pattern set

4 Aho-Corasick Algorithm

The Aho-Corasick algorithm [1] for multipattern matching uses a finite automaton to process the target string S. When a character of the target string is examined, one or more finite automaton moves are made. Aho and Corasick [1] propose two versions of their automaton–unoptimized and optimized–for multi-pattern matching. In the unoptimized version, there is a failure pointer for each state while in the optimized version, which we propose using for in-place file carving, no state has a failure pointer. In both versions, each state has success pointers and each success pointer has an associated label, which is a character from the string alphabet. Also, each state has a list of patterns/rules (from the pattern database) that are matched when that state is reached by following a success pointer. This is the list of matched rules.

In the unoptimized version, the search starts with the automaton start state designated as the current state and the first character in the text string, S, that is being searched designated as the current character. At each step, a state transition is made by examining the current character of S. If the current state has a success pointer labeled by the current character, a transition to the state pointed at by this success pointer is made and the next character of S becomes the current character. When there is no corresponding success pointer, a transition to the state pointed at by the failure pointer is made and the current character is not changed. Whenever a state is reached by following a success pointer, the rules in the list of matched rules for the reached state are output along with the position in S of the current character. This output is sufficient to identify all occurrences, in S, of all database strings. Aho and Corasick [1] have shown that when their unoptimized automaton is used, the total number of state transitions is $2n$, where n is the length of S.

In the optimized version, each state has a success pointer for every character in the alphabet and so, there is no failure pointer. Aho and Corasick [1] show how to compute the success pointer for pairs of states and characters for which there is no success pointer in the unoptimized automaton thereby transforming a unoptimized automaton into an optimized one. The number of state transitions made by an optimized automaton when searching for matches in a string of length n is n.

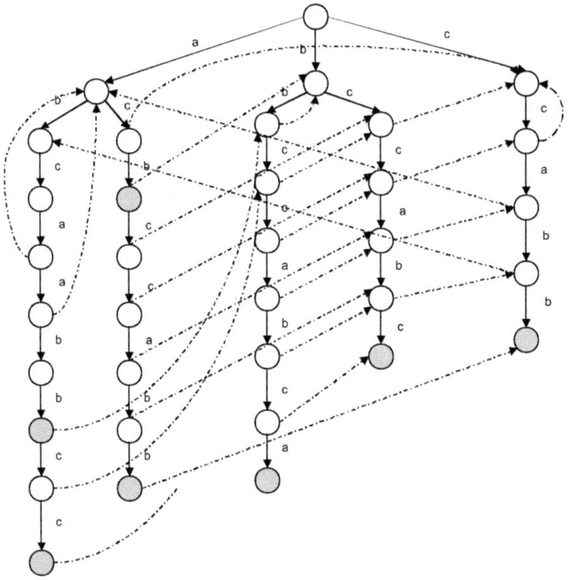

Fig. 5. Unoptimized Aho-Corasick automata for strings of Figure 4

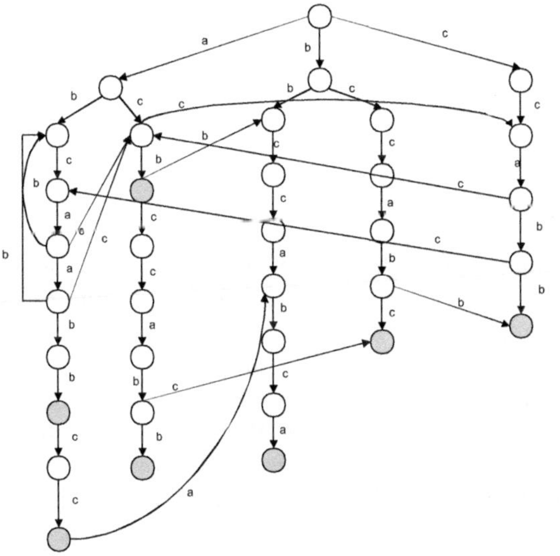

Fig. 6. Optimized Aho-Corasick automata for strings of Figure 4

Figure 4 shows an example set of patterns drawn from the 3-letter alphabet {a,b,c}. Figures 5 and 6, respectively, show the unoptimized and optimized Aho-Corasick automata for this set of patterns.

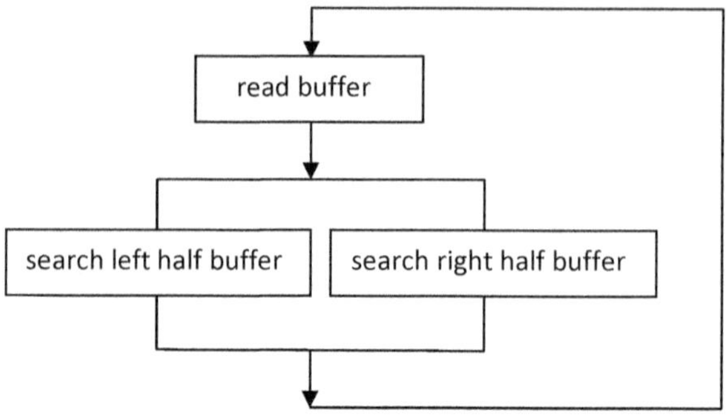

Fig. 7. Control flow for 2-threaded search

5 Multicore Searching

Contemporary commodity PCs have either a dualcore or quadcore processor. We may exploit the availability of more than one core to speed the search for headers and footers. This is done by creating as many threads as the number of cores (experiments indicate that there is no performance gain when we use more threads than the number of cores). Each thread searches a portion of the string S. So, if the number of threads is t, each thread searches a substring of size $|S|/t$ plus the length of the longest pattern minus 1. Figure 7 shows the control flow when two threads are used to do the search.

6 Asynchronous Read

Scalpel 1.6 fills its search buffer using *synchronous* (or blocking) reads of the target disk. In a synchronous read, the CPU is unable to do any computing while the read is in progress. Contemporary PCs, however, permit *asynchronous* (or non-blocking) reads of disk. When an asynchronous read is done, the CPU is able to perform computations that do not involve the data being read from disk while the disk read is in progress. When asynchronous reads are used, we need two buffers–active and inactive. In the steady state, our computer is doing an asynchronous read into the inactive buffer while simultaneously searching the active buffer. When the search of the active buffer completes, we wait for the ongoing asynchronous read to complete, swap the roles of the active and inactive buffers, initiate a new asynchronous read into the current inactive buffer, and proceed to search the current active buffer. This is stated more formally in Figure 8.

Let T_{read} be the time needed to read the target disk and let T_{search} be the time needed to search for headers and footers (exclusive of the time to read from disk). When synchronous reads are used as in Figure 3, the total time for in-place carving is approximately $T_{read} + T_{search}$ (note that the time required

```
Algorithm Asynchronous
begin
   read activebuffer
   repeat
    if there is more input
       asynchronous read inactivebuffer
    search activebuffer
    wait for asynchronous read (if any) to complete
    swap the roles of the 2 buffers
   until done
end
```

Fig. 8. In-place carving using asynchronous reads

for task (b) of in-place carving is relatively small). When asynchronous reads are used, all but the first buffer is read concurrently with the search of another buffer. So, the time for each iteration of the `repeat-until` loop is the larger of the time to read a buffer and that to search the buffer. When the buffer read time is consistently larger than the buffer search time or when the buffer search time is consistently larger than the buffer read time, the total in-place carving time using asynchronous reads is approximately $\max\{T_{read}, T_{search}\}$. Therefore, using asynchronous reads rather than synchronous reads has the potential to reduce run time by as much as 50%. The search algorithms of Sections 2 and 3, other than the Aho-Corasick algorithm, employ heuristics whose effectiveness depends on both the rule set and the actual contents of the buffer being searched. As a result, it is entirely possible that when we search one buffer, the read time exceeds the search time while when another buffer is searched, the read time exceeds the search time. So, when these search methods are used, it is possible that the in-place carving time is somewhat more than $\max\{T_{read}, T_{search}\}$.

7 Multicore in-Place Carving

In Section 5 we saw how to use multiple cores to speed the search for headers and footers. Task (a) of in-place carving, however, needs to both read data from disk and search the data that is read. There are several ways in which we can utilize the available cores to perform both these tasks. The first is to use synchronous reads followed by multicore searching as described in Section 5. We refer to this strategy as SRMS (synchronous read multicore search). Extension to a larger number of cores is straightforward.

The second possibility is to use one thread to read a buffer using a synchronous read and the second to do the search (Figure 9). We refer to this strategy as SRSS (single core read and single core search).

A third possibility is to use 4 buffers and have each thread run the asynchronous read algorithm of Figure 8 as shown in Figures 10 and 11. In Figure 10 the threads are synchronized for every pair of buffers searched while in Figure 11,

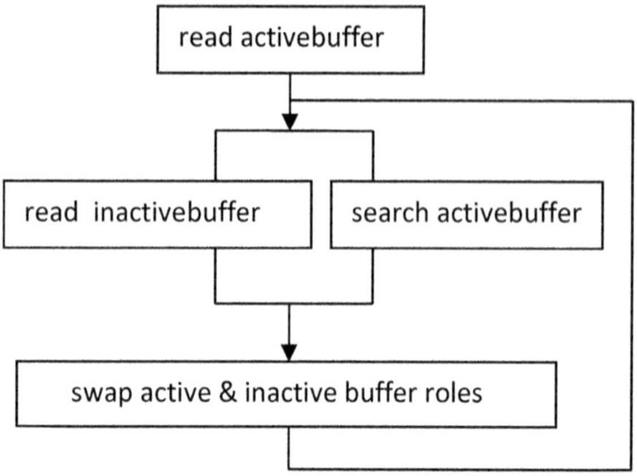

Fig. 9. Control flow for single core read and single core search (SRSS)

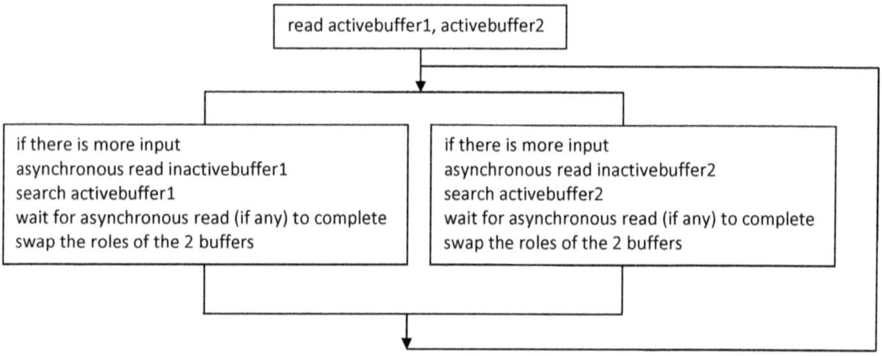

Fig. 10. Control flow for multicore asynchronous read and search (MARS1)

the synchronization is done only when the entire disk has been searched. So, using the strategy of Figure 10, each thread processes the same number of buffers (except when the number of buffers of data is odd). When the time to fill a buffer from disk consistently exceeds the time to search that buffer, the strategy of Figure 11 also processes the same number of buffers per thread. However, when the buffer fill time is less than the search time and there is sufficient variability in the time to search a buffer, it is possible, using the strategy of Figure 11, for one thread to process many more buffers than processed by the other thread. In this case, the strategy of Figure 11 will outperform that of Figure 10. For our application, the time to fill a buffer exceeds the time to search it excepts when the number of rules is large (more than 30) and the search is done using an algorithm such as Boyer Moore (as is the case in Scalpel 1.6), which is not

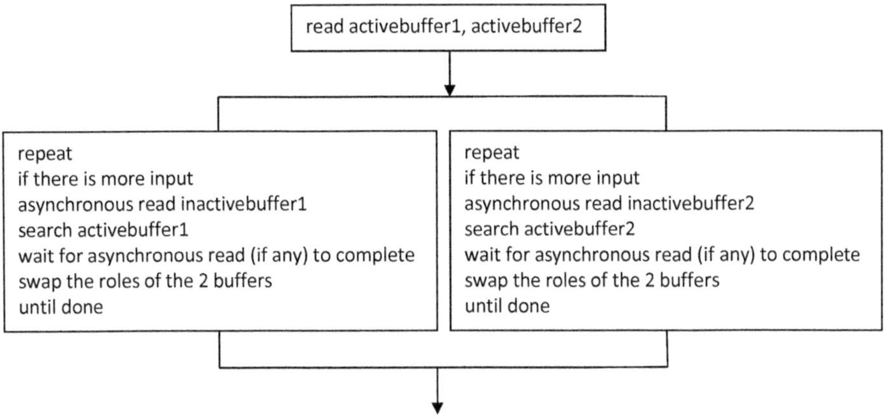

Fig. 11. Another control flow for multicore asynchronous read and search (MARS2)

designed for multipattern search. Hence, we expect both strategies to have similar performance. We refer to these strategies as MARS1 (multicore asynchronous read and search) and MARS2, respectively.

8 Experimental Results

We evaluated the strategies for in-place carving proposed in this paper using a dual processor,dual core AMD Athlon (2.6GHZ Core2Duo processor, 2GB RAM). We started with Scalpel 1.6 and shut off its second phase so that it stopped as soon as the metadata database of carved files was created. All our experiments used pattern/rule sets derived from the 48-rules in the configuration file in [12]. From this rule set we generated rule sets of smaller size by selecting the desired number of rules randomly from this set of 48 rules. We used the following search strategies: Boyer Moore as used in Scalpel 1.6 (BM); SBM-S (set-wise Boyer Moore-simple), which uses the combined bad character function given in Section 3 and the search algorithm employed in [14]; SBM-C (set-wise Boyer-Moore-complex) [15]; WuM [8]; and Aho Corasick (AC). Our experiments were designed to first measure the impact of each strategy proposed in the paper. These experiments were done using as our target disk a 16GB flash drive. All times reported in this paper are the average from repeating the experiment five times. A final experiment was conducted by coupling several strategies to obtain a new "best performance" Scalpel in-place carving program. This program is called FastScalpel. For this final experiment, we used flash drives and hard disks of varying capacity.

8.1 Run Time of Scalpel 1.6

Our first experiment analyzed the run time of in-place carving. Figure 12 shows the overall time to do an in-place carve of our 16GB flash drive as well as time

number of carving rules	6	12	24	36	48
total time	967s	1069s	1532s	1788s	1905s
disk read	833s	833s	833s	833s	833s
search	133s	232s	693s	947s	1063s
other	1s	4s	6s	8s	9s

Fig. 12. In-place carving time by Scalpel 1.6 for a 16GB falshdisk

buffer size	100KB	1MB	10MB	20MB
time	2030s	1895s	1905s	1916s

Fig. 13. In-place carving time by Scalpel 1.6 with different buffer size with 48 carving rules

spent to read the disk and that spent to search the disk for headers and footers. The time spent on other tasks (this is the difference between the total time and the sum of the read and search times) also is shown. As can be seen, the search time increases with the number of rules. However, the increase in search time isn't quite linear in the number of rules because the effectiveness of the bad character function varies from one rule to the next. For small rule sets (approximately 30 or less), the input time (time to read from disk) exceeds the search time while for larger rule sets, the search time exceeds the input time. The time spent on activities other than input and search is very small compared to that spent on search and input for all rule sets. So, to reduce overall time, we need to focus on reducing the time spent reading data from the disk and the time spent searching for headers and footers.

8.2 Buffer Size

Scalpel 1.6 spends almost all of its time reading the disk and searching for headers and footers (Figure 12). The time to read the disk is independent of the size of the processing buffer as this time depends on the disk block size used rather than the number of blocks per buffer. The search time too is relatively insensitive to the buffer size as changing the buffer size affects only the number of times the overhead of processing buffer boundaries is incurred. For large buffer sizes (say 100K and more), this overhead is negligible. Although the time spent on "other" tasks is relatively small when the buffer size is 10MB (as used in Scalpel 1.6), this time increases as the buffer size is reduced. For example, Scalpel 1.6 refreshes the progress bar following the processing of each buffer load. When the buffer size is reduced from 10MB to 100KB, this refresh is done 100 times as often. The variation in time spent on "other" activities results in a variation in the run time of Scalpel 1.6 with changing buffer size. Figure 13 shows the in-place carving time by Scalpel 1.6 with different buffer size with 48 carving rules. This variation may be virtually eliminated by altering the code for the

number of carving rules	6	12	24	36	48
BM	133s	232s	693s	947s	1063s
SBM-S	99s	108s	124s	132s	158s
SBM-C	107s	117s	142s	155s	178s
WuM	206s	205s	201s	219s	212s
AC	63s	62s	64s	65s	64s

Fig. 14. Search time for a 16GB flash drive

number of carving rules	6	12	24	36	48
SBM-S	1.34	2.15	5.59	7.17	6.73
SBM-C	1.24	1.98	4.88	6.09	5.97
WuM	0.64	1.13	3.45	4.32	5.01
AC	2.11	3.74	10.83	14.57	16.61

Fig. 15. Speedup in search time relative to Boyer-Moore

"other" components to (say) refresh the progress bar after every (say) 10 MB of data has been processed, thereby eliminating the dependency on buffer size. *So, we can get the same performance using a much smaller buffer size.*

8.3 Multipattern Matching

Figure 14 shows the time required to search our 16GB flash drive for headers and footers using different search methods. This time does not include the time needed to read from disk to buffer or the time to do other activities (see Figure 12). Figures 15 and 16 give the speedup achieved by the various multipattern search algorithms relative to the Boyer-Moore search algorithm that is used in Scalpel 1.6. As can be seen, the run time is fairly independent of the number of rules when the Aho-Corasick (AC) multipattern search algorithm is used. Although the theoretical expected run time of the remaining multipattern search algorithms (SBM-S, SBM-C, and WuM) is independent of the number of search patterns, the observed run time shows some increase with the increase in number of patterns. This is because of the variability in the effectiveness of the heuristics employed by these methods and the fact that our experiment is limited to a single rule set for each rule set size. Employing a large number of rule sets for each rule set size and searching over many different disks should result in an average time that does not increase with rule set size. The Aho-Corasick multipattern search algorithm is the clear winner for all rule set sizes. The speedup in search time when this method is used ranges from a low of 2.1 when we have 6 rules to a high of 17 when we have 48 rules.

8.4 Multicore Searching

Figure 17 gives the time to search our 16GB flash drive (exclusive of the time to read from the drive to the buffer and exclusive of the time spent on "other"

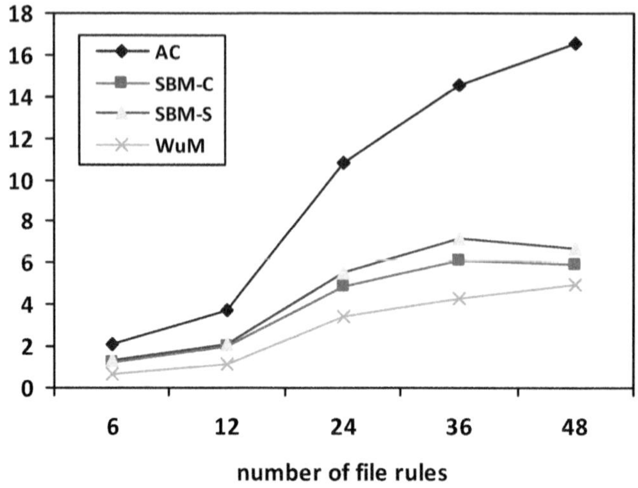

Fig. 16. Multi-Pattern Search Algorithms Speedup

Algorithms	unthreaded	2 threads	speedup
BM	693s	380s	1.82
SBM-S	124s	88s	1.41
SBM-C	142s	99s	1.43
WuM	201s	149s	1.35
AC	64s	58s	1.10

Fig. 17. Time to search using dualcore strategy with 24 rules

number of carving rules	6	12	24	36	48
BM	843s	855s	968s	966s	1100s
SBM-S	838s	837s	839s	888s	847s
SBM-C	832s	843s	837s	829s	847s
WuM	840s	841s	840s	843s	842s
AC	832s	834s	828s	833s	828s

Fig. 18. In-place carving time using Algorithm Asynchronous

activities) using 24 rules and the dualcore search strategy of Section 5. The column labeled "unthreaded" is the same as that labeled "24" in Figure 14. Although the search task is easily partitioned into 2 or more threads with little extra work required to ensure that matches that cross partition boundaries are not missed, the observed speedup from using 2 threads on a dualcore processor is quite a bit less than 2. This is due to the overhead associated with spawning and synchronizing threads. The impact of this overhead is very noticeable when the search time for each thread launch is relatively small as in the case of AC

number of carving rules	6	12	24	36	48
BM	961s	987s	1217s	1338s	1393s
SBM-S	942s	944s	953s	958s	944s
SBM-C	948s	937s	928s	935s	979s
WuM	978s	977s	975s	987s	1042s
AC	924s	925s	929s	927s	973s

Fig. 19. In-place carving time using SRMS

number of carving rules	6	12	24	36	48
BM	846	826	937s	932s	1006s
SBM-S	849s	850s	849s	844s	881s
SBM-C	852s	847s	844s	854s	845s
WuM	843s	837s	870s	843s	833s
AC	850s	852s	852s	852s	849s

Fig. 20. In-pace carving time using SRSS

number of carving rules	6	12	24	36	48
BM	909s	912s	943s	938s	1011s
SBM-S	907s	907s	908s	908s	909s
SBM-C	904s	906s	905s	907s	917s
WuM	906s	906s	907s	908s	908s
AC	904s	903s	902s	904s	904s

Fig. 21. In-place carving time using MARS2

and less noticeable when this search time is large as in the case of BM. In the case of AC, we get virtually no speedup in total search time using a dualcore search while for BM, the speedup is 1.8.

8.5 Asynchronous Read

Figure 18 gives the time taken to do an in-place carving of our 16GB disk using Algorithm Asynchronous (Figure 8). The measured time is generally quite close to the expected time of $\max\{T_{read}, T_{search}\}$. A notable exception is the time for BM with 24 rules where the in-place carving time is substantially more than $\max\{833, 693\} = 833$ (see Figure 12). This discrepancy has to do with variation in the effectiveness of the bad character heuristic used in BM from one buffer to the next as explained at the end of Section 6. Although using asynchronous reads, we are able to speedup Scalpel 1.6 by a factor of almost 2 when the number of rules is 48, this isn't sufficient to overcome the inherent inefficiency of using the Boyer-Moore search algorithm in this application over using one of the stated multipattern search algorithms.

number of carving rules	6	12	24	36	48
Scalpel 1.6(16GB)	967s	1069s	1532s	1788s	1905s
FastScalpel(16GB)	832s	834s	828s	833s	828s
Speedup(16GB)	1.16	1.28	1.85	2.15	2.31
Scalpel 1.6(32GB)	1581s	1737s	2573s	3263s	3386s
FastScalpel(32GB)	1443s	1460s	1448s	1447s	1438s
Speedup(32GB)	1.10	1.19	1.78	2.26	2.35
Scalpel 1.6(75GB)	3766s	4150s	6348s	7801s	8307s
FastScalpel(75GB)	3376s	3393s	3386s	3375s	3396s
Speedup(75GB)	1.12	1.22	1.87	2.31	2.45

Fig. 22. In-place carving time and speedup using FastScalpel and Scalpel 1.6

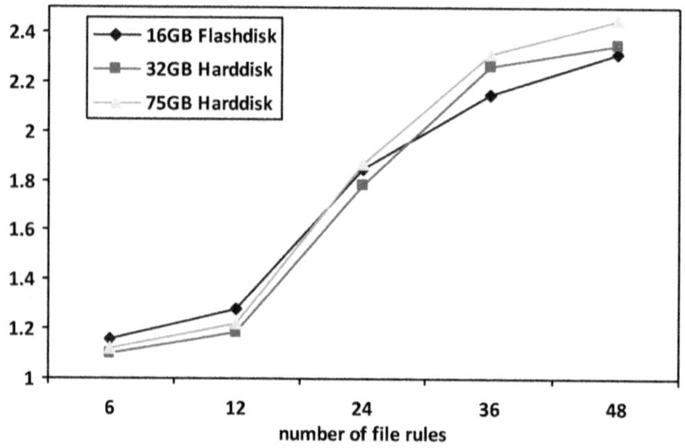

Fig. 23. Speedup of FastScalpel relative to Scalpel 1.6

8.6 Multicore in-Place Carving

Figures 19 through 21, respectively, give the time taken by the multicore carving strategies SRMS, SRSS, and MARS2 of Section 7. When the Boyer-Moore search algorithm is used, a multicore strategy results in some improvement over Algorithm Asynchronous only when we have a large number of rules (in our experiments, 24 or more rules) as when the number of rules is small, the search time is dominated by the read time and the overhead of spawning and synchronizing threads. When a multipattern search algorithm is used, no performance improvement results from the use of multiple cores. Although we experimented only with a dualcore, this conclusion applies to a large number of cores, GPUs, and other accelerators as the bottleneck is the read time from disk and not the time spent searching for headers and footers.

8.7 Scalpel 1.6 vs. FastScalpel

Based on our preliminary experiments, we modified the first phase of Scalpel 1.6 in the following way:

1. Replace the synchronous buffer reads of Scalpel 1.6 by asynchronous reads.
2. Replace the Boyer-Moore search algorithm used in Scalpel 1.6 by the Aho-Corasick multipattern search algorithm

We refer to this modified version as FastScalpel. Although FastScalpel uses the same buffer size (10MB) as used by Scalpel 1.6, we can reduce the buffer size to tens of KBs without impacting performance provided we modify the code for the "other" components of Scalpel 1.6 as described in Section 8.2. The performance of FastScalpel relative to Scalpel 1.6 was measured using a variety of target disks. Figure 22 gives the measured in-pace carving time as well as the speedup achieved by FastScalpel relative to Scalpel 1.6. Figure 23 plots the measured speedup. The 16GB disk used in these experiments is a flash disk while the 32GB and 75GB disks are hard drives. While speedup increases as we increase the size of the rule set, the speedup is relatively independent of the disk size and type. The speedup ranged from about 1.1 when the rule set size is 6 to about 2.4 when the rule set size is 48. For larger rule sets, we expect even greater speedup. Since the total time taken by FastScalpel is approximately equal to the time to read the disk being carved, further speedup is possible only by reducing the time to read the disk. This would require a higher bandwidth between the disk and buffer.

9 Conclusions

We have analyzed the performance of the popular file-carving software Scalpel 1.6 and determined that this software spend almost all of its time reading from disk and searching for headers and footers. The time spent on the latter activity may be drastically reduced (by a factor of 17 when we have 48 rules) by replacing Scalpel's current search algorithm (Boyer Moore) by the Aho-Corasick algorithm. Further, by using asynchronous disk reads, we can fully mask the search time by the read time and do in-place carving in essentially the time it takes to read the target disk. FastScalpel is an enhanced version of Scalpel 1.6 that uses asynchronous reads and the Aho-Corasick multipattern search algorithm. FastScalpel achieves a speedup of about 2.4 over Scalpel 1.6 with rule sets of size 48. Larger rule sets will result in a larger speedup. Further, our analysis and experiments show that the time to do in-place carving cannot be reduced through the use of multicores and GPUs as suggested in [11]. This is because the bottleneck is disk read and not header and footer search. The use of multicores, GPUs, and other accelerators can reduce only the search time. To improve the performance of in-place carving beyond that achieved by FastScalpel requires a reduction in the disk read time.

References

1. Aho, A., Corasick, M.: Efficient string matching: An aid to bibliographic search. CACM 18(6), 333–340 (1975)
2. Baeza-Yates, R.: Improved string searching. Software-Practice and Experience 19, 257–271 (1989)

3. Baeza-Yates, R., Gonnet, G.: A new approach to text searching. CACM 35(10), 74–82 (1992)
4. Boyer, R., Moore, J.: A fast string searching algorithm. CACM 20(10), 262–272 (1977)
5. Galil, Z.: On improving the worst case running time of Boyer-Moore string matching algorithm. In: 5th Colloquia on Automata, Languages and Programming. EATCS (1978)
6. Horspool, N.: Practical fast searching in strings. Software-Practice and Experience 10 (1980)
7. Pal, A., Memon, N.: The evolution of file carving. IEEE Signal Processing Magazine, 59–72 (2009)
8. Wu, S., Manber, U.: Agrep–a fast algorithm for multi-pattern searching, Technical Report, Department of Computer Science, University of Arizona (1994)
9. Richard III, G., Roussev, V.: Scalpel: A Frugal, High Performance FIle Carver. In: Digital Forensics Research Workshop (2005)
10. Marziale, L., Richard III, G., Roussev, V.: Massive Threading: Using GPUs to increase the performance of digit forensics tools. Science Direct (2007)
11. Richard III, G., Roussev, V., Marziale, L.: In-Place File Carving. Science Direct (2007)
12. `http://www.digitalforensicssolutions.com/Scalpel/`
13. `http://foremost.sourceforge.net/`
14. Fisk, M., Varghese, G.: Applying Fast String Matching to Intrusion Detection. Los Alamos National Lab NM (2002)
15. Commentz-Walter, B.: A String Matching Algorithm Fast on the Average. In: Maurer, H.A. (ed.) ICALP 1979. LNCS, vol. 71, pp. 118–132. Springer, Heidelberg (1979)

Live Memory Acquisition through FireWire

Lei Zhang, Lianhai Wang, Ruichao Zhang, Shuhui Zhang, and Yang Zhou

Shandong Provincial Key Laboratory of Computer Network,
Shandong Computer Science Center,
19 Keyuan Road, 250014 Jinan, Shandong, China
{zhanglei,wanglh,zhangrch,zhangshh,zhouy}@keylab.net

Abstract. Although FireWire-based memory acquisition method has been introduced for several years, the methodologies are not discussed in detail and still lack of practical tools. Besides, the existing method is not working stably when dealing with different versions of Windows. In this paper, we try to compare different memory acquisition methods and discuss their virtues and disadvantages. Then, the methodologies of FireWire-based memory acquisition are discussed. Finally, we give a practical implementation of FireWire-based acquisition tool that can work well with different versions of Windows without causing BSoD problems.

Keywords: live forensics; memory acquisition; FireWire; memory analysis; Windows registry.

1 Introduction

Live memory forensics, typically consists of live memory acquisition and memory analysis, is playing a more and more important role in modern computer forensics because of "in memory only" malwares, widely using of file and disk encrypting tools [1], and a lot of useful information that resides only in system memory and can't be acquired through traditional forensics methods [2].

To acquire volatile system memory, there are mainly two different ways, hardware-based and software-based [3]. Software-based methods are widely used because of their simplicity and freeness - many memory acquisition tools are available on internet and can be downloaded freely. This results in a boom of live memory forensics technologies.

Despite the virtues, software-based methods can not deal with locked systems when the unlock password is unknown since they need to run software application program(s) on the subject machine. At the same time, running of such software acquisition tools needs to use relative large memory (compared to hardware-based methods) of the subject system, this may overwrite useful data and destroy the integrity of system memory data and keep it from being evidence. Moreover, software based memory acquisition tools can be easily cheated by anti-forensic malwares since running of these tools is heavily based on services provided by the subject system OS which may have been manipulated by these malwares.

Hardware based memory acquisition tools could be used to resolve these problems or just to improve the performance, these tools typically do memory acquisition work

X. Lai et al. (Eds.): E-Forensics 2010, LNICST 56, pp. 159–167, 2011.

in DMA (Direct Memory Access) mode, by this way, the subject system OS is bypassed when they are working. At the same time, these methods do not need to run any software application in the subject system.

So far, there are two different hardware based methods to acquire system memory, one is using a PCI expansion card, the other is through a FireWire port. The PCI-card method needs a pre-installation of the acquisition card into the subject system before incidents happen, this narrows its usability. FireWire, also called IEEE 1394, is shipped with many modern notebooks or even desktop computers. Even if there are no FireWire ports directly equipped on the machine, they could be expanded through PCMCIA or PCI Express expansion cards. As the subject system OS is bypassed when these acquisition tools are accessing system memory in DMA mode, password is unneeded to dump system memory out of the locked machine. But how could FireWire-based tools get the right to access system memory, and what steps should be taken to dump the whole system memory? In this paper, we will discuss these problems and give an implementation of the FireWire-base memory acquisition method, and this tool can work stably with Windows operating systems.

The rest of this paper is organized as follows. Section 2 discusses base concepts of live memory acquisition and compare different acquisition methods. Section 3 discusses methodologies of FireWire-based memory acquisition and give a practical implementation of this method. Section 4 discusses what we can do in the future. Section 5 is the conclusion of this paper.

2 Live Memory Acquisition, Methods and Available Tools

Traditional computer forensics, also called "static forensics", is mainly based on static disk images acquired from a "dead" machine. There are many problems such as shut down process, unreadable encrypted data, and incomplete evidence [4] by using this traditional method. Live memory forensics could be used to try to resolve these problems.

Live memory acquisition, being the first step of memory forensics, is performed on a running subject machine. There are mainly two different ways to acquire system memory, software-based and hardware-based. A set of tools are associated to each of them. In this section, we will discuss virtues and limitations of each of them.

2.1 Software-Based Acquisition

System memory is managed as a special device in many modern operating systems. Table 1 shows the device name and user mode availability in different operating systems.

Table 1. Physical memory device name and availability in different operating systems

Operating system	Physical memory device	Availability in user mode
UNIX	/dev/mem	Available
Linux	/dev/mem	Available
MAC OS X	/dev/mem	Not available
Windows	\device\PhysicalMemory	Not available since Windows 2003 SP1

There are a set of software tools such as "*dd*", "*mdd*", "*Nigilant32*", "*Win32dd*", "*nc*", "*F-Response*", and "*HBGary FastDump*" that could be used to dump physical memory out from subject systems. As an example, the physical memory could be dumped through a simple command line by "*dd*":

```
dd if=/dev/mem of=mymem.img conv=noerror,sync
```

The physical memory could also be dumped to a remote system by "*nc*", the command line is listed below:

```
nc -v -n -I \\.\PhysicalMemory <ip> <port>
```

These software acquisition tools are very easy to use and can be downloaded from internet freely, but they also have many limitations such as need a full control right of the subject system and have relatively heavy footprint since they must be loaded into the subject system memory and running there. For Windows operating systems after Windows 2003 SP1, the \\.*PhysicalMemory* device is not available in user mode, thus memory acquisition tools that use this device and run in user mode can't work anymore. Moreover, these tools are based on services provided by the subject OS, so they could be easily cheated by anti-forensic malwares.

2.2 Hardware-Based Acquisition

Hardware-based memory acquisition tools are not that popular as software ones because they need additional hardware devices. The hardware device, in forms of a PCI expansion card, a dedicated Linux-based machine or a special-designed hardware is either very expensive or just not available on general markets. These tools, either pre-equipped or post-installed, could be attached to subject systems and dump the system memory in DMA mode. These tools need not to run any software agent in the subject system and could circumvent the subject system OS when they are working. Thus they could hardly be cheated by anti-forensic malwares (But also could be defeated by changing settings of registers in the North Bridge [5]) and have relatively light footprint in the subject system memory. There are typically two different kinds of hardware-based memory acquisition methods, one is through PCI bus, the other is through FireWire ports.

As to PCI bus method, a tool named "*Tribble*" [6] is introduced in February 2004 by *Brain Carrier*, et.al. This method uses a pre-installed PCI expansion card to acquire system memory when incidents happen. With a switch being turned on to start the dumping process, "*Tribble*" does not introduce any software to the subject system thus it has a good performance on protecting data integrity. But, the need of pre-installing of the acquisition card heavily limits its usage.

FireWire began to attract forensic experts' attention as a memory acquisition tool after the initial introduction as a way to hack into locked systems by the use of a modified "ipod" [7] in 2005. This method can only acquire memory of Linux-based systems until 2006, when Adam Boileau first gave a method to cheat the target Windows-based OS to give the acquisition tool Direct Memory Access right [8]. This method does not need any pre-installation. FireWire ports are equipped with many modern computers, even if there is not such a port that already integrated on the system motherboard, it could be expanded through a PCMCIA or PCI Express slot.

Although this method has emerged and has been used by forensic experts for some years, there are still problems such as weak stability in dealing with Windows-based systems and might run into a BSoD (Blue Screen of Death) state when try to access the UMA (Upper Memory Area) [9] or other spaces that were not mapped into system memory. We will discuss methods of how to resolve these problems in section 3.

3 Methodologies and an Implementation of FireWire-Based Memory Acquisition

FireWire-based devices communicate to host computers through FireWire bus by using a protocol stack, the structure of this stack is shown in Figure 1. The IEEE 1394 protocol mainly specifies the physical layer electrical and mechanical characteristics, and it also defines link layer protocols of FireWire bus. The OHCI (Open Host Controller Interface) standard specifies the implementation of IEEE 1394 protocol in the "host computer" side. The transport protocols, such as SBP-2 (Serial Bus Protocol 2), define the protocol of transferring commands and data over FireWire bus. The device-type specific command sets, such as RBC (Reduced Block Commands and SPC-2 (SCSI Primary Commands - 2), define the commands that should be implemented by the device.

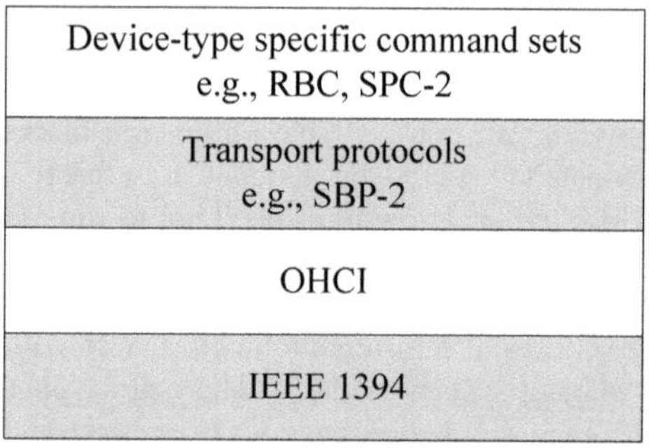

Fig. 1. Protocol stack of FireWire-based devices

To achieve best performance, the IEEE 1394 protocol gives the "target" device the ability to direct access system memory, by this way the host CPU could be freed from charging large amount of data transfers to or from system memory. According to IEEE 1394 protocol, read or write data packages are transferred from source nodes to destination nodes with a 64-bit destination address contained in these packages. The destination address consists of two parts, 16-bit *destination_ID* which consists of 10-bit bus address and 6-bit node address, and 48-bit *destination_offset.* The structure of a block read request package is shown in Figure 2.

The 16-bit *destination_ID* field contains the destination bus and node address, the 48-bit *destination_offset* is the destination address inside the target node. The OHCI standard gives an explaining of this 48-bit destination offset address. When the 48-bit address is below the address stored in the *Physical Upper Bound* register or less than the default value 0x000100000000 if the *Physical Upper Bound* register is not implemented, the 48-bit target address will be explained by the host OHCI controller as a physical memory address, and then the OHCI controller will perform a direct memory transfer using the *Physical Response Unit* inside it. By this way the "target" device could address the host computer's system memory and perform both physical memory read and write transfers. By our testing and reading on datasheets of different OHCI controllers, the *Physical Upper Bound* register is either unimplemented or has a default value of all 0s, this will cause the OHCI controller to take a default value of 0x000100000000 as physical upper bound. Till now the acquisition tool already can deal with Linux and MAC OS X based systems, but not to Windows-based ones, why? According to OHCI standard, besides the *Physical Upper Bound* register, there are also another two registers that should be set correctly to make the read or write transfers be of sense. These two registers are *PhysicalRequestFiltersHi* and *PhysicalRequestFiltersLo*. Each bit in these two registers is associated with a device node indicated by the 6-bit node address in the *source-ID* field. When the associated bit is cleared to "0", the OHCI controller will forward the request to the *Asynchronous Receive Request DMA context* instead of *Physical Response Unit*, and this request will be processed by the associated device driver and the *destination_offset* will be explained as virtual memory address, thus the "target" device can't get the actual physical memory contents.

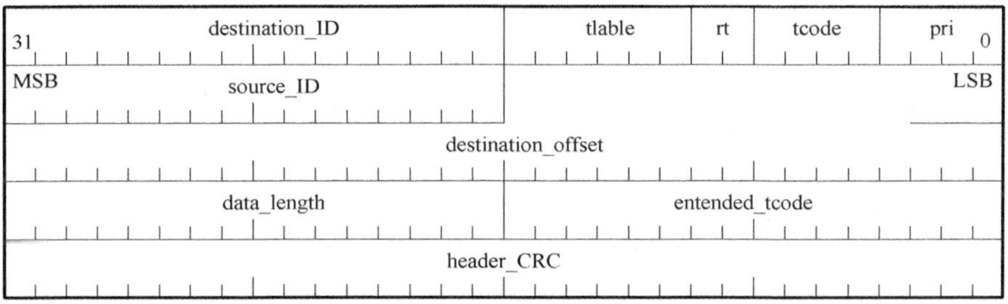

Fig. 2. Block read request package format

Fortunately, by the research of Adam Boileau, the physical DMA right could be gained if the "target" device pretends itself to be an ipod or a hard disk. By using the configure ROM of an ipod or hard disk, the "target" device could cheat the host computer to gain the DMA right. But, through our research, this method is not very stable towards different versions of Windows operating systems because of different implementations of file system drivers such as *disk.sys* and *partmgr.sys*. Since the file system is not implemented in the "target" device, it can't respond to commands sent from host computer, and to some versions of Windows, this will cause repeated sending of these commands and finally result in a bus reset with associated bit in the *PhysicalRequestFilterxx* registers being cleared to "0", this will prevent the acquisition tool from working. To resolve this problem, the mandatory commands associated with the device type given in the configure ROM should be implemented in the "target" device. The mandatory commands needed by a "Simplified direct-access" type device using a command set of RBC is listed in Table 2.

Table 2. Commands must be implemented in "Simplified direct-access" type devices

Command name	Opcode	Referenced command set
INQUIRY	12h	SPC-2
MODE SELECT	15h	SPC-2
MODE SENSE	1Ah	SPC-2
READ	28h	RBC
READ CAPACITY	25h	RBC
START STOP UNIT	1Bh	RBC
TEST UNIT READY	00h	SPC-2
VERIFY	2Fh	RBC
WRITE	2Ah	RBC
WRITE BUFFER	3Bh	SPC-2

Till now the acquisition tool could be attached to the host system and working stably. But, there is still another problem to acquire the whole subject system memory - since the length of the system memory is unknown, the acquisition tool does not know when to stop, and this may result into a BSoD state finally when the acquisition tool try to reading addresses not mapped into system memory. So the memory length information should be acquired before the address runs out of system memory range. To a subject system that in a locked state, the only information available is system memory, so the memory length information should be work out from the data stored in system memory.

As to a Windows operating system, the system registry is made up of a number of binary files called *hives*, among these *hives* there is a special one called *hardware* that stores information of hardware detected when the system was booting [10]. These information is only stored in system memory and thus could be acquired by the FireWire-based acquisition tool. There is a registry value named *.Translated* in the location of *HKEY_LOCAL_MACHIME/HARDWARE/RESOURCEMAP/System Resources/Physical Memory* in the *hardware hive* that stores base addresses and lengths of all memory segments. These memory segments could be accessed with no problem because they are mapped into truly physical memory. Figure 3 shows the *.Translated* registry value's contents, the *Physical Address* column shows the base addresses of different memory segments, and the *length* column shows the length of each memory segment. As an example, the "*0x001000*" in the *Physical Address* column is the base address of the first memory segment. The "*0x9e000*" in the *length* column is the first segment length. So, the address space of this memory segment is from *0x00001000* to *0x0009f000*. The first and last 4K bytes of the first 640K bytes system memory below UMA are not included in the first memory segment, but they could also be acquired properly. So we can use the first memory segment with its range from *0x00000000* to *0x000a0000*. We will use this fixed segment when we start memory acquisition work because the memory segments information is unknown in this stage. The second memory segment begins from the address *0x00100000*, between the first two segments is the UMA space. This space should be circumvented otherwise it may cause BSoD problem. In traditional computers, the memory space *0x00fff000-0x01000000* is used by some ISA cards and does not map into physical memory, this generates a memory hole. To be compatible with traditional computers, this memory hole is maintained by modern operating systems though there are no ISA cards in the computer and this space is actually mapped into physical memory. So, this "hole" can be neglected because it does not actually exist. The next segment begins from *0x01000000* contains all the rest of the physical memory. So, we just have to bypass the UMA space before we find the memory segments information.

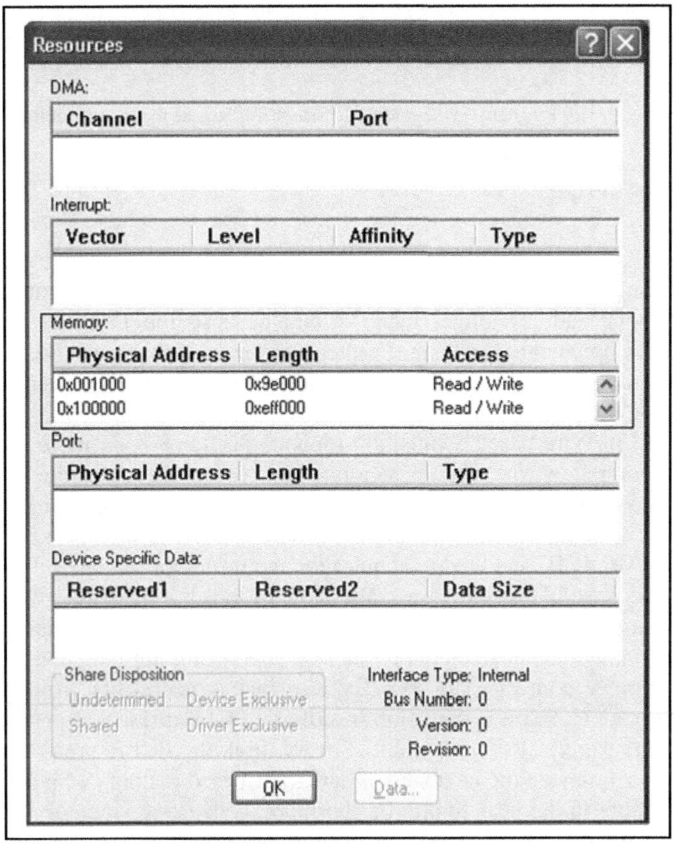

Fig. 3. Memory segments information contained in the *.Translated* registry value

The *.Translated* registry value data that stores in physical memory in a binary format is shown in Figure 4. So we can either search the registry value data using the character string "*.Translated*" or we can use the method provided by [10] to get this registry value data out from system memory.

Then, we could use the acquired information to generate base address and length of each memory segment. By this way, we never go into address spaces that are not mapped into physical memory thus the acquisition tool could work well without causing the target system to crash.

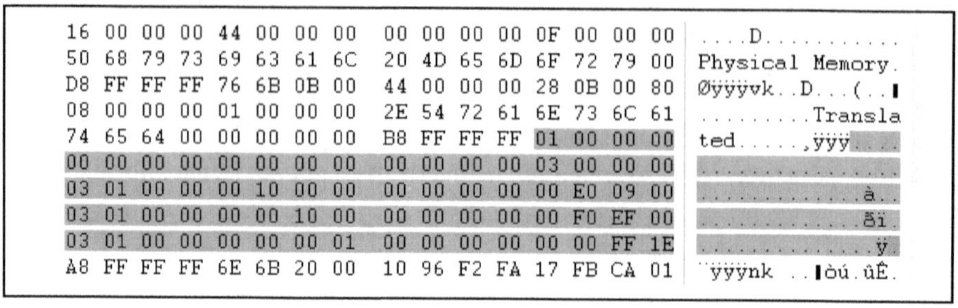

Fig. 4. Binary memory segments information stored in system memory

4 Future Work

Although OHCI protocol supports physical DMA in memory range over 4GB by properly setting the *Physical Upper Bound* register, most OHCI controllers do not support memory address longer than 32 bits because the *Physical Upper Bound* register is not implemented in them. Furthermore, even if this register is implemented in the OHCI controller, it can only be set by the OHCI controller driver from the host computer side and can't be accessed by the acquisition tool. So the amount of memory that FireWire-based acquisition tools can acquire is no more than 4GB. As for modern computers, the system memory becomes more and more large. Lots of computers have more than 4GB memory now, and modern operating systems are already capable of supporting systems with more than 4GB memory. So, how to get the memory over 4GB, and how to acquire the memory more rapidly? FireWire is not dependable because of its limitations. We have to look for substitute ways to resolve these problems. PCI Express bus, a serial version of the most popular used parallel PCI bus, has many new characteristics such as supporting hot-plug and supporting up to 64-bit memory address. The PCI Express bus is accessible from outside of a notebook through an Express card slot. Inserting a PCI Express add-in card to a "*live*" desktop or server may also be operable. So, we think the PCI Express-based memory acquisition tools may be the next step of hardware-based memory acquisition and will become available in the near future. Furthermore, because the memory contents keep changing while the acquisition tool is working, the consistency of the acquired data is not guaranteed. If the target system could be halted before acquisition work begins, the consistency of memory data will be protected. So methods of how to halt the target machine deserve further research.

5 Conclusion

In this paper, we discussed methodologies of FireWire-based memory acquisition and gave a method of how to get memory segment information from Windows registry to avoid access spaces that were not mapped into physical memory. We have worked out a proof-of-concept tool based on these methods, and now it can deal with Linux, MAC OS X, and almost all versions of Windows newer than Windows XP SP0. But because of the limitations of FireWire, memory above 4GB can't be acquired, and the acquisition speed is relatively low. So substitute ways such as PCI Express bus should be considered in the future work.

Acknowledgement. We would like to express thanks to the following people who assisted in the proofing, testing and live demonstrations of the methods described above. Shandong Computer Science Center: Qiuxiang Guo, Shumian Yang and Lijuan Xu.

References

1. Casey, E.: The impact of full disk encryption on digital forensics. ACM SIGOPS Operating Systems Review 42(3), 93–98 (2008)
2. Brown, C.L.: Computer Evidence: Collection & Preservation. Charles River Media, Hingham (2005)
3. Ruff, N.: Windows memory forensics. Journal in Computer Virology 4(2), 83–100 (2008)
4. Hay, B., Bishop, M., Nance, K.: Live Analysis: Progress and Challenges. IEEE Security and Privacy 7, 30–37 (2009)
5. Rutkowska, J.: Beyond The CPU: Defeating Hardware Based RAM Acquisition Tools (Part I: AMD case), http://invisiblethings.org/papers/cheating-hardware-memoryacquisition-updated.ppt
6. Carrier, B., Grand, J.: A Hardware-based Memory Acquisition Procedure for Digital Investigations. Digital Investigation 1(1), 50–60 (2004)
7. Dornseif, M.: FireWire - all your memory are belong to us, http://md.hudora.de/presentations/
8. Boileau, A.: Hit by a Bus: Physical Access Attacks with FireWire. Security-Assessment.com, http://www.security-assessment.com/files/presentations/ab_firewire_rux2k6-final.pdf
9. Upper Memory Area Memory dumping over FireWire—UMA issues, http://ntsecurity.nu/onmymind/2006/2006-09-02.html
10. Dolan-Gavitt, B.: Forensic analysis of the Windows registry in memory. Digital Investigation 5(supplement 1), 26–32 (2008)

Digital Forensic Analysis on Runtime Instruction Flow*

Juanru Li, Dawu Gu, Chaoguo Deng, and Yuhao Luo

Shanghai Jiao Tong University, Shanghai 200240, China
jarod@sjtu.edu.cn

Abstract. Computer system's runtime information is an essential part of the digital evidence. Current digital forensic approaches mainly focus on memory and I/O data, while the runtime instructions from processes are often ignored. We present a novel approach on runtime instruction forensic analysis and have developed a forensic system which collects instruction flow and extracts digital evidence. The system is based on whole-system emulation technique and analysts are allowed to define analysis strategy to improve analysis efficiency and reduce overhead. This forensic approach and system are applicable to binary code analysis, information retrieval and malware forensics.

Keywords: Digital forensics, Dynamic analysis, Instruction flow, Virtual machine, Emulation.

1 Introduction

Dynamic runtime information such as instructions, memory data and I/O data is a valuable source of the digital evidence, and is suitable for reconstructing system events due to its dynamic characteristic. Traditional digital forensic techniques are sufficient to extract information from memory and I/O data, but to observe runtime instruction flow, a low-level description of a program's behavior, more studies are needed. Network intrusion and malicious behavior are often carried out by a set of program instruction, leaving few evidence on hard disk, reducing the effectiveness of media forensics and increasing the importance of instruction analysis in digital investigations.

Two challenges in extracting evidence from instruction flow are the difficulties of data tracing and evidence distinguishing. Compared to other types of dynamic information, instruction flow is hard to be captured. Instructions are executed on the CPU instantaneously and are more volatile than memory data. Meanwhile, the CPU will produce a huge amount of instructions because of the high execution speed. Known techniques on capturing instruction flow are in two different ways. The First and the most well researched is the debugging technique. A debugger could control a process or even an operation system, and could trace the runtime information. But it is hard to record instruction flow

* Supported by SafeNet Northeast Asia grant awards.

X. Lai et al. (Eds.): E-Forensics 2010, LNICST 56, pp. 168–178, 2011.

completely. Moreover, debugging will affect debuggee's behavior. So apparently, debugging is not suitable for evidence collecting on instruction flow. The second technique is virtual machine monitoring. Virtualization is widely used in security analysis, it could observe and capture the privileged operations. But to collect the whole set of instructions using virtualization is not so convenient. Even if the instruction flow could be traced, the huge number of instructions are in form of opcode. It is impossible to manually analyze the flow. Automatic analysis technique must be used to extract useful information. Current technique of binary analysis couldn't be operated directly on instruction flow. Advances in tools and techniques to perform instruction flow forensics are needed.

To solute the problems above, we have developed a series of techniques and tools. The main contributions of this paper are:

- *Evidence from the instruction flow.* Forensic analysis requires the acquisition of many different types of evidence. We have proposed a novel view on capturing and analyzing instruction flow, which extends the range of digital evidence.
- *Emulator with generic analysis capability.* We have implemented a whole-system emulator based on bochs[2] to achieve instruction capturing. Windows and Linux application could be analyzed on this emulator. And our forensic analysis is compatible to various application.
- *Conditional instruction record and automatic data recovering.* We've provided an extensible interface to let analyst define which instruction should be captured, so as to to reduce the amount of record data. Conditions include time, memory Address, operands value and types of instructions. We've provided a series of tools and scripts to deal with the captured instruction flow. The functions of these tools include string searching, simple structure recognition and related data searching. We have also proposed some universal patterns related to certain encrypt algorithm like DES, which helps analyzing such algorithm more effectively based on instruction flow.
- *Efficiency and accuracy.* We have evaluated the capabilities, efficiency and accuracy of our forensic system. The result shows that the running speed of the system with instruction record is acceptable and the pattern based analysis could locate the accurate event or algorithm automatically.

The remainder of the paper is organized as follows. Section 2 introduces the characteristic of the instruction flow and how to use instruction flow as digital evidence. Section 3 describes our forensic analysis technique in detail. Section 4 gives the implementation of our forensic system. Experimental evaluation is described in Section 5 and Section 6 offers conclusion.

2 Background

The instruction flow is an abstract concept that describes a stream of instructions from the process of program execution. When programs are executed, static instructions are loaded into memory and fetched by the CPU. After each clock cycle of the CPU, the executed instruction with its operands is determined. Thus the sequence of the executed instructions composes a flow. Instruction flow contains not only data, but also how data is operated, thus is helpful on reconstructing system events. Additionally, recent researches on virtual machine security shows that instruction level analysis is an important aspect of computer security[10][13]. This section describes the characteristic of the instruction flow and how to extract digital evidence from the instruction flow.

2.1 Characteristics of the Instruction Flow

The instruction flow is different from the information flow or the data flow. It is a flow that contains information about low-level operation yet provides more details about the system's status. Like packet in a network dataflow, the basic unit in an instruction flow is the single instruction. Properties of the instruction are important for analysis. First, instructions in a flow are ordered by time, and the same instruction could be executed repeatedly and appears in different positions of the flow. Notice that in the instruction flow, operands are bind to instructions, as illustrated in Figure 1. So even two instructions in the different places of a flow are the same, analyst could learn more from the position and operands. What's more, an instruction could be loaded into different memory addresses of different processes. Same instruction performs distinctly at different virtual memory addresses. Another property is that branch instruction is useless during analysis because the execution path is determined when the flow is generated. Finally, the form of the instruction flow remains the same despite of the changing of upper level operation system. So the same forensic analysis technique could be used ignoring platform differences.

2.2 Instruction Flow as Digital Evidence

Individual disk drives, RAID sets, network packets, memory images, and extracted files are the main source of traditional digital evidence. But taking instruction flow as a source of digital evidence is practical. A typical scenario for the application of instruction flow analysis is the malware analysis[6], which allows analyst to use a controllable, isolated system to test the program and determines whether the behavior is malicious. Consider the event that a Trojan horse program acquires the password, encrypts it with a fix public key and sends it to a remote server. The public encrypt algorithm, public key and remote server's address are all useful evidences. Obviously these evidences are included in the instruction flow, but how to effectively recognize them in a huge quantity of instructions is a problem. Our work gives an approach on how to analyze instruction flow and search digital evidence.

3 Forensic Analysis on Runtime Instruction Flow

Two main steps are essential to perform forensic analysis on runtime instruction flow. First, the instructions are recorded and the instruction flow is generated.

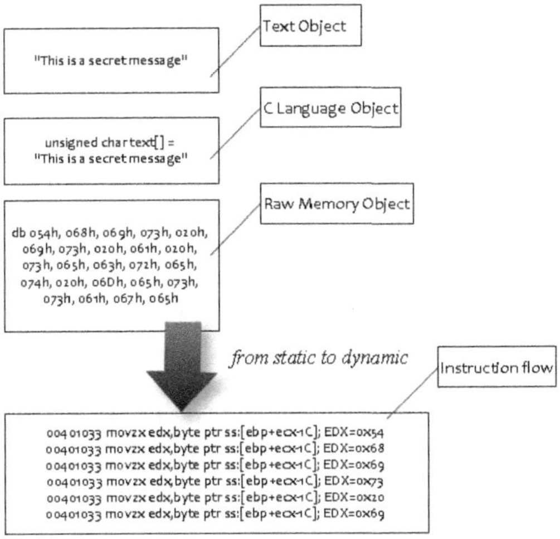

Fig. 1. From string to instruction flow

Second, after the instruction flow data is acquired, automatic analysis should be introduced to efficiently process the data and find out useful information. The following two subsections discuss these two steps and then a standard form of evidence from instruction flow is proposed.

3.1 Instruction Flow Generating

To capture instructions directly from the execution process, the CPU must be interrupted on every instruction. A trap flag based approach is introduced in [4]. We choose emulation to fulfil the capture function because it is simple and clear, the implementation detail of the system is described in Section 4. Another important problem is to decide the form of recorded instruction flow. We choose a data-instruction mixed form to record the flow, that is to say, each instruction's opcode, operands and memory address are recorded as a single unit and these units are ordered by time to compose a flow. Two modes are supported in instruction flow generating process:

Complete Record. In this mode, the instruction flow contains every instruction executed by the CPU. The data amount is huge and the running speed of the emulated system will be affected. This mode could bring the most precise record, yet sacrifice efficiency and storage space. Although the amount of instruction flow is large, to collect it is practical. In our experiment, the execution will produce about 1G Byte raw data per minute. That is almost the same volume a raw video stream produced by a DV camera, thus acceptable to store. When analyzing, it is suggested that the conditional record mode introduced below be used first to get some clues, and use these clues to guide the complete record.

Conditional Record. In the execution process, many instructions are useless for analyzing. To reduce the redundant data, various conditions could be used to filter the instruction flow. We've designed an open interface which allows analyst to define their own filtering conditions and the combination. Conditions supported by our system are listed below:

- *Time.* If the analyst knows the start and the end of a specific behavior, the record process could be set to start and stop at certain time point. One situation is to start recording after the boot of operation system.
- *Memory Address.* The CPU executes instruction by fetching it from memory, and the virtual memory address of the instruction is a special feature. For system calls, their entry points are already known and could be used as a condition to determine program behavior. More flexibly, analysts are allowed to capture or filter a range of memory address. A very effective strategy to monitor application on Windows is to filter off instructions with memory address higher than 0x70000000, which belongs to Kernel and system service processes. The same strategy is applicable on analyzing Linux(See Figure 2)
- *Instruction type.* Different analysts may concern different types of instructions. Analysts could determine which types of instructions should be captured, thus constructing specific instruction flow. For instance, if the forensic analysis focuses on encrypt algorithms, arithmetic instruction such as XOR is important while others could be filtered off.

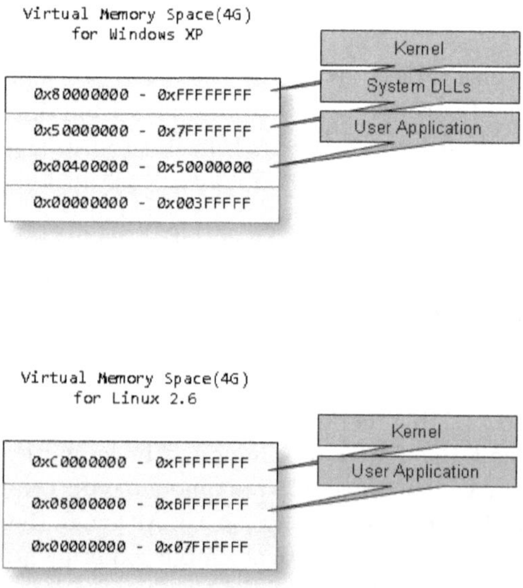

Fig. 2. Memory Allocation in Windows and Linux

– *Operands.* The value of Operands illustrates the content of an operation. To search a string in an instruction flow, analyst could first focus on the instructions with certain value of operands. And operands are a good feature that seldom change if the algorithm and input data are fixed. So code protection is invalid to hide information when using operands value as feature.

Using such conditions and their combination to filter the instruction flow, the data amount could be reduced to a considerably small size.

3.2 Analysis of the Instruction Flow

After collecting of instruction flow, analysis is ready to start. The aim of traditional binary analysis is to reconstruct high-level abstraction of the code. But in the instruction flow analysis process, the core part is data abstraction. The main purpose of the analysis is to express data in a clear form, and to find evidence through data. Two modes are supported in our analysis environment: offline analysis and online analysis. When the analysis runs in the offline analysis mode, saved instruction flow is analyzed, while in online analysis, our system directly analyzes instruction flow in memory.

Offline Analysis. In offline analysis mode, instruction flow is saved first and then scanned multiple times. We developed a series of tools and scripts to deal with the collected instruction flow. The first step is to analyze the data recorded in conditional mode. The provided automatic tools check the data bind to each instruction and maintain a sequence of data related. In low-level language most of the strings and arrays are operated with the same instruction for many times, so a large part of the data information can be recognized after this operation. The second step is to find useful information. Readable strings are automatically listed and are related to instructions. The related instructions are selected as clues of digital evidence. The final step is to run a complete record to gather a full set of instructions that operates the information, and use the selected instructions to slice the program and extract useful fragments.

Online Analysis. Although to analyze realtime instruction flow loses lots of context information, the profit is apparent. Less storage space is needed and running speed of emulation is expected to be faster. Online analysis is a debug-like analysis, which allows analyst to use some strong pattern(e.g. specific memory address, certain opcode) to quickly locate the suspicious instructions. In this mode the forensic system also plays the role of a debugger and supports all traditional debugging technologies.

3.3 Evidence from the Instruction Flow

One question about the instruction flow forensic analysis is how to give a convincing evidence. We propose a format of evidence from the instruction flow which the extracted evidence should follow:

1. **Data information from the instructions**
   Data information from the instruction is the core part of the digital evidence. It can be string information, IP address, URL or any other readable information. These kinds of data illustrate the analyzed events' properties.
2. **Related instruction set**
   The instructions that operate the data information should be provided as supporting evidence to illustrate the generation and transformation of the data.
3. **External supporting data**
   External supporting data such as Memory dump, Network flow, I/O data is collected via black box analysis. These kinds of data could be analyzed by traditional forensic analysis to support the evidence from the instructions.
4. **Testing environment**
   Testing environment should also be provided so that other analysts could replay the analysis.

4 Implementation

In this section we describe the implementation detail. To monitor the program's behavior and capture its instruction flow, a virtual environment is necessary. We choose bochs[2], which is an open source IA-32 (x86) PC emulator written in C++, to build this environment. In bochs we can run most operating systems inside the emulation, including Linux, DOS and Windows. Moreover, bochs is a typical CPU emulator that has a well designed structure for adding monitoring function with little performance overhead[7]. By using CPU emulation, analysts could collect instruction flow and trace software's activity, while the risk of evidence tampering is reduced.

Figure 3 shows the architecture of our forensic system. We have designed an engine on the bochs emulator to deal with the instruction flow. The engine will read parameters from a configuration file first, and analysts are able to set conditional filter parameters in this file. Then, when the emulation starts, the engine filters each instruction according to the configuration and fulfil a conditional record. A buffer in memory is maintained to record the instruction flow, and the data isn't written back to hard disk unless it reaches the buffer's capacity. Real-time data compression mechanism is optional for the buffered data to reduce the storage. We've also provided scripts in perl and python to automatically analyze instruction flow.

5 Evaluation

For digital forensics, accuracy is the most important factor. The using of emulation imports less interference to the analyzed object, yet sacrifices the efficiency. So one essential target of forensic emulation is to decrease emulation overhead. Several measures have been adapted. First, we use Windows PE and SliTaz GNU/Linux as testing operation system platform because these two systems are

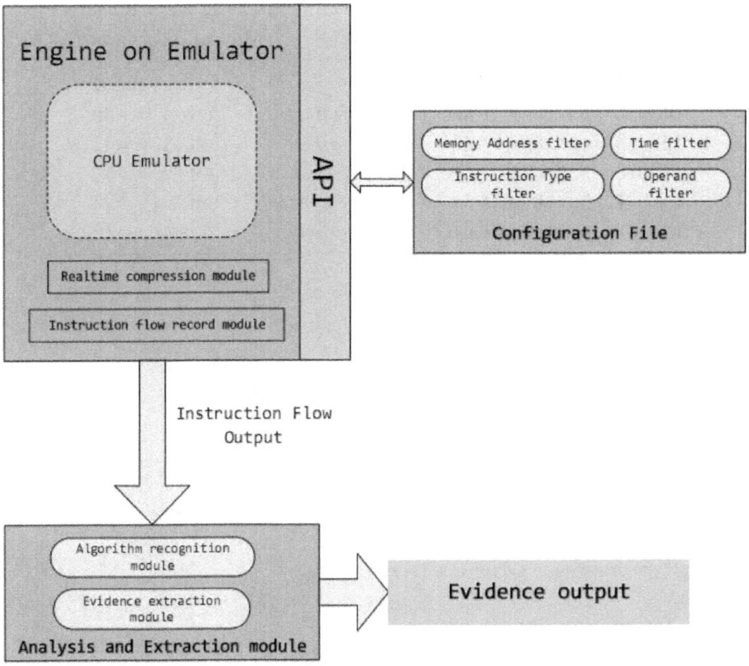

Fig. 3. The architecture of the forensic system

the lightweight version of the currently most widely used OS, and provide complete environment with GUI. Second, the running speed is 10-100 times slower in complete record mode than the original emulation due to the delay of hard disk writing. In order to improve the speed, an SSD driver is used to collect instruction flow and conditional record mode is suggested to be used. A typical configuration for Windows program analysis is shown in Table 1:

Table 1. An typical configuration on analyzing Windows program

Parameter	Configuration
Platform	Windows PE 1.5 (with kernel same as Windows XP SP2)
Range of Memory address	instruction with address $\leq$ 0x70000000
Instruction type	arithmetic, logical and bit operation
Record Time	-
Range of Operands	-

In real world, a program may use crypto algorithm to hide information. The private key and the algorithm are the most important evidences[5]. We give a forensic analysis on a Linux program that hides string information through DES encryption to show how our system works.

Table 2. Search result of the instruction flow

Seq No.	address	opcode	value of operands
143001	0x80486C9	*MOV EAX,[offset]*	[offset]==57
143025	0x80486C9	*MOV EAX,[offset]*	[offset]==49
143049	0x80486C9	*MOV EAX,[offset]*	[offset]==41
143073	0x80486C9	*MOV EAX,[offset]*	[offset]==33
143097	0x80486C9	*MOV EAX,[offset]*	[offset]==25
143112	0x80486C9	*MOV EAX,[offset]*	[offset]==17

```
0x80486C9    MOV32  EAX,[0x804A2A4](57)
0x80486D0    LEA  EDX,0xE4                <----key
0x80486D7    MOV32  EAX,[0xBFFFFD60](0x804B2C0)
0x80486DA    MOV32  EAX,[0x804B3A4](1)
0x80486DD    MOV32  [0x804B1C4],EAX(1)
0x80486E4    LEA  EAX,0xBFFFFD54
0x80486E7    INC  [0xBFFFFD54](1)         <----counter
0x80486BB    CMP  [0xBFFFFD54](2),56      <----key length
0x80486C3    MOV32  ECX,[0xBFFFFD54](2)  <----counter
```

Fig. 4. A DES encryption loop

The tested program is a Linux ELF file. Before checking up the private key, we should first determine whether this program uses the DES algorithm. We configure the forensic system for Linux environment, restricting the range of memory address from 0x08000000 to 0x10000000 and the value of operands: only the instructions with operands less than 0x100 are to be record. Then the system records the running process of the program on Slitaz Linux 3.0. We collect an instruction flow and use scripts to search for the *Permuted choice 1* of DES[3]: $\{57, 49, 41, 33, 25, 17, 9, 1, 58, 50, 42, 34, 26, 18, 10, 2, 59, 51, 43, 35, 27, 19, 11, 3, 60, 52, 44, 36, 63, 55, 47, 39, 31, 23, 15, 7, 62, 54, 46, 38, 30, 22, 14, 6, 61, 53, 45, 37, 29, 21, 13, 5, 28, 20, 12, 4\}$ The search gives a solitary result shown in Table 2. The result shows a strong feature of DES encryption. After the search we run the system again in complete record mode and locate the address 0x80486C9. According to the specification of DES, Permuted choice 1 is directly linked to main key. A simple program slicing on 0x80486C9 will give a loop of 56 times. Check the loop(see Figure 4), the private key is easily extracted.

6 Related Work

The topic of forensic analysis on low-level, dynamic information has attracted many researchers. Tools for volatile memory analysis and for program behavioral analysis have been developed. FATKit[8] provides the capability to extract higher level objects from low-level memory images. But memory image can't describe the behavior of program in detail. Capture[9] is a behavioral analysis tool based on kernel monitoring, which could analyze binary behavior. One shortage of Capture is that it focuses on system call rather than program's instruction. Although this would bring abstraction and convenience for analysis, a more fine-grained analysis on binary code is required.

Our work is to introduce low-level instruction analysis to forensic system. Prior to our work, some tools have provided analysis functions focusing on certain aspects. Rotalumé[10] and TEMU[13] are emulation systems based on the QEMU emulator[1]. The target of these systems is to provide syntax and semantics of the binary code, in other words, they try to transfer binary code to a high-level abstraction concept rather than collect detail evidence. Our system targets at collecting data from the instruction flow, providing not only an emulator but also a series of tools and methods to do forensic analysis on dynamic instructions.

7 Conclusion

In this paper we have presented a novel approach for forensic analysis and digital evidence collection on the instruction flow. We have presented details of a forensic system based on emulation. This forensic system deals with dynamic instructions. Functions of the system include: (1) generation of instruction flow, (2) automatical analysis of the instruction flow, (3) extraction of digital evidence. The system also provides a flexible interface which enables analysts to define their own strategy and augment analysis.

References

1. Bellard, F.: QEMU, a fast and portable dynamic translator. In: Proceedings of the Annual Conference on USENIX Annual Technical Conference, p. 41 (2010)
2. bochs: The Open Source IA-32 Emulation Project, `http://bochs.sourceforge.net`
3. FIPS 46-2 - (DES), Data Encryption Standard, `http://www.itl.nist.gov/fipspubs/fip46-2.htm`
4. Dinaburg, A., Royal, P., Sharif, M., Lee, W.: Ether: malware analysis via hardware virtualization extensions. In: Proceedings of the 15th ACM Conference on Computer and Communications Security, pp. 51–62 (2008)
5. Maartmann-Moe, C., Thorkildsen, S., Årnes, A.: The persistence of memory Forensic identification and extraction of cryptographic keys. Digital Investigation 6 (supplement 1), 132–140 (2009)
6. Malin, C., Casey, E., Aquilina, J.: Malware forensics: investigating and analyzing malicious code. Syngress (2008)
7. Martignoni, A., Paleari, R., Roglia, G., Bruschi, D.: Testing CPU emulators. In: Proceedings of the Eighteenth International Symposium on Software Testing and Analysis, pp. 261–272 (2009)
8. Petroni, N., Walters, A., Fraser, T., Arbaugh, W.: FATKit: A framework for the extraction and analysis of digital forensic data from volatile system memory. Digital Investigation 3(4), 197–210 (2006)

9. Seiferta, C., Steensona, R., Welcha, I., Komisarczuka, P., Popovskyb, B.: Capture - A behavioral analysis tool for applications and documents. Digital Investigation 4 (supplement 1), 23–30 (2007)
10. Sharif, M., Lanzi, A., Giffin, J., Lee, W.: Automatic Reverse Engineering of Malware Emulators. In: 30th IEEE Symposium on Security and Privacy, pp. 94–109 (2009)
11. SliTaz GNU/Linux (en), http://www.slitaz.org/en/
12. What Is Windows PE?, http://technet.microsoft.com/en-us/library/dd799308WS.10.aspx
13. Yin, H., Song, D.: TEMU: Binary Code Analysis via WholeSystem Layered Annotative Execution. Submitted to: VEE 2010, Pittsburgh, PA, USA (2010)

Enhance Information Flow Tracking with Function Recognition

Kan Zhou[1], Shiqiu Huang[1], Zhengwei Qi[1], Jian Gu[2], and Beijun Shen[1]

[1] School of software, Shanghai JiaoTong University
Shanghai, 200240, China
[2] Key Lab of Information Network Security, Ministry of Public Security
Shanghai, 200031, China
{zhoukan,hsqfire,qizhwei,bjshen}@sjtu.edu.cn,
gujian@mail.mctc.gov.cn

Abstract. With the spread use of the computers, a new crime space and method are presented for criminals. Computer evidence plays a key part in criminal cases. Traditional computer evidence searches require that the computer specialists know what is stored in the given computer. Binary-based information flow tracking which concerns on the changes of control flow is an effective way to analyze the behavior of a program. The existing systems ignore the modifications of the data flow, which may be also a malicious behavior. Function recognition is introduced to improve the information flow tracking, which recognizes the function body from the software binary. And no false positive and false negative in our experiment strongly prove that our approach is effective.

Keywords: function recognition, information flow tracking.

1 Introduction

With the spread use of the computers, the number of crimes with computers has been increasing rapidly in recent years. Computer evidence is useful in criminal cases, civil disputes, and so on. Traditional computer evidence searches require that the computer specialists know what is stored in a given computer. Information Flow Tracking (IFT) [7] is introduced and applied to our work to analyze the behavior of a program specially the malicious behavior.

Given program source code, there are already some techniques and tools that can perform IFT [5]. While the source code is not always available to the computer forensics, the techniques have to rely on the binary to detect the malicious behaviors [4]. Existing binary-based IFT systems ignore the modifications of the data flow, which may be also a malicious behavior [2]. Thus the Function Recognition (FR) [6] is applied to improve the accuracy of IFT.

We enhance IFT with FR for computer forensics. Our contributions include:

- We implement FR which recognize the functions from the software binary. A method of enhancing IFT in executables with FR is proposed.
- IFT with FR is applied into the computer forensics area.

X. Lai et al. (Eds.): E-Forensics 2010, LNICST 56, pp. 179–184, 2011.

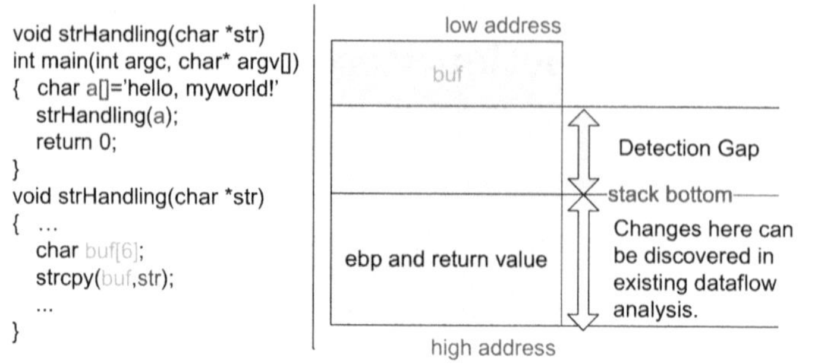

Fig. 1. An example of an overflow and the detection gap. In function *strHandling*, the size of the buffer is smaller than the size of the string assigned to it. When an overflow happens, it can be discovered only when it modified the value of *ebp* and the return address in the regular systems.

2 Motivation

When operations that results in a value greater than the maximum value which causes the value to wrap-around, the overflow happens as same as the one shown in Figure 1. This example is in C for clarity but our tool works with the binary code. The existing systems only concern on whether the control flow is modified or not, while the modifications of data flow are ignored. Thus a detection gap between the existing systems and our tool comes up just like Figure 1 shows. In our work, FR is introduced to address the detection gap. Take the Figure 1 as example, by comparing the lengths of the two parameters of *strcpy*, this kind of overflow can be easily detected.

3 Key Technique

3.1 Challenges

Memory Usage. The sheer quantity of functions and the size of the memory they occupy is a obstacle in FR [3]. If all versions of all libraries produced by all compiler vendors for different memory models are evaluated, the tens of gigabytes range is easily to wrap around. When we try to consider *MFC* and similar libraries, the size of the memory needed is huge. The requirement is beyond what the present personal computer can afford [3]. Thus a strategy is implemented to diminish the size of the information needed to recognize the functions. Not all the functions are recognized, only the functions related to the program behavior recognition are recognized and analyzed.

Signature Conflict. The relocation information of the call instruction will be replaced with "00". If most of two functions are same except for one call instructions, the two functions will have the same signature, which we call signature conflict. To resolve this, the original general signature will be linked by the special symbol "&" with the machine code of callee functions, the addresses of which can be found in the corresponding *.obj* file. After that a new unique signature is generated.

Algorithm: *General Signature Extraction*

```
Input: the set of signature samples:
       A {f1,f2,f3,f4......},
Output: the general signature fr,

procedure GeneralExtract
fr=Func(f1,f2)
while (A≠NULL)
{
fr=Func(fr,fn);
n++;
}

procedure Func(fr,fn)
GetSuperSequence(fr,fn);
//Get the most related general subsequence.
fr=RestructSig();
//Restructure the signatures to a new one.
```

3.2 Steps

Generation of General Signatures. The common parts of the machine code are extracted as a general signature. The algorithm using in our work has been presented below. The signature is separated to several subsequence with special symbols like "HHHH" and "&&". That the original signatures produced for different parameter types may have different lengths should been taken in account. Thus symbols like "00"s will be inserted into the shorter one where difference in successive bytes are detected, and different bytes of them are also replaced with "00"s to extract the common parts of original signatures. The procedure of the generation is as follows. Firstly a *.cpp* file that contains all the related functions are compiled by compilers with options, and a series of *.obj* files are generated. Then each *.obj* file will be analyzed and the machine codes of the functions are taken to generate the signatures.

Function Recognition with Signatures. When function calls (FCs) happen, FCs will be compared with the signatures, and the matched result is considered as an identified function. FC is identified by comparing the machine code with the signatures. It needs to match all these signatures to identify a FC.

3.3 Enhanced Information Flow Tracking

IFT usually tracks the information flow to analyze the modifications of the control flow by the input. Generally this technique labels the input from unsafe channels as "tainted", then any data derived from the tainted data are labeled

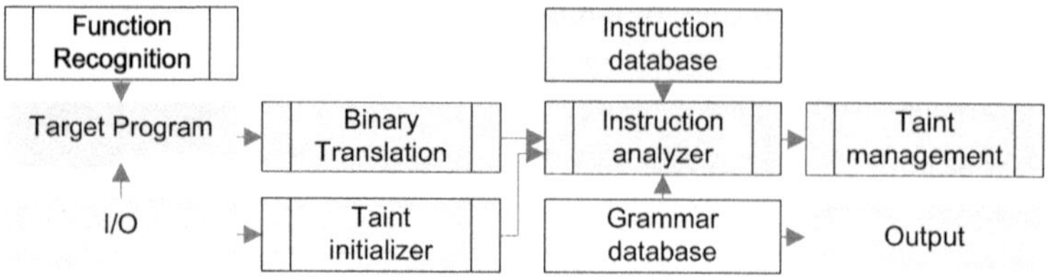

Fig. 2. The structure of the enhanced IFT system. Function Recognition is the module to recognize the functions. Taint Initializer initializes other modules and starts up the system. Instruction Analyzer analyzes the propagation and communicates with Taint Management module.

as tainted. In this way the behavior of a program can be analyzed and presented. General IFT focuses on the changes of the control flow, while the changes of data flow are always ignored. In our work, FR is introduced into IFT to solve the problem referred in the section 2, and the structure of the tool has been shown in Figure 2. Most of the structure is the same as the regular binary IFT. FR is the an important part different from other systems.

4 Experimental Results

4.1 Accuracy

To test our work, we have used 7 applications listed in Figure 3, also the results of FR are shown. All the functions appeared in the code can be divided into 2 types, *User-Defined Function* (*UDF*) and *Windows API*. In our experiments, the false positive rate and the false negative rate are both 0%. Experiment results prove that our work can recognize the functions accurately.

Application	*UDFs in source*	*Identified UDFs*	*APIs in source*	*Identified APIs*	*fp% / fn%*
Win32.exe	4	4	17	17	0% / 0%
Fibo.exe	0	0	0	0	0% / 0%
BenchFunc.exe	4	4	11	11	0% / 0%
Valstring.exe	0	0	0	0	0% / 0%
StrAPI.exe	4	4	11	11	0% / 0%
Hallint.exe	4	4	11	11	0% / 0%
Notepad_prime.exe	52	52	62	62	0% / 0%

Fig. 3. The results of the FR. *fp%* and *fn%* interprets the false positive rate and false negative rate. *UDFs in source* is the number of *UDFs* in the source code, and *Identified UDFs* shows the number of *UDFs* our tool identified. *APIs in source* and *Identified APIs* demonstrates the number of *APIs* in the source code and *APIs* identified by our tool respectively. *Notepad_prime* is a third-party program, which has the same functions and a similar interface with *Microsoft notepad.exe*.

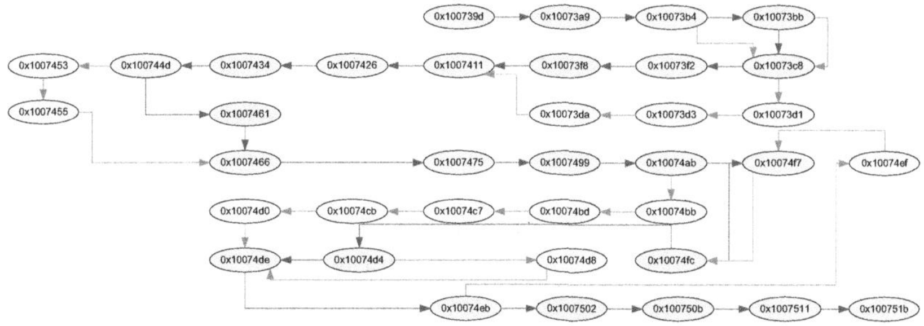

Fig. 4. A behavior graph that presents how *Microsoft notepad.exe* works. Different colors mean the different execution paths.

4.2 Behavior Graph

The behavior graph is a graph to illuminate the behavior of a program. It is useful for the computer specialists to understand the behavior of a program. Figure 4 shows the behavior graph of *Microsoft notepad*. Different colors of the ellipses and the lines mean they are from different execution paths separately. For example we track the information flow and get the purple path, while the malicious behaviors are not included in this path. Then we could change the input according to the behavior graph, and another path like the green one can be tracked and labeled in the graph.

4.3 Performance

Figure 5 demonstrates the performance of the tool when it is used in *SPEC CINT2006* applications. The results show that FR incurs the low overhead. *DynamoRIO*[1] is the binary translation our tool based on. In the results, FR does not significantly increase the execution time of IFT. The main reason is that we only track the functions related to the program behavior.

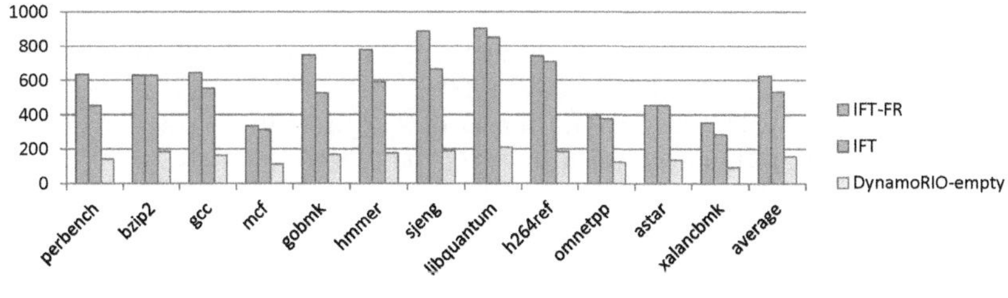

Fig. 5. The comparison of normalized execution time. "*DynamoRIO*-empty" bars show the *dynamoRIO* without any extra function. "*IFT*" bars interpret IFT system without FR. "*IFT-FR*" means the technique with FR.

[1] `http://dynamorio.org/`

5 Conclusion

In this paper we provide a way to analyze the behavior of a program to assist people to understand the program. The accuracy is an important issue in computer forensics, thus we implement the FR to improve IFT. FR is the strategy we applied to address the detection gap problem. And experimental results prove the method we implement the FR is effective. Zero false positive and zero false negative in our experiment illuminate the accuracy. Also the experiment results on the performance demonstrate that our tool is practical.

Acknowledgement. This work is supported by Key Lab of Information Network Security, Ministry of Public Security, and the Opening Project of Shanghai Key Lab of Advanced Manufacturing Environment (No. KF200902) and National Natural Science Foundation of China (Grant No.60773093, 60873209, and 60970107), the Key Program for Basic Research of Shanghai (Grant No.09JC1407900, 09510701600), and the foundation of inter-discipline of medical and engineering.

References

1. Baek, E., Kim, Y., Sung, J., Lee, S.: The Design of Framework for Detecting an Insiders Leak of Confidential Information. e-Forensics (2008)
2. Pan, L., Margaret Batten, L.: Robust Correctness Testing for Digital Forensic Tools. e-Forensics (2009)
3. Guilfanov, I.: Fast Library Identification and Recognition Technology, `http://www.hex-rays.com`
4. Song, D.X., Brumley, D., Yin, H., Caballero, J., Jager, I., Kang, M.G., Liang, Z., Newsome, J., Poosankam, P., Saxena, P.: BitBlaze: A new approach to computer security via binary analysis. In: Sekar, R., Pujari, A.K. (eds.) ICISS 2008. LNCS, vol. 5352, pp. 1–25. Springer, Heidelberg (2008)
5. Clause, J.A., Li, W., Orso, A.: Dytan: a generic dynamic taint analysis framework. In: ISSTA 2007 (2007)
6. Cifuentes, C., Simon, D.: Procedure Abstraction Recovery from Binary Code. In: CSMR 2000 (2000)
7. Clause, J.A., Orso, A.: Penumbra: automatically identifying failure-relevant inputs using dynamic tainting. In: ISSTA 2009 (2009)
8. Mittal, G., Zaretsky, D., Memik, G., Banerjee, P.: Automatic extraction of function bodies from software binaries. In: ASP-DAC 2005 (2005)

A Privilege Separation Method for Security Commercial Transactions

Yasha Chen[1,2], Jun Hu[3], Xinmao Gai[4], and Yu Sun[3]

[1] Department of Electrical and Information Engineering, Naval University of Engineering, 430033, Wuhan, Hubei, China
[2] Key Lab of Information Network Security, Ministry of Public Security, 201204, Shanghai, China
cys925@hotmail.com
[3] School of Computer, Beijing University of Technology, 100124, Beijing, China
[4] School of Computer, National University of Defense Technology, 410073, Changsha, Hunan, China

Abstract. Privilege user is needed to manage the commercial transactions, but a super-administrator may have monopolize power and cause serious security problem. Relied on trusted computing technology, a privilege separation method is proposed to satisfy the security management requirement for information systems. It authorizes the system privilege to three different managers, and none of it can be interfered by others. Process algebra Communication Sequential Processes is used to model the three powers mechanism, and safety effect is analyzed and compared.

Keywords: privilege separation, fraud management, security commercial transactions, formal method.

1 Introduction

Information systems are widely used in commerce activities, business transactions and government services. Privilege user is needed to manage the commercial transactions in those systems, but a super-administrator may have monopolize power and cause serious security problem. In order to avoid it, security criteria is specified in GB17859[1] and TCSEC[2], in which stringent figuration management controls are imposed, and trusted facility management is provided in the form of support for system administrator and operator functions. Privilege control mechanism provides appropriate security assurance for commercial transactions system.

"Separation of privilege" is one of the eight principles Saltzer and Schroeder [3] specified for the design and implementation of security mechanisms. Separations of duty rules are normally associated with integrity policies and models [4, 5, 6]. Recent work in security management [7, 8, 9] designed multi-layered privilege control mechanism and implemented in security operating system. However, formal methods are hardly used to describe their methods, and the effects is not well proved.

X. Lai et al. (Eds.): E-Forensics 2010, LNICST 56, pp. 185–192, 2011.

Process algebra is a structure in the sense of universal algebra that satisfied a particular set of axioms, which was coined in 1982 by Klop and Bergstra [10]. Its tools are algebraically languages for the specification of processes and the formulation of statements about them, together with calculi for the verification of these statements. Communicating Sequential Processes (CSP) [11] specify system as a set of parallel state machines that sometimes synchronize on events, so it can mathematically precise statement of a security policy. [12] modeled the first noninterference security argument for a practical security operating system using the CSP formalism, and proved that the model fulfills an end-to-end property that protects secrecy and integrity even against subtle covert channel attacks.

The paper is organized as follows. Section 2 analysis the relationship with privilege control, security management and commercial transactions system, and then give a review of the three powers separation mechanism. Section 3 specifies each manager's privilege and the assembled model with CSP. Section 4 analyzes the security effect of the method, and proves that is safer than monopolize power mechanism.

2 Review of the Model

The separation of powers, is a model for the governance of democratic states, which constituted by the separation of "executive, legislative, and judicial powers". With the help of information system, commercial transactions can be conducted automatically, but privilege user is needed to manage the system. We have introduced this approach to implement privilege control mechanism which provides three different types of managers to exercise "decision making, enforcement, audit" privilege respectively, thus avoiding power of abuse. If a system exist only one monopolize administrator, he can subvert easily the security of the system, in Section 4, we'll prove that after adopting the approach of "separation of power" no administrator can use his own privilege to subvert the security of system.

The privilege users undertaking such a logic function named as "*system manager*, *security manage*r and *audit manager*". Their responsibility specified as

security manager-Unified mark all the subjects and objects of the system, and manage authorization of subjects.

system manager-Manage the system subject's identities and resources, configure the system.

audit manager-Manage various types of audit records of the storage, management and query, etc.

A monopolized privilege user can do anything he likes, so it is evident then, that our three powers mechanism is safer than monopolize power mechanism.

3 Formal Description

3.1 Mechanism Analysis

Reference monitor is a part of trusted computing base (TCB), always running, temper-resistant, and cannot be bypassed. In our model, the relationship between the reference monitor, operators and three types of managers are described as Fig 1:

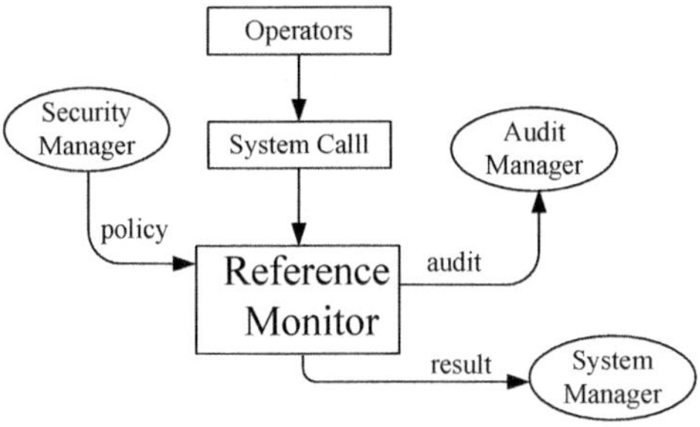

Fig. 1. Relation of all users and reference monitor

a). *Security manager* specify the policy that the reference monitor need to excute;
b). Reference monitor executes the policy and send the result to *system manager*;
c). *Audit manager* audits all system actions through reference monitor.

3.2 Communicating Sequential Processes

CSP is well suited to the description and analysis of operation system, because operation system and the relevant aspects of the users all can be described as processes within CSP. Our model investigates three managers' actions and their interactions, and then verifies certain aspects of their behavior through use of the theory.

The word *process* stand for the behavior pattern of an object [11]. A process is a mathematical abstraction of the interactions between a system and its environment. The set of names of events which are considered relevant for a particular description of the object is called its *alphabet*. Processes can be assembled together into systems, in which the components interact with each other and with their external environment.

In the traces model of CSP, a *trace* of a process is a finite sequence of symbols recording the events in which the process has engaged up to some moment in time.

We offer a brief glossary of symbols here:

αP	the alphabet of process *P*
$a \rightarrow P$	*a* then *P*
$(a \rightarrow P \vert b \rightarrow Q)$	*a* then *P* choice *b* then *Q* (provide $a \neq b$)
$P \vert\vert Q$	*P* in parallel with *Q*
$P \sqcap Q$	*P* or *Q*(non-deterministic)
$P \Box Q$	*P* choice *Q*
$P \setminus C$	*P* without *C*(hiding)
$P \vert\vert\vert Q$	*P* interleave *Q*
$P // Q$	*P* subordinate to *Q*
$b!e$	on channel *b* output *e*
$b?x$	on channel *b* input *x*

3.3 Privilege Separation

System manager, *security manager* and *audit manager* are denoted as CSP processes M_{SE}, M_{AU}, M_{SY}. We define their privilege as follows;

1) The privilege of *security manager* is defined as.

$$M_{SE} = TAGMGR|AUTMGR$$

$$TAGMGR = NEWTAG| \\ DELTAG| \\ MODTAG$$

$$NEWTAG = choose : CHOOSE|| \\ |\forall_i(i.g?(t,+)) \rightarrow \\ i.g!t \rightarrow TAGMGR$$

$$DELTAG = choose : CHOOSE|| \\ |\forall_i(i.g?(t,-)) \rightarrow \\ i.g!t \rightarrow TAGMGR$$

$$MODTAG = choose : CHOOSE|| \\ |\forall_i(i.g?(t,t')) \rightarrow \\ i.g!t' \rightarrow TAGMGR$$

$$AUTMGR = AUTHORIZE| \\ WITHDRAW$$

TAGMGR and *AUTMGR* are sub processes of M_{SE}.*TAGMGR* tags any system subject and object, which received from *SYSMGR*. It uses *NEWTAG* to create a tag, *DELTAG* to delete a tag and *MODTAG* to modify the original tag. *AUTMGR* uses *AUTHORIZE* to give access right for a subject, and uses *WITHDRAW* to cancel it.

2) The privilege of *audit manager* is defined as.

$$M_{AU} = ADATAMGR$$

$$ADATAMGR = EXPORT| \\ DELETE| \\ CHECK$$

$$EXPORT = choose : SELECT|| \\ |\forall_i(i.a?m) \rightarrow \\ i.a!m \rightarrow ADATAMGR$$

$$DELETE = choose : SELECT|| \\ |\forall_i(i.a?(m,-)) \rightarrow \\ i.g!r \rightarrow ADATAMGR$$

$$CHECK = choose : SELECT|| \\ |\forall_i(i.a?m) \rightarrow \\ i.a!m \rightarrow ADATAMGR$$

AUMGR uses *ADATAMGR* to manger audit data, *EXPORT* to export audit data, *DELETE* to clear useless audit files. *CHECK* can browse all data.

3) The privilege of *system manager* is defined as.

$$M_{SY} = USERMGR|PROMGR|COFMGR$$

$$\begin{aligned} USERMGR =& ADDUSER| \\ & DELUSER \\ ADDUSER =& choose : LIST|| \\ & |_{\forall i}(i.u?(m,+)) \rightarrow \\ & i.u!m \rightarrow USERMGR \\ DELUSER =& choose : LIST|| \\ & |_{\forall i}(i.u?(m,-)) \rightarrow \\ & i.u!m \rightarrow USERMGR \\ PROMGR =& INSTALL| \\ & UNISTALL \end{aligned}$$

USERGMGR, *PROTMGR* and *COFMGR* are sub-processes of M_{SE}. *USERMGR* manages the information of system users. *ADDUSER* add a new system user and *DELUSER* delete a user and corresponding resource. *PROMG* manages the application program. It uses setup to add new program, and use *UNISTLL* to remove it. *COFMGR* manages all the configuration files.

3.4 Communication

Except executing self-responsibility, those three managers need to interact with others. The communication events between them can be clearly showed (Fig.2). Those communications are:

1) All the operations of *system manager* will be audited by *audit manager*.
2) All the operations of *security manager* will be audited by *audit manager*.
3) *system manage*r submit request to *audit manager* before the state transition.

We split each process $M_i(i \in \{SE, SY, AU\})$ into two logical components: a *application half* A_i, and a *TOOL half* $i{:}T$. A_i represents the behaviors of people (similarly to a user interface). $i{:}T$ represents the trusted system tool, it behaves according to a strict state machine. The two halves of the same manager communicate via the channel *s*. (CSP processes use *channel* to communicate. A channel is used in only one direction and between only two processes).

Those communications can be specified as processes *SEND* and *SWITCH*.

$$\begin{aligned} |_{\forall i}SEND_i =& (i.p?(j,m)) \rightarrow \\ & ((AU.p!(i.m) \rightarrow SKIP)||| \qquad (i \in \{SE, SY\}) \\ & SWITCH) \end{aligned}$$

M_{SE} and M_{SY} use process *SEND* to communicate with M_{AU}, where *m* is an arbitrary string.

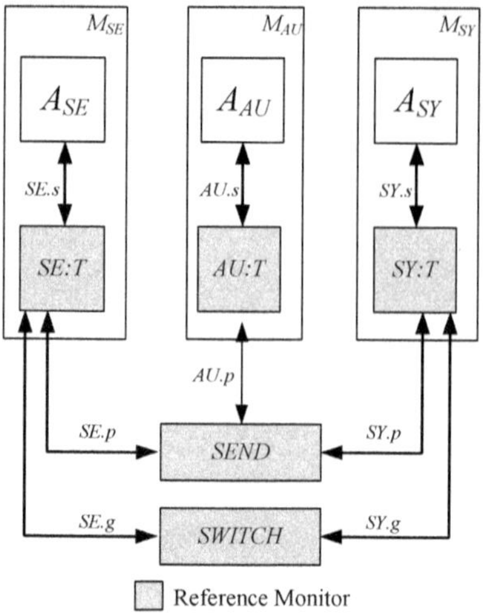

Fig. 2. Events of communication

$$SWITCH = |_{\forall i}(i.g?(j, S, O, M)) \rightarrow ((j.g!(i.r) \rightarrow SKIP)||| \quad (i, \in \{SY, SE\}) \; SWITCH)$$

M_{SE} and M_{SY} use process *SWITCH* to communicate, where *S* is subject sets and *O* is object set. *M* is a tabular data. This information as M_{SE}*can provide identification of* M_{SY}.

3.5 Cooperate Functioning

System manager, *security manager* and *audit manager* have to cooperate. for functioning An interleaving of all these processes specified as follows. Let *P* be the assembled process,

$$\begin{aligned} P = & M_{SE}|||M_{AU}|||M_{SY}||| \\ & A_{SE}|||A_{AU}|||A_{SY}||| \\ & (SEND||(SE:T|AT:T) \setminus \alpha SEND)||| \\ & (SE:T||SY:T) \setminus \alpha SWITCH) \end{aligned}$$

The direct evidence of internal state transitions will not be shown as the CSP hiding operator ("\") can hide the events in the alphabet.

4 Security Analysis and Implement

We will prove the three powers privilege separation mechanism can avoid the damage which happened in the monopolize power mechanism system.

Definition 1 (Secure manager state). The manager is secure if and only if:

$$\forall i \neq j \cdot tr, tr' \in traces(M_j) :$$
$$tr \upharpoonright \alpha M_i = tr' \upharpoonright \alpha M_i \Rightarrow$$
$$\mathcal{SF}[[M_j/tr]] \upharpoonright \alpha M_i = \mathcal{SF}[[M_j/tr']] \upharpoonright \alpha M_i$$

This definition of equivalence follows the *stable failures model*. For a process *P*, the stable failure of *P*, [13] [14] written $\mathcal{SF}[[P]]$, is defined as:

$$\mathcal{SF}[[P]] = \{(s, X) \mid s \in traces(P) \wedge P/s \downarrow \wedge X \in refusals(P/s)\}$$

For each pair of traces, two experiments traces by M_j. If two resulting processes look equivalent from the managerM_j's perspective, than M_i is secure.

Definition 2 (Safe initial state). The initial state is safe if and only if:

$$\forall M_i \in M \cdot M_{i_0} = (b?m) \rightarrow M_i \wedge m \in TRUST$$
$$M = \{M_{SE}, M_{AU}, M_{SY}\}$$

M_{i_0} is the start process of M_i. M_{i_0} uses channel *b* to listen on for its initial message *m*. Relied on Trusted Computing technology, the set *TRUST* can be fully trusted, any message picked from it is safe.

As the initial state of manager and the definition of a secure state of the manager have give, and the way in which the manager progresses from one state to another defined in section 3, than all future states of manager will be secure.

We implement this mechanism in Debian5.0 with LSM architecture. LSM provides a solution for security access control model in Linux. Based on operating system security mechanisms, our security management framework replaces original Linux hooks with loadable module in order to implement our security mechanism. Major security capability of the system meets the Structured-Protection criteria in [1] and [2].

5 Discussion

Although our privilege separation mechanism is safer than monopolize power, there is still much work to research. First, the formal prove of our mechanism has not be done in this paper, and we should do a machine-checkable proof (using FDR theorem proof checker in our future work. Second, conspiring situation has not been considered, which deserved to investigate.

Acknowledgement. This article is supported by the National High Technology Research and Development Program of China (2009AA01Z437), the National Key Basic Research Program of China (2007CB311100) and the Opening Project of Key Lab of Information Network Security, Ministry of Public Security.

References

1. Classified criteria for security protection of computer information system. GB17859-1999 (1999)
2. Trusted Computer System Evaluation Criteria (TCSEC), DoD (1985)

3. Saltzer, J., Schroeder, M.: The Protection of Information in Computer Systems. Proceedings of the IEEE 63(9), 1278–1308 (1975)
4. Clark, D.D., Wilson, D.R.: A Comparison of Commercial and Military Computer Security models. In: Proceedings 1987 Symposium on Security and Privacy. IEEE Computer Society, Oakland (1987)
5. Lee, T.M.P.: Using Mandatory Integrity to Enforce "Commercial Security". In: 1988 IEEE Symposium on Security and Privacy. IEEE Computer Society, Oakland (1988)
6. Shockley, W.R.: Implement Clark/Wilson Integrity Policy Using Current Technology. In: Proceedings 11th National Computer Security Conference (October 1988)
7. Qing, S.H., Shen, C.X.: Designing of High Security Level Operating System. Science in China Ser. E. Information Sciences 37(2) (2007)
8. Ji, Q.G., Qing, S.H., He, Y.P.: A New Privilege Control Formal Model Supporting POSIX. Science in China Ser. E. Information Sciences 34(6) (2004)
9. Sheng, Q.M., Qing, S.H., Li, L.P.: Design and Implementation of a Multi-Layered Privilege Control Mechanism. Journal of Computer Research and Development (3) (2006)
10. Bergstra, J.A., Klop, J.W.: Fixed Point Semantics in Process Algebras, Report IW 206. Mathematisch Centrum, Amsterdam (1982)
11. Hoare, C.A.R.: Communicating Sequential Processes. Prentice/Hall International, Englewood Cliffs (1985)
12. Krohn, M., Tromer, E.: Non-interference for a Practical DIFC-Based Operating System. In: 2009 IEEE Symposium on Security and Privacy. IEEE Computer Society, Oakland (2009)
13. Roscoe, A.W.: A Theory and Practice of Concurrency. Prentice Hall, London (1998)
14. Schneider, S.: Concurrent and Real-Time Systems: The CSP Approach. John Wiley & Sons, LTD., Chichester (2000)

Data Recovery Based on Intelligent Pattern Matching

JunKai Yi, Shuo Tang, and Hui Li

College of Information Science and Technology,
Beijing University of Chemical Technology, China
yijk@mail.buct.edu.cn, tangshuo2005@126.com,
leehuui@163.com

Abstract. To solve the problem of data recovery on free disk sectors, an approach of data recovering based on intelligent pattern matching is proposed in this paper. Different from the methods based on the file directory, this approach utilizes the consistency among the data on the disk. A feature pattern library is established based on different types of files according to the internal constructions of text. Data on sectors will be classified automatically by data clustering and evaluating. When the conflict happens on data classification, the digestion will be initiated by adopting context pattern. Based on this approach, the paper achieved the data recovery system aiming at pattern matching of txt, word and pdf files. Raw and formatting recovery tests proved that the system works well.

Keywords: Data recovery, Fuzzy matching, Bayesian.

1 Introduction

Computer data missing often occurs by personal mistakes or incidental reasons. Sometimes the data are too precious to be evaluated by money. So data recovery is very important. Currently, there are many kinds of good and useful data recovery software, most of which are developed based on file directory [1] which could not make full use of data on free sectors. So the data could be missed. This disadvantage is also utilized by criminals to make anti-restore data [2] so that neither data could be collected as evidence nor valuable clues could be found.

By taking advantage of the data on free sectors, this paper is proposing a data recovery method based on intelligent pattern matching, aiming to restore text files, such as *txt*, *doc* and *pdf* files. Firstly, a binary feature pattern library is established for different file categories by analyzing their internal format [3]. Secondly, in order to determine which kind of file they may belong to, data on sectors are classified by clustering [4] and evaluating automatically and the types of the files are identified. Here, each sector is a unit. When conflict of sector data classification happens, it will digest with the reference of the context of the sector and the encoding pattern [5]. Finally, data are organized into different files and recovered according to the data feature pattern library.

X. Lai et al. (Eds.): E-Forensics 2010, LNICST 56, pp. 193–199, 2011.

2 Data Recovery

Data recovery is to restore data which are lost or damaged by hardware-disable, incorrect operation and/or other reasons, in other words, is to restore them back to its original state. For most of cases, it is able to be restored as long as the data isn't covered. If the sector can be read and written normally, data recovery can be divided into three classes. They are respectively base on file directory, file data character and incomplete data. Functionally, data recovery can be classified into deletion recovery, format recovery and Raw recovery. Deletion recovery means to find and recover deleted file; Format recovery means to recover files on formatted disk; Raw recovery means to restore files ignoring any file information system.

3 Specific File Structure and Feature Pattern Library

3.1 Specific File Structure

Each specific file has its own format. File format is a special encoding pattern of information used for the computer to store and identify information [6]. For instance, it can be used to store pictures, procedures, and text messages. Meanwhile, each type of information can be stored in the computer by one or more file formats. Each file format usually has one or more extension names for identification or no extension name in some cases. File structures are defined as follows:

<file>|*<code>*{*<header>* : *<body>* : *<trailer>*}

For instance : *<txt>* *<Unicode* | *UTF>* {*<0xFFFE>*▯ *<body>* ▯ <>}

file: file type; *code*: encoding pattern; *header*: file head; *body*: file content; *trailer*: file tail.

(1) Word Document Structure

Word file's structure is more complicated than the *txt* file's. It is made up of several virtual streams including Header, Data, Fat Sectors, MiniFat Sectors and DIF Sectors. Word pattern is as follows:

<word><Unicode>{*<header><stream1, stream2…><trailer>*}

(2) PDF Structure

Generally speaking, a *PDF* file can be divided into four parts. The first is file header, in the first line of the PDF file, specifies the version number of a *PDF* specification that the file obeys. The second is file body, the main part of *PDF* files, which is formed by a series of objects. The third is cross-reference table, an address index table of indirect object, which is used to realize the random access to indirect objects. The last is file tail, which declares the address of the cross-reference table, points out the file catalog, so that the location of each object body in *PDF* file can be found and random access can be achieved. It also stores encryption and other security information of the *PDF* file. *PDF* pattern is as follows:

<pdf>{<Header><Body><xref table><trailer>}

3.2 The Definition of Feature Pattern Library

Feature pattern is seen as an ordered sequence composed of items and each item corresponds to a set of binary sequences [7]. During the pattern matching, items can be divided into three types according to the role they play. They are feature item P, data item D, optional item H.

1) Feature items P: To identify common features of different files, such as the feature item of A *Word* file always begins with 0xD0CF11E0.

2) Data items D: To show the body of the file.

3) Optional items H: the data used to fulfill the integrity of file.

3.3 Pattern Library Generation

The processes of pattern library generation are listed as follow steps. Firstly, compare different files with the same type and generate candidate pattern set; Secondly, apply it to the procedure of training data recovery; Thirdly, compare the recovery result with the original file in order to evaluate the candidate patterns and then screen out patterns which meet the requirements; Lastly, the pattern library of this type of file is achieved. There are three files provided, they are 1.doc, 2.doc and 3.doc. Three patterns can be obtained after binary comparison with each other. The three patterns are E_1, E_2, *and E3*.

$$E_1 = P_1 H_1 P_2 D_1 H_2 \quad ....D_n P_n E_n$$

$$E_2 = P_1 H_1 P_2 D_1 H_2 \quad ....D_n P_n E_n$$

$$E_3 = P_1 H_1 P_2 D_1 H_2 \quad ....D_n P_n E_n$$

3.4 Cluster Analysis of Pattern

(1) Pattern Similarity Calculation

The pattern generated by existing files is an ordered sequence of items which are made up of binary sequences. With pattern E_1, E_2, the definition of similarity is

$Sim(E_i, E_j)$: $Sim(E_i, E_j) = \max(Score(Comm(E_i, E_j)))$. In the definition, $Comm(E_i, E_j)$ is the common subsequence of E_i and E_j. $Score(Comm(E_i, E_j))$ is the score of the common subsequence.

(2) The Definition of the Common Subsequence Score

There are two given sequences $A=\{a_1, a_2, a_3.....a_n\}$ and $B=\{b_1, b_2, b_3......b_n\}$. If there exist two monotone increasing sequences of integers $i_1< i_2< i_3......< i_n$ and $j_1< j_2<$

j_3......< j_n satisfying $a_{ik}=b_{jk}=c_k$ (k=1,2.......), then we can call $C=\{c_1, c_2, c_3......c_n\}$ is the common subsequence of A and B, and C can be denoted by symbol $Comm(A, B)$.

The expression of common subsequence score defines as follow:

$$Score(Comm(E_i, E_j)) = \frac{\sum_{i,j=1}^{n} Num(Comm(E_i, E_j))}{|E_i| + |E_j| - Num(Comm(E_i, E_j))}$$

Among them, $Num(Comm(E_i, E_j))$ denotes the account of items contained in the $Comm(E_i, E_j)$.

(3) Set the Similarity Threshold

According to threshold, patterns are classified and form the pattern library of corresponding documentation. For instance, *txt* pattern library: $\{E_1, E_2\}$, $E_1 = D_1$ (When *txt* is stored in *ASCII*, store the file body directly. $P = \{\}$); $E_2 = P_1\ D_1$(When txt is stored in UNICODE or UTF8, the file begins with 0xFFFE, that is, P_1 = 0xFFFE);

(4) The Classification of Sector Data

The current file system is distributed by clusters and a cluster as the smallest units; moreover the cluster is composed by many sectors. Typically, the size of a sector is 512 bytes. However, in order to exclude the affection of file systems, this system recovers files in sectors. Furthermore, since most files are not stored continuously, it is necessary to match the data on sector with the feature pattern library one by one in order to determine the file type stored inside.

If the data A of a sector is given, to determine which type of document the sector data belongs to and make $P(A/S)$maximum, then $\hat{S} = \arg\max_s P(A/S)$

According to Bayesian formula

$\hat{S} = \arg\max_S \frac{P(S)P(A/S)}{P(A)}$, $P(A)$ is constant when A is given, therefore,

$\hat{S} = \arg\max_s P(A/S)P(S)$.

According to the result, the ones with the maximum probability can be classified into certain kind of file. However, this method does not include the match of data items D, because data items are abstracted from file body, while the body of the document is uncertain, so it will not be able to measure the matching degree. Consequently, with regard to the process of data item, the main idea is to determine its property determine its properties by checking its encoding mode and the context of its neighbor sectors. So, $\hat{S}_n = \arg\max\{P(S_{n-1}), P(S_n), P(S_{n+1})\}$.

(5) Pattern Evaluation

After comparing the result of data recovery with standard document, we can divide files into successfully restored ones and unsuccessfully restored ones according to the result matched with pattern E. So, we can calculate the credibility of selected pattern E [8]:

$$R(E) = \frac{Corr(E)}{Corr(E) + Err(E)}$$

Among them, $R(E)$ is the credibility of the selected pattern E, $Corr(E)$ is the number of files which are successful recovered by selected pattern E, and $Err(E)$ is the number of files which are unsuccessful recovered. According to the result, patterns are sequenced and the one with higher credibility will get priority.

4 Recovery Process

4.1 Recovery Process

By analyzing the internal structure of documents, a data recovery method based on pattern matching is proposed. It combines feature pattern of files with data association. (Figure 1)

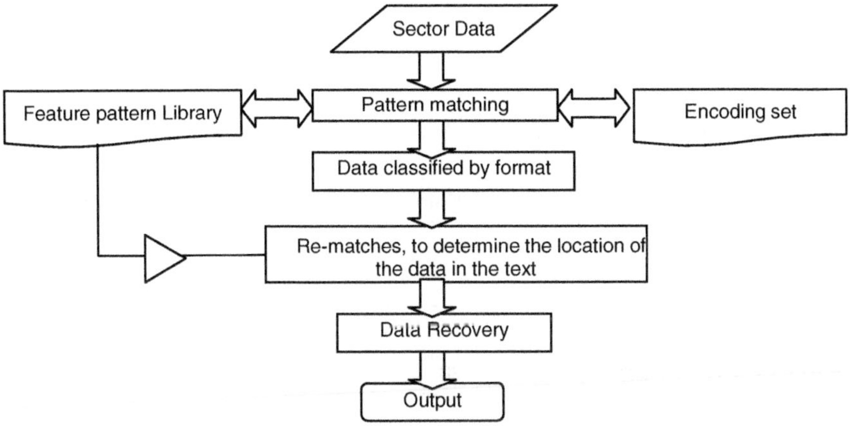

Fig. 1. Data recovery flow chart

4.2 Solving Data Conflict

Data conflicts are mainly caused by the fact that there is more than one file with the same type on hard disk. The conflicts have two kinds. One is the data which has almost the same similarity with pattern matching and the other is the data which cannot match with pattern matching.

For data conflicts, an approach based on context pattern is adopted [8]. The context pattern is seen as an ordered sequence which is composed of neighbor sectors where the data is stored, i.e., $W_{-n}W_{-n-1}...W_{-2}\ W_{-1}$<PN> $W_1\ W_2...W_n$.

<*PN*> represents data conflict, W refers to context data of *PN*, n represents the index of the sector.

Algorithm processes are as follows.

Set the similarity threshold l=0.5, n=1, n<8

1. Expand data PN into $W_{-n}W_{-n-1}\ldots W_{-2}\, W_{-1}<PN>\, W_1\, W_2\ldots W_n$;
2. Match with the feature pattern library, if l <0.5, then n ++, and return 1.
3. If $n \neq 8$, $W_{-n}W_{-n-1}\ldots W_{-2}\, W_{-1}<PN>\, W_1\, W_2\ldots W_n$ will be classified, the position in the pattern is recorded; If $n = 8$, it means that there is no appropriate place, then the data on this sector will be treated as useless data and been abandoned.

5 Experimental Result and Analysis

Feature pattern library is generated by 3 *txt* documents, 6 *word* documents and 6 *pdf* documents, and the pattern similarity threshold S = 0.4. After making internal testing on generated patterns, six of them are selected to form feature pattern library. It includes 2 *txt* patterns, 2 *word* patterns and 2 *pdf* patterns, respectively named E_1, E_2, E_3, E_4, E_5 and E_6.

A hard disk and both a new and an old USB flash disks are selected to make Raw and formatted recovery respectively. Each disk has 10 files on it. The results are showed in Table 1, Table 2:

Table 1. Result of Raw Data Recovery Based on pattern Matching

Disk	Size	Number of recovery files	successful rate
New USB flash disk	128M	8	80%
USB flash disk	128M	14	50%
USB flash disk	256M	20	30%
Hard disk	5G	31	10%

Table 2. Result of Formatted Recovery Based on pattern Matching

Disk	Size	Number of recovery files	successful rate
USB flash disk	128M	9	60%
USB flash disk	256M	13	35%
Hard disk	5G	25	90%

As we can see from the tables, the recovery result of a new USB flash disk is the best. It is because the majority sectors of a new USB flash disk have not been written yet and most files are stored continuously. This reduces the conflicts on data classification, and it is convenient for pattern matching. While the disk has been used for a long time, the sector data becomes very complicated because of the increasing number of user operations, which will make the matching more complicated.

It is obviously that the effect of file recovery is related to disk capacity and serving time. The larger disk capacity and the more files it stores, the more conflicts would be caused on data classification; the longer serving time, the more complicated the data would become, which results in more difficulties in pattern matching.

6 Conclusion

Making full use of data on free sectors, data recovery based on intelligent pattern matching has a good effect on restoration of text files, provides a new approach to the development of data recovery software in the future, and also improves the efficiency of computer forensics. However, there are lots of works to further improve, including to improve the accuracy of extraction of feature patterns, to expand the scope of the pattern library, to further improve the intelligent processing of related sectors, to extract the central meaning of the text and enhance the matching accuracy. Currently this approach only deals with text files, but it is feasible to expand the scope to other files because other files also have their own file formats and encoding patterns, based on which their characteristic pattern library can be developed. With this data recovery approach, the data utilization ratio of free sectors can be enhanced, the risk of data loss can be reduced and the recovery efficiency can be improved.

References

[1] Riloff, E.: Automatically Constructing a Dictionary for Information Extraction Tasks. In: Proceedings of the Eleventh National Conference on Artificial Intelligence, pp. 811–816. AAAI Press / The MIT Press (1993)

[2] Yangarber, R., Grishman, R., Tapanainen, P.: Unsupervised Discovery of Scenario Level Patterns for Information Extraction. In: Proceedings of Sixth Applied Natural Language Processing Conference (ANLP - 2000), Seattle WA, pp. 282–289 (2000)

[3] Zheng, J.h., Wang, X.y., Li, F.: Research on Automatic Generation of Extraction Patterns. Journal of Chinese Information Processing 18(1), 48–54 (2004)

[4] Qiu, Z.-h., Gong, L.-g.: Improved Text Clustering Using Context. Journal of Chinese Information Processing 21(6), 109–115 (2007)

[5] Liu, Y.-c., Wang, X.-l., Xu, Z.-m., Guan, Y.: A Survey of Document Clustering. Journal of Chinese Information Processing 20(3), 55–62 (2006)

[6] Abdel-Galil, T.K., Hegazy, Y.G., Salama, M.M.A.: Fast match-based vector quantization partial discharge pulse pattern recognition. IEEE Transactions on Instrumentation and Measurement 54(1), 3–9 (2005)

[7] Perruisseau-Carrier, J., Llorens Del Rio, D., Mosig, J.R.: A new integrated match for CPW-FED slot antennas. Microwave and Optical Technology Letters 42(6), 444–448 (2004)

[8] Papadimit riou, C.H.: Latent Semantic Indexing:A Probabilistic Analysis. Journal of Computer and System Sciences 61(2), 217–235 (2000)

Study on Supervision of Integrity of Chain of Custody in Computer Forensics*

Yi Wang

East China University of Political Science and Law,
Department of Information Science and Technology,
Shanghai, P.R. China, 201620
wangyi@ecupl.edu.cn

Abstract. Electronic evidence becomes more and more popular in case handling. In order to maintain its original effect and be accepted by court, its integrity has to be supervised by judges. This paper studies on how to reduce the burden of judges' task to determine the integrity of chain of custody, even there is no technique experts on the spot.

Keywords: Electronic evidence, chain of custody, computer forensics.

1 Introduction

Nowadays, electronic evidence becomes more and more popular in cases handling. Sometimes it is even unique and only evidence. However, current Laws are not suitable enough to treat this kind of cases. Academia and practitioners are devoted themselves to facing the challenges. Besides, experts in field of information science and technology are also engaged in solving these problems, since it is complicated and referring to cross field research.

In technical field, several typical models for computer forensics had been proposed since last century. They are Basic Process Model, Incident Response Process Model, [1] Law Enforcement Process Model, an Abstract Process Model, the Integrated Digital Investigation Model and Enhanced Forensics Model, etc. Chinese scholars also put forward their achievements, such as Requirement Based Forensics model, Multi-Dimension Forensics Model, and Layer Forensics Model. Above researches are concentrated on regular technique operations during forensic process. [2] Some of the models are designed for specific environment, and can not be popularized to other situations.

In legislation, there are debates on many questions, such as classification of electronic evidence, rules of evidence, the effect of electronic evidence, etc. They try to establish a framework, guide lines or criterions to regular and direct operations and process.[3] However, since there are so many uncertain things need to be clarified, it

* This paper is supported by Innovation Program of Shanghai Municipal Education Commission, project number: 10YS152, and Program of National Social Science Fund, project number: 06BFX051, and Key Subject of Shanghai Education Commission (fifth) Forensic Project, project number J51102.

X. Lai et al. (Eds.): E-Forensics 2010, LNICST 56, pp. 200–206, 2011.

needs time to solve them one by one. It has been widely accepted that current laws lag behind the technology development, and need to be modified or appended to adapt new circumstances. But innovation can't be finished in one day.

One of the main reasons on slowness of current law innovation is lack of seamless integration between legislation and computer science field. Lawyers are not familiar with computer science and technology, when it comes to technique area, they can not write or discuss deeply. On the opposite, the computer experts are facing the same problem, when it comes to law, they are laymen. Therefore, when standing on the border of the two fields, there is no enough guidance telling you what to do next, and there is no explicit rules directing you how to operate exactly. Judges and forensic officers sustain heavy burden when they facing cases dealing with electronic evidences, on one hand they have no enough guidelines, and on the other hand, they have to push cases forward.

This paper first considers how to divding duty clearly between legislation and computer science. That is to say which areas are concerned by law, and which ones are left for technique. It is the base of further discussion. Then let things go ahead naturally.

2 Analysis of Forensic Process

In computer forensic, many forensic models are suggested to regular forensic process, which is related to a lot of technical tasks. The models considered more on technique problems. In order to apply these models properly, it is necessary to have forensic officers with strong technical background. On the other hand, from the lawyers' point of view, this is a legal process and should follow the legal program and must within certain restraints. Considering technique experts' and legislation experts' viewpoint, there is no discrepancy between them. Forensic process can be divided into different stages. Technical experts are focusing on how to divide the whole process reasonably and make each stage clearly and easy to manage. Some models introduce the thinking of software engineer into them.

Judges concerns more on whether the forensic process is performed under the legal disciplines, whether captured evidences are maintained their integrity attribute, and whether these evidences are relative with the case. Therefore, judges don't need to be proficient in every detail of forensic process, but they can supervise the chain of custody if necessary.

So regardless which forensic model is used, when chain of custody is checked, there should be enough data to prove whether the integrity is held or not. Of course the supervision needs technique support. But it doesn't mean if there is no technical expert on the spot, the supervision task can't be executed. Besides the technical details, other aspects should be censored in a standardized way, and after that, judges can draw the conclusion whether the integrity attribute is maintained. If they need to clarify some technical problems, they could decide whether it is necessary to ask technical experts for help.

Therefore, the boundary of technique and law is clear, that is the data offered during the supervision and the standardized way of supervision. As there is no unified forensic model, the data given should not be fixed tightly. In the following, we call these give data as interface data. According to technical doctrine of equivalents, the interface data can't incline to certain technique. And the standardized supervision is also principle, not specific for any technique or model(s).

3 Interface Data and Supervision

From above analysis, the core of the problem is how to supply interface data and how to design a standardized supervision way. In order not to be lost in detail, we first divide forensic process into five phases. They are preparation, evidence capture and collection, evidence analysis, evidence depository, and evidence submission. In some models, the stage division is different, but it is not the point. Here logic order is important. Once the logic order is right, a step belongs to previous phase or next phase is not critical.

Through discuss the inner relationship between different steps and stages, this paper gives a logic order table, which declares that forensic progress has to comply certain programs in order to guarantee the integrity of whole chain of custody, and during the programs, interface data can be determined, which is the important information for supervision.

3.1 Interface Data

According to the five stages mentioned above, let's discuss them one by one.

1. Preparation
In this phase, the main task includes selecting qualified people or training people to satisfy computer forensic tasks, acquiring legal permission for investigation and evidence collection, planning how to execute forensics in detail, such as background information collection, environment analysis, and arrangement, etc.

2. Evidence Capture and Collection
This stage is engaged in evidence fixing, capture and collection. The evidences include physical evidences and digital evidences. The former can use traditional evidences capture technique, and the latter need computer forensic technique to get stationary and dynamic electronic evidences. Then the collected evidences need to be fixed, and electronic evidences need to calculate digital signature to avoid original data is tampered.

3. Evidence Analysis
It is based on former phase. Evidences captured on second phase are analyzed in this stage. The main tasks are finding out useful and hidden evidences from amount of physical materials and digital data. Through IT technology and other traditional evidence analyzing technique, extract and make up evidences.

4. Evidence Depository
When evidences are collected in second phase, and up to they are submitted in court, during this period of time, the evidences should be put in a secure and good environment. It can guarantee that they will not be destroyed, tampered and become invalid. Evidences stored here are managed well.

5. Evidence Submission
In this phase, evidences collected and analyzed from above phase will be demonstrated and cross examined in court. Besides necessary reports written on evidences analysis phase, evidences should be submitted follow certain format required by law. When it comes to electronic evidences, the data which guarantee the integrity of chain of custody are also need to submit.

From above analysis, the basic data generated from each phase are clear, and demonstrated in table one.

Table 1. Interface data

Phase Num.	Interface data
Preparation	1. Certificate for proofing person who does forensic tasks is qualified. 2. Legal permission for investigation and evidence collection. 3. Other data if needed by special requirements.
	Comments: Except emergency formulated by law that could obtain legal permission after evidence capture and collection, other cases are not permitted.
Evidence Capture and Collection	1. Investigation and captured evidences are within the legal permission. 2. Traditional evidences capturer and collection follow current law's regulation. They should supply spot records, notes, take photos, and sign signatures etc. 3. For each of electronic evidence, it should calculate digital signature so as to guarantee the originality and integrity. 4. For dynamic data capture, if condition permitted, it should take video to record the whole collection process. Or 2 or more people should on the spot, and record the whole procedure.
	Comments: In this phase, if during executing tasks, accident happens, such as finding out unexpected evidences but without legal permission, criminals take extreme actions to destroy or damage evidences, and other unpredictable things, forensic officers could take measures agilely according to current law.
Evidence Analysis	1. Traditional evidence analysis follows current law. 2. Electronic evidence analysis should be taken by qualified organizations, and they should not be delegated by personal people. 3. During electronic evidence analysis, if condition permit, examination and analysis should be under monitor. If there is no video, there should be a complete report on how examination and analysis are going on, 2 or more people should sign their signature. The report should meet the format requirements needed by law.

Table 1. (*continued*)

Evidence Depository	1. The depository should have proper environment to store electronic evidences. 2. During the storage time, there should have complete record for in and out, and the state of electronic evidence for each time.
Evidence Submission	1. Since electronic evidence cannot be perceived directly from the storage medium, in order to make it clear and easy to understand, necessity transformation should be taken. 2. Interface data generated on above phases relevant to proof the integrity of electronic evidences should be demonstrated in court.

Table one gives an overview of the framework of the interface data, if refine them further, there will be a lot of tables and documents need to standardize and define. This paper doesn't intend to regular every rule in every place, but suggests a boundary between law and computer technology. Once the boundary is clear, two sides can devote them to their work. The details and imperfect field can be remedy gradually.

3.2 Supervision

After realizing whole forensic procedure, judges can make up their mind based on fundamental rules, and don't need sink into technique details. According to the logic order in forensic process, judges are mainly concerned on following aspects.

1. Collected evidences should be within legal permission.
Through check the range of legal permission and its valid date, this one can be determined. Investigating the method of obtaining evidences to make sure evidences are legal. For example, judges can check out whether the forensic officers have certificates to proof they are qualified for computer forensic tasks. Before investigation and evidence collection, whether they have applied legal permission or there is any emergency exceptions.

2. Evidences collected on spot should have complete formality.
Traditional evidence collecting has formed a set of formal programs and regulations. As for electronic evidence, the program and regulation are not perfect, some fields are still blank. During the transition, if it refers technique problems, judges can ask technique experts for help. If it refers legal questions, judges have to follow current law. The difficulty is when current law doesn't formulate the solution, what can judges do? Our suggestion is creation. If the situation is never meet before, then it is mainly based on judges' experience and their comprehensive quality, with the help of technique experts, they give a new solution. If this case handles well, the solution can be the reference for other cases. And later, it is a good reference material for making new legislation.

3. Report from evidence analysis should be standardized and regular.
In this phase, tasks are mainly technical. Qualified organizations are delegated to do the evidence analysis. The interface data in this stage are often report. The person who writes the report should have certificate and be authorized, he or she knows the obligation when issued reports to court. Constrains and supervision are mainly on organization audit and assessor audit. Judges are concerned on whether the organization and assessor follow the regulations.

4. Evidence depository should have complete supervision and management records.
Evidence depository runs through the whole forensic procedure. If there is a link loose, or there is a time period is blank, there is a possibility the evidences lose their integrity. Judges should check the records carefully to make sure that the evidences are not damaged or tampered. If there is technique questions, judges can ask technique experts for help.

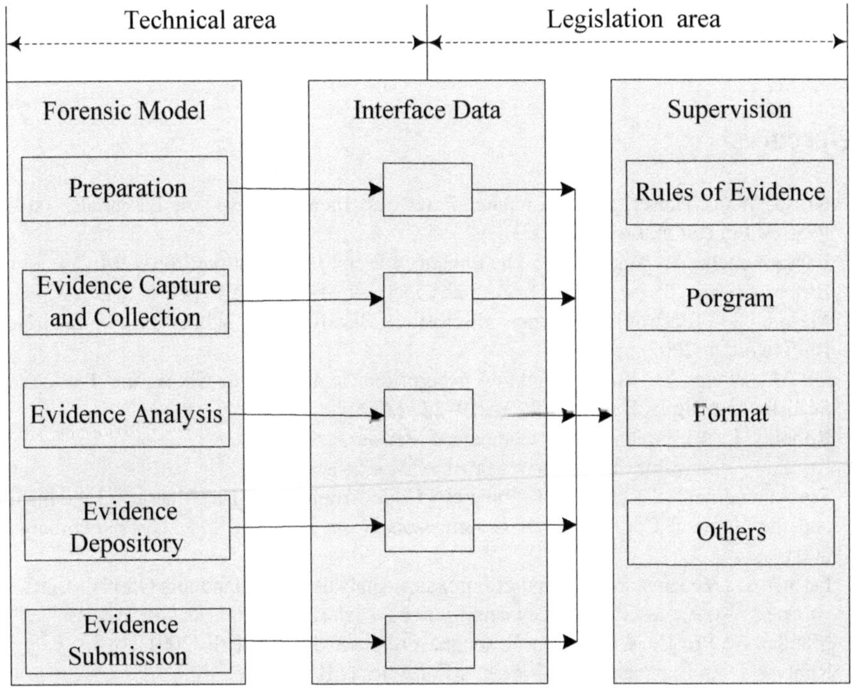

Fig. 1. Border of Technique and Legislation

5. Evidence submission should link above phase and factors together to obtain a chain of custody.
In this phase, valid evidences are displayed in court. Besides the evidences themselves, the chain of custody maintains integrity is also very important. Therefore, two aspects

are concerned in this stage, evidences and proof of integrity of evidences. Lawyers have the duty to arrange these evidences and their relevant proof materials, and let judges to determine the result.

Let's summarize the supervision procedure briefly: first legality examination, next normative examination, then standardization examination, finally integrity overview and check. Figure 1 displays the relationship between technique and legislation, which indicates that the cross field locates on interface data. If two sides define interface data clearly and can operate easily, the problem will be almost solved.

4 Conclusions

Nowadays more and more cases referring to electronic evidences appear. The contradiction between high incidences and inefficient handling gives huge pressure to the society. Both lawful professionals and technique experts are working together to face such challenges. This paper based on previous studies, gives some suggestions on how to reduce the burden of judges' task to determine the integrity of chain of custody to improve the speed of case handling.

References

1. Kruse, W.G., Heiser, J.G.: Computer Forensics: Incident Response Essentials, 1st edn. Pearson Educaiton, London (2003)
2. Baryamureeba, V., Tushabe, F.: The Enhanced Distal Investigation Process Model, `http://www.dfrws.org/bios/dayl/Tushabe_EIDIP.pdf`
3. Mason, S.: Electronic evidence disclosure, discovery & admissibility, LexisNexis Butterworths (2007)
4. Qi, M., Wang, Y., Xu, R.: Fighting cybercrime: legislation in China. Int. J. Electronic Security and Digital Forensics 2(2), 219–227 (2009)
5. Robbins, J.: An Explanation of Computer Forensics, `http://computerforensics.net/forensics.htm`
6. See Amendments To Uniform Commercial Code Article 2, by The American Law Institute and the National Conference Of Commissioners On Uniform State Laws (February 19, 2004)
7. Farmer, D., Venema, W.: Computer Forensics Analysis Class Handouts (1999), `http://www.fish.com/forensics/class.html`
8. Mandia, K., Prosise, C.: Incident Response. Osborne/McGraw-Hill (2001)
9. Robbins J. An Explanation of Computer Forensics [EB/OL], `http://computerforensics.net/forensics.htm`
10. Gahtan, A.M.: Electronic Evidence, pp. 157–167. The Thomson Professional Publishing (1999)

On the Feasibility of Carrying Out Live Real-Time Forensics for Modern Intelligent Vehicles

Saif Al-Kuwari[1,2] and Stephen D. Wolthusen[1,3]

[1] Information Security Group, Department of Mathematics, Royal Holloway, University of London, Egham Hill, Egham TW20 0EX, United Kingdom
[2] Information Technology Center, Department of Information and Research, Ministry of Foreign Affairs, P.O. Box 22711, Doha, Qatar
[3] Norwegian Information Security Laboratory, Gjøvik University College, P.O. Box 191, N-2802 Gjøvik, Norway

Summary. Modern vehicular systems exhibit a number of networked electronic components ranging from sensors and actuators to dedicated vehicular subsystems. These components/systems, and the fact that they are interconnected, raise questions as to whether they are suitable for digital forensic investigations. We found that this is indeed the case especially when the data produced by such components are properly obtained and fused (such as fusing location with audio/video data). In this paper we therefore investigate the relevant advanced automotive electronic components and their respective network configurations and functions with particular emphasis on the suitability for *live* (real time) forensic investigations and surveillance based on augmented software and/or hardware configurations related to passenger behaviour analysis. To this end, we describe subsystems from which sensor data can be obtained directly or with suitable modifications; we also discuss different automotive network and bus structures, and then proceed by describing several scenarios for the application of such behavioural analysis.

Keywords: Live Vehicular Forensics, Surveillance, Crime Investigation.

1 Introduction

Although high-speed local area networks connecting the various vehicular subsystems have been used, e.g. in the U.S. M1A2 main battle tank[1], complex wiring harnesses is increasingly being replaced by bus systems in smaller vehicles. This means that functions that had previously been controlled by mechanical/hydraulic components are now electronic-based, giving raise to the X-by-Wire technology [1], potentially turning the vehicle into a collection of embedded interconnected Electronic Control Unites (ECU). However, much of the recent increase in complexity has arisen from comfort, driving aid, communication, and

[1] Personal communication, Col. J. James (USA, retd.).

X. Lai et al. (Eds.): E-Forensics 2010, LNICST 56, pp. 207–223, 2011.

entertainment systems. We argue that these systems provide a powerful but as-yet under-utilised resource for criminal and intelligence investigations. Although dedicated surveillance devices can be installed at the in-vehicle system, these are neither convenient nor economical. On the other hand, the mechanisms proposed here can be implemented purely in *software* and suitably obfuscated. Moreover, some advanced automotive sensors may also provide redundant measurements that are not being fully used by the corresponding function, such as vision-based sensors used for object detection where images/video from the sensor's measurements are inspected to detect the presence of objects or obstacles. With appropriate modifications to the vehicular electronic systems, this (redundant) sensor information can then be used in forensics investigation. However, the fact that components are interconnected by bus systems implies that only central nodes, such as navigation and entertainment systems, will need to be modified and can themselves collect sensor data either passively or acquire data as needed. We also note the need for awareness of such manipulations in counter-forensic activity, particularly as external vehicular network connectivity is becoming more prevalent, increasing the risk, e.g., of industrial espionage.

The paper is structured as follows: in section 2 related works are presented. We then provide a brief overview of modern automotive architecture, communication and functions (in sections 3 - 7), followed by a thorough investigation on the feasibility of carrying out vehicular live forensics (in sections 8 - 9). The paper finally concludes in section 10 with conclusions and final remarks.

2 Related Work

Most vehicular forensic procedures today mainly concentrate on crash/accident investigations and scene reconstruction. Traditionally, this used to be carried out by physically examining the vehicular modules, but since these are increasingly being transformed into electronic systems, digital examination is now required, too. Moreover, most modern vehicles are equipped with an *Event Data Recorder (EDR)* [2,3] module or colloquially *black box*. Data collected by the EDR units include pre-crash information such as pre-crash system state and acceleration, driver input, and post-crash warnings. This information is clearly suitable for accident investigation, but not for criminal ones as ongoing surveillance requires data other than the operational state of the vehicle and selective longer-term retention. Nilsson and Larson have investigated the feasibility of combining both physical and digital vehicular evidence [4], showing that such approach improves typical crime investigations. They also carried out a series of related studies, mainly concerned with the security of the in-vehicle networks and how to detect attacks against them [5]. However, the focus of our work is somewhat different in that we take a more active role in our forensic examination and try to observe, in real-time, the behaviours of drivers and passengers, taking advantage of the recently introduced advanced electronic components and functions in typical modern higher-end vehicles.

3 Intelligent Vehicles Technology

The term *Intelligent vehicle* generally comprises the ability of the vehicle to sense the surrounding environment and provide auxiliary information in which the driver or the vehicular control systems can make judgments and take suitable actions. These technologies mainly involve passenger safety, comfort and convenience. Most modern vehicles implementing telematics (e.g. navigation) and driver assistance functions (e.g. parking assist), can be considered intelligent in this sense. Evidently, these functions are very rapidly spreading while becoming common even in moderately priced vehicles. This has highly motivated this research since, for the best of our knowledge, no previous work has been undertaken to exclusively investigate these new sources of information vehicles can offer for digital forensics examiners. However, before discussing such applications and functions, we first briefly review basic general design and functional principles of automotive electronic systems.

4 Automotive Functional Domains

When electronic control systems were first used in the 1970's vehicles, individual functions were typically associated with separate ECU. Although this unified ECU-function association was feasible for basic vehicle operation (with minor economical implications), it quickly became apparent that networking the ECUs was required as the complexity of systems increased and information had to be exchanged among units. However, different parts of the vehicle have different requirements in terms of performance, transmission and bandwidth, and also have different regulatory and safety requirements. Vehicular electronic systems may hence be broadly divided into several functional domains [6]: *(1) Power train domain:* also called drivetrain, controls most engine functions, *(2) Chassis domain:* controls suspension, steering and braking, *(3) Body domain:* also called interior domain, controls basic comfort functions like the dashboard, lights, doors and windows; these applications are usually called multiplexed applications, *(4) Telematics & multimedia domain:* controls auxiliary functions such as GPS navigation, hands-free telephony, and video-based functions, *(5) Safety domain:* controls functions that improve passenger safety such as belt pretensioners and tyre pressure monitoring.

Communication in the power train, chassis and safety domains is required to be in real-time for obvious reasons (operation and safety), while communication in the telematics & multimedia needs to provide sufficiently high data rates capable of transmitting bulk multimedia data. Communication in the body domain, however, does not require high bandwidth and usually involves limited amounts of data. In this paper, we are interested in functions that can provide a forensically useful data about driver and passenger behaviour; such data is mostly generated by comfort and convenience functions within the telematics & multimedia domain, though some functions in the body and safety domains are also of interest, as will be discussed later.

5 Automotive Networks and Bus Systems

Early interconnection requirements between ECUs were initially addressed by point-to-point links. This approach, however, increased the inter-ECU links exponentially as the number of ECUs increased, which introduced many reliability, complexity, and economical implications. Consequently, automotive networks emerged to reduce the number of connections while improving overall reliability and efficiency. Generally, automotive networks are either event-triggered (where data is transmitted only when a particular event occurs) or time-triggered (where data is periodically transmitted in time slots) [7]. In an attempt to formalise the distinction between these networks, the society of Automotive Engineers (SAE) classified automotive networks into four main classes: *(1) Class A:* for functions requiring low data rate (up to 10kbps), such as lights, doors and windows. An example of class A is LIN network. *(2) Class B:* mostly for data exchange between ECUs and has data rate of up to 125 kbps. An example of class B is Low speed CAN network. *(3) Class C:* for functions demanding high data rate up to 1Mbps (most functions in the Power train and Chassis domains). An example of class C is High speed CAN network. *(4) Class D:* for functions requiring data rate of more than 1Mbps, such as most functions in the Telematics & Multimedia domain, and some functions in the safety domain. Example of class D are FlexRay and MOST networks.

We note that a typical vehicle today consists of a number of different interconnected networks, thus any information generated by any ECU can be received at any other ECU [8]. However, since ECUs are classified into functional domains and each domain may deploy a different network type, *gateways* are used for inter-domain communication. In the following subsections we provide a brief overview of an example network from each class; table 1 presents a summary comparison between these networks [9].

LIN. Local Interconnect Network (LIN) was founded in 1998 by the LIN Consortium [10] as an economical alternative for CAN bus system and is mainly targeted for non-critical functions in the body domain that usually exchange low-volume data and thus does not require high data rates; such data is also not required to be delivered in real-time. LIN is based on master-slave architecture and is a time-driven network. Using an unshielded copper single wire, LIN bus can extend up to 40m while connecting up to 16 nodes. Typical LIN applications include: rain sensor, sun roof, door locks and heating controls [11].

CAN. Controller Area Network (CAN) [12] is an event-driven automotive bus system developed by Bosch and released in 1986 (latest version is CAN 2.0 released in 1991). CAN is the most widely used automotive bus system, usually connecting ECUs of the body, power train and chassis domains, as well as inter-domain connections. There are two types of CAN: *(1) Low-speed CAN:* standardized in ISO11519-2 [13], supports data rate of up to 125kbit/s and mostly operates in the body domain for applications requiring slightly higher transmission rate than LIN; example applications include: mirror adjustment, seat

Table 1. Comparison between the most popular automotive networks

	LIN	Low-CAN	High-CAN	FlexRay	MOST
Class	Class A	Class B	Class C	Class C & D	Class D
Domain	Body	Body, Power Train, chassis	Power Train, chassis	Power train, Chassis, Telematics & Mult., Safety	Telematics and Multimedia
Standard	LIN Consortium	ISO 11519-2	ISO 1198	FlexRay Consortium	MOST Consortium
Max. Data rate	19.2 kbit/s	125 kbit/s	1 Mbit/s	20 Mbit/s	22.5 Mbit/s
Topology	Bus	Bus	Bus	Star (mostly)	Ring
Max. node no.	16	24	10	22 per bus/star	64
Applications	windows, doors	lights, wipers	Engine, Transmission	airbag	CD/DVD player
Control Mechanism	Time-driven	Event-driven	Event-driven	Time/Event-driven	Time/Event-driven

adjustment, and air-conditioning. *(2) High-speed CAN:* standardized in ISO11898 [14], supports data rate of up to 1 Mbit/s and mostly operates in the power train and chassis domains for applications requiring real-time transmission; example applications include: engine and transmission management.

FlexRay. Founded by the FlexRay consortium in 2000, FlexRay [15] was intended as an enhanced alternative to CAN. FlexRay was originally targeted for X-by-Wire systems which require higher transmission rates than what CAN typically supports. Unlike CAN, FlexRay is a time-triggered network (although event-triggering is supported) operating on TDMA (Time Division Multiple Access) basis, and is mainly used by applications in the power train and safety domains, while some applications in the body domain are also supported [9]. FlexRay is equipped with two transmission channels, each having a capacity of up to 10 Mbit/s and can transmit data in parallel, achieving an overall data rate of up to 20 Mbit/s. FlexRay supports point-to-point, bus, star and hybrid network topologies.

MOST. Recent years have witnessed a proliferation of in-vehicle multimedia-based applications. These applications usually require high bandwidth to support real-time delivery of the large multimedia data. As a result, the Media Oriented Systems Transport (MOST) bus system [16] was developed in 1998 and is today the most dominant automotive multimedia bus system. Unlike CAN (which only defines the physical and data link layers), MOST comprises all the OSI reference model layers and even provides various standard application interfaces for improved interoperability. MOST can connect up to 64 nodes in a ring topology with a maximum bandwidth of 22.5 Mbit/s using an optical bus (though recent

MOST revisions support even higher data rate). Data in MOST network is sent in 1,024 bits frames, which suits the demanding multimedia functions. MOST supports both time-driven and event-driven paradigms. Applications of MOST including audio-based (e.g. radio), video-based (e.g. DVD), and telematics.

6 Automotive Sensors

A typical vehicle integrates at least several hundred sensors (and actuators, although this is not a concern for the present paper), with increasing number of sensors even in economical vehicles to provide new safety, comfort and convenience functions. Typically, ECUs are built from microcontrollers which control actuators based on sensor inputs. In this paper, we are not concerned with technical sensor technology issues such as how sensor information is measured and the accuracy or reliability of measurements, but rather in either the raw sensor information or the output of the ECU microcontrollers based on information from those sensors; for a comprehensive discussion about automotive sensors, the reader is referred to, e.g., [17].

7 Advanced Automotive Applications

Currently, typical modern vehicles contain around 30–70 Electronic Control Units (ECU) [18], most of which are part of the power train and the chassis domains and thus usually connected by CAN buses. However, while different vehicles maintain approximately similar number of these essential ECUs, the number of ECUs in other domains (especially the telematics & multimedia and safety domains) significantly differ for different vehicle models and they are mostly what constitute the intelligent vehicle technology. In the following we discuss examples of functions integrated in most modern, intelligent vehicles. Most of these functions are connected via MOST or FlexRay networks with few exceptions for functions that may be implemented in the body domain (and hence are typically connected by LIN or CAN links).

Adaptive Cruise Control. One of the fundamental intelligent vehicle functions is Adaptive Cruise Control (ACC). Unlike static cruise, which fixes the traveling speed of the vehicle, in ACC, the vehicle senses its surrounding environment and adjusts its speed appropriately; advanced ACC systems can also access the navigation system, identify the current location and adhere to the speed limit of the corresponding roadway and respond to road conditions. ACC can be based on Radar (radio waves measurements), LADAR (laser measurements), or computer vision (image/video analysis) [19]. In Radar and LADAR based ACC, radio waves and laser beams, respectively, are emitted to measure the range (the distance between the hosting vehicle and the vehicle ahead) and the range rate (how fast the vehicle ahead is moving), and adapt the traveling speed accordingly. In vision-based ACC, a camera mounted behind the windshield or the front bumper captures video images of the front scene in which computer vision algorithms are applied on to estimate the range and range rate [20]. Note that there are a few variants of ACC, e.g. high-speed ACC, low-speed ACC etc. While all of these variants are based on the same basic principles as outlined above, some of them take more active roles, such as automatic steering.

Lane Keeping Assist. Lane Keeping Assist (LKA) is an application of Lane Departure Warning Systems (LDWS) and Road Departure Warning Systems (RDWS). Motivated by safety reasons, LKA is now a key function in intelligent vehicles. The most widely used approach of implementing LKA is by processing camera images for the road surface and identifying lane edges (usually represented by white dashed lines), then either warn the driver or automatically adjust the steering away from the lane edge; similar process is applied when departing from roads. Other approaches to implement LKA include roadway magnetic markers detection, and using digital GPS maps [19], but these are less commonly used since not all roadways are equipped with magnetic markers (which is extremely expensive), while GPS lane tracking does not always produce acceptably accurate measures and may also be based on inaccurate maps.

Parking Assist. Parking assist systems are rapidly becoming an expected feature. Implementations range from basic ultrasonic sensor alerts to an automated steering for parallel parking as introduced in Toyota's Intelligent Parking Assist (IPS) system in 2003. Usually, these systems have an integrated camera mounted at the rear bumper of the vehicle to provide a wide angle rear-view for the driver and can be accompanied with visual or audible manoeuvre instructions to guide the vehicle into parking spaces.

Blind Spot Monitoring. Between the driver's side view and the driver's rearview, there is an angle of restricted vision usually called the *blind spot*. For obvious safety reasons, when changing the lane, vehicles passing through the blind spot should be detected, which is accomplished by the Blind Spot Monitoring (BSM) systems. Such systems detect vehicles in the blind spot by Radar, LADAR or Ultrasonic emitters, with vision-based approaches (i.e. camera image processing) also becoming increasingly common. Most of these systems initiate warnings to the driver once a vehicle is detected in the blind spot, but future models may take a more active role to prevent collisions by automatically control the steering. Note that blind spot monitoring may also refer to systems that implement an adjustable side mirrors to reveal the blind spot to the driver, e.g. [21], but here we refer to the more advanced (and convenient) RF- and/or vision-based systems.

Head-up Display and Night Vision. Head-Up Display (HUD) technology was originally developed for aircrafts. HUD projects an image on a vehicle's front glass (in aviation applications this was originally a separate translucent pane), which will appear for the driver to be at the tip of the bonnet, and can be used to display the various information such as dashboard information or even navigation instructions. Beginning in the mid-1990s, General Motors (GM) used

HUD technology to enhance visibility at night by adding night vision functions to the HUD. In this technology, the front bumper of the vehicle is equipped with an infrared camera which provides enhanced night vision images of the road ahead and projects it for the driver. Infrared cameras detect objects by measuring the heat emitted from other vehicles, humans or animals. Recent trends use Near-Infrared (NIR) cameras instead which are also able to detect cold objects like trees and road signs [19]. However, the range of NIR is shorter and extends for only around 100m compared to around 500m in the case of the conventional (thermal) infrared cameras.

Telematics and Multimedia. Originally motivated by location-based services, telematics is now a more general term and comprises all wireless communication to and from the vehicle to exchange various types of information, including navigation, traffic warnings, vehicle-to-vehicle communication and, recently, mobile Internet and mobile TV. Telematics services have seamlessly found their way to intelligent vehicles becoming totally indispensable from them. However, it is not clear whether multimedia-based services should be classified under telematics and indeed there is a fine line between the two; for brevity, and to prevent confusion, we here merge them under a single class and assume that they use similar bus technology (typically MOST or FlexRay). Multimedia-based services involve the transmission of large (and sometimes real-time) data, which require high data rates; examples of multimedia applications include hands-free phones, CD/DVD players, radio and voice recognition.

Navigation. Automotive navigation systems are among the most essential telematics applications in modern vehicles and can be either integrated or standalone. Off-the-shelf (aftermarket) standalone navigation systems operate independently from other in-vehicle automotive components; this type of portable systems is largely irrelevant for our discussion since it can be easily removed or tampered with, although some integration with other components via, e.g., Bluetooth may occur. Built-in navigation systems, on the other hand, are often tightly integrated with other in-vehicle ECUs. In this case, navigation is not solely dependant on GPS technology, instead it takes advantage of its in-vehicle integration by receiving inputs from other automotive sensors; this is especially advantageous as GPS signals are not always available. Built-in navigation systems use the *Vehicle Speed Sensor (VSS)* or *tachometer sensor* to calculate the vehicle's speed, the *yaw rate sensor* to detect changes in direction, and GPS to determine the absolute direction movement of the vehicle. Integration also provides further benefits in applications such as *Adaptive Light Control*, automatically adjusting headlight settings to, e.g., anticipate turns, or simply by highlighting points of interest such as petrol stations in low-fuel situations.

Occupant Sensors. For safety reasons, it is important to detect the presence of occupants inside the vehicle. This is usually accomplished by mounting sensors under the seats to detect occupancy by measuring the pressure of an occupant's weight against the seat [22]. More advanced systems can even estimate the size of the occupant and consequently adjust the inflation force of the airbag in case of an accident since inflating the airbag with sufficiently high pressure can sometimes lead to severe injuries or even fatalities for children. Occupant detection can also be used for heating and seat belt alerts. However, rear seats may not always be equipped with such sensors, so another type of occupancy sensing primarily intended for security based on motion detectors is usually used [23]. These sensors can be based on infrared, ultrasonic, microwave, or radar and will detect any movements within the interior of the entire vehicle.

8 Live Forensics

Digital forensic examinations have rapidly become a routine procedure of crime and crime scene investigations even where the alleged criminal acts were not themselves technology-based. Although vehicular forensic procedures are slightly less mature than conventional digital forensics in personal computers and mobile (smart) phones, for example, we argue that the rich set of sensors and information obtainable from vehicles, as outlined above, can provide important evidence. Forensic examiners, therefore, are now starting to realise the importance of vehicular-based forensics and evidence. Moreover, as the same techniques can also be used, e.g., in (industrial) espionage, awareness of forensic techniques and counter-forensics in this domain are also becoming relevant. Typical forensic examinations are carried out either *offline* or *online* (live). Offline forensics involves examining the vehicle after an event while online forensics observe and report on the behaviour of a target in real-time. Note that this taxonomy may not agree with the literature where sometimes both offline and online forensics are assumed to take place post hoc and differ only by whether the vehicle is turned on or off, respectively, at the time of examination. Live forensics in this context is slightly different from surveillance as the latter may not always refer to exclusively observing criminals/suspects.

When adopting an online forensic approach, live data can be collected *actively* or *passively*. In either case, the system has to be *observed* appropriately before initiating the data collection process. In active live forensics, we have partial control over the system and can trigger functions to be executed without occupant knowledge. In passive live forensics, on the other hand, data are collected passively by intercepting traffic on vehicular networks. The observation process can be either hardware or software-based as discussed in sections 8.1 and 8.2, respectively. In both cases, data is collected by entities called *collectors*; while passive forensics may be approached by both software and hardware-based solutions, active forensics may only be feasible in a software-based approach owing to the (usually) limited time available to prepare a target vehicle for the hardware-based one.

As discussed in section 7, a typical intelligent vehicle integrates numerous functions usable for evidence collection and surveillance; this is a natural approach even for normal operation. For example, parking assist units are sometimes used by the automatic steel folding roof systems in convertibles to first monitor the area behind the vehicle and assesses whether folding the roof is possible. Similarly, we can observe and collect the output of relevant functions and draw conclusions about the behaviour of the occupants while using such data as evidence. We generally classify the functions we are interested in as vision-based and RF-based functions, noting that some functions can use a complementary vision-RF approach, or have different modes supporting either, while other functions based on neither vision or RF measurement can still provide useful information as shown in section 9:

(1) Vision-based functions: these are applications based on video streams (or still images) and employ computer vision algorithms – sometimes we are interested in the original video data rather than the processed results. Examples of these applications include: ACC, LKA, parking assist, blind spot monitoring, night vision, and some telematics applications. Vision-based applications are generally based on externally mounted cameras, which is especially useful to capture external criminal activities (e.g. exchanging/selling drugs), even allowing to capture evidence on associates of the target. Furthermore, newer telematics models may have built-in internal cameras (e.g. for video conferencing) that can capture a vehicle's interior.
(2) RF-based functions: similarly, these are applications based on wireless measurements such as ultrasonic, radar, LADAR, laser or Bluetooth. Unlike vision-based applications, here we are mostly interested in post-analysis of these measurements as raw RF measurements are typically not forensically meaningful.

8.1 Hardware-Based Live Forensics

The most straightforward solution for live forensics is to adopt a hardware-based data collection approach which involves installing special intercepting devices (*collectors*) around the vehicle to *observe* and collect the various types of data flowing through the vehicular networks. The collectors can be attached to ECU's or other components and capture outbound and/or inbound traffic. This information may then be locally stored inside the collectors or in a central location such as an entertainment system for later retrieval if sufficient local storage is available, or otherwise, the collectors can be configured to establish a private connection to an external location (i.e. federated network) for constant data transmission. This private network can, e.g., be setup through GSM/UMTS in cooperation with the carrier.

It is of utmost importance to carefully decide where to install these collectors, thus a good understanding of the data flow within the in-vehicle automotive system is required. Since different vehicle makes and even models have slightly different specifications, in this section we try to discuss the most attractive *observation loci* within the vehicle. As described above, vehicular systems contain several networks of different types that are interconnected by gateways, which can be considered the automotive equivalent of routers in conventional networks. Either a central gateway is used where all networks are connected to a single gateway (see figure 1(a)), or these networks are connected by several gateways (see figure 1(b)). In our live forensics examination, we are only interested in data generated by specific ECU's (mostly those that are part of MOST or FlexRay networks which correspond to functions in the body, telematics and safety domains), thus only those gateways connecting such networks need to be observed. However, in some cases, observing the gateways only may not be sufficient because in some applications we may also be interested in the raw ECU sensor readings (such as camera video/images) which may be inaccessible from gateways. For example, in vision-based blind spot monitoring application, the information relevant to the driver is whether there is an obstacle at the left/right side of the vehicle, but we are not interested in this information, we are only interested in the video/image that the corresponding sensors capture to be used to detect the presence of an obstacle (i.e. we are interested in the ECU input, while only the output is what normally sent through the gateway). Thus, in such cases, we may need to observe individual ECU's rather than gateways. Note, however, that observing gateways only may work for some applications where the input and the output are similar, such as parking assist where the parking camera transmits a live video stream to the driver.

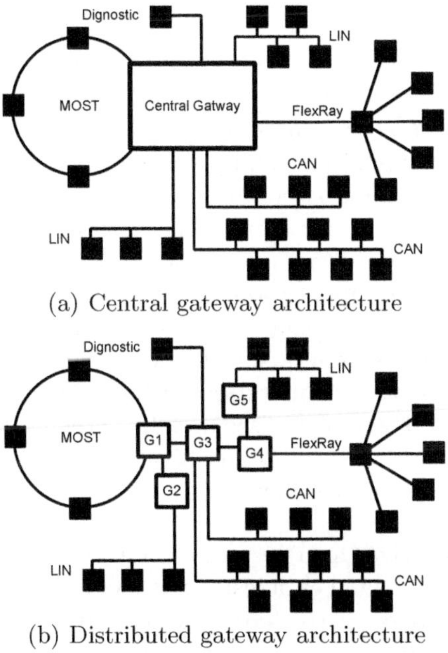

(a) Central gateway architecture

(b) Distributed gateway architecture

Fig. 1. Sample Automotive Network Architectures

8.2 Software-Based Live Forensics

Although by simply installing hardware collectors at particular ECU's or gateways, we will be able to collect live forensic data, such an approach may be limited due to aspects: *(1) Flexibility:* Since installation and removal of the hardware collectors need to be carried out manually and physically, they are inflexible in terms of reconfigurability and mobility; that is, once a devices is installed, it cannot be easily reconfigured or moved without physical intervention, which is not convenient or even (sometimes) possible. *(2) Installation:* The installation process of these devices will pose a serious challenge as locating and identifying the relevant ECU's or gateways is often difficult especially when some functions use information from several ECU's and sensors. Moreover, physical devices may be observable by an investigating target. *(3) Inspection:* the collectors will very likely collect large amount of possibly irrelevant data (such as channel management data); although this can be mitigated by using slightly more sophisticated collectors that filter observed traffic before interception, this introduces cost and efficiency implications.

Software based solutions, on the other hand, seem to alleviate these problems. Traditionally, the in-vehicle software (firmware) is updated manually via the vehicle's on-board diagnostic port. However, with the introduction of wireless communication, most manufacturers are now updating the firmware wirelessly, which, in turn, introduced several security concerns. Indeed, a recent work [24] showed that automotive networks are still lacking sufficient security measures. Thus, in our scenario, and following a particular set of legal procedures (see section 10), we can install the collectors as firmware updates with relative ease. These updates are then injected into the in-vehicle networks wirelessly and routed to the appropriate ECU.

Although software-based live forensics may be flexible and efficient, it poses a whole new class of compatibility and potentially safety issues. Unfortunately, most of the current software-based automotive solutions are proprietary and hardware dependant; thus, it may appear that unless we have knowledge of the automotive software and hardware architecture we are targeting, we will not be able to develop a software application to carry out our live forensics process, and even if we have such knowledge, we will be able to develop such software that will only work in the system it was developed for (lack of interoperability). However, these interoperability limitations (which also affect other automotive applications) have recently been realised and drove the leading automotive manufacturers and suppliers to establish an alliance for developing a standardized software architecture, named AUTOSAR.

AUTOSAR. AUTomotive Open System ARchitecture (AUTOSAR) is a newly established initiative by a number of leading automotive manufacturers and suppliers that jointly cooperated to develop a standardized automotive software architecture under the principle "cooperate on the standard, compete on the implementation". The first vehicle containing AUTOSAR components was launched in 2008 while a fully AUTOSAR supported vehicle is expected in 2010.

AUTOSAR aims to seamlessly separate applications from infrastructure so automotive applications developers do not have to be concerned about hardware peculiarities, which will greatly mitigate the complexity of integrating new and emerging automotive technologies. AUTOSAR covers all vehicle domains and functions from engine and transmission to wipers and lights. The main design principle of AUTOSAR is to abstract the automotive software development process and adopt a component-based model where applications are composed of software components that are all connected using a Virtual Functional Bus (VFB), which handles all communication requirements. AUTOSAR transforms ECUs into a layered architecture on top of the actual ECU hardware, as shown in figure 2 (a simplified view of the AUTOSAR layers). Below are brief descriptions of each layer:

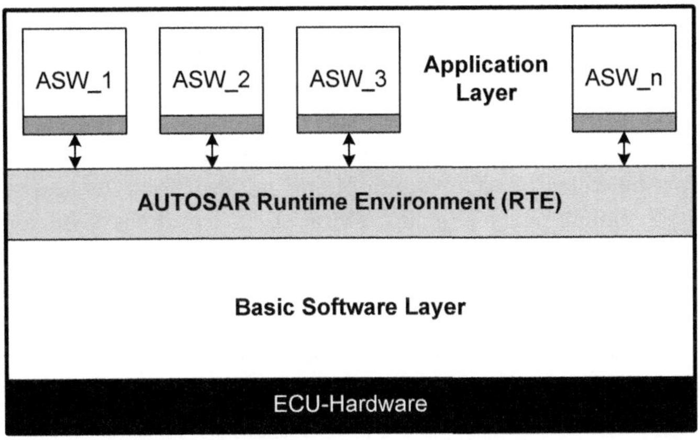

Fig. 2. AUTOSAR layered architecture

(1) AUTOSAR application layer: composed of a number of AUTOSAR software components (ASW). These components are not standardized (although their interfaces with the RTE are) and their implementation depends on the application functions. *(2) AUTOSAR Runtime Environment:* provides communication means to exchange information between the software components of the same ECU (intra-ECU) and with software components of other ECUs (inter-ECU). *(3) Basic software layer:* provides services to the AUTOSAR software components and contains both ECU independent (e.g. communication/network management) and ECU dependent (e.g. ECU abstraction) components. AUTOSAR standardises 63 basic software modules [25].

All software components are connected through the Virtual Functional Bus (VFB) which is implemented by the RTE at each ECU (VFB can be thought of as the concatenation of all RTE's). This paradigm potentially hides the underlying hardware from the application view, which, clearly, has advantageous consequences when collecting evidence for forensic examination. Thus an AUTOSAR-based collection tool will be compatible with all AUTOSAR supported vehicles. Furthermore, since the VFB allows seamless collection via different software components at different ECUs, a single live forensic software will be able to communicate with different software components and retrieve data from other applications and functions without having to be concerned with communication and other ECU-dependant issues.

Active Software-Based Live forensics. As discussed above, active live forensics appears feasible mainly when collectors are based on software, and is further facilitated by architectures such as AUTOSAR. An example of a typical application where active live forensics can be carried out is the vehicle's built-in hands-free telephony system. Although features and functions offered by the hands-free system may be different from a particular vehicle model to another, most recent models of hands-free system will synchronise some information with the phone it is paired with, including address books (contacts list) and call history. One benefit of this synchronisation process is allowing the driver to interact with the phone through the vehicle entertainment and communication system instead of the handset itself. This functionality is particularly useful for our live forensic investigation since it means that once the phone is paired with the hands-free system, the hands-free system can control it. Thus, an obvious active live forensic scenario is for the collector to initiate a phone call (without the knowledge of the driver) to a particular party (e.g. law enforcement) and carry out a live audio-based surveillance, the police can then cooperate with the carrier to suppress the relevant call charges. This can also occur in a side-band without affecting the ability to conduct further calls or in bursts.

We also note that the ability to scan for Bluetooth (or other RF such as 802.11) devices within a vehicle provides further potential to establish circumstantial evidence of the presence of individuals in a vehicle's proximity, even if, e.g., a passenger's mobile phone is never paired with the vehicle's communication system, allowing further tracking as reported in previous research [26].

9 Sensor Fusion

Forensic investigations can be significantly improved by fusing information from different sources (sensors). Many functions already implement sensor fusion as part of their normal operation, where two sensor measurements are fused, e.g. park assist uses ultrasonic and camera sensors. Similarly, while carrying out live forensic, we can fuse sensor data from even different functions that are not usually fused, such as video streams from blind spot monitoring with GPS measurements, where the location of the vehicle can be supported by visual images. Generally, however, data fusion is a post hoc process since it usually requires more resources than what the collectors are capable of. Below we discuss two applications of data fusion.

Visual Observation. Fusing video streams from different applications may result in a full view of the vehicle's surrounding environment. This is possible as the front view is captured by ACC, the side views by blind spot monitoring, and back view by parking assist cameras, while some vehicles provide further surround views. Note, however, that some of these cameras are only activated when the corresponding function is activated (e.g. the parking assist camera is only activated when the driver is trying to park); but obviously, active forensics can surmount this problem as it can actively control (activate/deactivate) the relevant functions.

Occupant Detection. As discussed in section 7, occupancy can be detected through existing sensors. However, further identifying the individuals on-board is even more desirable than just detecting their presence. While the approach of scanning for Bluetooth MAC addresses mentioned in section 8.2 may possibly identify the occupants passively, audio and, potentially, video recordings can provide further evidence even about individuals approaching or leaving the vehicle. Furthermore, In an active live forensic scenario, both the hands-free system and the occupant detection sensors can be associated such that if the occupant sensor detected a new occupant, the hands-free system automatically (and without the knowledge of the driver) initiates a pairing search to detect all MAC addresses in range. Note that hands-free search may detect Bluetooth devices of nearby vehicles or pedestrians and must hence be fused with occupant detection sensors information and repeated regularly, augmented by cameras where possible.

10 Discussion and Conclusion

The mechanisms (both active and passive) described in this paper have significant privacy and legal implications, yet while presenting this work we assume that such procedures are undertaken by law enforcement officials following appropriate procedures. We note that in some jurisdictions, it may not be necessary to obtain warrants, which is of particular relevance when persons other than the driver or vehicle owner are observed; this is, e.g., the case under the United Kingdom's Regulation of Investigatory Powers Act (2000).

In this paper, we presented a general overview of modern automotive systems and further discussed the various advanced functions resulting in what is commonly known today as an *Intelligent Vehicle*. We showed that functions available in modern automotive systems can significantly improve our live (real-time) digital forensic investigations. Most driver/passenger comfort and convenience functions such as telematics, parking assist and Adoptive Cruise Control (ACC) use multimedia sensors capturing the surrounding scene, which, if properly intercepted, can provide substantial evidence. Similarly, other sensors, like seat occupant sensors and hands-free phone systems, can be used for driver/passenger identification.

Future work will concentrate on characterising and fusing sensor data sources, while a natural extension to this work is to look at the feasibility of offline forensics (post hoc extraction of data) and investigate what kind of non-volatile data (other than Event Data Record (EDR) data, which is not always interesting or relevant for forensic investigations) that the vehicular system preserves and stores in-memory. Our expectation is that most of such data is not forensically relevant to investigating behavioural analysis of individuals in a court of law. However, we note that some functions may be capable of storing useful information as part of their normal operation, possibly with user interaction. For example, most navigation systems maintain historical records for previous destinations entered by the user in addition to a *favourite locations* list and a *home* location bookmark configured by the user; these records and configurations are likely to be non-volatile and can be easily retrieved at later times. Moreover, these systems may also contain information on *intended* movement, which is of particular interest if it can be communicated in real-time to investigators and enables anticipating target movements. Finally, future work will investigate counter-forensics mechanisms, which may also be relevant to investigate that vehicles such as hire cars have not been tampered with in anticipation of industrial espionage operations.

References

1. Wilwert, C., Navet, N., Song, Y., Simonot-Lion, F.: Design of Automotive X-by-Wire Systems. In: Zurawski, R. (ed.) The Industrial Communication Technology Handbook. CRC Press, Boca Raton (2005)
2. Singleton, N., Daily, J., Manes, G.: Automobile Event Data Recorder Forensics. In: Shenoi, S. (ed.) Advances in Digital Foreniscs IV. IFIP, vol. 285, pp. 261–272. Springer, Heidelberg (2008)
3. Daily, J., Singleton, N., Downing, B., Manes, G.: Light Vehicle Event Data Recorder Forensics. In: Advances in Computer and Information Sciences and Engineering, pp. 172–177 (2008)
4. Nilsson, D., Larson, U.: Combining Physical and Digital Evidence in Vehicle Environments. In: 3rd International Workshop on Systematic Approaches to Digital Forensic Engineering, pp. 10–14 (2008)
5. Nilsson, D., Larson, U.: Conducting Forensic Investigations of Cyber Attacks on Automobile in-Vehicle Network. In: e-Foreniscs 2008 (2008)
6. Navet, N., Simonot-Lion, F.: Review of Embedded Automotive Protocols. In: Automotive Embedded Systems Handbook. CRC Press, Boca Raton (2008)
7. Shaheen, S., Heffernan, D., Leen, G.: A Comparison of Emerging Time-Triggered Protocols for Automotive X-by-Wire Control Networks. Journal of Automobile Engineering 217(2), 12–22 (2002)
8. Leen, C., Heffernan, D., Dunne, A.: Digital Networks in the Automotive Vehicle. Computing and Control Journal 10(6), 257–266 (1999)
9. Dietsche, K.H. (ed.): Automotive Networking. Robert Bosch GmbH (2007)
10. LIN Consortium: LIN Specification Package, revision 2.1 (2006), `http://www.lin-subbus.org`
11. Schmid, M.: Automotive Bus Systems. Atmel Applications Journal 6, 29–32 (2006)
12. Robert Bosch GmbH: CAN Specification, Version 2.0 (1991)
13. International Standard Organization: Road Vehicles - Low Speed Serial Data Communication - Part 2: Low Speed Controller Area Network, ISO 11519-2 (1994)
14. International Standard Organization: Road Vehicles - Interchange of Digital Informaiton - Controller Aera Nework for High-speed Communication, ISO 11898 (1994)
15. FlexRay Consortium.: FlexRay Communications Systems, Protocol Specification, Version 2.1, Revision A. (2005), `www.flexray.com`
16. MOST Cooperation: MOST Specifications, revision 3.0 (2008), `http://www.mostnet.de`
17. Dietsche, K.H. (ed.): Automotive Sensors. Robert Bosch GmbH (2007)
18. Prosser, S.: Automotive Sensors: Past, Present and Future. Journal of Physics: Conference Series 76 (2007)

19. Bishop, R.: Intelligent Vehicle Technology and Trends. Artech House, Boston (2005)
20. Stein, G., Mano, O., Shashua, A.: Vision-based ACC with a Single Camera: Bounds on Range and Range Rate Accuracy. In: IEEE Intelligent Vehicle Symosium (2003)
21. Suggs, T.: Vehicle Blind Spot Monitoring System (Patent no. 6880941) (2005)
22. Henze, K., Baur, R.: Seat Occupancy Sensor (Patent no. 7595735) (2009)
23. Redfern, S.: A Radar Based Mass Movement Sensor for Automotive Security Applications. IEE Colloquium on Vehicle Security Systems, 5/1–5/3 (1993)
24. Nilsson, D., Larson, U.: Simulated Attacks on CAN Busses: Vehicle Virus. In: AsiaCSN 2008 (2008)
25. Voget, S., Golm, M., Sanchez, B., Stappert, F.: Application of the AUTOSAR Standard. In: Navet, N., Simonot-Lion, F. (eds.) Automotive Embedded Systems Handbook. CRC Press, Boca Raton (2008)
26. Al-Kuwari, S., Wolthusen, S.: Algorithms for Advanced Clandestine Tracking in Short-Range Ad Hoc Networks. In: MobiSec 2010. ICST. Springer, Heidelberg (2010)

Research and Review on Computer Forensics*

Hong Guo, Bo Jin, and Daoli Huang

Key Laboratory of Information Network Security, Ministry of Public Security, People's Republic of China (The 3rd Research Institute of Ministry of Public Security)
Room 304, BiSheng Road 339, Shanghai 201204, China
{guohong,jinbo,huangdaoli}@stars.org.cn

Abstract. With the development of Internet and information technology, the digital crimes are also on the rise. Computer forensics is an emerging research area that applies computer investigation and analysis techniques to help detection of these crimes and gathering of digital evidence suitable for presentation in courts. This paper provides foundational concept of computer forensics, outlines various principles of computer forensics, discusses the model of computer forensics and presents a proposed model.

Keywords: Computer forensics, computer crime, digital evidence.

1 Introduction

The use of Internet and information technology has grown rapidly all over the world in the 21st century. Directly correlated to this growth is the increased amount of criminal activities that involve digital crimes or e-crimes worldwide. These digital crimes impose new challenges on prevention, detection, investigation, and prosecution of the corresponding offences.

The emergence of highly technical nature of digital crimes was created a new branch of forensic science known as computer forensics. Computer forensics is an emerging research area that applies computer investigation and analysis techniques to help detection of these crimes and gathering of digital evidence suitable for presentation in courts. This new area combines the knowledge of information technology, forensics science, and law and gives rise to a number of interesting and challenging problems related to computer security and cryptography that are yet to be solved [1].

Computer forensics has recently gained significant popularity with many local law enforcement agencies. It is currently employed for judicial expertise in almost every enforcement activity. However, it is still behind other methods such as fingerprint analysis, because there have been fewer efforts to improve its accuracy. Therefore, the legal system is often in the dark as to the validity, or even the significance, of digital evidence [2].

* This paper is supported by the Special Basic Research, Ministry of Science and Technology of the People's Republic of China, project number: 2008FY240200.

X. Lai et al. (Eds.): E-Forensics 2010, LNICST 56, pp. 224–233, 2011.

This paper provides foundational concept of computer forensics, outlines various principles of computer forensics, discusses the model of computer forensics and presents a proposed model.

2 Definition of Computer Forensics

Those involved in computer forensics often do not understand the exact definition of computer forensics. In fact, computer forensics is a branch of forensic science pertaining to legal evidence found in computers and digital storage media.

2.1 Definition of Forensics and Forensic Science

The term forensics derives from the Latin "forensis", which means "in open court or public", which itself comes from the Latin "of the forum", referring to an actual location—a "public squarer marketplace used for judicial and other business". [3] In dictionaries forensics is defined as the process of using scientific knowledge for collecting, analyzing, and presenting evidence to the courts.

The term forensic science is "the application of scientific techniques and principles to provide evidence to legal or related investigations and determinations". [4] It aims to determining the evidential value of crime scene and related evidence.

2.2 Definition of Computer Forensics

Computer forensics is a branch of forensic science. The term computer forensics originated in the late 1980s with early law enforcement practitioners who used it to refer to examining standalone computers for digital evidence of crime.

Indeed, the language used to describe computer forensics and even the definition of the term itself varies considerably among those who study and practice it. [5] Legal specialists commonly refer only to the analysis, rather than the collection, of enhanced data. By way of contrast, computer scientists have defined it as valid tools and techniques applied against computer networks, systems, peripherals, software, data, and/or users -to identify actors, actions, and/or states of interest [6].

According to Steve Hailey, Cyber security Institute, computer forensics is "The preservation, identification, extraction, interpretation, and documentation of computer evidence, to include the rules of evidence, legal processes, integrity of evidence, factual reporting of the information found, and providing expert opinion in a court of law or other legal and/or administrative proceeding as to what was found." [7].

In Digital Forensics Research Workshop held in 2001, computer forensics is defined as "the use of scientifically derived and proven methods towards the preservation, collection, validation, identification, analysis, interpretation, documentation and presentation of digital evidence derived from digital source for the purpose of facilitating or furthering the reconstruction of events found to be criminal, or helping to anticipate unauthorized actions shown to be disruptive to planned operations. "

However, many experts feel that a precise definition is not yet possible because digital evidence is recovered from devices that are not traditionally considered to be computers. Some researchers prefer to expand the definition such as definition by Palmer to include the collection and examination of all forms of digital data, including that found in cell phones, PDAs, iPods and other electronic devices [8].

From a technical standpoint, Computer Forensics is formulated as an established set of disciplines and the very high standards in place for uncovering digital evidence extracted from personal computers and electronic devices (including those from large corporate systems and networks, across the Internet and the emerging families of cell phones, PDAs, iPods and other electronic devices) for court proceedings.

3 Principles of Computer Forensics

When dealing with computer forensics, the term "evidence" has the following meaning: "Any information and data of value to an investigation that is stored on, received, or transmitted by an electronic device. This evidence is acquired in physical or binary (digital) form that may be used to support or prove the facts of an incident.

According to NIJ, the properties of digital evidence as follows: [9]

- Is latent, like fingerprints or DNA evidence.
- Crosses jurisdictional borders quickly and easily.
- Is easily altered, damaged, or destroyed.
- Can be time sensitive.

3.1 Rules of Evidence

Dye to the properties of digital evidence, the rules of evidence are very precise and exist to ensure that evidence is properly acquired, stored and unaltered when it is presented in the courtroom. RFC 3227 describes legal considerations related to gathering evidence. The rules require digital evidence to be:

- Admissible: It must conform to certain legal rules before it can be put before a court.
- Authentic: The integrity and chain of custody of the evidence must be intact.[10]
- Complete: All evidence supporting or contradicting any evidence that incriminates a suspect must be considered and evaluated. It is also necessary to collect evidence that eliminates other suspects.
- Reliable: Evidence collection, examination, analysis, preservation and reporting procedures and tools must be able to replicate the same results over time. The procedures must not cast doubt on the evidence's authenticity and/or on conclusions drawn after analysis.
- Believable: Evidence should be clear, easy to understand and believable. The version of evidence presented in court must be linked back to the original binary evidence otherwise there is no way to know if the evidence has been fabricated.

3.2 Guidelines for Evidence Handling

It is s important to follow the rules of evidence in computer forensics investigations. There are a number of guidelines for handling digital evidence throughout the process of computer forensics, published by various groups, for example, Best Practices for Computer Forensics by SWGDE, Guidelines for Best Practice in the Forensic Examination of Digital Technology by IOCE, Electronic Crime Scene Investigation:

A Guide for First Responders by NIJ and Guide to Integrating Forensic Techniques into Incident Response by NIST. Of all the guidelines referred to above, the G8 principles proposed by IOCE is considered the most authoritative one.

In March 2000, the G8 put forward a set of proposed principles for procedures relating to digital evidence. These principles provide a solid base from which to work during any examination done before law enforcement attends.

G8 Principles – Procedures Relating to Digital Evidence [11]

1. When dealing with digital evidence, all general forensic and procedural principles must be applied.
2. Upon seizing digital evidence, actions taken should not change that evidence.
3. When it is necessary for a person to access original digital evidence, that person should be trained for the purpose.
4. All activity relating to the seizure, access, storage or transfer of digital evidence must be fully documented, preserved, and available for review.
5. An individual is responsible for all actions taken with respect to digital evidence whilst the digital evidence is in their possession.
6. Any agency, which is responsible for seizing, accessing, storing or transferring digital evidence is responsible for compliance with these principles.

This set of principles can act as a solid foundation. However, as one principle states, if someone must touch evidence they should be properly trained. Training helps reduce the likelihood of unintended alteration of evidence. It also increases one's credibility in a court of law if called to testify about actions taken before the arrival and/or involvement of the police.

3.3 Proposed Principles

According to the properties of digital evidences, we summarized the principles of computer forensics as follows:

- Practice in a timely manner
- Practice in a legal way
- Chain of custody
- Obey rules of evidence
- Minimize handling of the original evidence
- Document any changes in evidence
- Audit throughout the process

4 Models of Computer Forensics

Forensic practitioners and computer scientists both agree that "forensic models" are important for guiding the development in the computer forensics field. Models enable people to understand what that process does, and does not do.

There are many models for the forensic process, such as Kruse and Heiser Model (2002), Forensics Process Model (NIJ, 2001), Yale University Model (Eoghan Casey, 2000), KPMG Model (McKemmish, 1999), Dittrich and Brezinski Model (2000),

Mitre Model (Gary L. Palmer, 2002). Although the exact phases of the models vary somewhat, the models reflect the same basic principles and the same overall methodology.

Most of models reviewed have element identification, collection, preservation, analysis, and presentation. To make the step more clear and precise, some of them added addition detail steps into the element. Organizations should choose the specific forensic model that is most appropriate for their needs.

4.1 Kruse and Heiser Model

Kruse and Heiser have developed a methodology for computer forensics referred to as three basic components that is acquire, authenticate and analyze[12](Kruse and Heiser, 2002). These components focus on maintaining the integrity of the evidence during the investigation. In detail the steps are:

1. Acquire the evidence without altering or damaging the original. Consisting of the following steps:

a. Handling the evidence
b. Chain of custody
c. Collection
d. Identification
e. Storage
f. Documenting the investigation

2. Authenticate that your recovered evidence is the same as the originally seized data;
3. Analyze the data without modifying it.

Kruse and Heiser suggest that in computer forensics is the most essential element to fully document your investigation including all your steps taken. This is particularly important if due to the circumstances you did not maintain absolute forensic integrity then you can at least show the steps you did take. It is true that proper documentation of a computer forensic investigation is the most essential element and is commonly inadequately executed.

4.2 Forensics Process Model

The United States of America's Department of Justice proposed a process model in the Electronic Crime Scene Investigation: A guide to first responders. [13] This model is abstracted from technology. This model consists four phases:

1. Collection; The first phase in the process is to identify, label, record, and acquire data from the possible sources of relevant data, while following guidelines and procedures that preserve the integrity of the data.
2. Examination; Examinations involve forensically processing large amounts of collected data using a combination of automated and manual methods to assess and extract data of particular interest, while preserving the integrity of the data.

3. Analysis; The next phase of the process is to analyze the results of the examination, using legally justifiable methods and techniques, to derive useful information that addresses the questions that were the impetus for performing the collection and examination.

4. Reporting; The final phase is reporting the results of the analysis, which may include describing the actions used, explaining how tools and procedures were selected, determining what other actions need to be performed and providing recommendations for improvement to policies, guidelines, procedures, tools, and other aspects of the forensic process.

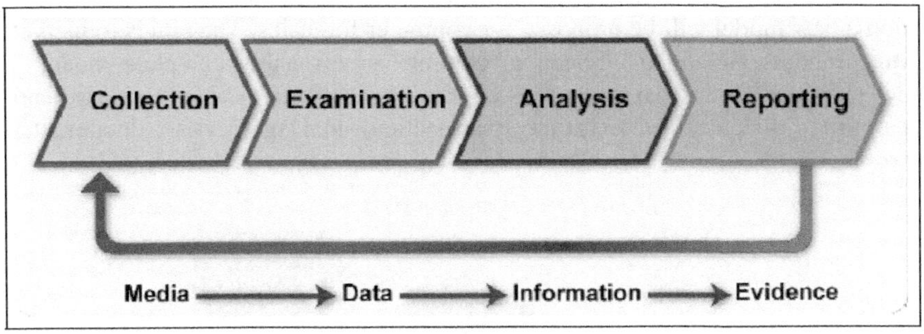

Fig. 1. Forensic Process [14]

There is a correlation between the 'acquiring the evidence' stage identified by Kruse and Heiser and the 'collection' stage proposed here. 'Analyzing the data' and 'analysis' are the same in both frameworks. Kruse has, however, neglected to include a vital component: reporting. This is included by the Department of Justice model.

4.3 Yale University Model

Eoghan Casey, a System Security Administrator at Yale University, also the author of Digital Evidence and Computer Crime (Casey, 2000) and the editor of the Handbook of Computer Crime Investigation (Casey, 2002), has developed the following digital evidence guidelines (Casey, 2000).

Casey: Digital Evidence Guidelines. [15]

1. Preliminary Considerations
2. Planning
3. Recognition
4. Preservation, collection and documentation
a. If you need to collect the entire computer (image)
b. If you need all the digital evidence on a computer but not the hardware (image)
c. If you only need a portion of the evidence on a computer (logical copy)
5. Classification, Comparison and Individualization
6. Reconstruction

This model focuses on processing and examining digital evidence. In Casey's models, the first and last steps are identical. Casey also places the focus of the forensic process on the investigation itself.

4.4 DFRW Model

The Digital Forensics Research Working Group (DFRW) developed a model with the following steps: identification; preservation; collection; examination; analysis; presentation, and decision. [16] This model puts in place an important foundation for future work and includes two crucial stages of the investigation. Components of an investigation stage as well as presentation stage are present.

4.5 Proposed Model

The previous sections outline several important computer forensic models. In this section a new model will be proposed for computer forensics. The aim is to merge the existing models already mentioned to compile a reasonably complete model. The model proposed in this paper consists of nine components. They are: identification, preparation, collection, preservation, examination, analysis, review, documentation and report.

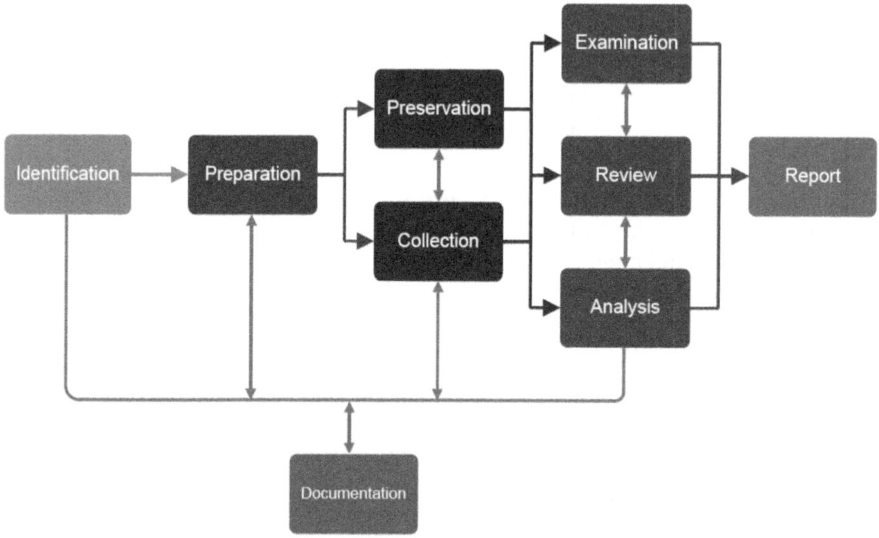

Fig. 2. Proposed Model of computer forensics

4.5.1 Identification

1. Identify the purpose of investigation.
2. Indentify resources required.
3. Indentify sources of digital evidence.
4. Indentify tools and techniques to use.

4.5.2 Preparation

The Preparation stage should include the following:

1. All equipment employed should be suitable for its purpose and maintained in a fully operational condition.

2. People accessing the original digital evidence should be trained to do so.

3. Preparation of search warrants, and monitoring authorizations and management support if necessary.

4. Develop a plan that prioritizes the sources, establishes the order in which the data should be acquired and determines the amount of effort required.

4.5.3 Collection

Methods of acquiring evidence should be forensically sound and verifiable.

1. Ensures no changes are made to the original data.

2. Security algorithms are provided to take an initial measurement of each file, as well as an entire collection of files. These algorithms are known as "hash" methodologies.

3. There are two methods for performing the copy process:

- Bit-by-Bit Copy:

This process, in order to be forensically sound, must use write blocker hardware or software to prevent any change to the data during the investigation. Once completed, this copy may be examined for evidence just as if it were the original.

- Forensic "Image"

The examiner uses special software and procedures to create the image file. An image file cannot be altered without altering the hash algorithm. None of the files contained within the image file can be altered without altering the hash algorithm. Furthermore, a cross validation test should be performed to ensure the validity of the process.

4.5.4 Preservation

1. Ensure that all digital evidence collected is properly documented, labeled, marked, photographed, video recorded or sketched, and inventoried.

2. Ensure that special care is taken with the digital evidences material during transportation to avoid physical damage, vibration and the effects of magnetic fields, electrical static and large variation of temperature and humidity.

3. Ensure that the digital evidence is stored in a secure, climate-controlled environment or a location that is not subject to extreme temperature or humidity. Ensure that the digital evidence is not exposed to magnetic fields, moisture, dust, vibration, or any other elements that may damage or destroy it.

4.5.5 Examination

1. Examiner should review documentation provided by the requestor to determine the processes necessary to complete the examination.

2. The strategy of the examination should be agreed upon and documented between the requestor and examiner.

3. Only appropriate standards, techniques and procedures and properly evaluated tools should be used for the forensic examination.

4. All standard forensic and procedural principles must be applied.

5. Avoid conducting an examination on the original evidence media if possible. Examinations should be conducted on forensic copies or via forensic image files.

6. All items submitted for forensic examination should first be reviewed for the integrity.

4.5.6 Analysis

The foundation of forensics is using a methodical approach to reach appropriate conclusions based on the evidence found or determine that no conclusion can yet be drawn. The analysis should include identifying people, places, items, and events, and determining how these elements are related so that a conclusion can be reached.

4.5.7 Review

The examiner's agency should have a written policy to establishing the protocols for technical and administrative review. All work undertaken should be subjected to both technical and administrative review.

1. Technical Review

Technical review should include consideration of the validity of all the critical examination findings and all the raw data used in preparation of the statement/report. It should also consider whether the conclusions drawn are justified by the work done and the information available. The review may include an element of independent testing, if circumstances warrant it.

2. Administrative Review

Administrative review should ensure that the requester's needs have been properly addressed, editorial correctness and adherence to policies.

4.5.8 Documentation

1. All activities relating to collection, preservation, examination or analysis of digital evidence must be completely documented.

2. Documentation should include evidence handling and examination documentation as well as administrative documentation. Appropriate standardized forms should be used to document.

3. Documentation should be preserved according to the examiner's agency policy.

4.5.9 Report

1. The style and content of written reports must meet the requirements of the criminal justice system for the country of jurisdiction, such as General Principles of Judicial Expertise Procedure in China.

2. Reports issued by the examiner should address the requestor's needs.

3. The report is to provide the reader with all the relevant information in a clear, concise, structured and unambiguous manner.

5 Conclusion

In this paper, we have reviewed the definition, the principles and several main categories models of computer forensics. In addition, we proposed a practical model that establishes a clear guideline of what steps should be followed in a forensic process. We suggest that such a model could be of great value to legal practitioners.

With more and more criminal behavior becomes linked to technology and the Internet, the necessity of digital evidence in litigation has increased. This evolution of evidence means that investigative strategies also must evolve in order to be applicable today and in the not so distant future. Due to this trend, the field of computer forensics will, no doubt, become more important to help curb the occurrences of crimes.

References

1. Hui, L.C.K., Chow, K.P., Yiu, S.M.: Tools and technology for computer forensics: research and development in Hong Kong. In: Proceedings of the 3rd International Conference on Information Security Practice and Experience, Hong Kong (2007)
2. Wagner, E.J.: The Science of Sherlock Holmes. Wiley, Chichester (2006)
3. New Oxford American Dictionary. 2nd edn.
4. Tilstone, W.J.: Forensic science: an encyclopedia of history, methods, and techniques (2006)
5. Peisert, S., Bishop, M., Marzullo, K.: Computer forensics in forensis. ACM SIGOPS Operating Systems Review 42(3) (2008)
6. Ziese, K.J.: Computer based forensics-a case study-U.S. support to the U.N. In: Proceedings of CMAD IV: Computer Misuse and Anomaly Detection (1996)
7. Hailey, S.: What is Computer Forensics (2003), http://www.cybersecurityinstitute.biz/forensics.htm
8. Abdullah, M.T., Mahmod, R., Ghani, A.A.A., Abdullah, M.Z., Sultan, A.B.M.: Advances in computer forensics. International Journal of Computer Science and Network Security 8(2), 215–219 (2008)
9. National Institute of Justice.: Electronic Crime Scene Investigation A Guide for First Responders, 2nd edn. (2001), http://www.ncjrs.gov/pdffiles1/nij/219941.pdf
10. RCMP: Computer Forensics: A Guide for IT Security Incident Responders (2008)
11. International Organization on Computer Evidence. G8 Proposed Principles for the Procedures Relating to Digital Evidence (1998)
12. Baryamureeba, V., Tushabe, F.: The Enhanced Digital Investigation Process Model Digital Forensics Research Workshop (2004)
13. National Institute of Justice.: Electronic Crime Scene Investigation A Guide for First Responders (2001), http://www.ncjrs.org/pdffiles1/nij/187736.pdf
14. National Institute of Standards and Technology.: Guide to Interating Forensic Techniques into Incident Response (2006)
15. Casey, E.: Digital Evidence and Computer Crime, 2nd edn. Elsevier Academic Press, Amsterdam (2004)
16. National Institute of Justice.: Results from Tools and Technologie Working Group, Goverors Summit on Cybercrime and Cyberterrorism, Princeton NJ (2002)

Text Content Filtering Based on Chinese Character Reconstruction from Radicals

Wenlei He[1], Gongshen Liu[1], Jun Luo[2], and Jiuchuan Lin[2]

[1] School of Information Security Engineering
Shanghai Jiao Tong University
[2] Key Lab of Information Network Security of Ministry of Public Security
The Third Research Institute of Ministry of Public Security

Abstract. Content filtering through keyword matching is widely adopted in network censoring, and proven to be successful. However, a technique to bypass this kind of censorship by decomposing Chinese characters appears recently. Chinese characters are combinations of radicals, and splitting characters into radicals pose a big obstacle to keyword filtering. To tackle this challenge, we proposed the first filtering technology based on combination of Chinese character radicals. We use a modified Rabin-Karp algorithm to reconstruct characters from radicals according to Chinese character structure library. Then we use another modified Rabin-Karp algorithm to filter keywords among massive text content. Experiment shows that our approach can identify most of the keywords in the form of combination of radicals and yields a visible improvement in the filtering result compared to traditional keyword filtering.

Keywords: Chinese character radical, multi-pattern matching, text filtering.

1 Introduction

In the past decades, Internet has evolved from an emerging technology to a ubiquitous service. The Internet can fulfill people's need for knowledge in today's information society by its quick spread of all kinds of information. However, due to its virtuality and arbitrariness nature, Internet conveys fruitful information as well as harmful information. The uncontrolled spread of harmful information may have bad influence on social stability. Thus, it's important to effectively manage the information resources of web media, which is also a big technical challenge due to the massive amount of information on the web.

Various kinds of information are available on the web, text, image, video, etc. Text is the dominant among all of them. Netizens are accustomed to negotiating through e-mails, participating in discussion on forums or BBS, recording seeing or feeling on blogs. Since everyone can participate in those activities and create shared text content on the web, it's quite easy for evils to create and share harmful texts. To keep a healthy network environment, it's essential to censor and filter text content on the web so as to keep netizens away from the infestation of harmful information.

The most prominent feature of harmful information is that they are always closely related to several keywords. Thus, keyword filtering is widely adopted to filter text

X. Lai et al. (Eds.): E-Forensics 2010, LNICST 56, pp. 234–240, 2011.

content [1], and proven to be quite successful. While the priest climbs a post, the devil climbs ten, keyword filtering are not always effective. Since Chinese characters are combinations of character radicals [2], many characters can be decomposed into radicals, some characters are themselves radicals. This made it possible to bypass keyword filtering without affecting understanding the meaning of those keywords by replacing one or more characters in keyword with combination of character radicals. E.g. use "运云力" to represent "运动".

Traditionally, we can filter harmful document related to "法轮功" by matching keyword, but some evil sites replaced "法轮功" with "三去车仑工力", causing the current filtering mechanism to fail. Even worse, since the filtering mechanism has failed, people can search for harmful keywords like "三去车仑工力" in commodity search engines, and get plenty of harmful documents from search result. Many evil sites are now aware of this weakness of the current filtering mechanism, and the trick mentioned above to bypass keyword filtering is becoming more and more popular. We analyzed a sample of harmful documents collected by National Engineering Laboratory of Content Analysis. Our analysis shows that:

- A visible portion of harmful documents has adopted the decomposing trick to bypass the filtering mechanism, see Table 1.
- Most of the documents involving decomposed characters contain harmful information.

Table 1. Statistic of sampled harmful documents

Category	Proportion	Sample Size
Reactionary	9%	893
Adult	8%	2781
Political Criticism	10%	1470
Public Hazard	6%	1322

The second column in the table shows the proportion of harmful documents containing intentionally decomposed Chinese characters in a category (number of harmful documents containing decomposed characters / number of harmful documents).

Decomposing Chinese characters into radicals is a new phenomenon on the web. The idea behind this trick is simple, but it can completely fail the traditional keyword filtering. Filtering against this trick is a new research topic without much attention now. In this paper, we proposed the first filtering technology against those intentionally decomposed characters. We first set up a Chinese character decomposing structure library. Section 2 gives an overview on the principles of how to decompose Chinese characters. Section 3 gives an overview of our filtering system. We used a modified Rabin-Karp [3] multi-pattern matching algorithm to reconstruct characters from radicals before applying keyword filtering. After reconstruction, we used another modified Rabin-Karp algorithm to filter keywords. We described our modification to Rabin-Karp in Section 3.1, 3.2. In Section 4, we compared our filtering results with traditional filtering, and also showed the efficiency improvement of our modified Rabin-Karp algorithm in reconstruction. We gave a conclusion of our work in Section 5.

2 Principles for Chinese Character Decomposing

Chinese character is structured two-dimension character. Every Chinese character is composed of several character radicals. Chinese Linguistics and Language Administration gave an official definition for character radical in <GB13000.1 Chinese Character Specification for Information Processing>: composing unit of Chinese characters that is made up of strokes [4]. Character radical has a hierarchy structure. A character radical can be made up of several smaller character radicals. E.g. Chinese character "想" is composed of "相" and "心", these two are level 1 radicals for "想". "相" is made up of "木" and "目", and these two are level 2 radicals for "想". Since level 1 decomposing is more intuitive than level 2 decomposing, e.g." 木目" looks like "相", but it's hard for people to think of "想" when looking at "木目心", in order to make words understandable, usually only level 1 decomposing is used in bypass filtering. We see no level 2 decomposing in the harmful document collection from National Engineering Laboratory of Content Analysis. Accordingly, we consider only level 1 decomposing.

The structure of a Chinese character usually falls into the following categories: left-right, up-down, left-center-right, up-center-down, surrounded, half-surrounded, monolith. Intuitively, left-right, left-center-right structure characters are more understandable after decomposing. Statistics [5] shows that left-right structure counts for over 60 percent of all Chinese characters; up-down structure counts for over 20 percent. We summarize these observations as the following conclusions:

- Level 1 decomposing is more intuitive
- Left-right, left-center-right decomposing is more intuitive

We manually decomposed some Chinese characters defined in GB2312 charset which are easily understandable after decomposing. Based on the above conclusions, most of the characters we choose to decompose are left-right characters, and we use only level 1 decomposing. The outcome of our decomposing work is a Chinese character decomposing structure library (character structure library for short) in the form of character-structure-radical triplets, as shown in Table 2.

Table 2. Sample of Chinese character decomposing structure library

Character	Structure	Radicals
权	Left-right	木又
格	Left-right	木各
就	Left-right	京尤
动	Left-right	云力
树	Left-center-right	木又寸
起	Half-surrounded	走己

Some radicals are variants of characters, some are not. Take "河" for example, if we decompose it into "水" and "可", it would be confusing and not understandable. Instead, we choose to decompose it into "氵" and "可", which is more meaningful.

3 Keyword Filtering Based on Chinese Character Reconstruction

Figure 1 gives an overview on our filtering system. HTML files shown in Figure 1 are collected via collectors in network. Preprocessing will remove all HTML tags, punctuations, and white-spaces. If punctuations and white-spaces are not removed, those punctuations in between characters of a keyword may cause keyword matching to fail. Next, we take the decomposed characters in character structure library as patterns, and use multi-pattern matching algorithm to find out and recombine all intentionally decomposed characters. After character reconstruction, we use another multi-pattern matching algorithm to search for keywords, and filter out all documents that contain any keywords.

In the above process, we used two multi-pattern matching algorithms, and the efficiency of the two algorithms is vital to the performance of the whole filtering system. We carefully selected the two algorithms. We modified Rabin-Karp [3] algorithm to better fit our scenario of character reconstruction and keyword filtering. We describe our modification to Rabin-Karp algorithm in Section 3.1 and 3.2.

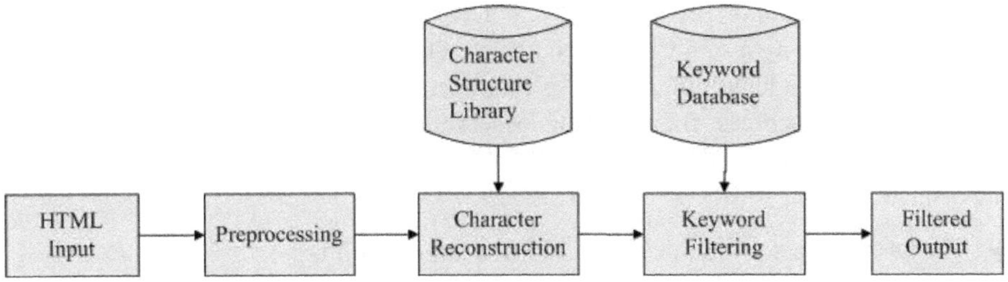

Fig. 1. Overview of filtering system

3.1 Chinese Character Reconstruction

Recombining Chinese character from character radicals is a multi-pattern matching problem in nature. Pattern matching [6] can be divided into single pattern matching and multi-pattern matching. Let $P = \{p_1, p_2,...,p_k\}$ be a set of patterns, which are strings of characters from a fixed alphabet $\sum$. Let $T=t_1, t_2,...,t_N$ be a large text, again consisting of characters from $\sum$. Multi-pattern matching is to find all occurrences of all the patterns of P in T. Single pattern matching is to find all occurrences of one pattern p_i in T. KMP (Knuth-Morris-Pratt) [7] and BM (Boyer-Moore) [8] are classical algorithms for single pattern matching. AC (Ano-Corasick) [9] and Wu-Manber [10] are algorithms for multi-pattern matching. AC is a state machine based algorithm, which requires large amount of memory resources. WM is an extension of BM, and it has the best performance in average case.

[11] proposed an improved WM algorithm. The algorithm eliminates the functional overlap of the table HASH and SHIFT, and computes the shift distances in an aggressive manner. After each test, the algorithm examines the character next to the scan window to maximize the shift distance. The idea behind this improvement is consistent with that of the quick-search (QS) algorithm [12].

From the observations in Section 2, we know that most patterns in character structure library are of length 2, few are of length 3. Since the prefix and suffix of WM algorithm overlaps a lot for patterns of length 2 and 3, it's not efficient to use WM. On the other hand, WM algorithm for such short patterns will act similar to Rabin-Karp algorithm, except that it's less efficient due to the tedious and duplicated computation and comparison of prefix and suffix hash. Rabin-Karp seems suitable for our purpose, but it requires the patterns to have a fixed length, thus we cannot use it directly.

Here we modified Rabin-Karp so that it can search for multi-patterns of both length 2 and 3. We replaced the set of hash values of pattern prefix with a hash map. The keys of hash map are hash values of pattern prefixes (prefix length is 2); the value of hash map is 0 for patterns of length 2; the one character following the prefix (the last character) for patterns of length 3. When current substring's hash equals any key in the hash map, we retrieve the corresponding value in the hash map. If a non-zero value is encountered, just compare the non-zero value (the third character in pattern) with the character following the prefix, a match (pattern of length 3) is found if the two equals. If the value we get is zero, a match is found immediately (pattern of length 2).

We further optimized Rabin-Karp by selecting a natural rolling hash function. In our modified version of RK, hash is calculated on two Chinese characters since prefix length is 2. The length of a Chinese character is two bytes in Unicode and many other encoding, thus the length of 2 Chinese characters equals the length a natural WORD (int) on 32-bit machines. Based on this observation, we take the four bytes code of 2 Chinese characters directly as its hash. This straightforward hashing has the following advantages:

- The hash value does not need any addition computation
- The probability of collision is zero.

Experiment shows that our modified RK outperforms the improved WM [11] in character reconstruction.

3.2 Keyword Filtering

Keyword filtering is also a problem of multi-pattern matching. Since the minimum length of all keywords is 2, WM is still not a good choice for keyword filtering due to the overlapping of prefix and suffix. We still choose to use RK. We need to modify RK further, since length of keywords (patterns) is mostly between 2 and 5 this time. We used the same straightforward rolling hash as in section 3.1, since prefix length is still 2. We still replace the set of hash values of pattern prefix with a hash map. We keep keys as the same in section 3.1, but use pointers pointing to the character following the prefix as values. When current substring's hash equals any key in the hash map, we retrieve the corresponding value in the hash map as before. Then compare the string pointed to by the retrieved pointer with the string starting from the character following the prefix to see if they are a match. Since most of our keywords are short, there won't be plenty of character comparisons, thus the algorithm is quite efficient.

4 Experiments

To demonstrate the effectiveness of our filtering system, we used the same harmful document collection from National Engineering Laboratory of Content Analysis as mentioned in Section 1, 2 as test data. We selected 752 words in all documents as the keywords to filter. These words show up 21973 times in all documents.

We input the document collection (6466 documents in all) into the filtering system. Our filtering system reconstructed those decomposed characters, and then applied keyword filtering on the processed text. A document is filtered out if it contains any keywords. The result in table 3 shows that our filtering system can recognize most of the keywords even if characters of these keywords are decomposed into radicals. As a comparison, we applied keyword filtering on the input without reconstructing characters from radicals.

Table 3. Effect of our filtering based on Character Reconstruction

	Keyword Matches	Filtered Documents
Filtering based on character reconstruction	99.57% (21878)	99.77% (6451)
Filtering without reconstruction	91.36% (20074)	92.11% (5956)

As shown in table 3, our approach can effective identify most of the keywords even in the form on combination of radicals. It yields a visible improvement in the filtering result compared to traditional filtering without character reconstruction. As more and more evil sites begin to use this trick, and the proportion of harmful documents containing intentionally decomposed characters increases, the improvement will be more significant in the future.

However, our approach also has its drawbacks. From table 3, we can see that there're still some keywords that cannot be identified with our approach (about 0.23%). Since the first radical of a character might be combined with character left to it mistakenly, some keywords cannot be identified. E.g. for "大小和卓木半反乱", "木" and "半" is combined into "柈" mistakenly, thus keyword "叛乱" cannot be identified after reconstruction. Our current approach cannot handle this kind of situations. To eliminate such kind of wrong combinations in future work, we can take semantic into consideration when recombining radicals.

We also tested the performance of our character reconstruction algorithm. It shows that our modified Rabin-Karp algorithm outperforms the improved Wu-Manber algorithm proposed in [11] by 35% on average in character reconstruction. To further improve the performance of the whole system, we can even consider combining character reconstruction and keyword filtering into one step in future work, using decomposed keywords as patterns. This would cause the hash table in Rabin-Karp to blow, since there might be several ways to decompose a single keyword. And it's trading space for speed.

5 Conclusions

Decomposing Chinese characters to bypass traditional keyword filtering has become a popular trick that many evil sites use now. In this paper we proposed a filtering technology against this kind of trick. We first use a modified Rabin-Karp algorithm to reconstruct Chinese characters from radicals. Then apply keyword filtering on the processed text. This is the first filtering system ever known against the trick. Experiment has showed the effectiveness and efficiency of our approach. In the future, we can further improve the filtering technology by taking semantic into consideration when recombining characters or even try to combine reconstruction and filtering into a single step.

Acknowledgement. The work described in this paper is fully supported by the National Natural Science Foundation of China (No.60703032), and the Opening Project of Key Lab of Information Network Security of Ministry of Public Security.

References

1. Oard, D.W.: The State of the Art in Text Filtering. User Modeling and User-Adapted Interaction 7(3) (1997)
2. Zhang, X.: Research of Chinese Character Structure of 20th Century. Language Research and Education (5), 75–79 (2004)
3. Karp, R.M., Rabin, M.O.: Efficient randomized pattern-matching algorithms. IBM Journal of Research and Development 31(2) (March 1987)
4. Chinese Linguistics and Language Administration. GB13000.1 Chinese Character Specification for Information Processing. Language and Literature Press, Beijing (1998)
5. Li, X.: Discussion and Opinion of the Evaluation Criterion of Chinese Calligraphy, `http://www.wenhuacn.com/`
6. Lee, R.J.: Analysis of Fundamental Exact and Inexact Pattern Matching Algorithms
7. Knuth, D.E.: Fast Pattern Matching in Strings. SIAM J. Comput. 6(2) (June 1977)
8. Boyer, R.S., Moore, J.S.: A Fast String Searching Algorithm. Communications of ACM 20(10) (October 1977)
9. Aho, A.V., Margaret, J.C.: Efficient string matching: An aid to bibliographic search. Communications of the ACM 18(6), 333–340 (1975)
10. Wu, S., Manber, U.: A Fast Algorithm for Multi-Pattern Searching. Technical Report TR 94-17, University of Arizona at Tuscon (May 1994)
11. Yang, D., Xu, K., Cui, Y.: An Improved Wu-Manber Multiple Patterns Matching Algorithm. IPCCC (April 2006)
12. Sunday, D.M.: A very fast substring search algorithm. Communications of the ACM 33(8), 132–142 (1990)

Disguisable Symmetric Encryption Schemes for an Anti-forensics Purpose*

Ning Ding, Dawu Gu, and Zhiqiang Liu

Department of Computer Science and Engineering
Shanghai Jiao Tong University
Shanghai, 200240, China
{dingning,dwgu,ilu_zq}@sjtu.edu.cn

Abstract. In this paper, we propose a new notion of secure disguisable symmetric encryption schemes, which captures the idea that the attacker can decrypt a cipher text he encrypted to different meaningful values when different keys are put to the decryption algorithm. This notion is aimed for the following anti-forensics purpose: the attacker can cheat the forensics investigator by decrypting an encrypted file to a meaningful file other than that one he encrypted, in the case that he is catched by the forensics investigator and ordered to hand over the key for decryption.

We then present a construction of secure disguisable symmetric encryption schemes. Typically, when an attacker uses such encryption schemes, he can achieve the following two goals: if the file he encrypted is an executable malicious file, he can use fake keys to decrypt it to a benign executable file, or if the file he encrypted is a data file which records his malicious activities, he can also use fake keys to decrypt it to an ordinary data file, e.g. a song or novel file.

Keywords: Symmetric Encryption, Obfuscation, Anti-forensics.

1 Introduction

Computer forensics is usually defined as the set of techniques that can be applied to understand if and how a system has been used or abused to commit mischief [8]. The increasing use of forensics techniques has led to the development of "anti-forensics" techniques that can make this process difficult, or impossible [2][7][6]. That is, the goal of anti-forensics techniques is to frustrate forensics investigators and their techniques.

In general, the anti-forensics techniques mainly contains those towards data wiping, data encryption, data steganography and techniques for frustrating forensics software etc. When an attacker performs an attack on a machine (called the target machine), there are much evidence of the attack left in the target machine and his own machine (called the tool machine). The evidence usually includes malicious data, malicious programs etc. used throughout the attack. To frustrate

* This work was supported by the Specialized Research Fund for the Doctoral Program of Higher Education (No. 200802480019).

X. Lai et al. (Eds.): E-Forensics 2010, LNICST 56, pp. 241–255, 2011.

forensics investigators to gather such evidence, the attacker usually tries to erase these evidence from the target machine and the tool machine after or during the attack. Although erasing the evidence may be the most efficient way to prevent the attacker from being traced by the forensics investigator, the attacker sometimes needs to store some data and malicious programs in the target machine or the tool machine so as to continue the attack later. In this case the attacker may choose to encrypt the evidence and then later decrypt it when needed.

A typical encryption operation for a file (called the plain text) is to first encrypt it and then erase the plain text. Thus after this encrypting operation, it seems that there is only the encrypted file (called the cipher text) in the hard disk and does not exist the plain text. However, some forensics software can recover the seemingly erased file or retrieve the plain text corresponding to a cipher text in the hard disk by making use of the physical properties of hard disks and the vulnerability of the operation systems. Thus, some anti-forensics researchers proposed some techniques on how to really erase or encrypt data such that no copy of the data or plain text still exists in the hard disk. By adopting such anti-forensics techniques, it can be ensured that there exist only encrypted data left in the machine. Thus, if the encryption scheme is secure in cryptographic sense, the forensics investigator cannot find any information on the data if he does not know the private key. Hence it seems that by employing the really erasing techniques and a secure encryption scheme, the attacker could realize secure encryption of malicious data and programs and avoid accusation even if the forensics investigator can gather cipher texts from the target machine or the tool machine since none can find any information from these cipher texts. But is this really true in all cases?

Consider such a case. The attacker uses a secure encryption scheme to encrypt a malicious executable file. But later the forensics investigator catches him and also controls the tool or target machines absolutely. Suppose the forensics investigator can further find the encrypted file of the malicious program by scanning the machine. Then the forensics investigator orders the attacker to hand over the private key so as to decrypt the file to obtain the malicious program. In this case, the attacker cannot hand over a fake key to the investigator since by using this fake key as the decryption key, either the decryption cannot proceed successfully or even if the decryption can proceed successfully, the decrypted file is usually not an executable file. This shows to the investigator that the attacker lies to him. Thus the inquest process will not end unless the attacker hands over the real key. So it can be seen that the secrecy of the cipher text cannot be ensured in this case.

The above discussion shows that ordinary encryption schemes may be insufficient for this anti-forensics purpose even if they possess strong security in cryptographic sense (e.g. IND-CCA2). One method of making the attacker able of cheating the forensics investigator is to let the encrypted file has multiple valid decryptions. Namely, each encryption of an executable file can be decrypted to more than one different executable files. Assuming such encryption schemes exist, in the above case when ordered to hand over the real key, the attacker can hand over one or more fake keys to the forensics investigator and the cipher text can be correspondingly decrypted to one or many benign executable programs, which are not the malicious program. Then the attacker can cheat the investigator that the program encrypted previously would be actually a benign program instead of a malicious program. Thus, the forensics investigator cannot accuse the attacker that he lies to the investigator. We say that an encryption scheme with such security is disguisable (in anti-forensics setting).

It can be seen that the disguisable encryption may be only motivated for the anti-forensics purpose and thus the standard encryption study does not investigate it explicitly and to our knowledge no existing encryption scheme is disguisable. Thus, in this paper we are interested in the question how to construct disguisable encryption schemes and try to provide an answer to this question.

1.1 Our Result

We provide a positive answer to the above question with respect to the symmetric encryption. That is, we first put forward a definition of secure disguisable symmetric encryption which captures the idea that a cipher text generated by the attacker can be decrypted to different meaningful plain texts when using different keys to the decryption algorithm. A bit more precisely, the attacker holds a real key and several fake keys and uses the real key to encrypt a file to output the cipher text. Then if the attacker is controlled by the forensics investigator and ordered to hand over the key to decrypt the cipher text, the attacker can hand over one or more fake keys and claims that these keys include the real one. We also require that the forensics investigator cannot learn any information of the number of all the keys the attacker holds.

Then we present a construction of secure disguisable symmetric encryption schemes. Informally, our result can be described as follows.

Claim 1. There exists a secure disguisable symmetric encryption scheme.

When an attacker encrypted a file using such encryption schemes, he can cheat the forensics investigator later by decrypting the encryption of the malicious file to another file. In particular, if an attacker used a secure disguisable symmetric encryption scheme to encrypt a malicious executable file and later is ordered to decrypt the cipher text, then the attacker can decrypt the cipher text to a benign executable file, or decrypt it to a malicious program other than the real encrypted one which, however, is unrelated to the attack. Or, if the attacker encrypted some data file which records his malicious activities, then later he can decrypt this cipher text to an ordinary data file, such as a song or a novel file. In both cases, the forensics investigator cannot recognize attacker's cheating activities.

For an encryption scheme, all security is lost if the private key is lost. Thus the attacker who uses a disguisable encryption scheme should ensure that the keys (the real one and many fakes ones) can be stored in a secure way. In the last part of this paper, we also provide some discussion on how to securely manage the keys.

1.2 Our Technique

Our construction of disguisable symmetric encryption schemes heavily depends on the the recent result of obfuscating multiple-bit point and set-membership functions proposed by [4]. Loosely speaking, an obfuscation of a program P is a program that computes the same functionality as P computes, but any adversary can only use this functionality and cannot learn anything beyond it, i.e., the adversary cannot reverse-engineering nor understand the code of the obfuscated program. A multiple-bit point function $MBPF_{x,y}$ is the one that on input x outputs y and outputs $\perp$ on all other inputs. As shown by [4], an obfuscation for multiple-bit point functions can be applied to construct a symmetric encryption scheme: The encryption of a message m with key k is letting $O(MBPF_{k,m})$ be the cipher text. To decrypt the cipher text with k is to compute $O(MBPF_{k,m})(k)$, which output is m.

Inspired by [4], we find that an obfuscation for multiple-bit set-membership functions can be used to construct a disguisable symmetric encryption scheme. A multiple-bit set-membership function $MBSF_{(x_1,y_1),(x_2,y_2),\cdots,(x_t,y_t)}$ is the one that on input x_i outputs y_i for. Our idea for constructing a disguisable symmetric encryption scheme is as follows: to encrypt y_1 with the key x_1, we choose $t-1$ more fake keys $x_2,\cdots,x_t$ and arbitrary $y_2,\cdots,y_t$ and let the obfuscation of $MBSF_{(x_1,y_1),(x_2,y_2),\cdots,(x_t,y_t)}$ be the cipher text. Thus the cipher text (also viewed as a program) on input x_i outputs y_i. This means the cipher text can be decrypted to many values. In this paper, we will formally illustrate and extend this basic idea as well as some necessary randomized techniques to construct a secure disguisable symmetric encryption scheme which can possess the required security.

1.3 Outline of This Paper

The rest of this paper is as follows. Section 2 presents the preliminaries. Section 3 presents our result, i.e. the definition and the construction of the disguisable symmetric encryption scheme as well as some discussion of how to securely store and manage keys for an attacker. Section 4 summarizes this paper.

2 Preliminaries

This section contains the notations and definitions used throughout this paper.

2.1 Basic Notions

A function $\mu(\cdot)$, where $\mu : \mathbb{N} \rightarrow [0,1]$ is called negligible if $\mu(n) = n^{-\omega(1)}$ (i.e., $\mu(n) < \frac{1}{p(n)}$ for all polynomial $p(\cdot)$ and large enough n's). We will sometimes use neg to denote an unspecified negligible function.

The shorthand "PPT" refers to probabilistic polynomial-time, and we denote by PPT machines non-uniform probabilistic polynomial-time algorithms unless stated explicitly.

We say that two probability ensembles $\{X_n\}_{n\in\mathbb{N}}$ and $\{Y_n\}_{n\in\mathbb{N}}$ are computationally indistinguishable if for every PPT algorithm A, it holds that $|\Pr[A(X_n) = 1] - \Pr[A(Y_n) = 1]| = \mathsf{neg}(n)$. We will sometimes abuse notation and say that the two random variables X_n and Y_n are computationally indistinguishable when each of them is a part of a probability ensemble such that these ensembles $\{X_n\}_{n\in\mathbb{N}}$ and $\{Y_n\}_{n\in\mathbb{N}}$ are computationally indistinguishable. We will also sometimes drop the index n from a random variable if it can be infer from the context. In most of these cases, the index n will be the security parameter.

2.2 Point Functions, Multi-bit Point and Set-Membership Functions

A point function, $PF_x : \{0,1\}^n \to \{0,1\}$, outputs 1 if and only if its input matches x, i.e., $PF_x(y) = 1$ iff $y = x$, and outputs 0 otherwise. A point function with multiple-bit output, $MBPF_{x,y} : \{0,1\}^n \to \{y, \perp\}$, outputs y if and only if its input matches x, i.e., $MBPF_{x,y}(z) = y$ iff $z = x$, and outputs $\perp$ otherwise. A multiple-bit set-membership function, $MBSF_{(x_1,y_1),\cdots,(x_t,y_t)} : \{0,1\}^n \to \{y_1, \cdots, y_t, \perp\}$ outputs y_i if and only if the input matches x_i and outputs $\perp$ otherwise, where t is at most a polynomial in n.

2.3 Obfuscation

Informally, an obfuscation of a program P is also a program that computes the same functionality as P but its code can hide all information beyond the functionality. That is, the obfuscated program is fully "unintelligent" and any adversary cannot understand nor reverse-engineering it. This paper adopts the definition of obfuscation proposed by [4][3][9].

Definition 1. *Let $\mathbb{F}$ be a family of functions. A uniform PPT O is called an obfuscator of $\mathbb{F}$, if:*

Approximate Functionality: *for any $F \in \mathbb{F}$, $\Pr[\exists x, O(F(x)) \neq F(x)]$ is negligible. Here the probability is taken over the coin tosses of O.*

Polynomial Slowdown: *There exists a polynomial p such that, for any $F \in \mathbb{F}$, $O(F)$ runs in time at most $p(T_F)$, where T_F is the worst-case running-time of F.*

Weak Virtual black-box property: *For every PPT distinguisher A and any polynomial p, there is an (non-uniform) PPT simulator S, such that for any $F \in \mathbb{F}$, $\Pr[A(O(F)) = 1] - \Pr[A(S^F(1^{|F|})) = 1] \leq \frac{1}{p(n)}$.*

The theoretical investigation of obfuscation was initialized by [1]. [4] presented a modular approach to construct an obfuscation for multiple-bit point and set-membership functions based on an obfuscation for point functions [3][5].

2.4 Symmetric Encryption

We recall the standard definitions of a symmetric (i.e. private-key) encryption scheme. We start by presenting the syntax definition as follows:

Definition 2. *(Symmetric encryption scheme). A symmetric or private-key encryption scheme* $\mathsf{SKE} = (G; E; D)$ *consists of three uniform PPT algorithms with the following semantics:*
1. The key generation algorithm G *samples a key* k. *We write* $k \leftarrow G(1^n)$ *where* n *is the security parameter.*
2. The encryption algorithm E *encrypts a message* $m \in \{0,1\}^{poly(n)}$ *and produces a cipher text* C. *We write* $C \leftarrow E(k; m)$.
3. The decryption algorithm D *decrypts a cipher text* C *to a message* m. *We write* $m \leftarrow D(k; C)$. *Usually, perfect correctness of the scheme is required, i.e., that* $D(k; E(k; m)) = m$ *for all* $m \in \{0,1\}^{poly(n)}$ *and all possible* k.

Security of encryption schemes. The standard security for encryption is computational indistinguishability, i.e., for any two different messages m_1, m_2 with equal bit length, their corresponding cipher texts are computationally indistinguishable.

3 Our Result

In this section we propose the definition and the construction of disguisable symmetric encryption schemes. As shown in Section 1.1, the two typical goals (or motivation) of this kind of encryption schemes is to either let the attacker disguise his malicious program as a benign program, or let the attacker disguise his malicious data as ordinary data.

Although we can present the definition of disguisable symmetric encryption schemes in a general sense without considering the goal it is intended to achieve, we still explicitly contain the goal in its definition to emphasis the motivation of such encryption schemes. In this section we illustrate the definition and construction with respect to the goal of disguising executable files in detail, and omit those counterparts with respect to the goal of disguising data files. Actually, the two definitions and constructions are same if we do not refer to the type of the underlying files.

In Section 3.1, we present the definition of disguisable symmetric encryption schemes and the security requirements. In Section 3.2 we present a construction of disguisable symmetric encryption schemes which can satisfy the required security requirements. In Section 3.3 we provide some discussion on how to securely store and manage the keys in practice.

3.1 Disguisable Symmetric Encryption

In this subsection we present the definition of secure disguisable symmetric encryption as follows.

Definition 3. *A disguisable symmetric encryption scheme* $\mathsf{DSKE} = (G; E; D)$ *(for encryption of executable files) consists of three uniform PPT algorithms with the following semantics:*

1. *The key generation algorithm G on input 1^n, where n is the security parameter, samples a real key k and several fake keys $\mathsf{FakeKey}_1, \cdots, \mathsf{FakeKey}_r$. (The fake keys are also inputs to the encryption algorithm.)*
2. *The encryption algorithm E on input k, an executable file $\mathsf{File} \in \{0,1\}^{poly(n)}$ to be encrypted, together with $\mathsf{FakeKey}_1, \cdots, \mathsf{FakeKey}_r$, produces a cipher text C.*
3. *The (deterministic) decryption algorithm D on input a key and a cipher text C (promised to be the encryption of the executable file File) outputs a plain text which value relies on the key. That is, if the key is k, D's output is File. If the key is any fake one generated previously, D's output is also an executable file other than File. Otherwise, D outputs $\perp$. We require computational correctness of the scheme. That is, for the random keys generated by G and E's internal coins, D works as required except negligible probability.*

We remark that in a different viewpoint, we can view that the very key used in encryption consists of k and all $\mathsf{FakeKey}_i$, and k, $\mathsf{FakeKey}_i$ can be named segments of this key. Thus in this viewpoint our definition essentially means that decryption operation only needs a segment of the key and behaves differently on input different segments of this key. However, since not all these segments are needed to perform correct decryption, i.e., there is no need for the users of such encryption schemes to remember all segments after performing the encryption, we still name k and all $\mathsf{FakeKey}_i$ keys in this paper. We only require computational correctness due to the obfuscation for MBSF functions underlying our construction which can only obtain computational approximate functionality (i.e., no PPT algorithm can output a x such that $O(F(x)) \neq F(x)$ with non-negligible probability).

Security of disguisable symmetric encryption schemes. We say DSKE is secure if the following conditions hold:

1. For any two different executable files $\mathsf{File}_1, \mathsf{File}_2$ with equal bit length, their corresponding cipher texts are computationally indistinguishable.
2. Assuming there is a public upper bound B on r known to everyone, any adversary on input a cipher text can correctly guess the value of r with probability no more than $\frac{1}{B} + \mathsf{neg}(n)$. (This means r should be uniform and independent of the cipher text.)
3. After the user hands over to the adversary $1 \leq r' \leq r$ fake key(s) and claims one of them is the real key and the remainders are fake keys (if $r' \geq 2$), the adversary cannot distinguish the cipher texts of $\mathsf{File}_1, \mathsf{File}_2$ either. Further,the conditional probability that the adversary can correctly guess the value of r is no more than $\frac{1}{B-r'} + \mathsf{neg}(n)$ if $r' < B$. (This means r is still uniform and independent of the cipher text on the occurrence that the adversary obtains the r' fake keys.)

We remark that the first requirement originates from the standard security of encryption, and that the second requirement basically says that the cipher text does not contain any information of r (beyond the public bound B), and that the third requirement says the requirements 1 and 2 still hold even if the adversary obtains some fake keys. In fact the second and third requirements are proposed for the anti-forensics purpose mentioned previously.

3.2 Construction of the Encryption Schemes

In this subsection we present a construction of the desired encryption scheme. Our scheme heavily depends on the current technique of obfuscating multiple-bit set-membership functions presented in [4]. The construction in [4] is modular based on the obfuscation for point functions. As shown by [4], this modularization construction is secure if the underlying obfuscation for point functions satisfies some composability. Actually, the known construction of obfuscation for point function in [3] when using the statistically indistinguishable perfectly one-way hash functions [5] satisfies such composability, which results in that the construction in [4] is a secure obfuscation with computational approximate functionality. We will not review the definitions and constructions of the obfuscation and perfectly one-way hash functions in [5][3] and several composability discussed in [4] here, and refer the readers to the original literature.

We first present a naive scheme in Construction 1 which can illustrate the basic idea how to construct a multiple-bit set-membership function to realize a disguisable symmetric encryption. But the drawback of this scheme is that it cannot possess the desired security. Then we present the final scheme in Construction 2 which can achieve the requirements of secure disguisable encryption schemes.

Construction 1: We construct a naive scheme $\mathsf{DSKE}' = (G; E; D)$ as follows:

1. G: on input 1^n, uniformly sample two n-bit strings independently from $\{0,1\}^n$, denoted k and $\mathsf{FakeKey}$ (note $\Pr[k = \mathsf{FakeKey}] = 2^{-n}$). k is the real symmetric key and $\mathsf{FakeKey}$ is the fake key. (r is 1 herein.)
2. E: on input $k, \mathsf{FakeKey}$ and an executable file $\mathsf{File} \in \{0,1\}^t$, perform the following computation:
   (a) Choose a fixed existing different executable file in the hard disk with bit length t (if its length is less than t, pad some dummy instructions to it to satisfy this requirement), denoted $\mathsf{FakeFile}$, and then compute the following program P.

   P's description:
   input: x
   1. in the case $x = k$, return File;
   2. in the case $x = \mathsf{FakeKey}$, return $\mathsf{FakeFile}$;
   3. return $\perp$;
   4. end.

   (b) Generate a program Q for P. (It differs from the obfuscation in [4] in that it does not use a random permutation on two blocks of Q, i.e. lines 1-3 and lines 4-6.)

That is, let y denote File and y_i denote the ith bit of y. For each i, if $y_i = 1$ E computes a program U_i as an obfuscation of PF_k (point function defined in Section 2.2), using the construction in [3] employing the statistically indistinguishable perfectly one-way hash functions in [5], otherwise E computes U_i as an obfuscation of PF_u where u is a uniformly random n-bit string. Generate a more program U_0 as an obfuscation of PF_k.

Similarly, E adopts the same method to compute t obfuscation according to each bit of FakeFile. Denote by FakeU_i these t obfuscation, $1 \le i \le t$. Generate a more program FakeU_0 as an obfuscation of PF_{FakeKey}.

Q's description:

input: x
1. in the case $U_0(x) = 1$
2.   for $i = 1$ to t let $y_i \leftarrow U_i(x)$;
3.   return y.
4. in the case $\mathsf{FakeU}_0(x) = 1$
5.   for $i = 1$ to t let $y_i \leftarrow \mathsf{FakeU}_i(x)$;
6.   return y;
7. return $\perp$.
8. end

Q is the cipher text.

3. D: on input a cipher text c and a key key, it views c as a program and executes c(key) to output what c outputs as the corresponding plain text.

It can be seen that P actually computes a multiple-bit set-membership function, defined in Section 2.2, and $Q \leftarrow E(k, \mathsf{File}, \mathsf{FakeKey})$ possesses the computational approximate functionality with P. Thus, except negligible probability, for any File that an attacker wants to encrypt, we have that $D(k, Q) = \mathsf{File}$, $D(\mathsf{Fakekey}, Q) = \mathsf{FakeFile}$. This shows that Definition 3 of disguisable symmetric encryption schemes is satisfied by DSKE'.

Now the next step is to verify if this encryption is secure with respect to the security of the disguisable symmetric encryption schemes. That is, we need to verify if the security requirements are satisfied. However, as we will point out, DSKE' is actually insecure with respect to the security requirements. First, since Q is not a secure obfuscation of P, we cannot establish the indistinguishability of encryption. Second, the secrecy of r cannot be satisfied. Instead, r is fixed as 1 herein. Thus if the forensics investigator knows the attacker adopts DSKE' to encrypt a malicious program and orders the attacker to hand over the two keys, the attacker may choose either to provide both k, FakeKey or to provide FakeKey (the attacker claims he only remembers one of the two keys) to the investigator. In the former case, the forensics investigator can immediately grasp the malicious program as well as another fake program. Notice that the execution traces of the two decryptions are not same, i.e. the decryption using the real key always occurs in Lines 2 and 3 of Q, while the one using the fake key occurs in Lines 5 and 6.

Thus the investigator can tell the real malicious program from the other one. In the latter case, the investigator can still judge if the attacker tells him the real key by checking the execution trace of Q. To achieve the security requirements, we should overcome the drawbacks of distinguishability of encryption, exposure of r and execution trace of Q, as the following shows.

We improve the naive scheme by randomizing r over some interval $[1, B]$ for a public constant B and adopt the secure obfuscation for multiple-bit set-membership functions in [4] etc. The construction of the desired encryption scheme is as follows.

Construction 2: The desired encryption scheme $\mathsf{DSKE} = (G; E; D)$ is as follows:

1. G: on input 1^n, uniformly sample $r + 1$ n-bit strings independently from $\{0,1\}^n$, denoted k and $\mathsf{FakeKey}_i$ for $1 \le i \le r$. k is the real symmetric key and $\mathsf{FakeKey}_i$ for each i is a fake key.
2. E: on input the secret key k, $\mathsf{FakeKey}_1, \cdots, \mathsf{FakeKey}_r$ and an executable file $\mathsf{File} \in \{0,1\}^t$, perform the following computation:
   (a) Choose a fixed existing executable file with bit length t in the hard disk, denoted File'. Let $u_0, \cdots, u_r$ denote $k, \mathsf{FakeKey}_1, \cdots, \mathsf{FakeKey}_r$. Then uniformly and independently choose $B-r$ more strings from $\{0,1\}^n$, denoted $u_{r+1}, \cdots, u_B$ (the probability that at least two elements in $\{u_0, \cdots, u_B\}$ are identical is only $\mathsf{neg}(n)$). Construct two $(B+1)$-cell tables K' and F' satisfying $K'[i] = u_i$ for $0 \le i \le B$ and $F'[0] = \mathsf{File}$ and $F'[i] = \mathsf{File}'$ for $1 \le i \le Q$.

   (b) Generate the following program P, which has the tables K', F' hardwired.

   input: x
   1. for $i = 0$ to B do the following
   2. if $x = K'[i]$, return $F'[i]$;
   3. return $\perp$;
   4. end.

   (c) Adopt the method presented in [4] to obfuscate P.
   That is, choose a random permutation π from $[0, B]$ to itself and let $K[i] = K'[\pi(i)]$ and $F[i] = F'[\pi(i)]$ for all i's. Then obfuscate the multiple-bit point functions $MBPF_{K[i],F[i]}$ for all i's. More concretely, let y_i denote $F[i]$ and $y_{i,j}$ denote the jth bit of y_i. For each j, if $y_{i,j} = 1$ E generates a program $U_{i,j}$ as an obfuscation of $PF_{K[i]}$ (point function), using the construction in [3] employing the statistically indistinguishable perfectly one-way hash functions in [5], otherwise E generates $U_{i,j}$ as an obfuscation of PF_u where u is a uniformly random n-bit string. Generate a more program $U_{i,0}$ as an obfuscation of $PF_{K[i]}$.

   Generate the following program Q, which is an obfuscation of P:

   input: x

for $i = 0$ to B do the following
    if $U_{i,0}(x) = 1$
        for $j = 1$ to t, let $y_{i,j} \leftarrow U_{i,j}(x)$;
        return $y_{i,j}$;
return $\perp$;
end.

Q is the cipher text.

3. D: on input a cipher text c and a key key, it views c as a program and executes $c(\mathsf{key})$ to output what c outputs as the corresponding plain text.

Since it is not hard to see that DSKE satisfies Definition 3, we now turn to show that DSKE can achieve the desired security requirements, as the following claims state.

Claim 2. *DSKE satisfies the computational indistinguishability of encryption.*

Proof. This claim follows from the result in [4] which ensures that Q is indeed an obfuscation of P. To prove this claim we need to show that for arbitrary two files f_1 and f_2 with equal bit length, letting Q_1 and Q_2 denote their cipher texts respectively generated by DSKE, Q_1 and Q_2 are indistinguishable. Formally, we need to show that for any PPT distinguisher A and any polynomial p, $|\Pr[A(Q_1) = 1] - \Pr[A(Q_2) = 1]| \leq \frac{1}{p(n)}$.

Let P_1 (resp. P_2) denote the intermediate program generated by the encryption algorithm in encrypting f_1 (resp. f_2) in step (b). Since Q_1 (resp. Q_2) is an obfuscation of P_1 (resp. P_2), by Definition 1 we have that for the polynomial $3p$ there exists a simulator S satisfying $|\Pr[A(Q_i) = 1] - \Pr[A(S^{P_i}(1^{|P_i|}) = 1]| \leq \frac{1}{3p(n)}$ for $i = 1, 2$.

As $|\Pr[A(Q_1) = 1] - \Pr[A(Q_2) = 1]| \leq |\Pr[A(Q_1) = 1] - \Pr[A(S^{P_1}(1^{|P_1|})) = 1]| + |\Pr[A(Q_2) = 1] - \Pr[A(S^{P_2}(1^{|P_2|})) = 1]| + |\Pr[A(S^{P_1}(1^{|P_1|})) = 1] - \Pr[A(S^{P_2}(1^{|P_2|})) = 1]|$, to show $|\Pr[A(Q_1) = 1] - \Pr[A(Q_2) = 1]| \leq \frac{1}{p(n)}$, it suffices to show $|\Pr[A(S^{P_1}(1^{|P_1|})) = 1] - \Pr[A(S^{P_2}(1^{|P_2|})) = 1]| = \mathsf{neg}(n)$.

Let bad_1 (resp. bad_2) denote the event that in the computation of $A(S^{P_1}(1^{|P_1|}))$ (resp. $A(S^{P_2}(1^{|P_2|}))$), S queries the oracle with an arbitrary one of the $B+1$ keys stored in table K.

It can be seen that on the occurrence of $\neg\mathsf{bad}_i$, the oracle P_i always responds $\perp$ to S in the respective computation for $i = 1, 2$. This results in that $\Pr[A(S^{P_1}) = 1|\neg\mathsf{bad}_1] = \Pr[A(S^{P_2}) = 1|\neg\mathsf{bad}_2]$. Further, since the $r+1$ keys in each computation are chosen uniformly, the probability that at least one of S's queries to its oracle equals one of the keys is $O(\frac{\mathrm{poly}(n)}{2^n})$, which is a negligible quantity, since S at most proposes polynomial queries. This means $\Pr[\mathsf{bad}_i] = \mathsf{neg}(n)$ for $i = 1, 2$.

Since $\Pr[\neg\mathsf{bad}_i] = 1 - \mathsf{neg}(n)$, $\Pr[A(S^{P_i}) = 1|\neg\mathsf{bad}_i] = \frac{\Pr[A(S^{P_i})=1,\neg\mathsf{bad}_i]}{\Pr[\neg\mathsf{bad}_i]} = \Pr[A(S^{P_i}) = 1] + \mathsf{neg}(n)$ or $\Pr[A(S^{P_i}) = 1] - \mathsf{neg}(n)$. Thus we have $|\Pr[A(S^{P_1}) = 1] - \Pr[A(S^{P_2}) = 1]| = \mathsf{neg}(n)$. So this claim follows as previously stated. □

Now we need to show that any adversary on input a cipher text can hardly obtain some information of r (beyond the public bound B).

Claim 3. *For any PPT adversary A, A on input a cipher text Q can correctly guess r with probability no more than $\frac{1}{B} + \mathsf{neg}(n)$.*

Proof. Since A's goal is to guess r (which was determined at the moment of generating Q), we can w.l.o.g. assume A's output is in $[1, B] \cup \{\perp\}$, where $\perp$ denotes the case that A outputs a value which is outside $[1, B]$ and thus viewed meaningless.

Then, we construct B PPT algorithms $A_1, \cdots, A_B$ with the following descriptions: A_i on input Q executes $A(Q)$ and finally outputs 1 if A outputs i and outputs 0 otherwise, $1 \leq i \leq B$. It can be seen each A_i can be viewed as a distinguisher and thus for any polynomial p there is a simulator S_i for A_i satisfying that $|\Pr[A_i(Q) = 1] - \Pr[A_i(S_i^P(1^{|P|})) = 1]| \leq \frac{1}{p(n)}$. Namely, $|\Pr[A(Q) = i] - \Pr[A(S_i^P(1^{|P|})) = i]| \leq \frac{1}{p(n)}$ for each i. Thus for random r, $|\Pr[A(Q) = r] - \Pr[A(S_r^P(1^{|P|})) = r]| \leq \frac{1}{p(n)}$.

Let good_i denote the event that S_i does not query its oracle with any one of the $r+1$ keys for each i. On the occurrence of good_i, the oracle P always responds $\perp$ to S_i and thus the computation of $A(S_i^P)$ is independent of the $r+1$ keys hidden in P. For the same reasons stated in the previous proof, $\Pr[A(S_i^P) = r|\mathsf{good}_i] = \frac{1}{B}$ and $\Pr[\mathsf{good}_i] = 1 - \mathsf{neg}(n)$. Thus it can be concluded $\Pr[A(S_i^P) = r] \leq \frac{1}{B} + \mathsf{neg}(n)$ for all i's. Thus for random r, $\Pr[A(S_r^P) = r] \leq \frac{1}{B} + \mathsf{neg}(n)$. Hence combining this with the result in the previous paragraph, we have for any p $\Pr[A(Q) = r] \leq \frac{1}{B} + \mathsf{neg}(n) + \frac{1}{p(n)}$. Thus $\Pr[A(Q) = r] \leq \frac{1}{B} + \mathsf{neg}(n)$. □

When the attacker is catched by the forensics investigator, and ordered to hand over the real key and all fake keys, he is supposed to provide r' fake keys and tries to convince the investigator that what he encrypted is an ordinary executable file. After obtaining these r' keys, the forensics investigator can verify if these keys are valid. Since Q outputs $\perp$ on input any other strings, we can assume that the attacker always hands over the valid fake keys, or else the investigator will no end the inquest until the r' keys the attacker provides are valid. Then we turn to show that the cipher texts of two plain texts with equal bit length are still indistinguishable.

Claim 4. *DSKE satisfies the computational indistinguishability of encryption, even if the adversary obtains $1 \leq r' \leq r$ valid fake keys.*

Proof. Assume an arbitrary A obtains a cipher text Q (Q_1 or Q_2) and r' fake keys. Since on input the r' fake keys as well as their decryptions and the subprogram in Q which consists of the obfuscated multi-bit point functions corresponding to those unexposed keys, denoted Q' (Q'_1 or Q'_2), A can generate a cipher text which is identically distributed to Q, it suffices to show that for any outcome of the r' fake keys as well as their decryptions, A', which is A with them hardwired, cannot tell Q'_1 from Q'_2. Notice that Q' is also an obfuscated multi-bit set-membership function. Then adopting the analogous method in the proof of Claim 2, we have for any polynomial p, $|\Pr[A'(Q_1') = 1] - \Pr[A'(Q_2') = 1]| \leq \frac{1}{p(n)}$. Details omitted. □

Lastly, we need to show that after the adversary obtains $1 \leq r' \leq r$ valid fake keys where $r' < B$, it can correctly guess r with probability nearly $\frac{1}{B-r'}$, as the following claim states.

Claim 5. *For any PPT adversary A, A on input a cipher text Q can correctly guess r with probability no more than $\frac{1}{B-r'} + \mathsf{neg}(n)$ on the occurrence that the adversary obtains $1 \leq r' \leq r$ valid fake keys for $r' < B$.*

Proof. The proof is almost the same as the one of Claim 3. Notice that there are $B - r'$ possible values left for r and for any outcome of the r' fake keys and their decryptions, A with them hardwired can be also viewed as an adversary, and Q' (referred to the previous proof) is an obfuscated multi-bit set-membership function. The remainder proof is analogous. □

Thus, we have shown that DSKE satisfies all the required security requirements of disguisable symmetric encryption.

Since for an encryption scheme all security is lost if the key is lost, to put it into practice we need to discuss the issue of securely storing and management of these keys, which will be shown in the next subsection.

3.3 Management of the Keys

Since all the keys are generated at random, these keys cannot be remembered by human's mind. Actually, by the requirement of the underlying obfuscation method presented in [4], the min-entropy of a key should be at least super-logarithmic and the available construction in [5] requires the min-entropy should be at least n^{ε}. By the algorithm of key generation in our scheme, this requirement can be satisfied.

If an attacker has the strong ability to remember the random keys with n^{ε} min-entropy, he can view these keys as the rememberable passwords and keeps all keys in his mind. Thus there is no need for him to store the keys (passwords) and manage them. But actually, we think that it is still hard for human's mind to remember several random strings with such min-entropy. On the other hand, keys or passwords generated by human's mind are of course not random enough and thus cannot ensure the security of the encryption schemes.

The above discussion shows that a secure management of keys should be introduced for attackers. The first attempt towards this goal is to store each key into a file and the attacker remembers the names of these files. When he needs to use the real key, he retrieves it from some file and then executes the encryption or decryption. When the encryption or decryption operation finishes, he should wipe all the information in the hard disk which records the read/write operation of this file. However, this attempt cannot eliminate the risk that the forensics investigator can scan the hard disk to gather all these files and obtain all keys.

Another solution is to use the obfuscation for multiple-bit set-membership functions one more time, as the construction 2 illustrates. That is, the attacker can arbitrarily choose r human-made passwords which can be easily remembered by himself. Let each password correspond to a key (the real one or a fake one). Then he constructs a program PWD which on each password outputs the corresponding key. It can be seen that the program PWD also computes a multiple-bit set-membership function, similar to the program P in Construction 2. Then obfuscate PWD using the similar way.

However, it should be emphasized that to achieve the theoretical security guarantee by this obfuscation the passwords should be random with min-entropy n^{ε}. In general the human-made rememberable ones cannot satisfy this requirement, or else we could directly replace the keys in Construction 2 by these passwords. So this solution only has a heuristic security guarantee that no forensics investigator can reverse-engineering nor understand PWD even if he obtains all its code.

The third solution is to let the attacker store the keys into a hardware device. However, we think putting all keys in a device is quite insecure since if the attacker is catched and ordered to hand over keys, he has to hand over this device and thus all the keys may expose to the investigator.

Actually, we think that it is the two assumptions that result in that we cannot provide a solution with a theoretical security guarantee. The two assumptions are that the human's mind cannot remember random strings with min-entropy n^{ε} and that the forensics investigator can always gather any file he desires from the attacker's machine or related devices. Thus to find a scheme for secure management of keys with a theoretical guarantee, we maybe need to relax at least one of the assumptions.

We suggest a solution by adopting such relaxation. Our relaxation is that we assume that the attacker has the ability to store at least a random string with such min-entropy in a secure way. For instance, this secure way may be to divide the string into several segments and store the different segments in his mind, the secret place in the hard disk and other auxiliary secure devices respectively. Under this assumption, the attacker can store the real key in this secure way and store some fake keys in different secret places in the hard disk using one or many solutions presented above or combining different solutions in storing these fake keys.

4 Conclusions

We now summarize our result as follows. To apply the disguisable symmetric encryption scheme, an attacker needs to perform the following ordered operations.

First, he runs the key generation algorithm to obtain a real key and several fake keys according to Construction 2. Second, he adopts a secure way to store the real key as well as storing some fake keys in his hard disk. Third, erase all possible information generated in the first and second steps. Fourth, prepare a benign executable file which is of the same length with the malicious program (resp. the data file) he wants to encrypt. Fifth, the attacker can encrypt the malicious program (resp. the data file) if needed. By Construction 2, the encryption is secure, i.e. indistinguishable.

If the attacker is catched by the forensics investigator and ordered to hand over keys to decrypt the cipher text of the malicious program (resp. the data file), he provides several fake keys to the investigator and claims that one of them is the real key and others are fake. Since all decryption are valid and the investigator has no idea of the number of the keys, the investigator cannot distinguish if the attacker lies to him.

References

1. Barak, B., Goldreich, O., Impagliazzo, R., Rudich, S., Sahai, A., Vadhan, S.P., Yang, K.: On the (Im)possibility of obfuscating programs. In: Kilian, J. (ed.) CRYPTO 2001. LNCS, vol. 2139, pp. 1–18. Springer, Heidelberg (2001)
2. Berghel, H.: Hiding Data, Forensics, and Anti-forensics. Commun. ACM 50(4), 15–20 (2007)
3. Canetti, R.: Towards realizing random oracles: Hash functions that hide all partial information. In: Kaliski Jr., B.S. (ed.) CRYPTO 1997. LNCS, vol. 1294, pp. 455–469. Springer, Heidelberg (1997)
4. Canetti, R., Dakdouk, R.R.: Obfuscating point functions with multibit output. In: Smart, N.P. (ed.) EUROCRYPT 2008. LNCS, vol. 4965, pp. 489–508. Springer, Heidelberg (2008)
5. Canetti, R., Micciancio, D., Reingold, O.: Perfectly One-way Probabilistic Hash Functions. In: The 30th ACM Symposium on Theory of Computing, pp. 131–140. ACM, New York (1998)
6. Garfinkel, S.: Anti-forensics: Techniques, Detection and Countermeasures. In: The 2nd International Conference on i-Warfare and Security (ICIW), ACI, pp. 8–9 (2007)
7. Cabrera, J.B.D., Lewis, L., Mehara, R.: Detection and Classification of Intrusion and Faults Using Sequences of System Calls. ACM SIGMOD Record 30, 25–34 (2001)
8. Mohay, G.M., Anderson, A., Collie, B., McKemmish, R.D., de Vel, O.: Computer and Intrusion Forensics. Artech House, Inc., Norwood (2003)
9. Wee, H.: On Obfuscating Point Functions. In: The 37th ACM Symposium on Theory of Computing, pp. 523–532. ACM, New York (2005)

Digital Signatures for e-Government – A Long-Term Security Architecture*

Przemysław Błaśkiewicz, Przemysław Kubiak, and Mirosław Kutyłowski

Institute of Mathematics and Computer Science,
Wrocław University of Technology
{przemyslaw.blaskiewicz,przemyslaw.kubiak,miroslaw.kutylowski}@pwr.wroc.pl

Abstract. The framework of digital signature based on qualified certificates and X.509 architecture is known to have many security risks. Moreover, the fraud prevention mechanism is fragile and does not provide strong guarantees that might be regarded necessary for flow of legal documents.

Recently, mediated signatures have been proposed as a mechanism to effectively disable signature cards. In this paper we propose further mechanisms that can be applied on top of mediated RSA, so that we obtain signatures compatible with the standard format, but providing security guarantees even in the case when RSA becomes broken or the keys are compromised. Our solution is well suited for deploying a large-scale, long-term digital signature system for signing legal documents. Moreover, the solution is immune to kleptographic attacks as only deterministic algorithms are used on user's side.

Keywords: mRSA, PSS padding, signatures based on hash functions, kleptography, deterministic signatures, pairing based signatures.

1 Introduction

Digital signature seems to be the key technology for securing electronic documents against unauthorized modifications and forgery. However, digital signatures require a broader framework, where cryptographic security of a signature scheme is only one of the components contributing to the security of the system.

Equally important are answers to the following questions:

- how to make sure that a given public key corresponds to an alleged signer?
- how to make sure that the private signing keys cannot be used by anybody else but its owner?

While there is a lot of research on the first question (with many proposals such as alternative PKI systems, identity based signatures, certificateless signatures), the second question is relatively neglected, despite that we have no really good answers for the following specific questions:

* The paper is partially supported by Polish Ministry of Science and Higher Education, grant N N206 2701 33, and by "MISTRZ" programme of Foundation for Polish Science.

X. Lai et al. (Eds.): E-Forensics 2010, LNICST 56, pp. 256–270, 2011.

1. how to make sure that a key generated outside a secure signature-creation device is not retained and occasionally used by the service provider?
2. how to make sure that an unauthorized person has not used a secure signature-creation device after guessing the PIN?
3. if a secure signature-creation device has no keypad, how to know that the signatures under arbitrary documents are created by the PC in cooperation with the signature creation device?
4. how to make sure that there are no trapdoors or just security gaps in secure signature-creation devices used?
5. how to make sure that a secure signature-creation device is immune to any kind of physical and side-channel attacks? In particular, how to make sure that a card does not generate faulty signatures giving room for fault cryptanalysis?
6. how to check the origin of a given signature-creation device, so that malicious replacement is impossible?

Many of these problems are particularly hard, if signature creation devices are cryptographic smart cards. Some surrogate solutions have been proposed:

ad 1) Retention of any such data has been declared as a criminal act. However, it is hard to trace any activity of this kind, if it is carefully hidden. Technical solutions, such as distributed key generation procedures have been proposed, so that a card must participate in key generation and the service provider does not learn the whole private key. However, in large scale applications these methods are not very attractive due to logistics problems (generation of keys at the moment of handing the card to its owner takes time and requires few manual operations).

ad 2) Three failures to provide a PIN usually lead to blocking the card. However, the attacker may return the card after two trials into the wallet of the owner and wait for another chance. This is particularly dangerous for office applications.

ad 3) This problem might be solved with new technologies for inputing data directly to a smart card. Alternatively, one may try to improve security of operating systems and processor architecture, but it seems to be extremely difficult, if possible at all.

ad 4) So far, a common practice is to depend on declarations of the producers (!) or examinations by specially designated bodies. In the latter case, the signer is fully dependant on honesty of the examiner and completeness of the verification procedure. So far, the possibilities of thorough security analysis of chips and trapdoor detection are more a myth than technical reality. What the examiner can do is to check if there are some security threats that follow from violating a closed set of rules.

ad 5) Securing a smart card against physical attacks is a never ending game between attacking possibilities and protection mechanisms. Evaluating the state of the art of attacking possibilities as well as effectiveness of hardware protection requires insider knowledge, where at least part of it is an industrial secret. So it is hard to say whether declarations of the manufacturers are dependable or, may be, they are based on their business goals.

ad 6) The main protection mechanism remains the protection of a supply chain and visual protection mechanisms on the surface of the card (such as holograms). This is effective, but not against powerful adversaries.

Kleptographic Channels. In the context of securing signature creation devices we especially focus on kleptographic attacks [1,2]. Kleptography is a set of cryptographic techniques that allow implementation of a kleptographic side channel within the framework of a randomized cryptographic protocol. Such channel is visible and usable only for its creator. Information transmitted in the channel is protected by a "public" key (i.e. asymmetric key used solely for encryption), information retrieval is possible with a matching "private" key. Let us assume that a manufacturer has planted a kleptographic channel in a batch of devices he produced. Then physical inspection of the tampered devices and extracting the "public" key do not give access to information hidden in the kleptographic channel of this or any other device.

There are techniques of setting a kleptographic channel in nondeterministic crypto protocols in such a way that the protocol runs according to the specification, the statistical properties of its output *are not altered*, and, on top of that, the time characteristics remain within acceptable interval [3]. In the case of a nondeterministic signature, the information can be hidden in the signature itself. For deterministic protocols (like RSA for example) the nondeterministic part is the key generation, so the information may be hidden there (for details see e.g. [4], [5]).

Mediated Signatures as Secure Signing Environment. The idea of mediated signatures is that signature creation requires not only using a private signing key, but also an additional key (or keys) held by a security mediator or mediators (SEM). Particularly straightforward is constructing mediated signatures on top of RSA. The idea is to split the original private key and give its parts to the signer and the mediator. It can be done in an additive way ([6,7,8]), or a multiplicative way ([7,9]). We focus on the former variant, because it broadens the set of ready-to-use algorithms for distributed generation of RSA keys and facilitates the procedure described in Sect. 4. Specifically, if d is the original private key, then the mediator gets $d - d_u$ and the signer gets d_u, where d_u is (pseudo)random generated and distributed according to private keys regime.

The idea presented in [8] is to use mediated signatures as a fundamental security mechanism for digital signatures. The mediator is located at a central server which keeps a black list of stolen/lost signature cards and refuses to finalize requests from such cards. Therefore, a withheld card cannot create a signature, even if there is no mechanism to block the card itself. It also allows for temporary disabling a card, for instance outside the office hours of the signer or just on request of the owner. Note that the mediator can also monitor activity of the card for accordance with its security policy (e.g. a limited number of signatures per day). Moreover, in this scenario recording of the time of the signature can be provided by the mediator which is not possible in the traditional mode of using signature cards.

1.1 Our Contribution

We propose a couple of additional security mechanisms that are backwards compatible: standard software can verify such signatures in the old way. We address the following issues:

- protection against kleptographic attacks on RSA signatures exploiting padding bits [5],

- combining RSA signature with a signature based on discrete logarithm problem, so that in case of breaking RSA a forged signature can be recognized,
- a method of generating signatures between the signer and the mediator, so that a powerful adversary cannot create signatures even if he knows the keys.

This paper is not on new signature schemes but rather on system architecture that should prevent or detect any misuse of cryptographic mechanisms.

2 Building Blocks

2.1 RSA Signatures and Message Encoding Functions

An RSA signature is a result of three functions: a hash function h applied to the message m to be signed, a coding function C converting the hash value to a number modulo RSA number N, and finally an exponentiation modulo N:

$$(C(h(m)))^d \bmod N.$$

The coding function must be chosen with care (see attacks [10], [11]).

In this paper we use EMSA-PSS coding [12]. A part of the coding, important in tightening security reduction (cf. [13]), is encoding a random *salt* string together with the hash value. Normally, this may lead to many problems due to kleptographic attacks, but we shall use the *salt* as place for embedding another signature. Embedding a signature does not violate the coding – according to Sect. 8.1 of [12]: as *salt* even "a fixed value or a sequence number could be employed (...), with the resulting provable security similar to that of FDH" (Full Domain Hashing).

Another issue, crucial for the embedded signature, is the length of *salt*. In Appendix A.2.3 of [12] a type `RSASSA-PSS-params` is described to include, among others, a field `saltLenght` (i.e. octet length of the *salt*). [12] specifies the default value of the field to be the octet length of the output of the function indicated in the `hashAlgorithm` field. However, `saltLength` may be different: let $modBits$ denote bitlength of N, and $hLen$ denotes the length in octets of the hash function output, then the following condition (see Sect. 9.1.1 of [12]) imposes an upper bound for *salt* length:

$$\lceil (modBits - 1)/8 \rceil - 2 \geq \texttt{saltLength} + hLen.$$

2.2 Deterministic Signatures Based on Discrete Logarithm

Most discrete logarithm based signatures are probabilistic ones. The problem with these solutions is that there are many kleptographic schemes taking advantage of the pseudorandom parameters for signature generation, that may be potentially used to leak keys from a signature creation device. On the other hand, DL based signatures are based on different algebraic structures than RSA and might help in the case when security of RSA becomes endangered.

Fortunetely, there are deterministic signatures based on DL Problem, see for instance the BLS [14] or [15].

In this paper we use BLS: Suppose that $\mathbb{G}_1$, $\mathbb{G}_2$ are cyclic additive groups of prime order q, and let P be a generator of $\mathbb{G}_1$. Assume that there is an efficiently computable isomorphism $\psi : \mathbb{G}_1 \to \mathbb{G}_2$, thus $\psi(P)$ is a generator of $\mathbb{G}_2$. Let $\mathbb{G}_T$ be a multiplicative group of prime order q, and $\hat{e} : \mathbb{G}_1 \times \mathbb{G}_2 \to \mathbb{G}_T$ be a non-degenerate bilinear map, that is:

1. for all $P \in \mathbb{G}_1$, $Q \in \mathbb{G}_2$ and $a, b \in \mathbb{Z}$, $\hat{e}([a]P, [b]Q) = \hat{e}(P, Q)^{ab}$, where $[k]P$ denotes scalar k multiplication of element P,
2. $\hat{e}(P, \psi(P)) \neq 1$.

For simplicity one may assume $\mathbb{G}_2 = \mathbb{G}_1$, and $\psi \equiv \mathrm{id}$. In the BLS scheme $\mathbb{G}_1$ is a subgroup of points of an elliptic curve E defined over some finite field $\mathbb{F}_{p^r}$, and $\mathbb{G}_T$ is a subgroup of the multiplicative group $\mathbb{F}^*_{p^{r\kappa}}$, where κ is a relatively small integer, say $\kappa \in \{12, \ldots, 40\}$. The number κ is usually called *the embedding degree*. Note that $q | \#E$, but for security reasons we require that $q^2 \not| \#E$.

The signature algorithm comprises of calculation of the first point $H(m) \in \langle P \rangle$ corresponding to a message m, and computing $[x_u]H(m)$, i.e. multiplication of elliptic curve point $H(m)$ by scalar x_u being the private key of the user making the signature. The signature is the x-coordinate of the point $[x_u]H(m)$. Verification of the signature (see Sect. 3) takes place in the group $\mathbb{F}^*_{p^{r\kappa}}$, and it is more costly than signature generation.

2.3 Signatures Based on Hash Functions

Apart from RSA and discrete logarithm based signatures there is a third family: signatures based on hash functions. Their main advantage is fast verification, their main disadvantage is limitation on the number of signatures one can create – basic schemes of this kind are usually one-time signatures. This drawback can be alleviated by employing *Merkle trees*, and the resulting schemes (*Merkle Signature Scheme – MSS*) offer multipe-time signatures. In this case however, the maximal number of signatures is determined at the time of key generation. This in turn causes complexity issues, since building a large, single Merkle tree is calculation demanding. In [16], the GMSS algorithm loosens this limitation: even 2^{80} signatures might be verified with the root of the main tree.

2.4 Overview of System Architecture

The system is based on security mediator SEM, as in [17]. However, we propose to split SEM into t sub-centers sub-SEM$_i$, $i = 1, \ldots, t$, $t \geq 2$ (such decomposition would alleviate the problems of information leakage from a SEM). System components on the signer's side are: a PC and a smart card used as a *secure signature creation device*.

When the signer wishes to compose a signature, then the smart card performes some operations in interaction with the SEMs. The final output of the SEMs is a high quality signature – its safety is based on many security mechanisms that on the whole address the problems and scenarios mentioned in the introduction.

3 Nested Signatures

Since long-term predictions about scheme's security are given with large amount of uncertainty, it seems reasonable to strengthen the RSA with another deterministic signature scheme — the BLS [14]. We combine them together using RSASSA-PSS, with the RSA signature layer being the mediated one, while BLS is composed solely by the smart card of the signer. Thanks to the way the message is coded the resulting signature can be input to a standard RSA verification software which will still verify the RSA layer in the regular way. However, software aware of the nesting can perform a thorough verification and check both signatures.

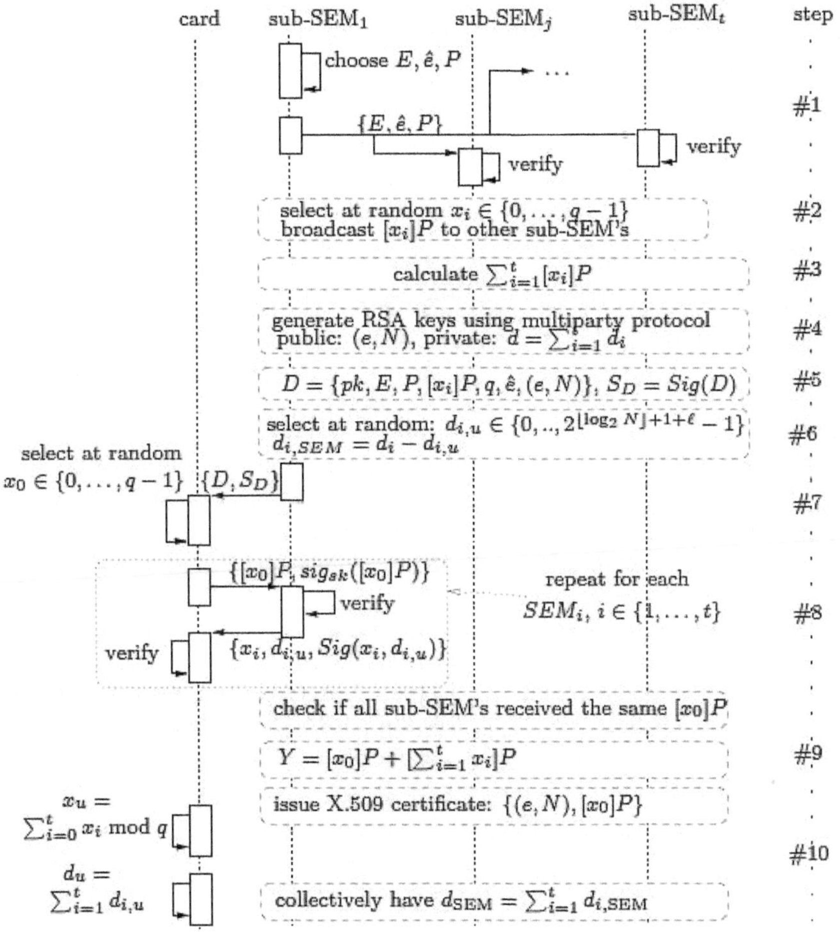

Fig. 1. Data flow for key generation. Operations in rounded rectangles are performed distributively.

Key Generation. We propose that the modulus N and the secret exponent d of RSA should be generated outside the card in a multiparty protocol (accordingly, we divide the security mediator SEM into t sub-SEMs, $t \geq 2$). This prevents any trapdoor or kleptography possibilities on the side of the smart card, and makes it possible to use high quality randomness. Last not least, it may speed up logistics issues (generation of RSA keys is relatively slow and the time delay may be annoying for an average user).

Multiparty generation of RSA keys has been described in the literature: [18] – for at least 3 participants (for real implementation issues see [19], for a robust version see [20]), [21] – for two participants, or a different approach in [22].

Let us describe the steps of generating the RSA and BLS keys in some more detail (see also Fig. 1):

Suppose that the card holds some single, initial, unique priate key sk (set by the card's producer) for deterministic one-time signature scheme. Let the public part pk of the key be given to SEM before the following protocol is executed. Assume also that the card's manufacturer has placed into the card SEM's public key for verification of SEM's signatures.

1. sub-SEM$_1$ selects an elliptic curve defined over some finite field (the choice determines also a bilinear mapping $\hat{e}$) and a basepoint P of prime order q. Then sub-SEM$_1$ transmits this data together with definition of $\hat{e}$ to the other sub-SEM's for verification.
2. If the verification succeeded, each sub-SEM$_i$ picks $x_i \in \{0, \ldots, q-1\}$ at random and broadcasts the point $[x_i]P$ to other sub-SEMs.
3. Each sub-SEM calculates $\sum_{i=1}^{t}[x_i]P$, i.e. calculates $[\sum_{i=1}^{t} x_i]P$.
4. The sub-SEMs generate the RSA-keys using a multiparty protocol: let the resulting public part be (e, N) and the secret exponent be $d = \sum_{i=1}^{t} \tilde{d}_i$, where $\tilde{d}_i \in \mathbb{Z}$ is known only to sub-SEM$_i$.
5. All sub-SEMs now distributively sign all public data D generated so far, i.e.: the public one time key pk (which serves as identifier of the addressee of data D), the definition of the field, curve E, points P, $[x_i]P$, $i = 1, \ldots, t$, order q of P, map $\hat{e}$ and RSA public key (e, N). The signature might also be a nested signature, even with the inner signature being a probabilistic one, e.g. ECDSA (to mitigate the threat of klepto channel each sub-SEM might xor outputs from a few random number generators).
6. Let ℓ is a fixed element from the set $\{128, \ldots, 160\}$ (see e.g. the range of additive sharing over $\mathbb{Z}$ in Sect. 3.2 of [22], and Δ in S-RSA-DEL delegation protocol in Fig. 2 of [23]). Each sub-SEM$_i$, $i = 1, \ldots, t$ picks $d_{i,u} \in \{0, \ldots, 2^{\lfloor \log_2 N \rfloor + 1 + \ell} - 1\}$ at random and calculates integer $d_{i,\mathrm{SEM}} = \tilde{d}_i - d_{i,u}$. Note that $d_{i,u}$ can be calculated independently of N (e.g. before N), only the length of N must be known.
7. The card contacts sub-SEM$_1$ over a secure channel and receives the signed data D. If verification of the signature succeeds the card picks its random element $x_0 \in \{0, \ldots, q-1\}$, and calculates $[x_0]P$.
8. For each $i \in \{1, \ldots, t\}$ the card contacts sub-SEM$_i$ over a secure channel and sends it $[x_0]P$ and $sig_{sk}([x_0]P)$. The sub-SEM$_i$ verifies the signature and only then does it respond with x_i and $d_{i,u}$ and a signature thereof (a certificate for the sub-SEM$_i$ signature key is distributiely signed by all sub-SEMs, and is transferred

to the card together with the signature). The card immediately checks x_i against P, $[x_i]P$ from D.

9. At this point all sub-SEMs compare the received element $[x_0]P \in E$ (i.e. they check if the sk was really used only once). If this is so, then the value is taken as ID-card's part of the BLS public key. Then the sub-SEMs complete calculation of the key: $E, P \in E, Y = [x_0]P + [\sum_{i=1}^{t} x_i]P$, and issue an X.509 certificate for the card that it possesses the RSA key (e, N). In some extension field the certificate must also contain card's BLS public key for the inner signature. The certificate is signed distributively. Sub-SEM$_t$ now transfer the certificate to the ID-card.
10. The card calculates its BLS private key as $x_u = \sum_{i=0}^{t} x_i \bmod q$ and its part of RSA private key as integer $d_u = \sum_{i=1}^{t} d_{i,u}$. Note that the remaining part $d_{\text{SEM}} = \sum_{i=1}^{t} d_{i,\text{SEM}}$ of the secret key d is distributed among sub-SEMs, who will participate in every signing procedure initiated by the user. Neither he nor the sub-SEMs can generate valid signatures on their own.
11. The card compares the certificate received from the last sub-SEM with D received from the first sub-SEM. As the last check the card initializes the signature generation protocol (see below) to sign the certificate. If the finalized signature is valid the card assumes that d_u is valid as well, and removes all partial $d_{i,u}$ and partial x_i together with their signatures. Otherwise the card discloses all data received, together with their signatures.

Each user should receive a different set of keys, i.e. different modulus N for RSA system and a unique (non-isomorphic with the ones so far generated) elliptic curve for the BLS signature. This can minimize damages that could result by breaking both systems using adequately large resources.

Signature Generation

1. The user's PC computes the hash value $h(m)$ of the message m to be signed, and sends it to the smartcard.
2. the smartcard signs $h(m)$ using BLS scheme: the first point $H(h(m))$ of the group $\langle P \rangle$, corresponding to $h(m)$, is calculated deterministically, according to the procedure from [14] (alternatively, the algorithm from [24] might be used, complemented by multiplication by scalar $\#E/q$ to get a point in the subgroup of order q), next $H(h(m))$ is multiplied by the scalar x_u, which yields point $[x_u]H(h(m))$. The BLS signature of $h(m)$ is the x-coordinate $x([x_u]H(h(m)))$ of the point $[x_u]H(h(m))$. The resulting signature is unpredictable to both the card's owner as well as other third parties. We call this signature the *salt*.
3. Both $h(m)$ and *salt* can now be used by the card as variables in execution of RSASSA-PSS scheme: they just need to be composed according to EMSA-PSS [12] and the result μ can now be simply RSA-exponentiated.
4. In the process of signature generation, the user's card calculates the d_u'th power of the result μ of EMSA-PSS padding and sends it, along with the message digest $h(m)$ and the padding result itself, to the SEM. That is, it sends the triple $(h(m), s_u, \mu)$, where $s_u = \mu^{d_u} \bmod N$.
5. The sub-SEMs finalize the RSA exponentiation: $s = s_u \cdot \prod_{i=1}^{t} \mu^{d_{i,\text{SEM}}} \bmod N$, thus finishing the procedure of RSA signature generation.

6. At this point a full verification is possible: SEM verifies the RSA signature, checks the EMSA-PSS coding – this includes *salt* recovering and verification of the inner signature (it also results in checking if the card had chosen *the first* possible point on the curve while encoding $h(m)$). If the checks succeed, the finalized signature is sent back to the user. A failure means that the card has malfunctioned or behaved maliciously – as we see, the system-internal verification is of vital importance.

Note that during the signature generation procedure the smartcard and sub-SEMs cannot use CRT, as in this case the factorization of N would be known to all parties. This increases signing time, especially on the side of the card. But, theoretically, this can be seen as an advantage. For example, the signing time longer than 10 sec. means that one cannot generate more than 2^{25} signatures over the period of 10 years; we therefore obtain an upper limit on power of the adversary in results of [25] and [13]. In fact the SEM might arbitrarily set a lower bound for the period of time it must pass between two consecutive finalizations of signatures of the same user. Moreover, if CRT is not in use, then some category of fault attacks is eliminated ([26,27]).

Signature Verification. For given m and its alleged signature s:

1. The verifier calculates $h(m)$ and the point $H(h(m)) \in \langle P \rangle$.
2. Given the RSA public key (e, N) the verifier first calculates $\mu = s^e \bmod N$, and checks the EMSA-PSS coding against $h(m)$ (this includes *salt* recovery).
3. If the coding is valid then, given BLS public key E, P, Y, q, and $\hat{e}$, the verifier checks the inner signature. From $salt = x([x_u]H(h(m)))$ one of the two points $\pm[x_u]H(h(m))$ is calculated, denote this point by Q. Next, it is checked whether the order of Q equals q. If it does, then the verifier checks if one of the conditions holds: $\hat{e}(Q, P) = \hat{e}(H(h(m)), Y)$ or $\hat{e}(Q, P) = (\hat{e}(H(h(m)), Y))^{-1}$.

4 Floating Exponents

Let us stress the fact that splitting the secret exponent d from the RSA algorithm between the user and the SEM has additional benefits. If the RSA and inner signature [14] keys are broken, it is still possible to verify if a given signature was mediated by the SEM or not, provided that the later keeps a record of operations it performed. Should this verification fail, it becomes obvious that both keys have been broken and, in particular, the adversary was able to extract the secret exponent d. On the other hand, if the adversary wants to trick the SEM by offering it a valid partial RSASSA-PSS signature with a valid inner signature [14], he must know the right part d_u of the exponent d of the user whose keys he had broken. Doing this equals solving a discrete logarithm problem taken modulus each factor of N (though the factors length equals half of that of N). Therefore it is vital that no constraints, in particular on length, be placed on exponents d and their parts.

To mitigate the problem of smaller length of the factors of N, which allows solving the discrete logarithm problem with relatively small effort, a technique of switching exponent parts can be used. Let the SEM and the card share the same secret key K, which is unique for each card. After a signature is generated, the key deterministically evolves on both sides. For each new signature, K is used as an initialization vector for a secure pseudo-random number generator (PRNG) to obtain a value that is added by the card to the part of the exponent it stores, and subtracted by the SEM from the part stored therein. This way, for each signature different exponents are used, but they still sum up to the same value. A one-time success at finding the discrete logarithm brings no advantage to the attacker as long as PRNG is strong and K remains secret.

To state the problem more formally, let K_i be a unique key shared by the card and sub-SEM$_i$, $i = 1, \ldots, t$ $(t \geq 1)$. To generate an RSA signature the card does the exponentiation of the result of EMSA-PSS coding to the exponent equal to

$$d_u \pm \sum_{i=1}^{t} (-1)^i \cdot GEN(K_i), \tag{1}$$

where $GEN(K_i)$ is an integer output of a cryptographically safe PRNG (see e.g. generators in [28], *excluding* the Dual_EC_DRBG generator – for the reason see [29]). It suffices if length of $GEN(K_i)$ equals $\ell + \lfloor \log_2 N \rfloor + 1$, where ℓ is a fixed element from the set $\{128, \ldots, 160\}$. Operator "$\pm$" in Eq. (1) means that the exponent is alternately "increased" and "decreased" every second signature: this and multiplier $(-1)^i$ lessen changes of length of the exponent. Next, for each K_i the card performs a deterministic key evolution (sufficiently many steps of key evolution seem to be feasible on nowadays smart cards, cf. [30] claiming on p. 4, Sect. "E^{2}PROM Technology", even $5 \cdot 10^5$ write/erase cycles). To calculate its part of the signature, each sub-SEM$_i$ exponentiates the result μ of EMSA-PSS coding (as received from the user along with the partial result of exponentiation) to the power of $d_{i,\mathrm{SEM}} \mp (-1)^i \cdot GEN(K_i)$. Next, the sub-SEM$_i$ performs a deterministic evolution of the key K_i.

Note that should the card be cloned it will be revealed after the first generation of a signature by the clone – the SEM will make one key-evolution step further than the original card and the keys will not match. Each sub-SEM$_i$ shall keep apart from its current state, the initial value of K_i to facilitate the process of investigation in case the keys get de-synchronized. To guarantee that the initial K_i will not be changed by sub-SEM$_i$, the following procedure might be applied: At point 2 of key generation procedure each sub-SEM commits to the initial K_i by broadcasting its hash $h(K_i)$ to other sub-SEMs. Next, at point 5 all broadcasted hashes are included in data set D, and are distributively signed by sub-SEMs with all the public data. Note that these hashes are sent to the card at point 7, and at points 7, 8 the card can check K_i against its commitment $h(K_i)$, $i = 1, \ldots, t$.

In order to force the adversary into tricking the SEM (i.e. make it even harder for him to generate a valid signature without participation of the SEM), one of the sub-SEMs may be required to place a timestamp under the documents (the timestamp would contain this sub-SEM's signature under the document and under the user's signature finalized by all the sub-SEMs) and only timestamped documents can be assumed valid. Such outer signature in the timestamp *must* be applied *both* to the document *and* to the finalized signature of the user. The best solution for it seems to be to use a scheme based on a completely different problem, to use a hash function signature scheme for instance. The Merkle tree traversal algorithm provides additional features with respect to timestamping: if a given sub-SEM faithfully follows the algorithm for any two document signatures it is possible to reconstruct (based on the signature only, without an additional timestamp) the succession in which the documents have been signed. Note that other sub-SEMs will verify the outer hash-based signature as well as the tree traversal order.

If hash-based signatures are implemented in SEM, it is important to separate the source of randomness from implementation of the signatures (i.e. from key generation — apart from key generation this signature scheme is purely deterministic). Instead of one, at least two independent sources of randomness should be utilized and their outputs combined.

5 Forensic Analysis

As an example of forensic analysis consider the case of malicious behavior of one of the sub-SEMs. Suppose that the procedure of distributed RSA key generation bounds each sub-SEM$_i$ to its secret exponent $\tilde{d}_i$ (see point 4 of the ID-card's key generation procedure), for example by some checking signature made at the end of the internal procedure of generating the RSA key.

As we could see, the sub-SEM$_i$ cannot claim that the initial value of K_i was different than the one passed to the card. If correct elements $d_{i,\mathrm{SEM}}$, K_i, $i = 1, \ldots, t$, were used in RSA signature generation at point 11 of the key generation procedure, and correct $d_{i,u}$ were passed to the ID-card, then the signature is valid. The sub-SEMs should then save all values $\beta_i = \mu^{\alpha_i} \bmod N$ generated by sub-SEM$_i$, $i = 1, \ldots, t$, to finalize the first cards partial signature s_u:

$$s = s_u \prod_{i=1}^{t} \mu^{\alpha_i} \bmod N.$$

Since $\alpha_i = d_{i,\mathrm{SEM}} - (-1)^i \cdot GEN(K_i)$, and the initial value of K_i is bounded by $h(K_i)$, value β_i is a commitment of correct $d_{i,\mathrm{SEM}}$.

Now consider the case of the first signature being invalid. First, the ID-card is checked: it reveals all values received: K_i, as well as received $d'_{i,u}$, $i = 1, \ldots, t$. Next, raising μ to power $(\sum_{i=1}^{t} d'_{i,u}) + \sum_{i=1}^{t} (-1)^i \cdot GEN(K_i)$ is repeated to check if partial signature s_u was correct. If it was, it is obvious that at least one sub-SEM behaved maliciously. All $\tilde{d}_i$ must be revealed, and integers $d'_{i,\mathrm{SEM}} = \tilde{d}_i - d'_{i,u}$ are calculated. Having $d'_{i,\mathrm{SEM}}$ and K_i it is easy to check correctness of each exponentiation $\mu^{\alpha_i} \bmod N$.

6 Implementation Recommendations

Hash Functions. Taking into account security aspects of long-term certificates used for digital signatures a hash function h used to make digests $h(m)$ should have long-term collision resistance. Therfore we propose to use the zipper hash construction [31], which utilizes two hash functions that are feed with the same message.

To harden the zipper hash against general techniques described in [32], we propose to use as the first hash function some non-iterative one, e.g. a hash function working analogously to MD6, when MD6's optional, mode control parameter L is greater than 27 (see Sect. 2.4.1 in [33]) – note that $L = 64$ by default.

RSA. It is advisable that modulus N of the RSA algorithm be a product of two *strong primes* [22]. Let us assume that the adversary succeeded in factorizing N into q and p. We do not want him to be able to gain any knowledge on the sum (1), that is indirectly on outputs of $GEN(K_i)$ for $i = 1, \ldots, t$. However, if $p-1$ or $q-1$ has a large smooth divisor, then by applying Pohling-Hellman algorithm he might be able to recover the value of sum (1) modulo the smooth divisor. Here "smooth" depends on adversary's computational power, but if p, q are of the form $2p' + 1$, $2q' + 1$, respectively, where p', q' are prime, then the smooth divisors for this case equal two only. Additionally, if the card and all the sub-SEM$_i$ unset the least significant bit of $GEN(K_i)$ then the output of the generator will not be visible in the subgroups of order two. In order to learn anything about (1), the adversary needs to perform an attack on discrete logarithm problem in the subgroup of large prime order (i.e. p' or q'). A single value does not bring much information and the same calculations must be carried out for many other intercepted signatures in order to launch cryptanalysis recovering keys K_i.

Elliptic Curves. The elliptic curve for the inner signature should have *embedding degree* ensuring at least 128-bit security (cf. [34]). Note that the security of the inner signature may not be entirely independent of the security of RSA – a progress made in attacks utilizing GNFS may have serious impact on *index calculations* (see last paragraph on p. 29 of online version [35]). Meanwhile, using pairing we need to take into account the fact, that the adversary may try to attack the discrete logarithm problem in the field in which verification of the inner signature takes place. Therefore we recommend a relatively high degree of security for the inner signature (see that according to Table 7.2 from [36], 128-bit security is achieved by RSA for 3248-bit modulus N, and such long N could distinctly slow down calculations done on the side of a smart card).

The proposed nested signature scheme with the zipper hash construction, extended with the secret keys shared between the card and sub-SEMs used for altering the exponent, and the SEM hash-signature under a timestamp, taken together increase the probability of outlasting the crypto analytical efforts of the (alleged) adversary. We hope that on each link (card → SEM, SEM → finalized signature with a timestamp) at least one out of three safeguards will last.

6.1 Resources and Logistics

If the computational and communication costs of distributed computation of strong RSA keys are prohibitively big to use this method on a large scale, one could consider the following alternative solution. Suppose there is a dealer who generates the RSA keys and splits each of them into parts that are distributed to the card and a number of sub-SEMs. When parts of the key are distributed, the dealer destroys its copy of the key.

Assume that the whole procedure of keys generation and secret exponents partition is deterministic, dependent of a random *seed* that is distributively generated by the dealer and sub-SEMs. For the purpose of verification for each key the parties must first commit to the shares of the *seed* they generated for that key. Next, some portion of the keys produced by the dealer as well as the partition of the secret exponents undergo a verification against commited shares of the *seed*. The verified values are destroyed afterwards.

The BLS key should be generated as described in Subsect. 3, necessarily *before* the RSA key is distributed.

Furthermore, each sub-SEM$_i$ generates its own secret key K_i to be used for altering the exponent, and sends it to the card (each sub-SEM$_i$ should generate K_i *before* it has obtained its part of the RSA exponent). One of the sub-SEMs or a separate entity designated for timestamping, generates its public key for timestamp signing (also *before* the RSA key is distributed). Note that this way there are components of the protocol beyond the influence of the trusted dealer (the same applies to each of the sub-SEMs).

Another issue are resources of the platform on which the system is implemented on signer's side. If the ID-card does not allow to generate the additional, inner signature efficiently, when the non-CRT implementation of RSA signatures must be executed, HMAC [37] function might be used as a source of a salt for the EMSA-PSS encoding. Let K_{MAC} be a key shared by the ID-card and *one* of the sub-SEM's, say sub-SEM$_j$. To generate a signature under message's digest $h(m)$, $salt$ = HMAC$(h(m), K_{MAC})$ is calculated by the ID-card, and the signature generation on the user's side proceeds further as described above. On the SEM's side, after finalization of the RSA signature the EMSA-PSS encoding value μ is verified. The sub-SEM$_j$ possessing K_{MAC} can now check validity of *salt*. Note that K_{MAC} might evolve as keys K_i do, and K_{MAC} might be used instead of K_j (thus one key might be dropped from Eq. (1)). In case of key-evolution the initial value of K_{MAC} should also be stored by sub-SEM$_j$, to facilitate a possible investigation.

If BLS is replaced by HMAC, then a more space-efficient encoding function [38] may be used instead of EMSA-PSS. The scheme uses a single bit value produced by a pseudorandom number generator on the basis of a secret key (the value is duplicated by the encoding function). Thus this bit value might be calculated from HMAC$(h(m), K_{MAC})$. Note that also in this case the evolution of K_{MAC} is enough to detect the fact that ID-card has been cloned, even if other keys K_i from (1) are not used in the system: usually a pseudorandom sequence and its shift differ every few possitions.

Yet another aspect that influences the system is the problem of trusted communication channels between the dealer and the card, and between each sub-SEM and the card. If these are cryptographic (remote) channels, then, above all, *security of the whole system will depend on the security of the cipher in use*. Moreover, if a public-key cipher is to be used, the question remains as to who is going to generate the public key (and the corresponding *secret* key) of the card? It *should not* be the card itself, neither its manufacturer. If, on the other hand, a symmetric cipher was used, then how to deliver the key to the card remains an open question. A distinct symmetric key is needed on the card for each sub-SEM and, possibly, for the dealer.

Therefore (above all, in order to eliminate the dependence of the signing schemes from the cipher scheme(s)), the best solution would be to transfer the secret data into the card directly on site where the data is generated (i.e. at the possible dealer and all the subsequent sub-SEMs). Such a solution can have its influence on the physical location of sub-SEMs and/or means of transportation of the cards.

Final Remarks

In this paper we have shown that a number of practical threats for PKI infrastructures can be avoided. In this way we can address most of the technical and legal challenges for proof value of electronic signatures. Moreover, our solutions are obtained by crytpographic means, so they are independent from hardware security mechanisms, which are hard to evaluate by parties having no sufficient technical insight. In contrast, our cryptographic solutions against hardware problems are platform independent and self-evident.

References

1. Young, A., Yung, M.: The dark side of "Black-box" cryptography, or: Should we trust capstone? In: Koblitz, N. (ed.) CRYPTO 1996. LNCS, vol. 1109, pp. 89–103. Springer, Heidelberg (1996)
2. Young, A., Yung, M.: The prevalence of kleptographic attacks on discrete-log based cryptosystems. In: Kaliski Jr., B.S. (ed.) CRYPTO 1997. LNCS, vol. 1294, pp. 264–276. Springer, Heidelberg (1997)
3. Young, A.L., Yung, M.: A timing-resistant elliptic curve backdoor in RSA. In: Pei, D., Yung, M., Lin, D., Wu, C. (eds.) Inscrypt 2007. LNCS, vol. 4990, pp. 427–441. Springer, Heidelberg (2008)
4. Young, A., Yung, M.: A space efficient backdoor in RSA and its applications. In: Preneel, B., Tavares, S. (eds.) SAC 2005. LNCS, vol. 3897, pp. 128–143. Springer, Heidelberg (2006)
5. Young, A., Yung, M.: An elliptic curve backdoor algorithm for RSASSA. In: Camenisch, J.L., Collberg, C.S., Johnson, N.F., Sallee, P. (eds.) IH 2006. LNCS, vol. 4437, pp. 355–374. Springer, Heidelberg (2007)
6. Boneh, D., Ding, X., Tsudik, G., Wong, C.M.: A method for fast revocation of public key certificates and security capabilities. In: SSYM 2001: Proceedings of the 10th Conference on USENIX Security Symposium, p. 22. USENIX Association, Berkeley (2001)
7. Tsudik, G.: Weak forward security in mediated RSA. In: Cimato, S., Galdi, C., Persiano, G. (eds.) SCN 2002. LNCS, vol. 2576, pp. 45–54. Springer, Heidelberg (2003)
8. Boneh, D., Ding, X., Tsudik, G.: Fine-grained control of security capabilities. ACM Trans. Internet Techn. 4(1), 60–82 (2004)
9. Bellare, M., Sandhu, R.: The security of practical two-party RSA signature schemes. Cryptology ePrint Archive, Report 2001/060 (2001)
10. Coppersmith, D., Coron, J.S., Grieu, F., Halevi, S., Jutla, C.S., Naccache, D., Stern, J.P.: Cryptanalysis of ISO/IEC 9796-1. J. Cryptology 21(1), 27–51 (2008)
11. Coron, J.S., Naccache, D., Tibouchi, M., Weinmann, R.P.: Practical cryptanalysis of ISO/IEC 9796-2 and EMV signatures. Cryptology ePrint Archive, Report 2009/203 (2009)
12. RSA Laboratories: PKCS#1 v2.1 — RSA Cryptography Standard + Errata (2005)
13. Jonsson, J.: Security proofs for the RSA-PSS signature scheme and its variants. Cryptology ePrint Archive, Report 2001/053 (2001)
14. Boneh, D., Lynn, B., Shacham, H.: Short signatures from the Weil pairing. J. Cryptology 17(4), 297–319 (2004)
15. Zhang, F., Safavi-Naini, R., Susilo, W.: An efficient signature scheme from bilinear pairings and its applications. In: Bao, F., Deng, R., Zhou, J. (eds.) PKC 2004. LNCS, vol. 2947, pp. 277–290. Springer, Heidelberg (2004)
16. Buchmann, J., Dahmen, E., Klintsevich, E., Okeya, K., Vuillaume, C.: Merkle signatures with virtually unlimited signature capacity. In: Katz, J., Yung, M. (eds.) ACNS 2007. LNCS, vol. 4521, pp. 31–45. Springer, Heidelberg (2007)
17. Kubiak, P., Kutyłowski, M., Lauks-Dutka, A., Tabor, M.: Mediated signatures - towards undeniability of digital data in technical and legal framework. In: 3rd Workshop on Legal Informatics and Legal Information Technology (LIT 2010). LNBIP. Springer, Heidelberg (2010)
18. Boneh, D., Franklin, M.: Efficient generation of shared RSA keys. J. ACM 48(4), 702–722 (2001)

19. Malkin, M., Wu, T.D., Boneh, D.: Experimenting with shared generation of RSA keys. In: NDSS. The Internet Society, San Diego (1999)
20. Frankel, Y., MacKenzie, P.D., Yung, M.: Robust efficient distributed RSA-key generation. In: PODC, vol. 320 (1998)
21. Gilboa, N.: Two party RSA key generation (Extended abstract). In: Wiener, M. (ed.) CRYPTO 1999. LNCS, vol. 1666, pp. 116–129. Springer, Heidelberg (1999)
22. Algesheimer, J., Camenisch, J., Shoup, V.: Efficient computation modulo a shared secret with application to the generation of shared safe-prime products. Cryptology ePrint Archive, Report 2002/029 (2002)
23. MacKenzie, P.D., Reiter, M.K.: Delegation of cryptographic servers for capture-resilient devices. Distributed Computing 16(4), 307–327 (2003)
24. Coron, J.S., Icart, T.: An indifferentiable hash function into elliptic curves. Cryptology ePrint Archive, Report 2009/340 (2009)
25. Coron, J.-S.: On the Exact Security of Full Domain Hash. In: Bellare, M. (ed.) CRYPTO 2000. LNCS, vol. 1880, pp. 229–235. Springer, Heidelberg (2000)
26. Coron, J.-S., Joux, A., Kizhvatov, I., Naccache, D., Paillier, P.: Fault attacks on RSA signatures with partially unknown messages. In: Clavier, C., Gaj, K. (eds.) CHES 2009. LNCS, vol. 5747, pp. 444–456. Springer, Heidelberg (2009)
27. Coron, J.-S., Naccache, D., Tibouchi, M.: Fault attacks against EMV signatures. In: Pieprzyk, J. (ed.) CT-RSA 2010. LNCS, vol. 5985, pp. 208–220. Springer, Heidelberg (2010)
28. Barker, E., Kelsey, J.: Recommendation for random number generation using deterministic random bit generators (revised). NIST Special Publication 800-90 (2007)
29. Shumow, D., Ferguson, N.: On the possibility of a back door in the NIST SP800-90 Dual EC Prng (2007), http://rump2007.cr.yp.to/15-shumow.pdf
30. Infineon Technologies AG: Chip Card & Security: SLE 66CLX800PE(M) Family, 8/16-Bit High Security Dual Interface Controller For Contact based and Contactless Applications (2009)
31. Liskov, M.: Constructing an ideal hash function from weak ideal compression functions. In: Biham, E., Youssef, A.M. (eds.) SAC 2006. LNCS, vol. 4356, pp. 358–375. Springer, Heidelberg (2007)
32. Joux, A.: Multicollisions in iterated hash functions. Application to cascaded constructions. In: Franklin, M. (ed.) CRYPTO 2004. LNCS, vol. 3152, pp. 306–316. Springer, Heidelberg (2004)
33. Rivest, R.L., Agre, B., Bailey, D.V., Crutchfield, C., Dodis, Y., Elliott, K., Khan, F.A., Krishnamurthy, J., Lin, Y., Reyzin, L., Shen, E., Sukha, J., Sutherland, D., Tromer, E., Yin, Y.L.: The MD6 hash function. a proposal to NIST for SHA-3 (2009)
34. Granger, R., Page, D.L., Smart, N.P.: High security pairing-based cryptography revisited. In: Hess, F., Pauli, S., Pohst, M. (eds.) ANTS 2006. LNCS, vol. 4076, pp. 480–494. Springer, Heidelberg (2006)
35. Lenstra, A.K.: Key lengths. In: The Handbook of Information Security, vol. 2, Wiley, Chichester (2005), http://www.keylength.com/biblio/Handbook_of_Information_Security_-_Keylength.pdf
36. Babbage, S., Catalano, D., Cid, C., de Weger, B., Dunkelman, O., Gehrmann, C., Granboulan, L., Lange, T., Lenstra, A., Mitchell, C., Näslund, M., Nguyen, P., Paar, C., Paterson, K., Pelzl, J., Pornin, T., Preneel, B., Rechberger, C., Rijmen, V., Robshaw, M., Rupp, A., Schläffer, M., Vaudenay, S., Ward, M.: ECRYPT2 yearly report on algorithms and keysizes (2008-2009) (2009)
37. Krawczyk, H., Bellare, M., Canetti, R.: HMAC: Keyed-Hashing for Message Authentication. RFC 2104 (Informational) (1997)
38. Qian, H., Li, Z.-b., Chen, Z.-j., Yang, S.: A practical optimal padding for signature schemes. In: Abe, M. (ed.) CT-RSA 2007. LNCS, vol. 4377, pp. 112–128. Springer, Heidelberg (2006)

SQL Injection Defense Mechanisms for IIS+ASP+MSSQL Web Applications

Beihua Wu*

East China University of Political Science and Law,
555 Longyuan Road, Shanghai, China, 201620
wubeihua@ecupl.edu.cn

Abstract. With the sharp increase of hacking attacks over the last couple of years, web application security has become a key concern. SQL injection is one of the most common types of web hacking and has been widely written and used in the wild. This paper analyzes the principle of SQL injection attacks on Web sites, presents methods available to prevent IIS+ASP+MSSQL web applications from these kinds of attacks, including secure coding within the web application, proper database configuration, deployment of IIS and other security techniques. The result is verified by WVS report.

Keywords: SQL Injection, Web sites, Security, Cybercrime.

1 Introduction

Together with the development of computer network and the advent of e-business (such as E-trade, cyber-banks, etc.) cybercrime continues to soar. The number of cyber attacks is doubling each year, aided by more and more skilled hackers and increasing easy-to-use hacking tools, as well as the fact that system and network administrators are exhausted and have inadequately trained. SQL injection is one of the most common types of web hacking and has been widely written and used in the wild. SQL injection attacks represent a serious threat to any database-driven sites and result in a great number of losses. This paper analyzes the principle of SQL injection attacks on Web sites, presents methods available to prevent IIS+ASP+MSSQL web applications from the attacks and implement those in practice. Finally, we draw the conclusions.

2 The Principle of SQL Injection

SQL injection is a code injection technique that exploits a security vulnerability occurring in the database layer of an application [1]. If user input, which is embedded in SQL statements, is incorrectly filtered for escape characters, attackers will take advantage of the present vulnerability. SQL injection exploit can allow attackers to obtain unrestricted access to the database, read sensitive data from the database, modify database data, and in some cases issue commands to the operating system.

* Academic Field: Network Security, Information Technology.

X. Lai et al. (Eds.): E-Forensics 2010, LNICST 56, pp. 271–276, 2011.

The multistep of SQL injection attack is as follows:

2.1 Finding Vulnerable Pages

In the first, try to look for pages that allow you to submit data, such as login pages with authentication forms, pages with search engines, feedback pages, etc. In general, Web pages use *post* or *get* command to send parameters to another ASP page. These pages include *<Form>* tag, and everything between the *<Form>* and *</Form>* has potential parameters that might be vulnerable [2]. You may find something like this in codes:

```
    <Form action="search.asp" method="post" id="search">
      <input type="text" size="12" name="t_name" />
      <input type="submit" name="Submit" value="search"
/>
    </Form>
```

Sometimes, you may not see the input box on the page directly, as the type of <input> can be set to hidden. However, the vulnerability is still present.

On the other hand, if you can't find any *<Form>* tag in HTML code, you should look for pages like ASP, PHP, or JSP web pages, especially for URL that takes parameters, such as: http://www.sqlinjection.com/news.asp?id=1020505.

2.2 SQL Injection Detection

How do you test if the web page is vulnerable? A simple test is to start with single quotation marks (‘) trick. Just enter an ‘ in a form that is vulnerable to SQL injection, or input it in the URL with parameters, such as: http:// www.sqlinjection.com/ news.asp ?id=1020505’, trying to interfere with the query and generate an error. If we get back an ODBC error, chances are that we are in the game.

Another usual method to be used is *Logic Judgement Method.* In others words, some SQL keywords like *and* and *or* can be used to try to modify the query and to detect whether it is vulnerable or not. Consider the following SQL query:

```
SELECT * FROM Admin WHERE Username='username' AND
Password='password'
```

A similar query is generally used in the login page for authenticating a user. However, if the *Username* and *Password* variable is crafted in a specific way by a malicious user, the SQL statement may do more than the programmer intended. For example, setting the *Username* and *Password* variables as *1' or '1' = '1* renders this SQL statement by the parent language:

```
SELECT * FROM Admin WHERE Username = '1' OR '1' = '1'
AND Password = '1' OR '1' = '1'
```

As a result, this query returns a value because the evaluation of '1'='1' is always true [3]. In this way, the system has authenticated the user without knowing the username and password.

2.3 SQL Injection Attacks Execution

Without user input sanitization, an attacker now has the ability to add/inject SQL commands, as mentioned in the source code snippet above. As default installation of MS SQL Server is running as SYSTEM, which is equivalent to administrator access in Windows, the attacker has the ability to use stored procedures like *master..xp_cmdshell* to perform remote execution:

```
exec master..xp-cmdshell "net user user1 psd1 /add"
exec master..xp-cmdshell "net localgroup administrators
user1 /add"
```

These inputs render the final SQL statements as follows:

```
SELECT * FROM Admin WHERE Username = '1' ; exec
master..xp_cmdshell "net user user1 psd1 /add"
SELECT * FROM Admin WHERE Username = '1' ; exec
master..xp_cmdshell "net localgroup administrators
user1 /add"
```

The semicolon will end the current SQL query and thus start a new SQL command. These above statements can create a new user named *user1* and add *user1* to the local *Administrators* group. In the result, SQL injection attacks succeed.

3 SQL Injection Defense

The major issue of web application security is SQL injection, which can give the attackers unrestricted access to the database that underlie web applications and has become increasingly frequent and serious. In this section, we present some methods available to prevent from SQL injection attacks and implement on the IIS+ASP+MSSQL web applications practically.

3.1 Secure Coding within the Web Application

Attackers take advantage of non-validated input vulnerabilities to inject SQL commands as an input via Web pages, thus execute arbitrary SQL queries on the backend database server. A straight-forward way to prevent injections is to enhance the reliability of program code.

Use Parameterized Statements. On most development platforms, parameterized statements can be used that work with parameters (sometimes called *placeholders* or *bind variables*) instead of embedding user input in the statement directly. For example, we construct the code as fallow:

```
searchid = request.querystring("id")
searched = checkStr(searchid)
sql = "SELECT Id, Title FROM News WHERE Id= '" &
searchid &"'"
```

Here, *checkStr* is a function for input validation. It is seen that the user input is assigned to a parameter, and then the SQL statement is fixed.

To protect against SQL injection, user input must not be embedded in SQL statements directly. Instead, parameterized statements are preferred to use.

Enhance Input Validation. It is imperative that we should use a standard input validation mechanism to validate all input data for length, type, syntax and business rules before accepting the data to be displayed or stored [4].

Firstly, limit the input length because most attacks depend on query strings. For instance, the length of I.D. card is limited to 15 or 18 in China.

Secondly, a crude defense is to restrict particular keywords used in SQL. It means that we should draw up a black list, which includes keywords such as *drop*, *insert*, *drop*, *exec*, *execute*, *truncate*, *xp_cmdshell* and *shutdown*. Also, ban SQL code such as single quotes, semicolon, --, %, =.

After checking the existence of normalized statement in the ready-sorted allowable list, we will be able to determine whether a SQL statement is legal or not. If the input data consists of illegal characters, the URL will redirect to a custom error page.

3.2 Proper Database Configuration

Enforce Least Privilege when Accessing the Database. Connecting to the database using the database's administrator account has the potential for attackers to execute almost unconfined commands with the database [5]. For instance, A system administrator account in MSSQL(sometimes called *sa*) is available to exploit *xp_cmdshell* command to perform remote execution.

To minimize the risk of attacks, we enforce the least privileges that are necessary to perform the functions of the application. Even though a malicious user is able to embed SQL commands inside the parameters, he will be confined by the permission set needed to run SQL Server.

Use Stored Procedures Carefully. As mentioned above, it is important to validate input data to ensure that no illegal characters are present. However, it is doubly important to restrict the application database user to execute the specified stored procedures. Validate the data if the stored procedure is going to use *exec(some_string)* where *some_string* is built up from data and string literals to form a new command [5].

Moreover, remove the extended stored procedure as follow:

```
use master
sp_dropextendedproc 'xp_cmdshell'
```

Visit the registry to store, and delete *Xp_regaddmultistring*, *Xp_regdeletekey*, *Xp_regdeletevalue*, *Xp_regenumvalues*, *Xp_regread*, *Xp_regwrite*, *Xp_regremovemultistring* extended procedures.

Release Security Patches. Last but not least, deploy database patches as they are released. It is an essential part in the defense against external threats.

3.3 Deployment of IIS (Internet Information Services)

Avoid Detailed Error Messages. Error messages are useful to an attacker because they give some additional information about the database. It is helpful for the technical supporter to get some useful information when the application has something wrong. However, it tells the hacker much more. A better solution is that just display a generic error message instead, which does not compromise security.

To resolve this problem, we set a generic error page for individual pages, for a whole application, or for the whole Web site or Web server. Additionally, select *Send the following text error message to client* to enable IIS to send a default error message to the browser when any error prevents the Web server from processing the ASP page.

Improved File-System Access Controls. To ensure each Web site has a different anonymous impersonation account identity configured, we create a new user to be used as an anonymous Internet User Guest Account and grant the appropriate permissions for each site, and disable the built-in IIS anonymous user. Moreover, deny *write* access to any file or directory in the web root directory to the anonymous user unless it is necessary.

In addition, FTP users should be isolated in their own home directories. FTP provides a means for transferring data between a client and the web host's server. While the protocol is quite useful, FTP also presents many security risks. Such attacks may include Web site defacement by uploading files to the web document root and remote command execution via the execution of malicious executables that may be uploaded to the scripts directory [6]. So we configure the *Isolation mode* for an FTP site when creating the site through the FTP Site Creation Wizard.The limitation prevents a user from uploading malicious files to other parts of the server's file system.

3.4 Other Security Techniques

We can improve the security of our Web servers and applications by using the tools, such as URLScan Security Tool, IIS Lockdown Tool, IIS Security Planning Tool. Here, we use URLScan 2.5 on IIS in practice.

URLScan is a security tool that restricts the types of HTTP requests that Internet Information Services (IIS) will process. By blocking specific HTTP requests, URLScan helps to prevent potentially harmful requests from being processed by web applications on the server [7].

All configuration of URLScan is performed through the *URLScan.ini* file, which is located in the *%WINDIR%\System32\Inetsrv\URLscan* folder. Define the *AllowVerbs* section as *get*, *post*, *head*. And permit the requests that use the verbs which are listed in the *AllowVerbs* section. Furthermore, configure URLScan to reject requests for *.exe*, *.asa*, *.bat*, *.log*, *.shtml*, *.printer* files to prevent Web users from executing applications on the system. In addition, we configure it to block requests that contain certain sequences of characters in the URL, Such as '..', './', '\', ':', '%', '&'. It is seen that URLScan includes the ability to filter based on query strings, which can help reduce the effect of SQL injection attacks.

4 Conclusion

Scanning our Web site with Acunetix WVS6.5, three low-severity vulnerabilities have been discovered by the scanner. The result is given in Table 1. It is seen that *possible sensitive directories* have been found, and these directories are not directly linked from the Web site. To fix the vulnerabilities, we restrict access to these directories. For instance, *admin* directory is confined to access only for appointed IP address, and deny write access to *cms* and *data* directory.

Table 1. Web vulnerability scanning report with Acunetix WVS6.5

Severity level	Quantity	Vulnerability description	Detail
High	0		
Medium	0		
Low	3	possible sensitive directory	/admin /cms /data

SQL injection has been one of the most widely used attack vectors for cyber attacks in recent years. In this paper, we pose SQL Injection Defense Mechanisms available to prevent IIS+ASP+MSSQL web applications, including secure coding within the web application, proper database configuration, deployment of IIS and other security techniques.

In the end, we must emphasize that each prevention technique cannot provide complete protection against SQL Injection Attacks, but a combination of the presented mechanisms will cover a wide range of these attacks.

References

1. Watson, C.: Beginning C# 2005, databases. Wrox, 201–205 (2005)
2. SQL Injection Walkthrough, `http://www.securiteam.com/securityreviews/5DP0N1P76E.html`
3. Pan, Q., Pan, J., Shi, Y., Peng, Z.: The Theory and Prevention Strategy of SQL Injection Attacks. Computer Knowledge and Technology 5(30), 8368–8370 (2009) (in Chinese)
4. Data Validation, `http://www.owasp.org/index.php/Data_Validation`
5. SQL Injection Attacks and Some Tips on How to Prevent Them, `http://www.codeproject.com/KB/database/SqlInjectionAttacks.aspx`
6. Belani, R., Muckin, M.: IIS 6.0 Security, `http://www.securityfocus.com/print/infocus/1765`
7. How to configure the URLScan Tool, `http://support.microsoft.com/kb/326444/en-us`

On Different Categories of Cybercrime in China*

Aidong Xu[1], Yan Gong[1], Yongquan Wang[1,2], and Nayan Ai[1]

[1] School of Criminal Justice
[2] Department of Information Science and Technology
East China University of Political Science and Law,
1575 Wan Hang Du Rd., Shanghai 200042, China
yukikung1022@gmail.com

Abstract. Cybercrimes have become an eye-catching social problem in not only China but also other countries of the world. Cybercrimes can be divided into two categories and different kinds of cybercrimes shall be treated differently. In this article, some typical cybercrimes are introduced in detail in order to set forth the characteristics of those cybercrimes. However, to defeat cybercrimes, joint efforts from countries all over the world shall be made.

Keywords: cybercrime, computer virus, gambling, fraud, pornography.

1 Introduction

Cybercrimes emerge with the development of the information networks. They are different from other crimes since they are hard to investigate in the information networks nowadays. Thus, special laws and regulations relevant to the investigation and conviction of cybercrimes should be made.

Cybercrimes are categorized according to different standards. French scholars, based on French legislation against cybercrimes, divide them into two large categories: crimes directly targeting computer systems and information networks, also called "pure computer crimes", and crimes committed through the use of computers and their related networks, in other words the use of computers in the commission of "conventional" crimes, which are also called "computer-related conventional crimes".[1] On the other hand, in the Convention on Cybercrime, the first international treaty seeking to address computer crime and Internet crime by harmonizing national laws, cybercrimes are classified into four categories: offences against the confidentiality, integrity and availability; computer-related offences; content-related offences; and offences related to infringements of copyright and related rights of computer data and systems.[2]

* This work was supported by National Social Science Foundation of China (No. 06BFX051) and Judicial Expertise Construction Project of 5th Key Discipline of Shanghai Education Committee (No. J51102).

[1] Yong Pi, Research on Cyber-Security Law, Chinese People's Public Security University Press, 2008, at 21-22.

[2] Council of Europe, Convention on Cybercrime, available at: http://conventions.coe.int/Treaty/Commun/QueVoulezVous.asp?NT=185&CM=8&DF=02/06/2010&CL=ENG

X. Lai et al. (Eds.): E-Forensics 2010, LNICST 56, pp. 277–281, 2011.

In China, however, there is no statute against cybercrimes specially. That is to say, there is no authoritative classification of cybercrimes. Despite all this, some scholars, based on the current situation of cybercrimes in China, classify them into four categories: offences against the order of network management; offences against the computer information system; offences against computer assets; and misuse of network.[3] They will be discussed in detail hereinafter.

2 Offences against the Order of Network Management

A network is setup and maintained for a normal order of network management. Offences in this category mean situations, in specific, when one uses or setups illegal channel(s) to get into international networking without authorization, when one manages international networking without the permission of the accessing unit, and when one infringes other's domain name. In common, those offences are related to network management. They influence the operation of network and usage of network resources.

In China, those offences violate regulations of the administration of international networking and measures on internet domain names. Up till now, they mainly include the 2001 *Measures for Managing Business Operations in Providing Internet Services*,[4] the 1997 *Provisional Administrative Measures on Registration of China Internet Domain Names*,[5] the 1997 *Implementing Measures on Registration of China Internet Domain Names*,[6] the 2002 *Proclamation of the Ministry of Information Industry of the People's Republic of China on China Internet Domain Name System*,[7] and the 2004 *Measures for the Administration of Internet Domain Names of China*.[8]

3 Offences against the Computer Information System

The computer information system is the heart of the computer network. Keeping the safety of it is the primary goal when fighting against cybercrimes. Those offences can be divided into two forms.

---

[3] Bingzhi Zhao, Current Situation of Cybercrime in China, available at: `http://www.lawtime.cn/info/xingfa/wangluofanzui/2007020231301.html`

[4] Man Qi, Yongquan Wang, Rongsheng Xu. "Fighting cybercrime: legislation in China", *International Journal of Electronic Security and Digital Forensics* (IJESDF), Inderscience Publication, Vol.2, No.2(2009), at 224.

[5] Available in Chinese at: `http://www.cnnic.net.cn/html/Dir/1997/05/30/0647.htm`

[6] Available in Chinese at: `http://www.cnnic.net.cn/html/Dir/1997/06/15/0648.htm`

[7] Man Qi, Yongquan Wang, Rongsheng Xu. "Fighting cybercrime: legislation in China", *International Journal of Electronic Security and Digital Forensics* (IJESDF), Inderscience Publication, Vol.2, No.2(2009), at 225.

[8] Available in Chinese at: `http://www.cnnic.net.cn/html/Dir/2004/11/25/2592.htm`, and in English at: `http://www.lawinfochina.com/law/display.asp?ID=3823&DB=1`

Unauthorized access to administrative controls over others' computers, which is commonly referred to as hacking, is one form. In China hacking is not an accusation that can be made under the Criminal Law of PRC., but it may constitute other accusations, such as the crime of destruction of the function of a computer information system, or the crime of illegal instruction of a computer information system.

Interrupting the normal operation of computer systems is the other form. Using computer virus is a way to commit the offence, and it is commonly happened not only in China but also all around the world. Computer viruses are defined in the *Regulations on the Protection of Computer Software*[9] as a set of computer instructions or program codes compiled or inserted in computer programs which damage computer functions or destroy data to impair the operation of computers. Computer viruses have become a problem since Internet access was available to most Chinese people. Most commonly, computer viruses can occupy the system resources, and slow down the operations, cause the computer to crash, damage and delete data. Furthermore they have the capacity to reproduce themselves. According to the *24th Statistical Report on Internet Development in China*, during the first six months of 2009, 57.6% of all the Internet users were attacked by viruses or Trojan horses while surfing the Internet.[10] Though people always feel headache on computer viruses, the *Criminal Law of the Prople's Republic of China* do define such activity as a crime from 1997. Article 286 punishes whoever in violation of State regulations, cancels, alters, increases or jams the functions of the computer information system, thereby making it impossible for the system to operate normally, and whoever in violation of State regulations, cancels, alters or increases the data stored in or handled or transmitted by the computer information system or its application program. The activities described in the article is what viruses do. Thus, whoever in violation of State regulations, creates and spreads computer viruses is punishable.

4 Offences against Computer Assets

Computer assets refer to the hardware configuration of the computer, the data saved in the computer and any other quantifiable information relating to the computer or the network. In practice, examples of those offences are activities damaging computer networking hardware and data, illegal usage of networking service, and illegal obtaining and using other's data information including infringing other's intellectual property.

---

[9] The Chinese version of the "Regulations" is available at: http://www.sipo.gov.cn/sipo2008/zcfg/flfg/bq/fljxzfg/200804/t20080403_369365.html. The English version is available at: http://www.lawinfochina.com/law/displayModeTwo.asp?ID=2161&DB=1&keyword=

[10] China Internet Network Information Centre, 24th Statistical Report on Internet Development, available at: http://www.cnnic.cn/uploadfiles/pdf/2009/10/13/94556.pdf

Laws and regulations against those offences mainly include the 2002 *Regulations on the Protection of Computer Software*,[11] the 2006 *Regulation on the Protection of the Right to Network Dissemination of Information*,[12] the 2009 *Administrative Measures for Software Products*,[13] etc.

5 Misuse of Network

Misuse of network means using computer network to commit conventional crimes. In this way network is just a tool. Most of the offences regulated in the Criminal Law of the People's Republic of China can be committed through network and, in fact, crimes in China are tending to be "webified". Within them, online fraud, online gambling and online pornography are crimes that are furiously expanded these days.

Like conventional fraud, online fraud is closely related to economic activity, but on the Internet. Online fraud occurs in different forms, such as Internet auction fraud, Internet credit card fraud, etc. Among them, Internet credit card fraud is the most common, and the most serious one in China. Internet credit card fraud is closely linked to the online payment business involving credit cards, a main method of online payment. It involves counterfeit and using of fake credit cards after cracking the keys of the real ones, counterfeit and masquerading as others by using their credit card numbers, and misusing others' credit cards by collaborating with specially-engaged commercial units.

Online gambling literally means gambling on the Internet. With the popularization and internationalization of the Internet, traditional forms of gambling, such as poker, casino gaming, sports betting and bingo are now available on the Internet. Gambling is prohibited on the mainland of China. So is online gambling, which is much harder to clamp down on considering the fact that those gambling websites may be legally established in countries where gambling is allowed. In online gambling, gamblers upload funds to the online gambling company, making bets or playing the games it offers, and then cash out any winnings. Usually, gamblers use credit cards to paying for their bets. Compared to traditional gambling, online gambling is more concealable, easier to be disguised and deceptive.

Conventional pornography is usually in the forms of words, paintings, photos and videos. Beginning in the 1990s, computer, Internet and multimedia technology have been widely used in the process of production and distribution of pornography. The visualization, informationization, and transnationality of the crime have aroused worldwide attention, making it one of the most serious cybercrimes in the world.

---

[11] Available in Chinese at: `http://www.sipo.gov.cn/sipo2008/zcfg/flfg/bq/fljxzfg/200804/t20080403_369365.html`, and in English at: `http://www.lawinfochina.com/law/displayModeTwo.asp?ID=2161&DB=1&keyword=`

[12] Available in Chinese at: `http://www.gov.cn/zwgk/2006-05/29/content_294000.htm`, and in English at: `http://www.lawinfochina.com/law/display.asp?ID=5224&DB=1`

[13] Available in Chinese at: `http://www.gov.cn/flfg/2009-03/10/content_1255724.htm`, and in English at: `http://www.lawinfochina.com/law/display.asp?ID=7348&DB=1`

6 Conclusion

Varieties of cybercrimes demand different methods to concur them. Cybercrimes are hard to defeat not only because of the changing cyber space, but also due to the globalization of the network. The one who commits a cybercrime in one country may live in another country. Thus joint efforts shall be made globally, and alliance shall be established to against cybercrimes in a more effective way.

References

1. Pi, Y.: Research on Cyber-Security Law. Chinese People's Public Security University, Beijing (2008)
2. Qi, M., Wang, Y., Xu, R., M.S.: Fighting Cybercrime: Legislation in China. International Journal of Electronic Security and Digital Forensics (IJESDF) 2(2), 219–227 (2009)
3. Criminal Law in PRC, `http://www.mps.gov.cn/n16/n1282/n3493/n3763/n493954/494322.html`
4. The Anti-Phishing Alliance of China has handled more than 6300 phishing websites, `http://www.cert.org.cn/articles/news/common/2009092724555.shtml`
5. 24th Statistical Report on Internet Development, `http://www.cnnic.cn/uploadfiles/pdf/2009/10/13/94556.pdf`
6. 25th Statistical Report on Internet Development, `http://www.cnnic.cn/uploadfiles/pdf/2010/1/15/101600.pdf`

Face and Lip Tracking for Person Identification*

Ying Zhang

Key Laboratory of Information Network Security, Ministry of Public Security,
People's Republic of China (The Third Research Institute of Ministry of Public Security),
339 Bisheng Road, Zhangjiang Hi-Tech Park, Pudong New Area, Shanghai, China
zhangying@stars.org.cn

Abstract. This paper addresses the issue of face and lip tracking via chromatic detector, CCL algorithm and canny edge detector. It aims to track face and lip region from static color images including frames read from videos, which is expected to be an important part of the robust and reliable person identification in the field of computer forensics. We use the M2VTS face database and pictures took from my colleagues as the test resource. This project is based on the concept of image processing and computer version.

Keywords: face recognition, lip tracking, computer forensics.

1 Introduction

Regarding the sustained increase of hi-tech crime, person authentication has aroused a lot of attentions in various fields especially in areas of high security. Thus there is an urgent requirement for robust and reliable identification technology from governments, the military, police, forensic scientists and commercial organizations. Based on the fact that most people are used to identify individuals by their faces, face recognition plays an important role during this process of identification.

Over the past ten years or so, face recognition has developed rapidly and become a popular area of research in computer vision and one of the most successful applications of image analysis and understanding [1]. For example, Chellappa et al. has demonstrated the survey of face detection as well as related psychological research in 1995. They considered static images and clips from videos respectively, generalized algorithms utilized for each one and analyzed their characteristics as well as advantages and disadvantages. [5]

Lip tracking is also an important tool for computer forensics. Sometimes the original evidences are possibly videos with strong noise while it is expected that the investigators could extract information from the voice. In this situation the technology will help forensic scientists make this via tracking the diversification of lip contour in real-time.

* This paper is supported by the Special Basic Research, Ministry of Science and Technology of the People's Republic of China, project number: 2008FY240200.

X. Lai et al. (Eds.): E-Forensics 2010, LNICST 56, pp. 282–286, 2011.

In this paper we will discuss a new way to implement face detection, which includes face detection, expression extraction and tracking of other features. And due to the importance of lip we select it as the representative from all the features and track its motion simultaneously.

2 Algorithms and Implementation

2.1 Face Region Segmentation

There are a lot of algorithms to segment face from the background image (e.g., pattern matching snakes, color localization and neural network). Here we use the chromatic method.

Rough Face Region Detection. Previous work [3] has proved that face region could be approximated via locating pixels in the following range:

$$L_{\lim} \leqslant \frac{R}{G} \leqslant U_{\lim} . \tag{1}$$

R and B stand for the red and green color component of each pixel respectively. And $L_{\lim}$ and $U_{\lim}$ are the thresholds which are dependent on the particular light over the facial part in the image [3].

The software ImageJ is utilized to split the color components and get two thresholds as shown in figure 1. After the segmentation, the candidate's points are marked by the color black and then we can get the rough face region.

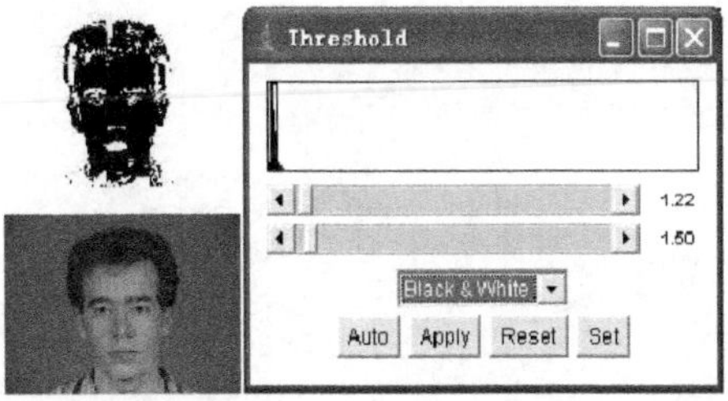

Fig. 1. The thresholds of face segmentation implemented by ImageJ

Accurate Face Region Segmentation. From the figure 2 we can see that there are some noises in the result image processed by previous step. Thus the elimination is expected to be performed. Via computing the frequency of marked points, if there are some points which are not located in the main block they will be treated as noise and will be removed from the candidate list.

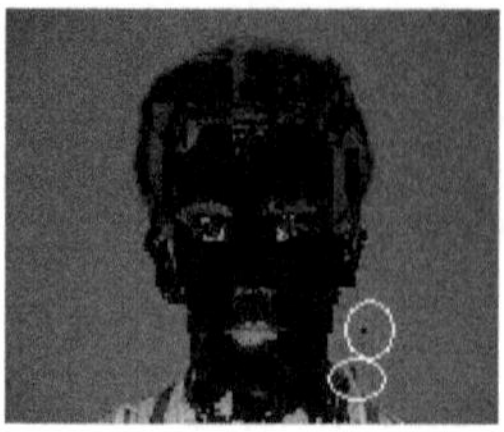

Fig. 2. Noise points

2.2 Lip Tracking

Rough Lip Region Detection. In this step, the two thresholds have been adjusted to locate lip pixels [3]. And then based on the theory that the lip is located in the lower half of face and it is usually symmetric about the vertical middle line of face, we could get rid of the extra points. In addition, we also need to merge broken lip regions which are brought about by the deficiency of lip thresholds.

Accurate Lip Region Detection. CCL (Connected Component Algorithm) is utilized here to find the largest blocks in the rough lip region.

Definition of CCL: The notation of pixel connectivity describes the relationship between two or more points. For two pixels to be connected they have to fulfill certain conditions on the pixel brightness and spatial adjacency [4].

Canny Edge Detector. We use Canny edge detector to describe the lip contour in the accurate lip region. The result of above steps is shown in figure 3.

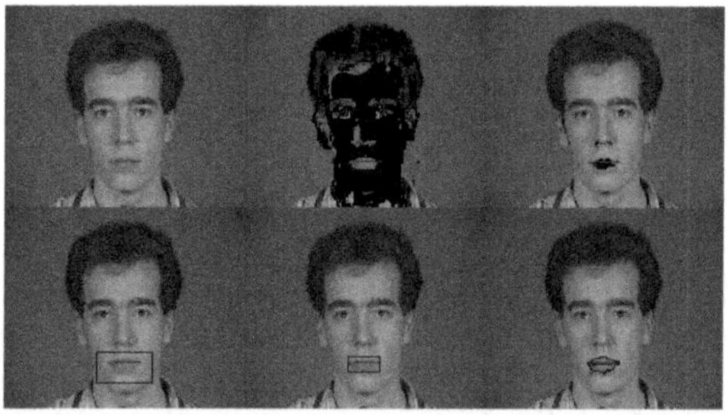

Fig. 3. Result images for face and lip tracking

3 Analysis of Results

3.1 Complexity of Algorithm

The complexity of this algorithm is O(facewidth×faceheight). This could be calculated by the following steps:

(1) Search the possible lip region, complexity here is O(facewidth*faceheight).
(2) Search the possible lip region, complexity here is O(facewidth*faceheight).
(3) Search the rough lip region, complexity here is O(half_faceheight*facewidth)
(4) Search the accurate lip region, complexity here is O(rough_lipwidth*rough_lipheight)
(5) Find the edge of lip, complexity here is O(accurate_lipwidth*accurate_lipheight)

According to the above deduction, the complexity is O(facewidth* faceheight). That means the consumptive time of this algorithm varies in the same manner as size of input image.

3.2 Veracity of Result

Here we evaluate the veracity via comparing the lip contour implemented by my algorithm to the one which is got by hand. The follow histograms show the distributions of lip edge points of the above two situations respectively.

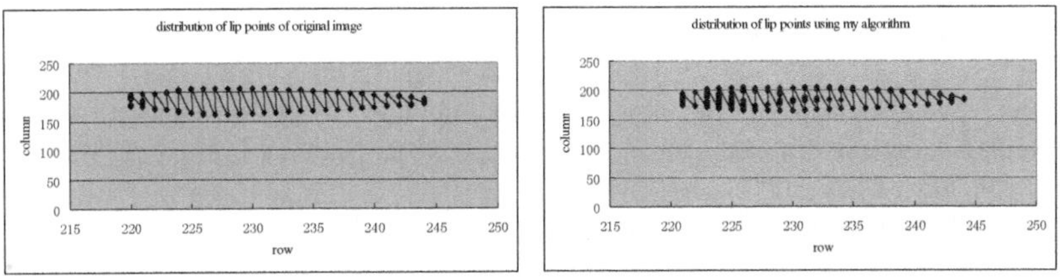

Fig. 4. Distribution of edge points by hand and my algorithm

And then we compare the pixels located in the edge of the two. According to the statistic data, 81.4% edge points have been included in the result.

3.3 Deficiencies

Easy to be Influenced by Other Conditions. The whole program is based on the chromatic algorithm. Point is that the chromatic difference is easy to be influenced by the camera series or the background light. For some images in which the rate of red and green color component didn't vary obviously the algorithm didn't work so well and sometimes even fails.

Only Suitable to Color Images. The basis of this algorithm is that the rate of red and green component is different for each part of the face. Hence it means that only color image is suitable instead of gray level image.

The Deficiency of Canny Edge Detector. Due to the shortage of canny edge detector there are some superfluous edges.

4 Future Application

The previous paper has mentioned that lip tracking system could be used in the security field especially for the field of computer forensics. For the reason that in some places where the speech signal is not so good or in the situation face detection is supposed to be helpful in the person authentication or in the case that lip reading is supposed to help the forensic scientists identify what people talk about in the videos, lip tracking is required to compensate the deficiency.

References

1. Grgic, M., Delac, K.: General Info (2005), http://www.face-rec.org/general-info/
2. Li, S.Z., Jain, A.K.: Handbook of Face Recognition, 10.1007/0-387-27257-7_17
3. Wark, T., Sridharan, S.: A Syntactic Approach to Automatic Lip Feature Extraction for Speaker Identification, Speech Research Laboratory, Signal Processing Research Centre, Queensland University of Technology, Australia (1998)
4. Fisher, R., Perkins, S., Walker, A., Wolfart, E.: Pixel Connectivity (2002), http://www.cee.hw.ac.uk/hipr/html/connect.html
5. Zhao, W., Chellappa, R., Phillips, P.J., Rosenfeld, A.: Face Recognition: A Literature Survey, University of Maryland, Sarnoff Corporation, National Institute of Standards and Technology, USA (2003)
6. Green, B.: Canny edge detector Tutorial (2002), http://www.pages.drexel.edu/~weg22/edge.html
7. Barnard, M., Holden, E.-J., Owens, R.: Lip tracking using pattern matching snakes. In: The 5th Asian Conference on Computer Vision (2002)
8. Mitsukura, Y., Fukumi, M., Akamatsu, N.: A Design of Face Detection System by using Lip Detection Neural Network and Skin Distinction Neural Network. Faculty of Engineering, University of Tokushima (2000)
9. Jiang, X., Wang, Y., Zhang, F.: Visual Speech Analysis and Synthesis with Application to Mandarin Speech Training, Department of Computer Science, Nanjing university, Nanjing Oral School (1999)
10. Gurney, K.: An Introductoin to Neural Networks. T.J. International Ltd., Padstow (1999)

An Anonymity Scheme Based on Pseudonym in P2P Networks*

Hao Peng[1], Songnian Lu[1], Jianhua Li[1], Aixin Zhang[2], and Dandan Zhao[1]

[1] Electrical Engineering Department
[2] Information Security Institute
Shanghai Jiao Tong University, Shanghai, China
{penghao2007,snlu,lijh888,axzhang,zhaodandan}@sjtu.edu.cn

Abstract. One of the fundamental challenges in P2P (Peer to Peer) networks is to protect peers' identity privacy. Adopting anonymity scheme is a good choice in most of networks such as the Internet, computer and communication networks. In this paper, we proposed an anonymity scheme based on pseudonym in which peers are motivated not to share their identity. Compared with precious anonymous scheme such as RuP (Reputation using Pseudonyms), our scheme can reduce the overhead and minimize the trusted center's involvement.

Keywords: anonymous, P2P networks, pseudonym.

1 Introduction

P2P networks are increasingly gaining acceptance on the internet as they provide an infrastructure in which the desired information and products can be located and traded. However, the open nature of the P2P networks also makes them vulnerable to malicious users trying to infect the network. In this case, peers' privacy requirements have become increasing urgent. However, the anonymity issues in P2P networks have not yet been fully addressed.

Current P2P networks achieve a certain degree of anonymity [1] [2] [3], which are mainly based on the following observations:

First, a peer's identity is exposed to all its neighbors. Some malicious peers can acquire information easily by monitoring packet flows, distinguishing packet types [4]. In this case, peers are not anonymous to their neighbors and then P2P networks fail to provide anonymity in each peer's local environment.

Second, in the communication transfer path, there are high risks that the identities of peers are exposed [5] [6]. In an open P2P network, when the files are transferred in a plain text model, the contents of the files also help the attackers on the path guess the identities of the communication parties.

Therefore, current P2P networks cannot provide anonymity guarantees. In this letter, utilizing pseudonym and aiming at providing all the peers' anonymity in P2P

* This work was supported by the Opening Project of Key Lab of Information Network Security of Ministry of Public Security under Grant No. C09607.

X. Lai et al. (Eds.): E-Forensics 2010, LNICST 56, pp. 287–293, 2011.

networks, we propose a new anonymity scheme. It can achieve all the peers' anonymity by changing pseudonym the contributions of our work are summarized as follows. 1) Our scheme reduces the server's cost by more than half in terms of numbers of RSA encryption operations. 2) The deficiency in the RuP protocol is avoided.

2 The Proposed Anonymity Scheme

Let S be the trusted third party server. It has a RSA key pair (K_S , k_s). Each peer *P* is identified by a self-generated and S-signed public key as its pseudonym. Each peer can change its S-signed current pseudonym to an *S*-signed new pseudonym to achieve anonymity. Let (K_P , k_P) and (K_{p} , k_{p}) denote the current and new RSA key pairs of peer P. Respectively $K\{M\}$ denote encrypting the message *M* with the public key *K* and $k\{M\}$ denote signing the message *M* with the private key *k*. We define *A* denote an AES (Advanced Encryption Standard) key. H (·) denotes a one-way hash function and "||" denotes the conventional binary string concatenation operation. v_P denote the macro value to be bound to *U*'s new pseudonym.

2.1 Overview

The main focus of this letter is the design of an anonymity scheme to achieve all the peers' anonymity in P2P networks by changing pseudonym with the help of a trusted server. From the design options provided in [7], we summarize two main challenges.

Linkage between Pseudonyms. Because each peer achieves anonymity by contacting the third trusted server to change its current pseudonym to a new pseudonym, the linkage of a peer's current and new pseudonyms should not be disclosed to the server and other peers.

Linked by the Rating Values. In P2P networks, each pseudonym is bound with one or more rating values. When a peer changes its pseudonym, its current and new pseudonyms may be linked by the rating values. If a requester changes its pseudonym and the rating values bound to the new pseudonym is unique to that of other peers, the requester's current and new pseudonyms can be linked by its unique rating values.

2.2 Review of the RuP Protocol

Here we assume peer *P* would like to change its pseudonym from K_p to k_p and *S*'s RSA key pair be (*e*, *d*) with modulo *n*. The pseudonym changing process of the RuP protocol includes two steps: anonymity step and translation step. In the former step, S first detaches the requester's rating values from the requester's current pseudonym and then binds a macro value to a blinded sequence number selected by the requester. In the latter step, S transfers the macro value from the unblinded sequence number to the requester's new pseudonym. Blind signature scheme is used to prevent the linkage between the requester's current and new pseudonyms from being disclosed to S. The details of the RuP protocol are shown below.

Step 1: P generates a new RSA key pair (K_P , k_P), selects a random number $r \in Z_n^*$.

$$m = r^e \bmod n. \tag{1}$$

Then $P \rightarrow S$: $k_P\{K_P \| m\}$.

Step 2: S uses P's pubic key K_P to verify whether the signature is valid. If it is valid, S computes P's macro value v_P and blindly signs $m * H(v_P)$.

$$m_b = (m * H(v_P))^d \bmod n. \tag{2}$$

Then S sends $\{m_b \| v_P\}$ to P and revokes P's current pseudonym K_P .Then $S \rightarrow P$: $\{m_b \| v_P\}$.

Step 3: P obtains S's signature $q * H(v_P)$ as follows:

$$(q * H(v_P))^d \bmod n = m_b * r^{-1} = (r^e * H(v_P))^d r^{-1}. \tag{3}$$

Then $P \rightarrow S$: $K_S\{m_b * r^{-1} \| v_P \| K_p\}$.

Step 4: S verifies whether the blind signature is valid. Then S generates a signature on U's new pseudonym K_u .

Then S→P: $k_S\{K_p \| H(v_P)\}$.

In this way, P obtains its new pseudonym K_p bound with a macro value v_P signed by S.

2.3 Our Proposed Anonymity Scheme

Firstly, the trusted server S selects a set of peers which need to communicate with each other to build a path. Secondly, S sends each peer on the path its next hop individually and directs each peer's new pseudonym through the path. Finally, S obtains all the new pseudonyms of the peers on the path at one time. Thus, S and other peers can not find out the linkage of the current and new pseudonyms of any peer who falls in the requester set.

We define each peer P_i would like to change its pseudonym from K_{P_i} to K_{p_i} . Our proposed scheme is described below.

Step 1: Each peer P_i sends a request to S. The request includes the current pseudonym K_{P_i} of P_i and an AES key A_i to be shared between S and P_i.

$$P_i \rightarrow S: K_S\{k_{P_i}\{K_{P_i}\} \| A_i\}. \tag{4}$$

Step 2: S first uses its private key k_S to decrypt the message to obtain P_i's current pseudonym K_{P_i} and the shared AES key A_i. Here we assume that P_1 is the first peer on the path and P_t is the last peer. An AES key A is also generated by S which is used to encrypt the new pseudonym of each peer on the path. Finally it sends each peer on the path a message. The message sent to P_i (0<i<t) includes the address of its next hop P_{i+1} on the path and the AES key A encrypted with the AES key A_i. The message sent to P_t includes the AES key A encrypted with the AES key A_t shared between P_t and S.

$$S \rightarrow P_i \ (0<i<t): A_i \{P_{i+1} || A\}. \tag{5}$$

$$S \rightarrow P_t: A_t \{A\}. \tag{6}$$

Step 3: For the first peer P_1 on the path, it obtains P_2's address and A by decrypting the message $A_1 \{P_2//A\}$ sent from S. Then it generates a new RSA (public, private) key pair (K_{p_1}, k_{p_1}) and encrypts its new pseudonym K_{p_1} with A.

Step 4: P_2 obtains P_3's address and A by decrypting the message $A_2\{A_3//A\}$ sent from S, using the AES key A_2 shared with S; it uses A to decrypt K_{p_1}. We use $[K_{p_1} || K_{p_2} || \ldots || K_{p_i}]$ to represent any permutations of pseudonyms $K_{p_1}, K_{p_2}, \ldots, K_{p_i}$. Then it generates a new RSA (public, private) key pair (K_{p_2}, k_{p_2}), encrypts P_1's new pseudonym and its new pseudonym together with A and sends a message to P_3. Here the order of the encrypted new pseudonyms is permutated randomly, such that S can not find out each requester's new pseudonym.

$$P_2 \rightarrow P_3: A \{[K_{p_1} || K_{p_1}]\}. \tag{7}$$

Step 5: The last requester P_t obtains A using the AES key A_t to decrypt $A_t \{A\}$ sent from S, using the AES key A_t shared with S. After it receives the message $A \{[K_{p_1} || K_{p_2} || \ldots || K_{p_{t-1}}]\}$ sent from P_{t-1}, it uses A to decrypt the message. Then it generates a new RSA (public, private) key pair (K_{p_t} , k_{p_t}), encrypts $\{[K_{p_1} || K_{p_2} || \ldots || K_{p_t}]\}$ with the AES key A_t and sends a message to S.

$$P_t \rightarrow S: A_t \{[K_{p_1} || K_{p_2} || \ldots || K_{p_t}] || H(v_P) \}. \tag{8}$$

Step 6: S obtains the new pseudonyms of $P_1, P_2 \ldots P_t$ using the AES key A_t shared with P_t. It generates a signature on all the new pseudonyms using its private key and revokes all the current pseudonyms of $P_1, P_2 \ldots P_t$ and sends the signature to $P_1, P_2 \ldots P_t$. Finally, each requester P_i obtains its new pseudonym bound signed by S and its macro value v_P.

We omitted how P_1 knows that it is the first requester on the path. In step 2 of our scheme, S can encrypt a flag in the message sent to P_1. In our design, S selects several peers who have the same requester peer to build a path. In fact, S does not need to produce the path beforehand; it can select it when needed. Compared with the RuP protocol where S signs each requester a new pseudonym, in our anonymous scheme, S needs to generate a signature for a set of requesters who have the same request. In this way, S's cost is reduced.

2.4 The Macro Value

Let R_+ (K_A, K_B) and $R_-(K_A, K_B)$ denote the sum of positive rating values and the sum of negative rating values given by A to A. Respectively K_A and K_B are the current pseudonyms of peer A and peer B. Then we assume the positive rating ratio R (K_A, K_B) represents a ratio of total number of positive rating values A gives to B.This process can be defined as follows:

$$R(K_A,K_B)=\frac{R_+(K_A,K_B)}{R_+(K_A,K_B)+R\_(K_A,K_B)} \tag{9}$$

A macro value computed every time when its pseudonym changes. We assume the current macro value bound to peer A's current pseudonym K_A is v_A. Then its new macro value v_a bound to its new pseudonym K_a can be computed as follows:

$$v_a=\alpha*\frac{\sum_{i=1}^{t}R(K_A,K_i)}{t}+(1-\alpha)*v_A \tag{10}$$

In the formula (10), K_i is the current pseudonym of the peer i and t denotes the size of the set of peers. The parameter α is used to assign different weights to the average positive rating values ratio and current macro value according to anonymous needs.

3 Anonymity Analysis

We will describe how our proposed scheme can achieve anonymity and reduce cost in this section.

Proposition 1: Our proposed scheme can achieve anonymity

Proof: In our proposed scheme, each peer's anonymity degree is defined as the probability that a peer's pseudonyms are not linked by attackers in the time interval T_i. If we assume the anonymous have n peers on the path and a peer's pseudonym changes f times. For each peer, it does not know other peers' current pseudonyms. The probability for a peer to make a correct linkage of current and new pseudonyms of a peer on the path with t peers is no more than $1/n$. Hence each peer's anonymity degree is a_p:

$$a_p \geq 1-\prod_{i=1}^{t}\frac{1}{n} \tag{11}$$

Therefore in a certain time interval, the higher the frequency change pseudonyms and the larger anonymous set of peers on the path, the better anonymous degree.

***Proposition** 2:* Our proposed scheme can reduce cost

Proof: For our scheme, S performs t RSA encryption operations which is the same as that of the RuP protocol. However, S performs only $t+2$ RSA decryption operations, while in the RuP protocol S needs $3t$ decryption operations. Because RSA decryption is much slower than RSA encryption, the operation cost of the trusted server is reduced in our scheme.

In Table 1, we can see that our scheme introduces AES encryption and decryption operations compared with the RuP protocol. On the other hand, our protocol does not use blind signature, therefore no additional operation is involved. Compared with the RuP protocol, our protocol does not increase the message overhead.

Table 1. Cost comparison (t: number of peer set)

	Number of operations			
	AES (Enc., Dec.)		RSA (Enc., Dec.)	
	Set	Server	Set	Server
RuP	0	0	(t, t)	$(3t, 3t)$
Mine	$(t, 2t\text{-}1)$	$(t, 1)$	(t, t)	$(t+2, t+2)$

Our scheme is designed to provide anonymity guarantees even in the face of a large-scale attack by a coordinated set of malicious nodes. If the ultimate destination of the message is not part of the coordinated attack, the anonymity scheme still preserves beyond suspicion with respect to the destination.

4 Conclusions

In this letter, we discuss an anonymity scheme in P2P networks. The main contribution of this letter is that we present an anonymity scheme based on pseudonym which can provide all the peers' anonymity with the reduced overhead. The analysis has shown that the anonymity issue in our designed scheme can be solved in a very simple way.

References

1. Cohen, E., Shenker, S.: Replication Strategies in Unstructured Peer-to-peer Networks. In: Proceedings of ACM SIGCOMM (2002)
2. Freedman, M., Morris, R.: Tarzan: A Peer-to-Peer Anonymizing Network Layer. In: Proceedings of the 9th ACM Conference on Computer and Communications Security (CCS) (2002)
3. Liu, Y., Xiao, L., Liu, X., Ni, L.M., Zhang, X.: Location Awareness in Unstructured Peer-to-Peer Systems. IEEE Transactions on Parallel and Distributed Systems(TPDS) (2005)
4. Jøsang, A., Ismail, R., Boyd, C.A.: Survey of trust and reputation for online service provision. Decision Support Systems 43(2), 618–644 (2007)

5. Hao, L., Yang, S., Lu, S., Chen, G.: A dynamic anonymous P2P reputation system based on Trusted Computing technology. In: Proceedings of the IEEE Global Telecommunications Conference, Washington, DC USA (2007)
6. Miranda, H., Rodrigues, L.: A framework to provide anonymity in reputation systems. In: Proceedings of the 3rd Annual International Conference on Mobile and Ubiquitous Systems: Networks and Services, San Jose, California (2006)
7. Lua, E.K., Crowcroft, J., Pias, M., Sharma, R., Lim, S.: A survey and comparison of peer-to-peer overlay network schemes. IEEE Commun. Survey and Tutorial 7(2), 72–93 (2005)

Research on the Application Security Isolation Model

Lei Gong[1,2,3], Yong Zhao[3], and Jianhua Liao[4]

[1] Institute of Electronic Technology, Information Engineering University, Zhengzhou, China
[2] Key Lab of Information Network Security, Ministry of Public Security, Shanghai, China
gonglei_sky@sohu.com
[3] Institute of Computer Science, Beijing University of Technology, Beijing, China
zhaoyonge_mail@sina.com
[4] School of Electronics Engineering and Computer Science Peking University, Beijing, China
liao_jh@139.com

Abstract. With the rapid development of information technology, the secrutiy problems of information systems are being paid more and more attention, so the Chinese government is carrying out information security classified protection policy in the whole country. Considering computer application systems are the key componets for information system, this paper analyzes the typical security problems in computer application systems and points out that the cause for the problems is lack of safe and valid isolation protection mechanism. In order to resolve the issues, some widely used isolation models are studied in this paper, and a New Application Security Isolation model called NASI is proposed, which is based on trusted computing technology and the least privilege principle. After that, this paper introduces the design ideas of NASI, gives out formal description and safety analysis for the model, and finally describes the implementation of the prototype system based on NASI.

Keywords: Information security classified protection, Application security, Security model, Application isolation.

1 Introduction

Nowadays, information security problems are being paid more and more attention in the world. The Chinese government decreed classified criteria for security protection of computer information system in 1999, and since then a lot of regulations were being released, which confirm that information security classified protection is the basic policy for information security construction in China.

Computer application systems are the key components for information system. The typical security problems are followed. Firstly, hackers usually explore security vulnerabilities in application to compromise computer systems, promote their privileges, and then access sensitive information or tamper some significant data. Secondly, there is some interference among different application systems because of user's misoperation, mutual confusion system data and so on. Thirdly, malicious code (malware) such as viruses, worms and Trojan horses always infiltrates computer systems, and badly threats security of application systems.

X. Lai et al. (Eds.): E-Forensics 2010, LNICST 56, pp. 294–300, 2011.

The basic reasons of those security problems mentioned above are confusion of application environment and fuzzy application boundary. So the most effective way to resolve those security problems is application isolation [1].

2 Related Work

The typical security model focusing on application isolation mainly includes sandbox model, virtualization model and noninterference information flow model.

The sandbox model restricts the actions of an application process according to security policies, so the process can only influence limited areas. For instance, Java virtual machine [2][3], Sidewinder firewall [4] and Janus [5] are the typical sandboxes. The sandbox model can also record the behaviors of processes [6]. It utilizes copy-on-write technology to make the system recoverable after being attacked.

Virtualization model tends to project implementation. VM Ware, Virtual PC and Xen virtualization are on hardware layer, which virtualizes CPU, memory, peripheral interface and so forth. FreeBSD jail and Solaris Containers (including Solaris Zones) virtualization are on operating system, which intercepts system calls to build an independent execution environment.

Noninterference information flow model is based on noninterference theory, which is firstly proposed by Goguen and Meseguer [7]. Noninterference theories are significant means to analyze information flow among components and reveal covert channels [8], but it does not provide additional solution to isolate application.

In summary, sandbox model focuses on constraining behaviors of process and neglects the protection of sensitive objects. Virtualization model can carry out complete application isolation, but it is not easy to be deployed under the complex application circumstances. Noninterference information flow models are theory model and the interference behaviors in information system are very multiplex, so it is difficult to be implemented.

3 Application Security Isolation Model

In this section, we will introduce an application security isolation model called New Application Security Isolation (NASI) model, which is based on the trusted computing technology and the least privilege principle.

3.1 An Overview of NASI

The NASI model divides resources for application environment into several parts, and sets up trusted and untrusted domains. In Trusted Computer System Evaluation Criteria (TCSEC) [9], domain means objects set which subjects can access. While in NASI model, the concept of domain does not mean a single set of objects, but an execution environment in which subjects with the least privilege can access objects, as shows in figure 1. In the domain, subjects are the application processes and objects are the resources including memory spaces, configuration files, program files, data files and so on. Some of the resources are public and some of them are private, as a whole, both of which can be seen as an independent resource set mapping to a specific application program.

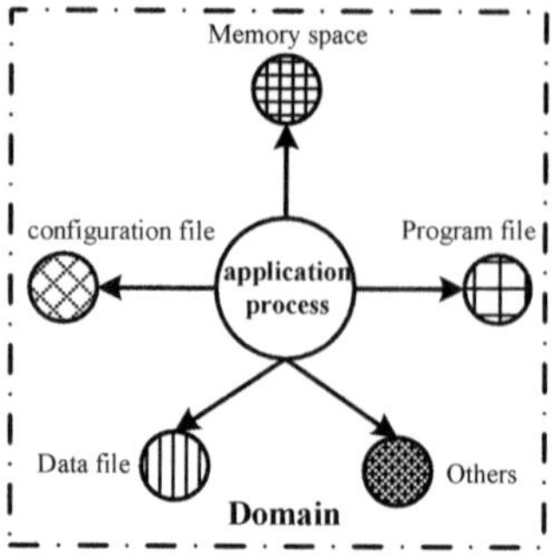

Fig. 1. Domain in NASI model can also be called application execution environment

The attribute of domains in NASI is either trusted or untrusted. In trusted domain, the program has normal and safe source, such as qualified software vendor. Processes in trusted domain can not only access the resources in the same domain, but also can access the resources in other trusted domains on the basis of security policies. In untrusted domain, the program has abnormal and unsafe source, such as Internet. Processes in untrusted domain can only access limited resources in their own and are unable to access resources in others.

3.2 Formal Description of NASI

Definition 1. Let Sub be a set of subjects in application environment, S for subjects in domains, then $Sub = \{S_1, S_2 \cdots S_n\}$; let Obj be a set of objects in application environment, O for objects in domains, O_{pub} for public objects, O_{pri} for private objects, then $O = O_{pub} + O_{pri}$, $Obj = \{O_1, O_2 \cdots O_n\}$; let $A = \{r, rw, w\}$ be a set of access modes, r for read only, rw for read/write, w for write; let R be requests for access, yes for allowed, no for deny, $error$ for illegal or error, so $D = \{yes, no, error\}$ denotes the set of outcomes for requests.

Definition 2 Trusted Domain. $TrustDom = \{N, S, O, A, P, TR\}$, N denotes domain ID, P denotes security policies, TR denotes trust relationship among domains.

Definition 3 unTrusted Domain. $unTrustDom = \{N, S, O, A, P\}$, the elements in untrusted domains are like trusted domains, except for lack of trust relationship TR .

Definition 4 Belonging relationship. $Host(O_i, t) = S_i, t \in T$, it means that the resources O_i belong to the process S_i at the moment t in a domain.

Property 1 Dynamic Property: $\exists(t_p, t_q \in T) t_p \neq t_q \wedge O_{it_p} \neq O_{it_q}$. This property means that during the procedure of program execution, some new resources will be created and some useless resources will be deleted.

Property 2 Belonging Property: $\forall(t_p \neq t_q \in T, O_i \in O)$, $Host(O_i, t_p) \equiv Host(O_i, t_q)$. This property indicates that although resources in domains are variational, they always belong to the process of their own, that is $Host(O_i, t) = Host(O_i)$.

Property 3 Base Property in Domains: if $\forall S_i, O_i \in unTrustDom, S_j, O_j \in TrustDom$, $\exists Host(O_i) = S_i, Host(O_j) = S_j$, then $S_i \times O_i \times A = \{yes\}$, $S_j \times O_j \times A = \{yes\}$. This property indicates that if processes and resources belong to the same domain, then the processes could access the resources.

Property 4 Base Property between Trusted Domain and Untrusted Domain: if $\forall S_i, O_i \in unTrustDom, S_j, O_j \in TrustDom$, $\exists Host(O_i) = S_i, Host(O_j) = S_j$, then $S_j \times O_i \times A = \{no\}$, $S_i \times O_j \times A = \{no\}$. This property indicates that there is no information flow between trusted and untrusted domain.

Property 5 Base Property among Trusted Domains:if $\exists TR_{ij} = TrustDom_i \succ TrustDom_j$, $\forall S_i, O_i \in TrustDom_i, S_j, O_j \in TrustDom_j$, $\exists Host(O_i) = S_i, Host(O_j) = S_j$,then $S_j \times O_i \times A = \{yes\}$. This property indicates that if one domain trusts another ($\succ$ means one-way trust), there will be information flow between them.

The properties above are very elementary, so NASI model has the following specific definitions and properties as complementarities.

Definition 5. Let C be a set of sensitivity level, L be the range of sensitivity level, and $L = \{[C_i, C_j] \mid C_i \in C \wedge C_j \in C \wedge (C_i \leq C_j)\}$, which means that its sensitivity level is between C_i and C_j .If $C_i = C_j$, then it represents single sensitivity level. Supposing $L_1 = [C_{1i}, C_{1j}] \in L$, $L_2 = [C_{2i}, C_{2j}] \in L$, then $L_2 \geq L_1 \Rightarrow (C_{2i} \geq C_{1j})$ and $L_2 \subseteq L_1 \Rightarrow (C_{2i} \geq C_{1i} \wedge C_{1j} \geq C_{2j})$; let $L_s L_o$ represent sensitivity level of subject and object respectively.

Definition 6. Let $V = B \times M \times F \times H$ be the set of system states, where $B \subseteq (Sub \times Obj \times A)$ denotes subjects access objects with privilege A , M is a set of access control matrices, $F \subseteq L_s \times L_o$ is the set of sensitivity levels for subjects and objects, $f = (f_s, f_o) \in F$, $f_s f_o$ denote sensitivity level of subject and object respectively, and H represents the set of hierarchy functions of objects. Furthermore, the set $W \subseteq R \times D \times V \times V$ is the set of behaviors of the system.

Property 6 Read Property: a state $v = (b, m, f, h) \in V$ satisfies this property if and only if, for each $(s, o, a) \in b$ the following holds: $a = r \Rightarrow$

$$\begin{cases} f_s(S) > f_o(O) \wedge S \in TrustDom_i \wedge O \in TrustDom_i \\ O = O_{pub} \wedge S \in TrustDom_i \wedge O \in TrustDom_j \wedge TrustDom_j \succ TrustDom_i \\ O = O_{pri} \wedge f_s(S) > f_o(O_{pri}) \wedge S \in TrustDom_i \wedge O \in TrustDom_j \wedge TrustDom_j \succ TrustDom_i \end{cases}$$

This property indicates that if processes and resources belong to the same trusted domain and subject dominates object, then S can read O. If processes and resources belong to different trusted domains, for the public resources, as long as the domains have trust relationship, S can read O; for the private resource, besides the conditions above, subject that is trusted must dominate object which is in the other domain.

Property 7 Write Property: a state $v = (b, m, f, h) \in V$ satisfies this property if and only if, for each $(s, o, a) \in b$ the following holds: $a = w \Rightarrow$

$$\begin{cases} f_o(O) > f_s(S) \wedge S \in TrustDom_i \wedge O \in TrustDom_i \\ f_o(O) > f_s(S) \wedge S \in TrustDom_i \wedge O \in TrustDom_j \wedge TrustDom_j \succ TrustDom_i \end{cases}$$

This property indicates that if processes and resources belong to the same trusted domain and object dominates the subject, then S can write O. If processes and resources belong to different trusted domains, besides the condition above, the domains must have trust relationship.

$a = rw \Rightarrow$

$$\begin{cases} f_s(S) = f_o(O) \wedge S \in TrustDom_i \wedge O \in TrustDom_i \\ f_s(S) = f_o(O) \wedge S \in TrustDom_i \wedge O \in TrustDom_j \wedge TrustDom_j \succ TrustDom_i \end{cases}$$

If processes and resources belong to the same trusted domain and the subject's sensitivity level is equal to the object's level, then S can read and write O. If processes and resources belong to different trusted domains, besides the condition above, the domains must have trust relationship.

3.3 Security Analysis

1. Defending Attack towards Software Vulnerability

NASI model can well cope with attack towards software vulnerabilities. With the least privilege principle, it can constrain permissions of a process by property 3 and 4. NASI model cannot prevent processes from being compromised, but can ensure that attack could not do anything out of permissions of compromised processes. So the permission that attacker gets is limited and it has no right to destroy the system or access sensitive resources of other applications.

2. Reducing Interference among Processes

NASI can provide separate environment for each application, prevent users from destroying systems by misoperation, and reduce interference among processes. For example, supposing there are two application systems called App1 and App2, which are deployed in two trusted domains separately. App1 supplies database resources for App2 to display. According to property 6, App2 could read the data file belonged to App1, but if App2 tries to modify the database resource, it will conflict with property 7. From this point of view, NASI model can reduce interference among applications if we set the security policies properly.

3. Resisting Malware Attack

NASI model can resist malwares and reduce the damages even if they get a chance to run. Because only legal processes have permissions to access sensitive information under protection of NASI model, it can prevent sensitive information from illegally being accessed by malwares. For example, supposing there is a malware which runs as process M and it tries to access O which is in another domain. Because M and O are not in the same domain, and they don't have trust relationship, according to property 3, 4 and 5, the access will be denied.

4 Implementation of NASI

The architecture of NASI prototype system is divided into four layers which are hardware layer, OS kernel layer, system layer and application layer, as shown in Fig.2. The main security mechanism is implemented in OS kernel layer and it is supported by TPM (Trusted Platform Module) chip as the root of trust, so we can guarantee the initial environment for applications to be safe, the procedure of which is from hardware power on to OS loading.

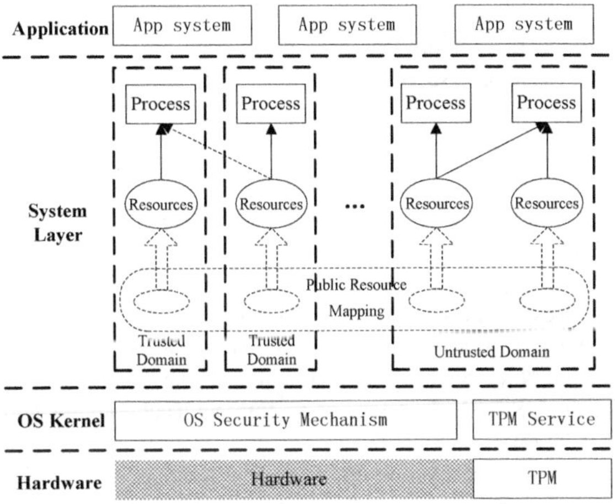

Fig. 2. The architecture of NASI prototype system

The NASI prototype system creates domains for each one of application. In the domain, the application process needs to utilize its own private resources and some of the public resources to accomplish the task effectively.

For private resources, the prototype system monitors them during the lifetime of application. The resources such as program files, configuration files and data files, which are created by application in deployment or in execution, belong to the same domain. For public resources, the prototype system uses virtualization technology to map public resources into different domains. When a process tries to access public resources, the prototype system will rename system resources at the OS system call interface [10]. For example, supposing an application in domain1 tries to access a file

/a/b, and then the prototype system will redirect it to access /domain1/a/b. When a process in domain2 accesses /a/b, it will try a different file /domain2/a/b, which is different from the file /a/b in domain1.

However, considering the performance overhead, a new created domain initially can share most of the public resources. Later on, if the processes in domain make only read requests, then they can directly access. But if they want to do some modification, the resources will be redirected to the domain to meet the requirement.

5 Conclusion and Future Work

In this paper, we introduced and implemented NASI model to satisfy the requirements of application security, which is very important in information security classified protection. From formalized description and security analysis, NASI can isolate application programs safely. Compared with other security model of related work, NASI can ensure not only security and validity, but also real feasibility.

In the future, we will pay more attention on how to measure trust degree for different domains and how to adjust trust degree during the application running.

Acknowledgement. This article is supported by the National High Technology Research and Development Program of China (2009AA01Z437), the National Key Basic Research Program of China (2007CB311100) and the Opening Project of Key Lab of Information Network Security, Ministry of Public Security.

References

1. Lampson, B.: A Note on the Confinement Problem. Communications of the ACM 16(10), 613–615 (1973)
2. Campione, M., Walrath, K., Huml, A.: and the Tutorial Team: The Java Tutorial Continued: The Rest of the JDK. Addison-Wesley, Reading (1999)
3. Gong, L., Mueller, M., Prafullchandra, H., Schemers, R.: Going Beyond the Sandbox: An Overview of the New Security Architecture in the Java Development Kit 1.2. In: Proceeding of the USENIX Symposium on Internet Technologies and Systems, pp. 103–112 (December 1997)
4. Thomsen, D.: Sidewinder: Combining Type Enforcement and UNIX. In: Proceedings of the 11th Annual Computer Security Application Conference, pp. 14–20 (December 1995)
5. Goldberg, I., Wagner, D., Thomas, R., Brewer, E.: A Secure Environment for Untrusted Helper Applications: Confining the Wily Hacker. In: Proceedings of the 6th USENIX Security Symposium, pp. 1–13 (July 1996)
6. Jain, S., Shafique, F., Djeric, V., Goel, A.: Application-level Isolation and Recovery with Solitude. In: EuroSys 2008, Glasgow, Scotland, UK, April 1-4 (2008)
7. Goguen, J., Meseguer, J.: Inference control and unwinding. In: Proc. Of the IEEE Symposium on Research in Security and Privacy, pp. 75–86 (1984)
8. Rushby, J.: Noninterference, Transitivity and Channel-Control Security Policies: Technical Report CSL-92-02, Computer Science Laboratory, SRI International, Menlo Park, CA (December 1992)
9. U.S. Department of Defense. Trusted Computer System Evaluation Criteria. DoD 5200.28-STD (1985)
10. Yu, Y., Guo, F., Nanda, S., Lam, L.-c.: A Feather-weight Virtual Machine for Windows Application. In: ACM Conference on VEE 2006, Ottawa, Ontario, Canada (2006)

Analysis of Telephone Call Detail Records Based on Fuzzy Decision Tree

Liping Ding[1], Jian Gu[2], Yongji Wang[1], and Jingzheng Wu[1]

[1] Institute of Software, Chinese Academy of Sciences, Beijing 100190, P.R. China
[2] Key Lab of Information Network Security of Ministry of Public Security
(The Third Research Institute of Ministry of Public Security),
Shanghai, 200031, P.R. China

Abstract. Digital evidences can be obtained from computers and various kinds of digital devices, such as telephones, mp3/mp4 players, printers, cameras, etc. Telephone Call Detail Records (CDRs) are one important source of digital evidences that can identify suspects and their partners. Law enforcement authorities may intercept and record specific conversations with a court order and CDRs can be obtained from telephone service providers. However, the CDRs of a suspect for a period of time are often fairly large in volume. To obtain useful information and make appropriate decisions automatically from such large amount of CDRs become more and more difficult. Current analysis tools are designed to present only numerical results rather than help us make useful decisions. In this paper, an algorithm based on fuzzy decision tree (FDT) for analyzing CDRs is proposed. We conducted experimental evaluation to verify the proposed algorithm and the result is very promising.

Keywords: Forensics, digital evidence, telephone call records, fuzzy decision tree.

1 Introduction

The global integration and interoperability of society's communication networks (i.e. the internet, public switched telephone networks, cellular networks etc.) means that any criminal with a laptop or a modern mobile phone may commit a crime, without any limitations on mobility [1]. There are more than 600 million cell phone users in China now. More and more frequently, investigators have to extract evidences from cell telephones for the case in hand. Telephone forensics is the science of recovering digital evidences from a telephone communication under forensically sound conditions using accepted methods. The information from CDRs includes content information and non-content information. Content information is the meaning of the conversation or message. Non-content information includes who communicated with whom, from where, when, for how long, and the type of communication (phone call, text message or page). Other information that is collected may include the name of the subscriber's service provider, service plan, and the type of communications device (traditional telephone, mobile telephone, PDA or pager) [2]. Once the law enforcement

X. Lai et al. (Eds.): E-Forensics 2010, LNICST 56, pp. 301–311, 2011.

agency obtains the telephone records, it may be important to employ forensic algorithm to discover correlations and patterns, such as identifying the key suspects and collaborators, obtaining insights into command and control techniques, etc. **Efficient and accurate** data mining algorithms are preferred in this case.

Software tools including I2's AN7 and our TRFS (Telephone Record Forensics System) are designed to filter and search data for forensic evidences. But these tools focus on presenting numerical analyzing results. The subsequent judgment, such as who is probably the criminal, who are probably the partners, and who has nothing to do with the event, will be made by the investigators based on their experiences. To address this issue, we propose a novel algorithm based on fuzzy decision trees to help the investigators make the final decision in this paper.

An investigator may analyze a suspect's telephone call records from two perspectives. One is global analysis in which we try to find all the relevant telephone numbers and their states that may be associated with a crimie incident. The other is local analysis in which we try to find a suspect's conversation content with someone and get important information. This paper focuses on the global analysis and tries to extract useful information (digital evidences) from non-content CDRs to help the investigator make decisions.

The rest of this paper is organized as follows. In Section 2, we introduce related work about telephone forensics, fuzzy decision trees, and our prototype of telephone forensics tool TRFS. We then present the algorithm based on fuzzy decision tree for CDR analysis in Section 3. In Section 4, we discuss our experimental evaluation and results. We conclude this paper and disucss future work in Section 5.

2 Related Work

2.1 Telephone Forensics

Mobile phones, especially those with advanced capabilities, are a relatively recent phenomenon, not usually covered in classical computer forensics. Wayne Jansen and Rick Ayers proposed guidelines on cell phone forensics in 2007 [3]. The guidelines focus on helping organizations evolve appropriate policies and procedures for dealing with cell phones, and preparing forensic specialists to contend with new circumstances involving cell phones. Most of the forensics tools that the guidelines proposed are designed to extract data from cell phones, and the function of data analysis is ignored. Keonwoo Kim, et al [4] provided a tool that copies file system of CDMA cellular phone and peeks data with an arbitrary address space from flash memory. But, their tool is not commonly applied to all cell phones since a different service code is needed to access to each cell phone and the logically accessible memory region is limited. I2's Analyst's Notebook 7(AN7, http://www.i2.co.uk) is a good tool that can visually analyze vast amounts of raw, multi-formatted data gathered from a wide variety of sources. However, AN7 is an aided tool for the investigator to find some patterns and relationships among suspects. Investigators have to reason themselves according to the visual result derived from AN7. In this paper, we propose an algorithm based on fuzzy decision tree to help investigators infer and make their decisions more justified and scientific.

2.2 Fuzzy Decision Tree

The decision tree is a well known technique in pattern recognition for making classification decisions. Its main advantage lies in the fact that we can maintain a large number of classes while at the same time minimize the time for making the final decision by a series of small local decisions [5]. Although decision tree technologies have already been shown to be interpretable, efficient, problem independent and able to treat large scale applications, they are also recognized as highly unstable classifiers with respect to minor perturbations in the training data. In other words, this type of methods presents high variance. Fuzzy logic brings in an improvement in these aspects due to the elasticity of fuzzy set formalism. Fuzzy sets and fuzzy logic allow the modeling of language-related uncertainties, while providing a symbolic framework for knowledge comprehensibility [6]. There have been a lot of algorithms for fuzzy decision tree [7-11]. One of the popular and efficient algorithms is based on ID3, but it is not able to deal with numerical data. Several improved algorithms based on C4.5 and C5.0 have been proposed. All of them have undergone a number of alterations to deal with language and measure uncertainties [12-15]. The algorithms are not compared and discussed in details in this paper due to space limit. Our fuzzy decision tree algorithm for CDRs analysis introduce in the following is based on some of these algorithms .

A fuzzy decision tree takes the fuzzy information entropy as heuristic and selects the attribute which has the biggest information gain on a node to generate a child node. The nodes of the tree are regarded as the fuzzy subsets in the decision-making space. The whole tree is equal to a series of "IF…THEN…"rules. Every path from the root to a leaf can be a rule. The precondition of a rule is made up of the nodes in the same path, while the conclusion is from the leaves of the path. The detail algorithm is presented in Section 3.

2.3 Introduction of TRFS

TRFS is now only a prototype and have some basic functions as illustrated in Fig. 1 and Fig.2. It consists of six components: data preprocessing, interface, general analysis, data transform, special analysis, and others. CDR analysis is included in the special analysis as illustrated in Fig. 2. For example, utilizing CDR analysis, the investigators can carry out local analysis to find the telephone numbers that communicate with a suspect's telephone for less than N seconds, more than N seconds, or the earliest N telephone calls and the latest N telephone calls in a special day, etc.

TRFS has two important differences from AN7. AN7 does not only focus on telephone number analysis but also implement various kinds of analysis as financial, supply chain, projects, and so on. TRFS is a special system only for telephone forensics. Moreover, TRFS is based on Chinese telephone features and is suitable for Chinese telephone forensics. However, similar to AN7, TRFS can only give the investigators numerical results and they have to make decisions based on their experiences. Therefore, we improve TRFS with fuzzy decision tree to support fuzzy decisions, e.g., who is probably the criminal, or who probably is the partner, etc.

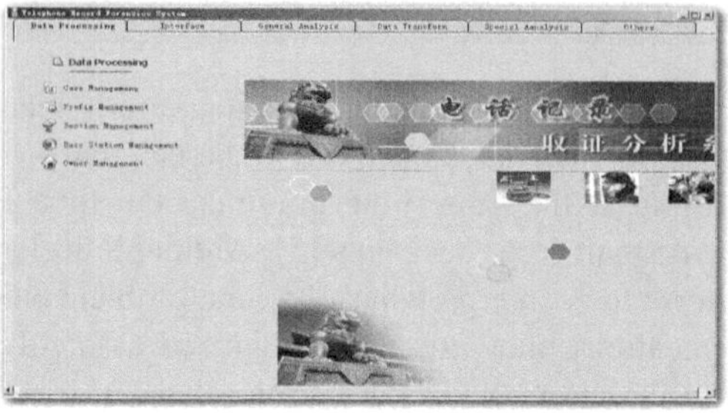

Fig. 1. The main interface of TRFS

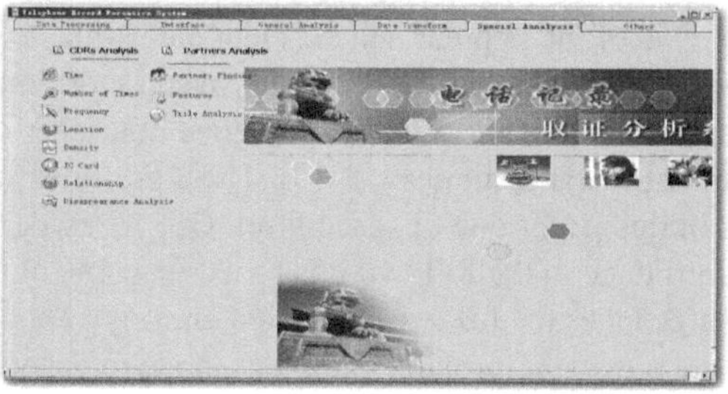

Fig. 2. The special analysis of TRFS

3 Proposed FDT Algorithm

A FDT algorithm is generally made up of three major components: a procedure to build a symbolic tree, a procedure to prune the tree, and an inference procedure to make decisions. Let us formally define FDT in the following. Suppose A_i (i=1,2,…,n) is the fuzzy attributes set of a training example data set D, $A_{i,j}$ (j=1,2,…,m) denotes the jth fuzzy subset of A_i (m is different with different i.), and C_k (k=1,2,…,l) is the classified classifications.

Definition 1. (the fuzzy decision tree)
A directed tree is a fuzzy decision tree if

1) Every node in the tree is a subset of D;
2) For each non-leaf node N in the tree, all of its child nodes will form a subset group of D which is denoted as T. Then there is a variable k ($1 \leq k \leq l$), enables $T = C_k \cap N$;
3) Each leaf node is one or more values of classification decision.

Definition 2. (the rule of fuzzy decision tree)

A rule from the root to a leaf of a fuzzy decision tree is presented as:

If $A_1=v_1$ with the degree p_1 and $A_2=v_2$ with the degree p_2 …and $A_n=v_n$ with the degree p_n, then $C=C_k$ with the degree p_0 (1)

Definition 3. (the fuzzy entropy).

For a certain classification, suppose s_k is the number of examples from D in class C_k, the expected information can be calculated by

$$I(D) = -\sum_{k=1}^{l} p_k \log_2 p_k \tag{2}$$

where p_k is the probability of a sample belongs to C_k.

$$p_k = \frac{s_k}{|D|} \tag{3}$$

Defintion 4. (the membership function).

The membership values of the fuzzy sets are relevant to the edges of the tree. For the discrete attributes, classical membership function is usually adopted:

$$\mu_k = \begin{cases} 1, & if \quad d \in D_k \\ 0, & if \quad d \notin D_k \end{cases} \tag{4}$$

For continuous attributes, the trapezoidal function (5) and triangle function (6) are the popular membership functions.

$$\mu_k(x) = \begin{cases} 0, & x \le d_1 \\ \frac{x-d_1}{d_2-d_1}, & d_1 < x \le d_2 \\ 1, & d_2 < x \le d_3 \\ \frac{d_4-x}{d_4-d_3}, & d_3 < x \le d_4 \\ 0, & d_4 < x \end{cases} \tag{5}$$

$$\mu_k(x) = \begin{cases} 0, & x \le a \\ \frac{x-a}{b-a}, & a < x \le b \\ \frac{c-x}{c-b}, & b < x \le c \\ 0, & c < x \end{cases} \tag{6}$$

Also, the membership values of the fuzzy sets can be calculated through statistic methods by carrying out questionnaire among domain experts. Our algorithm is adopted (4), (5) and finally modified by invited computer forensics experts and investigators through statistic method.

After the generation of fuzzy decision tree, decisions can be made through inference. According to [16], the operator(+,×) among four kinds of operators(+,×), (V,×), (V,^), and (+,^) is the most accurately operator for fuzzy decision tree inference. Therefore, we use (+,×) to perform the inference.

3.1 Data Preprocessing

The raw data from telephone service providers is the telephone numbers and their detail records of outgoing calls or incoming calls of the suspect's telephone to be investigated. Several main attributes of the data we examine are *Tele_number*, *Call_kinds*, *Start_time*, *Location*, and *Duration*. The classes are *suspect*, *partner* and *none*. To fuzzify the data, we defined several sub attributes:

1) In *Call_kinds*, *call* and *called* present that the owner of the telephone *call*ed the suspect or was *called* by the suspect;
2) *early*, *in-day*, and *later* in *Start_time* denote the telephone conversation took place before, at or after the day that the crime is conducted;
3) *inside* and *outside* in *Location* present that the owner of the telephone was or was not in the same city (the region of a base station) with the suspect during their telephone conversation;
4) *long*, *mid* and *short* in *Duration* present the time spending on a telephone conversation.

All the definitions above are showed in Table 2.in Section 4.

3.2 Generation of Fuzzy Decision Tree

The key of generating a fuzzy decision tree is attribute expansion. The algorithm of the fuzzy decision tree generation in our system is as follows:

Input: Training example set E.

Output: Fuzzy decision tree.

Procedures:

For $e_g \in E \quad (g=1,2,...p)$,
1) Calculate fuzzy classification entropy *I(E)*

$$P_k = \frac{\sum_{g=1}^{p} \mu_{gk}}{\sum_{k=1}^{l}\sum_{g=1}^{p} \mu_{gk}} \tag{7}$$

$$I(E) = -\sum_{k=1}^{l} p_k \log_2 p_k \tag{8}$$

where μ_{gk} is the membership of $e_g \in C_k$ $(g=1,2,...p, k=1,2,...l)$.

2) Calculate the average fuzzy classification entropy of the ith attribute $Q_i(E)$

$$P_{ij}(C_k) = \frac{\sum_{e_g \in C_k} \mu_{gk}(A_{ij})}{\sum_{g=1}^{p} \mu_{gk}(A_{ij})} \tag{9}$$

$$I_{ij} = -\sum_{k=1}^{l} P_{ij}(C_k) \log_2 P_{ij}(C_k) \tag{10}$$

$$Q_i(E) = \sum_{j=1}^{m} \frac{\sum_{g=1}^{p} \mu_{gk}(A_{ij})}{\sum_{j=1}^{m} \sum_{g=1}^{p} \mu_{gk}(A_{ij})} I_{ij} \tag{11}$$

where $\mu_{gk}(A_{ij})$ is the membership of $e_g \in C_k$ under the attribute of $A_{i,j}$ (g=1,2,…p. k=1,2,…l).

3) Calculate the information gain.

$$G_i(E) = I(E) - Q_i(E) \tag{12}$$

4) Find i_0 which satisfies to

$$G_{i_0} = \max_{1 \le i \le n} G_i(E) \tag{13}$$

Then select A_{i0}as the test node.

5) For i=1,2,…,n, j=1,2,…m, repeat 2-4, until (1) the proportion of a data set of a class C_k is not less than a threshold θ_r , (2) there are no attribute for more classifications, then it is a leaf node and assigned by the class names and the probabilities.

3.3 Pruning Fuzzy Decision Tree

Pruning is to provide a good compromise between simplicity and predictive accuracy of the fuzzy decision tree by removing irrelevant parts in it. Pruning also enhances the interpretability of a tree. It is obvious that a simpler tree will be easier to interpret. Our pruning algorithm is based on [9], which is an important part of our method and will be discussed in detail in another paper in the future.

3.4 FDT Inference

As mentioned above, we adopted (+,×) to carry out the inference of the fuzzy decision tree. The algorithm is as follows:

Suppose the final fuzzy decision tree have v paths, every path has w_h nodes, the probabilities of the nodes is labeled f_{ht} ($h=1, 2, \ldots, v.\ t=w_1, w_2, \ldots, w_v.$). Every leaf node belong to C_k at the probability of $f_h^{C_k}$ ($k=1,2,\ldots l$)

Then

$$f_h^k = \prod_{t=1}^{w_h-1} f_{ht} f_h^{c_k} \quad (h=1,2,\ldots v,\ k=1,2\ldots l) \tag{14}$$

The total probability of classification is:

$$f^k = \sum_{h=1}^{v} f_h^k \tag{15}$$

And

$$\sum_{k=1}^{l} f^k = 1 \tag{16}$$

The reasoning formalization maybe:

If A_{h1} is Z_{h1} with the degree more than f_{h1} and A_{h2} is Z_{h2} with the degree more than f_{h2} and A_{hw_h} is Z_{hw_h} with the degree more than f_{hw_h} then $C = C_k$ with the degree f_h^k.

4 Experiment and Analysis

In a case of murder, we got the suspect's telephone number and collected 50 CDRs of some relevant telephone numbers during a period of time. Some of them are showed in Table 1. In the column of *Call_kinds*, 1 denotes the telephone *call*ed the suspect's telephone, while 0 denotes the telephone was *called* by the suspect's telephone. In the column of *Location*, every number presents the base station number which matches a certain geographic location. The time of the murder is about 2004/10/02 13:25:00. According to the algorithm in the above, the raw data is fuzzified and the membership is calculated by (4), (5). However, it is very complicated to determine which telephone owner is the main suspect, who is the partner and who has nothing to do with the event. For example, e23's telephone number is 114, which is the service provider of telephone number searching. So the owner of 114 may have nothing to do with the crime with a high probability. In order to make the decision more accurate, we adopted a statistical method to imorve the calculated results. We invited 10 experienced investigators and 10 forensics experts to help us modify the membership values. The final result is illustrated in Table 2.

Using the data in Table 2 as the training example set and applying the method mentioned above, the entropies of the whole fuzzy set and the four fuzzy subsets are respectively:

$I(E)$=1.5685 $Q_1(E)$=1.8263 $Q_2(E)$=1.4830, $Q_3(E)$=1.5718, $Q_4(E)$=1.4146

Therefore the maximum information gain is *duration* and it is selected as the root node. The finally fuzzy decision tree is showed in Fig.3.

According to the inference method described in Section3, we can obtain the final probabilities of the three classes by operator (+,×) and get 21 rules from the fuzzy decision tree. For example, the path from the root to the left leaf node indicates 3 rules. One of them is:

If "Duration is short with the probability of more than 0.790" and "Start_ time is early with the probability of more than 0.443" then the owner of the telephone is suspect with the degree 0.473.

Following the rules derived from the FDT, investigators can determine the owner of an input telephone number is probably a suspect, or a partner, or has nothing to do with the case.

Table 1. Some of the original data

Telephone	*Call_kinds*	*Start_time*	*Location*	*Duration*
13061256***	0	2004/10/01 07:21:25	6	79
05323650***	0	2004/10/01 07:23:22	6	187
13605425***	1	2004/10/01 07:44:10	6	19
05324069***	0	2004/10/01 10:12:43	6	71
05324069***	0	2004/10/01 10:39:08	6	111
11*	0	2004/10/01 10:41:16	6	23
05322789***	0	2004/10/01 10:42:03	6	79
3650***	0	2004/10/01 11:59:02	6	69
13061256***	0	2004/10/01 13:44:36	6	120
13361227***	1	2004/10/01 14:03:51	6	35
13012515***	0	2004/10/01 17:36:00	6	50
13061229***	0	2004/10/01 17:37:23	6	20

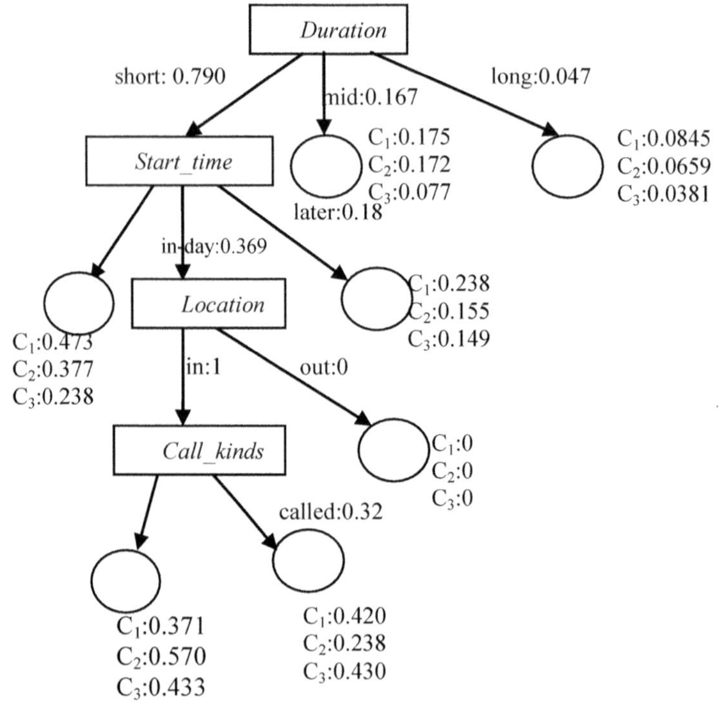

Fig. 3. The fuzzy decision tree

Table 2. Some of the original data

E	*Call_kinds*		*Start_time*			*Location*		*Duration*			*Classification*		
	called	call	early	in-day	later	In	out	short	mid	long	suspect	partner	non
e1	0.5	0.0	0.2	0.0	0.0	1	0	0.3	0.0	0.0	0.1	0.5	0.5
e2	0.5	0.0	0.0	0.3	0.3	1	0	0.6	0.0	0.0	0.2	0.6	0.3
e3	0.5	0.0	0.0	0.0	0.2	1	0	0.3	0.0	0.0	0.1	0.5	0.5
e4	0.0	0.3	0.0	0.0	0.2	1	0	0.3	0.0	0.0	0.3	0.4	0.5
e5	0.0	0.3	0.0	0.3	0.0	1	0	0.3	0.0	0.0	0.5	0.4	0.2
e6	0.5	0.3	0.6	0.6	0.0	1	0	0.6	0.0	0.0	0.5	0.5	0.1
e7	0.0	1.0	0.3	0.4	0.3	1	0	1.0	0.0	0.0	0.7	0.3	0.1
e8	0.5	0.0	0.0	0.3	0.0	1	0	0.3	0.0	0.0	0.1	0.7	0.5
e9	0	0.3	0.3	0.0	0.0	1	0	0.3	0.0	0.0	0.1	0.2	0.7
e10	0.0	0.3	0.3	0.0	0.0	1	0	0.0	1.0	0.0	0.3	0.3	0.4
e11	0.5	1.0	1.0	1.0	1.0	1	0	1.0	0.3	0.0	0.9	0.2	0.1
e12	0.6	0.0	0.6	0.0	0.0	1	0	0.6	0.0	0.0	0.3	0.5	0.4

5 Conclusions and Future Works

In this paper, we apply fuzzy decision tree to telephone forensics and enable investigators more justified reasoning. We discuss the related work of telephone forensics, FDT algorithms and our telephone record forensics system (TRFS). We then present our algorithm based on fuzzy decision tree. We further evaluate our algorithm with real experimental data. Currently, we are improving the algorithm by making FDT generating, pruning and reasoning completely automatic, and looking into better methods to obtain appropriate membership values, and integrating the algorithm with our TRFS. In addition, the algorithm will be assessed and compared with other similar algorithms.

Acknowledgement. This research was supported by following funds: Accessing-Verification-Protection oriented secure operating system prototype under Grant NO.KGCX2-YW-125, the Opening Project of Key Lab of Information Network Security of Ministry of Public Security (The Third Research Institute of Ministry of Public Security).

References

[1] McCarthy, P.: Forensic Analysis of Mobile Phones [Dissertation]. Mawson Lakes: School of Computer and Information Science, University of south Australia (2005)

[2] Swenson, C., Adams, C., Whitledge, A., Shenoi, S.: Advances in Digital Forensics III. In: Craiger, P., Shenoi, S. (eds.) IFIP International Federation for Information Processing, vol. (242), pp. 21–39. Springer, Boston (2007)

[3] Jansen, W., Ayers, R.: Guidelines on Cell Phone Forensics, `http://csrc.nist.gov/publications/nistpubs/800-101/SP800-101.pdf`

[4] Kim, K., Hong, D., Chung, K.: Forensics for Korean Cell Phone. In: Proceedings of e-Forensics 2008, Adelaide, Australia, January 21-23 (2008)

[5] Chang, R.L.P., Pavlidis, T.: Fuzzy decision tree algorithms. IEEE Trans. Syst. Man Cybern. SMC-7(1), 28–35 (1977)

[6] Zadeh, L.A.: Fuzzy logic and approximate reasoning. Synthese (30), 407–428 (1975)

[7] Quinlan, J.R.: Induction on decision trees. Machine Learning 1(1), 81–106 (1986)

[8] Doncescu, A., Martin, J.A., Atine, J.-C.: Image color segmentation using the fuzzy tree algorithm T-LAMDA. Fuzzy Sets and Systems (158), 230–238 (2007)

[9] Olaru, C., Wehenkel, L.: A complete fuzzy decision tree technique. Fuzzy Sets and Systems (138), 221–254 (2003)

[10] Umanol, M., Okamoto, H., Hatono, I., Tamura, H., Kawachi, F., Umedzu, S., Kinoshita, J.: Fuzzy decision trees by fuzzy ID3 algorithm and its application to diagnosis systems. In: IEEE World Congress on Computational Intelligence, Proceedings of the Third IEEE Conference on Fuzzy Systems, June 26-29, vol. (3), pp. 2113–2118 (1994)

[11] Kantardzic, M.: Data Mining Concepts, Models, Methods, and Algorithms. IEEE Press, Los Alamitos (2002)

[12] Ichihashi, H., Shirai, T., Nagasaka, K., Miyoshi, T.: Neuro-fuzzy ID3: a method of inducing fuzzy decision trees with linear programming for maximising entropy and an algebraic method for incremental learning. Fuzzy Sets and Systems (81), 157–167 (1996)

[13] Wehenkel, L.: On uncertainty measures used for decision tree induction. In: IPMU 1996 Info. Proc. and Manag. of Uncertainty in Knowledge-Based Systems, Granada, Spain (1996)

[14] Jeng, B., Jeng, Y., Liang, T.: FILM: a fuzzy inductive learning method for automated knowledge acquisition. Decision Support System (21), 61–73 (1997)

[15] Janikow, C.Z.: Fuzzy decision trees: issues and methods. IEEE Transactions on Systems, Man, and Cybernetics—Part B: Cybernetics 28(1), 1–14 (1998)

[16] Wang, X.Z., Yeung, D.S., Tsang, E.C.C.: A comparative study on heuristic algorithms for generating fuzzy decision trees. IEEE Transactions on Systems, Man and Cybernetics (31), 215–226 (2001)

Author Index

GPSR Compliance

The European Union's (EU) General Product Safety Regulation (GPSR) is a set of rules that requires consumer products to be safe and our obligations to ensure this.

If you have any concerns about our products, you can contact us on ProductSafety@springernature.com

In case Publisher is established outside the EU, the EU authorized representative is:

Springer Nature Customer Service Center GmbH
Europaplatz 3
69115 Heidelberg, Germany

Batch number: 10844669

Printed by Printforce, the Netherlands